LAND ROVER
EXPERIENCE TOUR

DAG ROGGE & ROLAND LÖWISCH

teNeues

INHALT
CONTENTS

INTRO

JORDANIEN | JORDAN

ISLAND | ICELAND

NAMIBIA

MUNDO MAYA

KANADA | CANADA

SCHOTTLAND | SCOTLAND

WINTER EXPERIENCE

ARGENTINIEN | ARGENTINA

MALAYSIA

BOLIVIEN | BOLIVIA

SEIDENSTRASSE | SILK ROAD

AUSTRALIEN | AUSTRALIA

PERU

OUTRO

VORWORT
FOREWORD

Liebe Leserin, lieber Leser, liebe Land-Rover-Freunde,

ein lang gehegter Traum sollte in Erfüllung gehen – Land Rover Experience hatte eine Reise nach Peru und zur Ruinenstadt Machu Picchu im Programm. Wir buchten sofort.

Wir starteten eine Reise voller Erwartungen. Jeder Tag überraschte und bereicherte uns mit ungeplanten und unvorhersehbaren neuen Erlebnissen. Mit vielen unvergesslichen Eindrücken kehrten wir zurück. Menschen, Natur und Kultur, Gemeinschaft: Diese Momente, diese Begegnungen und Erfahrungen zählen zum Wertvollsten, was wir in jüngster Zeit erleben durften.

Mit Peru wählten die Organisatoren der Tour um Dag Rogge eines der vielfältigsten und abwechslungsreichsten Ziele, reich an einem unglaublichen Farbspektrum, den vom Wind gezeichneten Formen der Atacama-Wüste, über 4 600 Meter hohen Bergen und Bergdörfern in den Anden voller freundlicher Peruaner, üppiger Artenvielfalt der Flora und Fauna im tropischen Regenwald und rabenschwarzen Nächten ohne Lichtverschmutzung am Pazifik.

Lagerfeuerromantik mit Campsites am Ozean, Übernachtungen in lokalen Gästehäusern und beste peruanische Verpflegung bereicherten unsere Tage. Als Höhepunkt feierten wir den Abschluss der Tour in der alten Inka-Hauptstadt Cusco und besuchten das UNESCO-Weltkulturerbe Machu Picchu.

Unser Konvoi aus weißen Land Rover Discovery erregte immer wieder Aufmerksamkeit. Wir reisten leichtfüßig, agil und sicher zu all unseren Zielen. Die Gruppe der Reisenden bestach durch Teamgeist und Hilfsbereitschaft.

Mit ein wenig Stolz dürfen wir feststellen: Land Rover Experience ermöglicht Abenteuer und Erlebnisse, die in dieser Form nur Land Rover bieten kann.

Herzlichst bedanken wir uns für die wunderschönen Tage bei den flexiblen und improvisationsfreudigen Organisatoren.

Wir kommen gerne wieder.

Prof. Dr. R. Speth
CEO Jaguar Land Rover

Dear Readers, Dear Land Rover Friends,

This has been the realization of a long-held dream of ours. Land Rover Experience was offering a tour to Peru and the ancient, ruined city of Machu Picchu. We booked immediately.

The sense of anticipation and excitement was overwhelming. Every day on the tour was a bountiful panoply of the unexpected and the spontaneous. We returned home all the richer for what we had seen and experienced. People, nature, culture and community – those are the elements that, in combination, made the trip one of our absolute highlights of recent years.

Dag Rogge and his team had come up with a country offering diversity, a wonderful variety of unbelievable colours, the wind-scarred shapes of the Atacama desert, mountains stretching to impressive 15,000 feet above sea level and villages full of welcoming locals. With its amazing mix of flora and fauna in the tropical rainforest and pitch-black nights devoid of any light pollution, Peru just has to be experienced to be believed.

The mix of romantic beach campfires, local lodges and enjoying the best of Peru's exquisite cuisine made our stay truly unforgettable. The absolute climax of the tour was a visit to the ancient Inca capital of Cusco and the famous UNESCO world heritage site Machu Picchu.

Our convoy of white Land Rover Discovery caused a stir wherever we went. At the same time we kept our footprint to a minimum, creating no fuss and stayed safe. It is with a sense of pride that we can confirm that the Experience Tour is an adventure made by Land Rover.

We wish to extend our grateful thanks to the team for their flexibility, improvization and for making our tour such a fantastic experience.

Until next time.

Prof. Dr R. Speth
CEO Jaguar Land Rover

VORWORT
FOREWORD

Die Land Rover Experience Tour ist einmalig in der Automobilwelt und eine Erfolgsgeschichte für die Marke Land Rover in Deutschland. Von Anfang an war es das Ziel, die Marke in ihrer eigentlichen Umgebung für eine breitere Öffentlichkeit erlebbar zu machen und gleichzeitig die Bandbreite an Fähigkeiten der Fahrzeuge unter Beweis zu stellen.

Die Offroad-Welt hat sich seit dem Start der Land Rover Experience Tour im Jahr 2000 dramatisch geändert. Seitdem die Camel Trophy den Abenteurer mit kaputten Schuhen und einem Land Rover an seiner Seite erfunden hatte und in unzähligen Werbespots präsentierte, wurden viele neue Nischen besetzt, neue Player und ein Wertewandel in der Gesellschaft haben den SUV- und Geländewagenmarkt zu einem überaus relevanten Segment werden lassen. Aber schon immer hat die automobile Konkurrenz respektvoll auf die Experience-Aktivitäten von Land Rover geschaut. Auch der einhellige Tenor der Journalisten war: „So eine Tour kann nur Land Rover durchführen, nur diese Marke steht authentisch für dieses Abenteuer."

Durch die Finanz- und Wirtschaftskrise ab 2007 wurden viele „Abenteuer-Projekte" in der Industrie eingestellt. Auch Land Rover Deutschland musste die Land Rover Experience Tour (LET) vehement gegenüber der Zentrale in Großbritannien verteidigen, aber mit dem Jaguar-Land-Rover-Besitzerwechsel von Ford zu Tata Motors war die LET wieder im Fokus und ist heute eine der wichtigsten Säulen der globalen Marketingstrategie von Land Rover.

Das schlüssige und kontinuierlich verfolgte Konzept ist das Erfolgsrezept für die Tour: Zunächst die Qualifikation mit teils mehr als 30 000 Bewerbungen, den intensiven Offroad-Testfahrten der Bewerber bei den nationalen Qualifikationscamps und der Zielgruppenansprache, die auch weitestgehend der Käuferzielgruppe entspricht. Wer hier dabei ist (bei der Qualifikation Peru mehr als 3 200 Teilnehmer), hat zwar das Tourziel vor Augen, ist aber alleine schon durch den Abenteuertag mit Land Rover und all den Modelllinien vom Defender bis zum Range Rover nachhaltig begeistert. Diejenigen, die sich durchgesetzt haben und als besonderes Extra dann bei der Endqualifikation in unserem Experience Center in Wülfrath dabei sein dürfen (in diesen Genuss kommen 60 Personen vor jeder Tour), sind beinahe auf dem Offroad-Olymp.

Ein einmaliges Erlebnis, das man nie mehr vergisst. Drei Tage im Gelände, sich mit anderen messen, immer nach dem Motto: „Dabei sein ist alles." Wer dann zu den sechs Finalisten gehört, hat viele Neider, denn diese Tour kann man für Geld nicht kaufen. Die Tour ist das Faszinosum, das einen ganz besonderen Reiz ausübt.

Wenn wir behaupten, die Tour sei nicht zu kaufen, ist das nicht ganz richtig, denn auch die gerade beendete Tour nach Peru, von der Wüste bis zum Machu Picchu, ist im aktuellen Reiseangebot, sozusagen „auf den Spuren der Tour". Dabei nutzen wir das durch unsere Profis erworbene Know-how in den Tourländern in Form eines exklusiven und individuellen Reiseprogramms. Erfolgreiche Beispiele für Experience-Reisen sind die Tourziele Island und Namibia, die seit Jahren im Programm sind und weiterhin sehr stark nachgefragt werden.

Wir sind überzeugt, dass unser Konzept so stark und einzigartig ist, dass es zahlreiche weitere Touren geben wird und wir gemeinsam mit Dag Rogge und seinem Team auch weiterhin neue Experience-Destinationen finden werden. Denn es gibt immer wieder ein neues faszinierendes Ziel, an dem Träume wahr werden können.

Christian Uhrig
Leiter Marketing Kommunikation Jaguar Land Rover Deutschland
Kronberg/Taunus, den 31.10.2017

In the automotive industry, the Land Rover Experience Tour is both unique and a runaway success for the Land Rover brand in Germany. From the start, it was intended to open up the brand to a greater portion of the general public by enabling them to experience Land Rover in its natural environment – and to demonstrate the sheer breadth of capability inherent in the vehicles themselves.

The world of off-road and 4x4 has changed dramatically since the first Experience Tour in 2000. After Camel Trophy virtually invented the globetrotter with his worn-out shoes and trusty Land Rover at his side in countless advertising slots, many new niches have sprung up. Society has experienced a change in values and the SUV (Sport Utility Vehicle) and off-road vehicle market in general have grown significantly in importance. The Experience programme, however, has always enjoyed the respect of the competition, with journalists agreeing unanimously that "only Land Rover can do this kind of tour, as it is the only brand which truly stands for adventure."

From 2007 onwards, however, the global, economic and financial crisis resulted in the cancellation of many car-industry-driven adventure projects. Land Rover Germany had to fight the good fight with the head office in Great Britain in order to keep the Land Rover Experience Tour (LET) alive. When Ford sold Jaguar Land Rover to Tata Motors, though, things looked up for the LET, and today it has become one of the most important cornerstones of Land Rover's global marketing strategy.

A coherent and rigorously applied concept is the secret behind the tour's success. Over 30,000 candidates apply to take part in national selection camps that involve intensive off-road driving and a target-group communication methodology that fits the Land Rover customer profile almost like a glove. Those who make it to this stage (in case of the Peru tour qualification well over 3,200 participants) are obviously focused on taking part in the tour, but by virtue of having participated in the selection phase, they have also had the privilege to drive the full range of Land Rover products, from Defender to Range Rover. Those who make it to the final selection camp held at our centre in Wülfrath (60 participants per tour), which is itself a highlight of the tour selection process, have nearly made it to the off-road equivalent of the 100 metres in the Olympic Games.

The experience is unique and unforgettable. Three days of total off-road, measuring up against your competitors and driven by the maxim: "It isn't winning that counts; it's taking part that matters." The final six will be the target of more than their fair share of envy, as the tour is something money can't buy. It is a fascinating journey with its own individual appeal.

When we say the tour is something money can't buy, that's not strictly accurate. The tour to Peru, driving through the desert all the way to Machu Picchu can also be booked by paying customers keen to follow in the footsteps of an LET. Our professional teams use the knowledge gained in the countries we explore to provide the backbone to a very exclusive, made-to-measure adventure holiday. Iceland and Namibia are very good examples of our Experience adventure tour destinations which have been in the programme for years and continue to be booked up year after year.

We believe that the concept is still so unique and robust enough to support further tours in the future. Together with Dag and his team, we will continue the search for new tour destinations. Experience has taught us time and again that there are new and fascinating locations just waiting to be the stuff of dreams.

Christian Uhrig
Head of Marketing Communication Jaguar Land Rover Germany
Kronberg/Taunus, Germany, 31 October 2017

ES BEGAB SICH ZU EINER ZEIT ...

... da war es noch cool, zu rauchen. Lässig die Fluppe im Mundwinkel, dazu noch ein bisschen Abenteuer und Cowboy-Märchen, fertig war das Camel-Image vom weit reisenden, unerschütterlichen Weltenbummler. Den höchstens ein Loch im Schuh bremste, wenn er im wildesten Westen, Osten, Süden oder Norden unterwegs war. Deswegen brauchte er Helfer.

Die stellte die gelbe Zigarettenmarke aus dem Hause Reynolds Tobacco Company zunächst in Form von uramerikanischen Jeeps. Die erste Camel Trophy im Jahr 1980 – der Versuch, harte und hart rauchende Männer durch noch härteres Gelände zu treiben, um sich das allerhärteste Image zu verleihen – führte mit vier Mietwagen entlang der Transamazônica, teils direkt durch den Urwald. Einzige Aufgabenstellung: Fahre bei A los und versuche, B zu erreichen.

Es gab keine lokalen Scouts und Guides, die mit Wissen, Sprache und landestypischen Lösungen aushelfen konnten. Es gab keine Vortouren zum Eruieren von Pisten, Hotels, Verkehr und Gefahren. Und es gab keine geplante Sicherheit – als würde harten Männern schon nichts passieren. Man brach durch den Dschungel, wo es ging. Zum Beispiel auf Forststraßen. Wo es nicht ging, musste man umkehren und man merkte: B ist manchmal ganz schön weit weg.

1981 stand plötzlich in der Kinowerbung kein Jeep mehr neben dem immer noch sehr abenteuerlustig wirkenden Herrn mit Loch in der Schuhsohle, sondern ein bis dato in Deutschland wenig beachteter Land Rover. Dass neben der Zigarette auch ein Land Rover plötzlich in aller Munde war, ermutigte den englischen Offroad-Spezialisten, 1982 fester Sponsor der Camel Trophy zu werden und die Autos für die Touren zu stellen. Um nicht nur mit schwerem Gasfuß irgendwo durch eine Gegend zu toben, waren nun auch spezielle Aufgaben in die Touren eingebaut worden: besonders schwierige Offroad-Parcours meistern, auf Zeit fahren, nach Roadbook navigieren.

Der Aufwand für die Camel Trophy wuchs stetig: Hubschrauber wurden zum Transport der Lead Scouts eingesetzt, und wenn die Aufgaben zum Beispiel auf der Insel Borneo stattfanden und Regen den Weg unpassierbar machte, wurden schon mal alle teilnehmenden 90er-Defender in ihre Einzelteile zerlegt, ums Hindernis herum geflogen und nach der Landung von den Teilnehmern wieder zusammengebaut. Geld spielte keine Rolle. Es war einfach da.

1990 reichte es den Veranstaltern nicht mehr, mit kleinen Spielchen im Gepäck durch die Gegend zu touren – sie stellten neue, diesmal sehr sportliche Aufgaben, zum Beispiel Kanufahrten, Orientierungsläufe oder Mountainbiken in den abenteuerlichsten Ecken der Welt. Diese Trophy gilt als letzte „Zigaretten-Trophy". Hier wurden noch Sieger und Vizemeister gekürt – ein gewisser Hans Hermann Ruthe erhielt als Teilnehmer den Master Driver Award und belegte in der Gesamtwertung Platz zwei.

Die Umfänge der folgenden Touren nahmen inzwischen gigantische Ausmaße an: 1996 in Argentinien und Chile bestand der Tross aus 56 Land Rover. Allein 36 davon bildeten einen Konvoi, inklusive zwei Ambulanzen, drei Technikwagen, 22 Teamfahrzeugen, drei Fotowagen und noch mal drei Autos für Videofilmer.

Ende des Jahrtausends war es nicht mehr cool, in Schlammschlachten durch die Welt zu pflügen. Die Trophy entwickelte sich mehr und mehr zum Adventure, die Autos wurden zu reinen Transportmitteln. Sport stand jetzt im Vordergrund: Biken, Snowboarden, Laufen, extrem zuschauerunfreundlich, weil nicht ein Journalist den Top-Athleten, welche die Teilnehmer inzwischen sein mussten,

folgen konnte. Außerdem wetterte ein Teil der Öffentlichkeit gegen diese Form von Tourismus, würde man doch nur die Umwelt platt walzen. Was die wenigsten wussten oder wissen wollten: Die Land Rover haben nie neue Wege geschaffen, sondern immer nur vorhandene genutzt und stets einen Benefit im Land gelassen. Wie etwa vier Millionen Dollar für den Nationalpark Baikalsee oder eine komplette Forschungsstation in Malaysia.

1998 wurde Reynolds nach Japan verkauft. Da war Land Rover als Sponsor bereits seit einem Jahr ausgestiegen, weil das Raucherumfeld nicht zum Land-Rover-Image passte und der neue Eigner, BMW, anderes mit der Marke vorhatte. Im Jahr 2000 wurde eine letzte Camel Trophy organisiert, die alle anderen in den Schatten stellen sollte: Samoa. Autos gab es gar nicht mehr, nun wurde in Booten um Punkte und Platzierungen gekämpft. 46 Teamschiffe düsten durchs Wasser, begleitet von einem Tankschiff, Kriegsschiffen als Sicherung, Beobachterschiffen und natürlich auch zwei Hubschraubern. Dann war Schluss.

Aber Land Rover ohne Abenteuer? Niemals.

1999 bestand das Portfolio der Marke aus Range Rover, Discovery, Freelander und Defender. Eigentlich perfekt für die Eroberung der Welt – aber dazu mussten wir reisen. Metaphorisch ausgedrückt: Wir hatten eine tolle Torte, doch es fehlte die Kirsche obendrauf.

So entwickelten wir 1999 ein neues Konzept. Basis war die Idee, dass sich nun Menschen für eine Tour bewerben können, die früher bei der Camel Trophy nur vorm Fernseher saßen und bedauerten, dass sie weder das richtige Alter noch die richtige Statur für so eine harte Rallye besaßen. Die Tortur schafften damals wirklich nur gestählte GSG-9-Beamte, Jet-Piloten oder Extremsportler. Außerdem erschien uns die ganz harte Tour nicht mehr zeitgemäß. Der Trend ging zum Nichtrauchen, zum ökologisch verantwortbaren Offroaden, zu Menschen und Kultur statt mit der Brechstange durch den Dschungel. Wir stellten uns ein kontrolliertes und kontrollierbares Abenteuer vor, die Entdeckung von Land und Leuten abseits touristischer Pfade mit hohem Erlebniswert.

Der Weg dorthin: Bekanntmachung einer solchen Tour über die damals rund 160 Land-Rover-Händler sowie Presse und Radio. Danach die Einrichtung von verschiedenen Qualifikationscamps, bei denen die Aufgaben niemanden abschrecken oder überfordern sollten. Nach denen aber auch diejenigen, die nicht ausgewählt wurden, zufrieden nach Hause fahren konnten – und das Erlebnis, in einem Land Rover gefahren zu sein, nicht vergaßen. Letztendlich sollten stets sechs geeignete Menschen mit uns auf die jeweilige Tour gehen. 1999 präsentierten wir das Konzept dem damaligen Eigner BMW. Von dort kam ein klares Nein. Niemand dort konnte sich solche Touren als imageförderndes Marketinginstrument vorstellen.

Doch kurz darauf, im April 2000, verkaufte BMW die Marke Land Rover an Ford. Die Amerikaner forderten noch in der Übergangsphase verkaufsunterstützende Marketingaktivitäten für die Offroad-Marke, für die zu dem Zeitpunkt noch eine BMW-Abteilung zuständig war. So bekam Land Rover im April/Mai 2000 einen Anruf aus Bayern: Konzept nun doch genehmigt. Die erste Tour führte – noch unter dem Namen „Land Rover Entdecker-Tour" – nach Jordanien.

Die englische Land-Rover-Sektion versuchte übrigens ebenfalls, ein eigenes Event auf die Beine zu stellen. 2003 und 2006 gab es die G4 Challenge (G4 = Global Four), eine Tour in vier Zeitzonen auf vier Kontinenten. Das Projekt erwies sich aber als zu aufwendig, für Journalisten war es so gut wie nicht mehr verfolgbar.

Und: Die Medienvertreter durften nie – wie schon bei allen früheren Camel Trophys – selbst ans Steuer. Was für die eher Komfort gewohnten Lifestyle-Schreiber nicht so dramatisch war, für die erlebnisorientierten Autojournalisten jedoch umso schlimmer. So oder so: Auf diese Weise war es für sie nur schwer vermittelbar, was so eine G4-Tour ausmachte.

2001 kam Christian Uhrig ins Marketing von Land Rover, mit ihm zusammen entwickelten wir das aktuelle Tour-Konzept aus Qualifikation, Tour und Reiseprogramm weiter. Im gleichen Jahr wurde die Land Rover Experience gegründet – als „Fahrschule" für Neukunden. Nach Festsetzung von Qualitätsstandards sollten alle Land Rover Experience Center die exakt gleichen Aus- und Fortbildungskriterien an die Kunden weitergeben, Händler schulen, die hohe Verantwortung beim Offroadfahren vermitteln und ein optimales Trainingsareal zur Verfügung stellen.

Die Ur-Ausbildungsstätten heißen Eastnor Castle und Solihull – die „homes of the legend". Hier waren Hans und ich schon in den 80er-Jahren zu Schulungen. Mittlerweile werden hier die neuen Instruktoren der Experience Center ausgebildet. Heute existieren weltweit 27 Experience Center. Die Land Rover Experience Tour aber gibt es nur in Deutschland. Darauf bin ich ein bisschen stolz.

Unseren Rückblick auf zwölf Land Rover Experience Touren und eine unvergessliche Winterveranstaltung für Journalisten beginnen wir chronologisch mit der Reise durch Jordanien. Die aufwendigste und längste Tour ist die Jubiläumstour durch elf Länder über Teile der legendären Seidenstraße von Deutschland nach Indien. Die jüngste Tour führte uns nach Peru – und sie war nicht weniger faszinierend als alle anderen Land Rover Experience Touren zuvor.

Sie werden sehen: Wir haben zwar die Abenteuertouren mit den besten Offroadern der Welt nicht neu erfunden – aber dramatisch professionalisiert, präzisiert und kultiviert.

Dag Rogge, *Chef der Land Rover Experience Deutschland*
Wülfrath, den 07.11.2017

THERE ONCE WAS A TIME...

... when smoking was still cool. Nonchalant, the cigarette dangling from the corner of one's mouth, a bit of adventure and cowboy chic thrown in, and there you had it – Camel's image of the intrepid globetrotter. The only thing that was stopping him on his way west, east, south or north was a hole in his shoe. It was time to get help.

Reynolds Tobacco Company, which owned the Camel brand, initially found help in the form of American Jeeps. The first Camel Trophy in 1980 was an attempt to get tough, smoking guys through even tougher terrain to bolster the tough-guy image in the ad campaign. Four rented vehicles battled their way along the Trans-Amazonian Highway, partly cutting their way through rainforest. The task was simple: start in A and try to get to B. There were no scouts or guides on hand to contribute local knowledge, language or any other skills indigenous to the region. There was no pre-scouting to determine the best possible routes, accommodation, traffic situation or possible dangers. And there was no risk management – where the going gets tough, the tough get going. Where necessary, the route was hacked through the jungle using forestry roads, for example, and where that wasn't possible, one simply turned round, noting that B was quite a long way away.

From 1981, however, cinema advertising no longer featured a Jeep alongside the globetrotting adventurer with the hole in his shoe. On display instead was a Land Rover, which thus far in Germany had not exactly been a sales or even PR success story. As people began talking not only about cigarettes but about Land Rover as well, it prompted the English maker of specialist off-road vehicles to become official sponsor of the Camel Trophy in 1982 and furnish the vehicles used in the competition. To avoid simply flattening the countryside, special tasks were now integrated into the event, including mastering particularly challenging off-road driving sections, time trials and road book navigation.

The logistics of the Camel Trophy grew exponentially year on year. Helicopters were used to transport the lead scouts; when, for example, during the event on the island of Borneo, incessant rain made the route impassable, the participating Defender 90s were taken apart, flown around the obstacle and rebuilt by the competitors. Money was no object.

By 1990, as far as the event organizers were concerned, simply driving through the countryside, with all manner of mini tasks for the participants, would no longer suffice. This time the focus was on real sporting tasks – with canoeing, orienteering and mountain bike events scheduled in the most exotic "back of beyond" locations on the planet. The 1990 event was known as the last "Cigarette Trophy". Winner and runner-up titles were awarded, with a certain Hans Hermann Ruthe winning the Master Driver Award and second place overall.

The following tours grew increasingly complex, assuming gargantuan dimensions. The 1996 event in Argentina and Chile had a fleet of 56 Land Rovers, of which 36 alone made up the main convoy with two ambulances, three technical support vehicles, 22 team cars, three photography cars and another three cars for video crews.

By the end of the century, global mud-plugging was no longer cool. The Trophy was increasingly adventure-focused, the vehicles reduced to the status of mere transport. The emphasis was on sport: biking, snowboarding, running – all of which was difficult for audience participation, as no journalist could keep up with the top athletes (who now made up the majority of the competitors). For the scribes, covering the event proved a struggle. Additionally, some sections of the general public were increasingly prone to rant and rail at this kind of tourism, which appeared to have no respect whatsoever for the environment. At the time, people were either unaware, or wished to remain ignorant, of the fact that the Land Rovers never hacked their way through virgin jungle. Instead, they drove routes that already existed and always made sure that when they left a country, some form of benefit remained, such as a four million dollar donation for the Lake Baikal National Park or a complete research station in Malaysia.

In 1998, Reynolds was sold to a company in Japan. The year prior, Land Rover had ended its sponsorship deal, as smoking no longer suited Land Rover's image and new owner BMW had other plans for the brand. In 2000, the final Camel Trophy event, designed to put all the previous Trophies in the shade, took part on Samoa. This time there were no vehicles involved. The competition was fought out in high-speed dirigibles. 46 team boats shot across the Pacific Ocean, supported by their own tanker and protected by warships, with the usual entourage of observers and of course two helicopters.

And then it was over. Still, the idea that Land Rover could do without adventure was simply intolerable.

In 1999, the brand consisted of four vehicle types: Range Rover, Discovery, Freelander and Defender. All designed to conquer the world – but to do so, you had to go travelling. Metaphorically speaking, the cake looked delicious but still needed the icing on top.

In 1999, we developed a new idea. The idea was that there were people out there who had seen Camel Trophy on TV but had been unable to take part because they were either too old or lacked the appropriate physique for such a demanding tour. Indeed, by the final running of the Camel Trophy, only jet fighter pilots, marines and extreme athletes were up to the task. Besides, we felt that the extreme tour was no longer in keeping with the zeitgeist. Not smoking was the new trend, and off-roading had gone ecologically responsible, with greater focus on understanding communities and culture rather than just ploughing one's way through the jungle. We planned a controlled and manageable adventure trip, one that would be a rich and varied experience, exploring countries and their ways of life off the beaten tourist trails.

How to get there: we had to spread the word about the new tour to the approximately 160 Land Rover dealers in Germany, and we had to generate the necessary PR through the media. After that, we had to set up a series of selection camps in which no one would be scared off by tasks deemed impossible, but that would also leave those not selected with a positive impression of the experience of having driven a Land Rover as they made their way home. In 1999, we presented the concept to the owner of Land Rover at the time – BMW. The answer was a very clear "No". Such tours were not seen in Munich as an appropriate image-building marketing tool.

Shortly afterwards, in April 2000, BMW sold the Land Rover brand to Ford. During the handover period, the Americans requested marketing events to directly support the off-road brand's sales operations in Germany. As this effort

was still being run by a BMW department, Land Rover received a phone call in April/May 2000 from the Bavarians informing them that the concept had been approved after all. The first Tour, which ran under the name "Land Rover Entdecker (Discoverer) Tour", was to Jordan.

Land Rover's head office in Great Britain was also planning its own event. 2003 and 2006 saw the global marketing department putting on the G4 Challenge (G4 stood for "Global Four"): an event held in four time zones on four continents. The logistics of the project were, as it turned out, too complex for the journalists to follow the entire competition. And to add insult to injury, the media weren't allowed to drive themselves (as had been the case on all the Camel Trophy events). For cosseted-lifestyle journalists, this wasn't too great a sacrifice, but for the automobile press focusing on the experience aspect of the event, it was a PR nightmare. Either way, it was difficult for them to convey to audiences what the buzz of the G4 Tour really was.

Christian Uhrig joined the marketing department at Land Rover Germany in 2001, and together we developed the current tour concept, consisting of selection, tour and travel programme. That same year, the Land Rover Experience was founded as a form of Driving Academy for new customers. Following centrally assigned quality standards, Land Rover Experience Centres the world over were to offer a common standard of driver and off-road training courses for customers and dealers, teaching people the need to act responsibly when driving off-road while also providing ideal locations in which to conduct training.

The original Land Rover training centres are located at Eastnor Castle (on the border between England and Wales) and at the home of Land Rover in Solihull, Birmingham, where they operate under the title "Home of the Legend". Hans and I completed our respective training courses there in the 1980s. Today, all Experience Centre instructors complete their training at Eastnor Castle. There are 27 Experience Centres in operation across the world. However, the "Land Rover Experience Tour" is a purely German operation, which leaves me with a sense of pride.

Our review of twelve Land Rover Experience Tours and an unforgettable winter driving event for journalists starts chronologically with our journey through Jordan. The most complicated and longest tour was our anniversary event through eleven countries traversing parts of the legendary Silk Road from Germany to India. Our most recent tour took us to Peru – a country that was just as fascinating as every Land Rover Experience Tour that has gone before. Obviously we haven't re-invented the adventure tour with the best off-road vehicles on the planet – what we have achieved, however, is this: an adventure tour with new impetus and significant improvements in the levels of professionalism and attention to detail.

Dag Rogge
Head of Land Rover Experience Germany
Wülfrath, Germany
07 November 2017

„Hans, Hans – Dag, Dag!"
„Dag, Hans!"
„Hans, geht's da weiter?"
„Dag, sieht so aus."
„Danke Hans, Dag."
„Dag, Dag – Hans, Hans?"
„Dag hört."
„Oder auch nicht."
„Danke Hans. Hans, Dag, Dag?"
„Hier Hans. Dag?"
„Hans, also was?"
„Dag, Hans, weiter."
„Hans, Dag, klar."
„Dag, Dag, Hans, Hans?"
„Hans, Dag."
„Wie immer."
„Genau, Hans. Bis später. Dag Ende."
„Bis später. Hans Ende."

PROLOG
PROLOGUE

"Hans, Hans – Dag, Dag!"
"Dag, Hans!"
"Hans, any movement up there?"
"Dag, looks like it."
"Thanks Hans, Dag."
"Dag, Dag – Hans, Hans?"
"Dag's listening."
"Or maybe not."
"Thanks Hans. Hans, Dag, Dag?"
"Hans here. Dag?"
"Hans, so what's happening?"
"Dag, Hans, off we go."
"Hans, Dag, understood."
"Dag, Dag, Hans, Hans?"
"Hans, Dag."
"As usual."
"Exactly, Hans. See you later. Dag out."
"See you later. Hans out."

Ich gebe zu, ob diese Unterhaltung über Funk tatsächlich so verlaufen ist und wann das war, vermag ich nicht mit hundertprozentiger Sicherheit zu sagen. Aber wer zum ersten Mal eine unserer Touren begleitet, hat zumindest den Eindruck, Hans und ich würden uns nur so unterhalten. Und da ist eine Menge Wahres dran.

Wir beide sind Seelenverwandte, der Hans Hermann Ruthe und ich, und wäre es anders, gäbe es vielleicht die Land Rover Experience Touren nicht. Dieser begnadete Werkzeugbauer organisierte seit 1991 die Camel Trophy mit, wurde 1992 Adjutant des Eventdirektors und ist heute bei den Land Rover Experience Touren nicht mehr wegzudenken – meine rechte und manchmal auch linke Hand, mein gutes und manchmal auch mein schlechtes Gewissen.

Aber selbst, wenn wir viel Spaß an unseren Touren haben – es steckt unendlich viel Arbeit darin, die wir alleine nicht leisten könnten. Deshalb möchte ich mich hier ganz besonders bei dem Team von Jaguar Land Rover Deutschland bedanken, das die Touren finanziert; bei meinem gesamten Land Rover Experience Team; bei den Ärzten, die seit zehn Jahren die Touren begleiten; bei den Fotografen und Journalisten, die dafür sorgen, dass die Welt von unseren unvergleichlichen Touren erfährt; bei den lokalen Guides, ohne die wir niemals die unvergesslichen Tracks und Pisten gefunden hätten; und bei den unzähligen anderen Helfern, die zum Erfolg der Land Rover Experience Touren beigetragen haben. Einige von ihnen lernen Sie in diesem Buch durch persönliche Interviews kennen.

Übrigens: Oft werde ich gefragt, ob wir uns schon mal so richtig verfahren haben. Erst seit der Jubiläumstour – der Seidenstraße – muss ich zugeben: Ja. Und peinlicherweise ausgerechnet in Deutschland: Am Startpunkt Wülfrath hatten wir Krakau in Polen ins von uns sonst nie benutzte Navigationssystem eingegeben, und als es uns in Dortmund „abbiegen" befahl, haben wir den Hinweis ignoriert. Wie sollte ein Navi es denn auch besser wissen können als gewiefte Weltreisende? Kurz: Es wusste es besser. Wir sind über Berlin nach Polen gereist statt über den kürzesten Weg.

Aber das ist wirklich nur eine Petitesse gegenüber den Anekdoten, Geschichten und Dramen, die ich als Leiter der Land Rover Experience in mehr als 17 Jahren Experience Tour erleben durfte. Lassen Sie sich in Wort und Bild einfach ein auf die zwölf „geilsten Touren der Welt" in insgesamt 25 Länder sowie den Versuch einer „Winter Experience" für Journalisten, die ich hier zusammengetragen habe – natürlich aus persönlichem Blickwinkel erzählt, aber immer hart an der Wahrheit. Ich habe nichts hinzugedichtet und keine Problematik, Unter- und Überschätzung ausgelassen.

Sie werden sehen: Trotz aller Erfahrung bin auch ich nicht unfehlbar.

I will admit that I can't recall with any certainty when or whether this conversation actually took place at all. However, anyone joining Hans and myself for the first time on a tour rapidly comes to the conclusion that this is how we talk to each other all the time. And there is a lot of truth in that.

Hans Hermann Ruthe and I are soulmates, and were this not the case, then we probably wouldn't have the Land Rover Experience Tour at all. From 1991 onwards, this gifted toolmaker was involved in the organization of the Camel Trophy, becoming adjutant to the event director in 1992. Today I can't image the Land Rover Experience Tour without him – he is my right hand and sometimes even my left. He is my conscience in the good times and the bad.

However much fun we have on the tours – there is a phenomenal amount of work involved in the organization of the event, which we couldn't achieve on our own. For this reason I would like to extend my thanks to the team at Jaguar Land Rover Germany, which finances the tours; to my own team at Land Rover Experience; to the doctors who have accompanied the tours for years; to the photographers and journalists who have seen to it that the world experiences our incomparable tours; to the local guides without whom we would never have discovered the unforgettable routes and tracks; and to countless others who have contributed to the success of the Land Rover Experience Tours. You will get to know some of them in interviews conducted for this book.

By the way, I have often been asked whether we have taken a wrong turn on a tour. Since the anniversary event on the Silk Road, I have to admit: yes. Embarrassingly enough, it happened in Germany. At our point of departure in Wülfrath we tapped Kraków in Poland into the navigation system (which we otherwise never really use), and as we approached Dortmund we ignored the instruction to turn off the motorway – as if a computer were better informed than two globetrotting professionals. Fact is, the computer was better informed, and we ended up driving to Poland via Berlin instead of taking the shorter route.

This, however, is a mere trifle when weighed up against the plethora of anecdotes, tales and dramas that I have been privileged to witness first-hand as head of the Land Rover Experience in over 17 years of the tour. Enjoy the words and pictures I have put together from twelve of the most awesome tours on the planet, crossing through a total of 25 countries and including a Media Winter Experience Tour we once attempted. Always from my personal perspective but as close to what really happened as possible. Nothing has been made up, and no problem, under- or overestimation of a situation has been omitted from the story.

As you will see, despite all my experience, I'm human, too.

JORDANIEN

JORDAN

2000

2000
LAND: JORDANIEN
STRECKE: 850 KM
COUNTRY: JORDAN
DISTANCE: 530 MILES

4 DEFENDER, 1 FREELANDER,
1 DISCOVERY

DAS ZIEL
THE DESTINATION

Der Anruf von BMW kommt unvermittelt, ist kurz und knochentrocken: Die erste Tour – sie heißt zunächst „Land Rover Entdecker-Tour" – startet in vier Monaten. Also hopphopp!

Es gibt kein verabschiedetes Gesamtkonzept, keine Kooperationspartner und keine geplanten Reisen nach der Tour. Das alles wird erst im Jahr 2001 passieren. Es gibt eigentlich gar nichts außer vier Monate Zeit. Für die Bekanntmachung, für Qualifikationscamps, für die Endqualifikation, für eine Vortour, für die gesamte Event-Organisation. Ich setze mich mit offenem Mund erst mal eine Weile hin und sage gar nichts. Auch wenn die Zeit drängt.

Und wie. Wir haben kein definiertes Ziel. Aber die Infos für die Bewerbungen müssen raus. Wie, bitteschön, bewirbt man eine Tour, von der man nur weiß, dass sie stattfinden muss? Liebe Leute, Land Rover befindet sich gerade in einer Umbauphase, und die beginnt damit, dass wir mit euch irgendwohin touren wollen, wo es nett ist, was zu der Marke passt, was euch ein bisschen mehr abverlangt, als nur einem Reiseleiter zu folgen, und was ihr nie vergessen werdet – aber wir haben keine Ahnung, wohin? Na prima.

Mit insgesamt acht Festangestellten und ein paar Freelancern gilt es, so schnell wie möglich sechs verschiedene Standorte für die Qualicamps aus dem Boden zu stampfen. Das Areal für die Endqualifikation ist dagegen schnell definiert: unser Steinbruch in Wülfrath. Perfekt für Fahrübungen aller Art, ein guter Startpunkt für Navigationsaufgaben in den Kohlenpott, und bei Mondschein kann ich die Reiselustigen wunderbar aus den Zelten schmeißen für Nachtaufgaben, ohne dass sich meine Nachbarn nachhaltig über die Action im Revier beschweren.

Die Zeit rennt. Noch drei Monate Zeit. 6 000 Menschen bewerben sich in aller Schnelle, 2 400 laden wir zu den Qualifikationscamps ein. Wohin es letztlich geht, verschleiern wir so gut wie möglich. Was nicht schwer ist, weil wir es selbst noch nicht wissen. Dabei sein kann dagegen fast jeder: Wir achten ein bisschen auf das jeweilige Hobby, auf das Alter, natürlich auf die Gültigkeit des Führerscheins, aber auf mehr auch nicht. Auch wenn wir keine so dramatischen Abenteuer wie bei der Camel Trophy planen, so können wir doch nicht das Risiko eingehen, Fahranfänger mitzunehmen (was sich bis heute nicht geändert hat). Die Hoffnungsfrohen müssen zeigen, dass sie mit den Autos umgehen können, Grundzüge der Navigation lernen, Erste-Hilfe-Kenntnisse beweisen. Jeder Trainer macht Aufzeichnungen, schmeißt seine Prüflinge wie geplant (und mit großer Freude) auch mal nachts aus dem Zelt, um ihnen eine Aufgabe zu stellen. Und schnell sind sechs Menschen gefunden, die auf die erste Reise gehen dürfen.

Aber wohin? Die Zeit wird immer knapper, und wir müssen schnell entscheiden: Was kennen wir? Wo müssen wir nicht bei Null mit der Recherche anfangen? In Jordanien! Hans und ich hatten dort unseren bislang letzten Urlaub verbracht. Eine Endqualifikation für die Camel Trophy (mit Hans als Organisator) fand dort auch schon mal statt. Fast 90 000 Quadratkilometer steinige Spielwiese, heißes, trockenes Sommerklima, das Tote Meer als perfekter Swimmingpool und schließlich eine reichhaltige Natur – Planerherz, was willst du mehr? Und der Schwager von Hans namens Hussein ist auch noch gebürtiger Jordanier – einen besseren Guide können wir uns nicht vorstellen. Das Land ist sicher, ruhig und damit erfüllt es einen der wichtigsten Grundsätze der Land Rover Experience: „Es darf nie etwas Schlimmes passieren!"

The call from BMW came unexpectedly and was short and to the point: the first tour is to kick off in four months and is provisionally called the "Land Rover Entdecker (Discoverer) Tour". So get on with it!

There was no overall concept that had been approved, no co-op partners and no customer trips planned for after the tour. All that would have to wait until 2001. We had four months to organize the event, including the pre-event PR and call-to-action campaign, selection camps, final selections and a pre-scout recce. Somewhat dumbstruck, I sat down for a while and said nothing. And that with the clock ticking inexorably. We had no clearly defined destination but at the same time we had to go public with the application information. How does one market a tour when all you have to talk about is the fact that it is going to happen at all?

"Dear potential candidate, Land Rover is currently restructuring itself, and part of this process is to take you on a tour to a nice place that matches the brand, that requires a bit more from you than just following the guide, and that will remain unforgettable. One other thing: we don't know where we're going." Nice idea.

With a total of eight permanent staff and a few freelancers, we had to create six locations for the selection camps out of nothing. Final selections were clarified almost immediately and would take place in our quarry site in Wülfrath near Düsseldorf. A perfect place for all manner of driving exercises, a good location for navigational tasks spreading across the Ruhr area and, in the middle of the night, ideal for pulling would-be globetrotters out of their tents to complete a night task without waking up the neighbours at the same time.

We were on a mission. Three months to go. 6,000 people applied almost spontaneously. We invited 2,400 to the selection camps. We said as little as possible regarding the tour's final destination, which wasn't difficult as we still hadn't decided where we were actually going. Almost all of the candidates had what it takes to accompany us. Hobbies that fitted our requirements, age and of course a valid driving licence were pretty much the only criteria. That said, even though we weren't planning a Camel Trophy-style adventure assault, we still couldn't afford to risk taking learner drivers with us (a criterion upon which we still insist to this day.) Our hopeful candidates needed to show that they could operate the vehicles safely, and that they understood the basics of navigation and first aid. Each trainer observed each and every candidate, took notes and with considerable gusto threw his fledglings out of their tents at some ungodly hour to confront them with a special task. In no time at all, we had six candidates who had earned the right to accompany us.

Yet we still didn't know where we were going. Time was running out, and we needed to come to a decision. Where had we been before? Was there somewhere where we wouldn't be starting with an empty page? How about Jordan? Hans and I had spent our last holiday there, and Hans had organized Camel Trophy final selections there, too. 35,000 square miles of stony playground; a dry, hot climate; the Dead Sea as a perfect swimming pool; and, not least, a rich and diverse environment – a planner's dream! Hans' brother-in-law is a native Jordanian – we wouldn't find a better guide. Political and social unrest was unheard-of, which enabled us to tick one of our most important prerequisites: "We should always avoid getting into trouble!"

DAS PROBLEM
THE PROBLEM

Während noch die Teilnehmer gesucht werden, gilt es, sich so schnell wie möglich über Import-/Exportvorschriften schlau zu machen, die Autos nach Jordanien zu verschiffen und diverse Genehmigungen einzuholen. Wir sind auf einem guten Weg – bis wir an den Zollchef im Hafen von Akaba, dem einzigen jordanischen Seehafen, geraten. Der Mann ist so beleibt wie stur. Er kennt zwar die Prozedur, Autos ins Land zu lassen, die dort bleiben, aber nicht diejenige, Autos ins Land und dann wieder ausreisen zu lassen. Kurz: Er setzt unsere für die Vortour dringend benötigten Allradler im Zollbereich des Hafens fest.

Hussein muss uns retten. Uns ist schon ganz anders, weil der Zollchef von Akaba uns bei den vielen Besprechungen unablässig mit viel zu viel heißem, irrsinnig süßem Tee füttert (nicht ohne dabei ständig Solitaire zu spielen). So fliegen wir mit Hussein nach Amman, um eine Unterredung mit dem Tourismusminister von Jordanien zu erbitten. Der Einsatz von Hans' Schwager ist Gold wert, denn es klappt: Nach einer vollen Woche persönlicher Blockade muss der Zollchef die Wagen auf Weisung der Regierung freigeben. Und weil er nach wie vor keine Ahnung hat, was er da eigentlich tut, setzt er einen Stempel auf das Ausfuhrdokument, das fortan regierungsgenehmigt besagt, dass die Wagen ein volles Jahr im Land bleiben dürfen. Damit hat er ungewollt die Grundlage für alle Land Rover Experience Reisen gelegt. Denn daraufhin können wir später Reisen für Journalisten und alle buchenden Land-Rover-Fans in dem wunderschönen Land anbieten, ohne uns Gedanken um die Autos machen zu müssen. Man kann eben auch mal Glück haben.

Nachteil der Hängepartie im jordanischen Hafen: Wir haben nur noch wenig Zeit, bis die Teilnehmer kommen. Und immer noch ist keine Vortour erledigt, um Hotels zu checken, interessante Trails zu suchen, Campsites vorzubereiten. So rasen Hans und ich in letzter Minute einen Tag und eine Nacht die Hauptstrecke ab und klären die wichtigsten offenen Fragen. Wir fallen zwar am Abend halbtot in die Betten, aber die Tour steht. Wie erwartet nach vier Monaten und keiner Stunde mehr.

While we were still selecting our participants, we needed to get to grips with the import/export regulations, ship the cars to Jordan and sort out numerous permits. We had made considerable progress until we made the acquaintance of the head of customs in Jordan's only port in Aqaba. Obese and obstinate in equal measure, he understood the procedure whereby vehicles are imported into the country to stay there. He had not, however, heard of any procedure facilitating the entry and exit of the same vehicles in and out of the country. In short, our four-wheel drive vehicles, which we urgently required for the pre-scout recce, were impounded and remained in the port's customs area under lock and key.

Hussein had to save our skins. We were at our wits' end, not least as a result of interminable conversations with the same customs chief who would serve us endless cups of unfathomably hot, extremely sweet tea while playing solitaire. We flew to Amman, taking Hussein along, with the intention of talking to Jordan's minister of tourism directly. Hans' brother-in-law's intervention was worth his weight in gold. For the plan worked. After a week of his personal blocking tactics, a government directive instructed the intransigent customs chief to release the vehicles. The moment he stamped the vehicle-release document, thereby putting a government seal of approval on the vehicles' staying in Jordan for a year, he unknowingly laid the foundations for all future Land Rover Experience Tours. We were now able to offer a tour package to media and Land Rover fans willing to pay without having to worry about the vehicles. A little luck never hurts.

The long stalemate in the port of Aqaba left us with another problem, though – there was now very little time left before the participants' arrival. We still had to finish up a pre-scouting: we needed to find hotels and interesting routes, and we needed to prepare campsites. Hans and I shot off at the last minute to drive the main route in 24 hours and sort out the remaining issues. The following day, we were both exhausted, but the tour was ready to roll as instructed in four months and not a day longer.

OB AUF KAMELEN DER WÜSTENPOLIZEI
ODER ÜBER ABENTEUERLICHE PISTEN
IN RUND 1 000 METERN HÖHE – DIE
ANGESTEUERTEN ZIELE SIND ALLE
STRAPAZEN WERT.
--
WHETHER ENJOYING THE SIGHT
OF CAMEL-MOUNTED POLICE IN
THE DESERT OR DRIVING ADVEN-
TUROUS TRACKS IN THE SAND AT
OVER 3,000 FEET, IT IS WORTH ALL THE
EFFORT GETTING THERE.

DAS WADI
THE WADI

Es ist perfekt: traumhafte Landschaften, wilde Vegetation, malerische Camps unterm Himmelszelt. Und viel Sand, gut zum Festfahren. Man darf in weichem Sand nicht anhalten, aber die nicht so gewieften Teams kommen um die von uns durchaus gewollte Erfahrung des Ausgrabens nicht herum. Größte Fahrunwissenheit: Bei eingeschalteter Untersetzung geben die Fahrer im soften Untergrund oft zu viel Gas. So verdichtet sich das lockere Sediment beim Anfahren hinter dem Rad, aber davor baut sich ein kleiner Sandhügel auf – der Wagen bleibt erneut stecken. Das passiert selbst bei den Defendern, man muss sie eben zu bewegen wissen. Alle 4 bis 5 Kilometer bleibt ein Wagen stecken – nur ausgerechnet nicht der mitgenommene Freelander. Der ist viel leichter als das Urvieh aller Offroader und gehorcht dadurch anderen physikalischen Gesetzen. So fährt Christian Uhrig, unser Marketingchef, mit dem recht neuen kleinen Landy Kreise in den Sanddünen um die von nur halbkundigen Händen bewegten Defender, was alle erstaunt. Mich eingeschlossen.

Nach so vielen Fragezeichen in den Augen unserer Erstteilnehmer denke ich, die nächste Aufgabe sollte einfach gestrickt sein. Sie lautet schließlich: Findet von Punkt A, dem Standort, zum Punkt B, dem Einstieg ins Wadi Rum. Und zwar in einer Nacht-Task.

Wer das traumhafte ausgetrocknete Flussbett nicht kennt: Das Wadi Rum ist das größte Wadi in Jordanien mit einer Länge von rund 100 und einer Breite von 60 Kilometern. Als Schutzgebiet mit einer Fläche von 74 000 Hektar wurde es 2011 in die Welterbeliste der UNESCO aufgenommen. Nachts wird es hier um diese Jahreszeit um die 3 Grad kühl, tagsüber bis zu 26 Grad heiß. Dank GPS und topografischem Kartenmaterial sollte der etwa 40 Kilometer lange Weg dorthin nicht so schwer zu finden sein.

Sollte. Denn statt sich mit den Karten zu beschäftigen, geben alle Teams einfach den GPS-Punkt für den Wadi-Einstieg ein und fahren los. Dass dazwischen vielleicht eine Schlucht liegen könnte, die den direkten Weg versperrt, daran denken sie nicht. Die einen fahren strikt geradeaus, die anderen im Kreis, die dritten eiern durch die Gegend wie ein wild gewordener Lunar Rover durchs Mare Imbrium. Hans guckt mich an, ich gucke Hans an, und wir beschließen, einzugreifen, bevor auch nur ein Team zu weit weg ist und damit außerhalb unseres Funkbereichs. Oder sogar kopfüber in die Schlucht stürzt.

Bis wir die so ahnungs- wie orientierungslosen Teams wieder eingesammelt haben, vergeht eine ganze Weile. Und nach wilden Einfangmanövern bilden wir einen Kreis – inzwischen haben alle Teilnehmer ihre Fahrzeuge verlassen. Ich will gerade in tiefster jordanischer Nacht ohne jedwede Lichtverschmutzung mit meiner Standpauke loslegen, da erschrecken wir alle fürchterlich – neben mir steht plötzlich ein völlig in schwarz gekleideter Beduine. Der Mann macht allerdings ein genauso erschrockenes Gesicht wie wir, er zittert wie ein Turbodiesel bei falscher Leerlaufdrehzahl. Bis sich alles aufklärt: Der arme Jordanier dachte, die dunklen, großen Autos seien von irgendeiner halbseidenen Behörde ausgesandt, um weiß der Geier was in dieser Wildnis anzustellen. Er führt uns zu einem großen Felsen – dahinter kauert ebenso zitternd sein Harem in einem kleinen Zeltdorf.

Aufgrund der sowieso schon überlangen Nacht leeren wir schließlich im Camp ein Outdoor-Case, füllen es mit Eis, kühlen den Champagner darin und feiern bis morgens um 4 Uhr.

Perfection: fantastic landscapes, wild vegetation, picturesque campsites under a painted sky. And sand in abundance – enough to get really stuck. Stopping in soft sand is ill-advised, but the teams are new to the experience and sooner or later they have to grab their shovels (which is what we wanted in the first place). It is perhaps the most common error in soft terrain: after having selected low-range, to then put your foot down on the gas, kicking the loose material to the rear, behind the wheel, whilst creating a mini sand escarpment in front of the wheel. As a result, the vehicle simply digs itself in again. Defenders are not exempt – the driver just needs to understand how to move the vehicle. Every 3 miles or so, one of our vehicles became stuck, with the exception of the Freelander. The latter is much lighter than Land Rover's iconic off-roader and interprets the rules of physics differently. Our head of marketing, Christian Uhrig, drove circles in the sand dunes around the Defenders that were admittedly being driven by relative newcomers to off-roading. The group was astounded. Myself included.

The questions on the faces of our first participants forced us to simplify the next task. And that was to drive from A (where we were) to B (the entrance to the Wadi Rum). At night.

For those who do not know this wonderful dry riverbed, the Wadi Rum is the largest wadi in Jordan, approximately 60 miles long and 40 miles wide. The protected reserve, with a surface area of some 285 square miles, was awarded UNESCO World Heritage Site status in 2011. From a daytime high of 26 degrees Celsius (79 degrees Fahrenheit) at this time of year, the temperature can drop to 3 degrees Celsius (37 degrees Fahrenheit) at night. Thanks to GPS navigation and topographical maps, one might think that finding the 25-mile route to the wadi would not be too difficult.

One might think … But rather than consult maps, the teams simply tapped in the GPS coordinates for the entrance into the wadi. They failed to consider that a gorge might be in the way, blocking the route. The first team headed straight as a plank into the distance, the second drove around in circles, and the third was all over the place like an out-of-control Lunar Rover heading over the moon's Mare Imbrium. Hans and I looked at each other and decided to put a stop to it either before the teams were out of range of our CB radios or one of them disappeared head first into a gorge.

It took a while before we had gathered up our clueless and completely disoriented teams. After having reeled them in – and doing so took some rather reckless manoeuvring in the sand – we parked the vehicles in a circle and everybody climbed down. As I wound myself up to rant at everyone in the dark of the Jordanian night, suddenly everyone jumped in fright. Standing literally right next to me was a Bedouin bedecked from head to toe in black. I think he was just as frightened as we were and was shivering and shaking like a poorly idling diesel engine. And then came the explanation. He thought the big dark cars were from some dubious government agency planning something equally dubious out here in the wilderness. Then he led us to a huge rock. Behind it, equally terrified, was his harem in a small tent village. As it was already way past bedtime by then, we returned to camp, filled one of our outdoor travel cases with ice, bedded the champagne in it and partied till 4 in the morning.

DIE FLUCHT
THE ESCAPE

Nicht alle Treffen in Jordanien klären sich so vorteilhaft für die Beteiligten auf wie die Begegnung mit dem verunsicherten Beduinen. In der streng islamischen Stadt Ma'an müssen wir erfahren, wie groß die Kluft zwischen Religionen, Volksgruppen, ja Welten sein kann.

Nachdem wir auf dem Weg durch Jordanien Kraftstoff in alten Olivenöldosen erworben und getreu unserem Motto „Jeden Tag eine gute Tat" einen liegengebliebenen Jordanier mit seinem Auto abgeschleppt haben (wobei sich dann herausstellt, dass sein Auto doch noch fährt), legen wir in Ma'an einen Stopp ein, um Brot und andere Lebensmittel zu kaufen. Die Teams und Hussein verschwinden im Supermarkt, wir anderen warten bei den Autos. Ich stehe oben auf dem Dachgepäckträger, um die Spannung der Sicherungsgurte zu überprüfen. Ein anscheinend ausgesprochen schlechter Standpunkt.

Dass auf den Straßen nur Männer spazieren, macht uns zunächst nicht misstrauisch. Ab und zu fliegt mal ein Steinchen gegen unsere Autos, es wird auch mal dagegen gespuckt, aber mit solchen Missfallenskundgebungen können wir leben. Plötzlich und völlig unvermittelt fängt allerdings ein Geistlicher an zu schimpfen und sich übermäßig aufzuregen. Immer mehr Männer versammeln sich wütend um unsere parkenden Autos. Immerhin sprechen die Männer noch mit uns, und mich fragt der aufgeregte Araber, was ich von „Saft" halten würde. Wahrheitsgemäß gebe ich an, dass ich Saft mag, und zwar sehr. Das regt den bärtigen Gottesmann nun erst recht auf, und auch die anderen Ma'anner scheinen eine Menge gegen „juice" zu haben. Und es dauert, bis wir alle begreifen, dass es den Jordaniern gar nicht um „juice" geht, sondern um „jews": Juden. Zur Deeskalation der Situation trägt zusätzlich nicht gerade bei, dass ich auf dem Defender-Dach stehe. Auf der anderen Straßenseite befindet sich eine Mädchenschule und ich werde beschuldigt, aufs Auto gestiegen zu sein, um über die hohe Mauer dort hineinzublicken. Leider kann ich kein Arabisch – so fällt mir zur Entspannung der Situation nur ein, die Flucht anzutreten.

Über Funk informieren wir Hussein, dass wir abhauen müssen. In aller Eile entern wir die Autos und rasen aus der Stadt – blinde Fährten legend und Finten schlagend, damit uns auch niemand verfolgt, denn der nächste Halt ist eine Campsite. Da möchte wohl niemand von religiösen Eiferern überrascht werden. Zum Glück folgt uns niemand.

Ausruhen von diesem Abenteuer – dafür ist die alte jordanische Felsenstadt Petra genau richtig. Mein persönlicher Held Indiana Jones war auch schon hier: Das muss ja ein magischer Ort sein! Die unglaubliche Stadt war früher Hauptstadt der Nabatäer, die Monumentalfassaden sind direkt aus dem Fels gemeißelt. Eigentlich kommt man nur zu Fuß durch einen engen Canyon des Wadi Musa dort hin, und so lassen wir die Teams auch zu Fuß laufen. Sie wissen nicht, dass wir eine Sondergenehmigung bekommen haben, mit zwei Wagen direkt vor das Weltkulturerbe zu fahren. Hier vertraut man uns, so wie übrigens sonst auch in diesem grundsätzlich sehr gastfreundlichen Land. Nachdem wir dann noch eine Offroad-Strecke finden, die selbst die Polizei als „unfahrbar" bezeichnet, und diese bewältigen, und nachdem wir mit einer bestellten Kamel-Polizeipatrouille samt Krummsäbel unsere Teilnehmer necken, haben Hans und ich endlich das Gefühl: Ja, wir sind auf dem richtigen Weg für die Land Rover Entdecker-Tour. So ungefähr haben wir uns das vorgestellt.

Not all encounters in Jordan are sorted out as easily as our run-in with the nervous Bedouin. In the strictly Islamic town of Ma'an we experienced firsthand just how great the differences in religions, ethnic groups and our worlds really are.

After having bought fuel in old olive oil tins and recovered a vehicle belonging to a Jordanian who had broken down (according to the maxim "a good deed every day") – though it later turned out that his vehicle could move under its own power – we stopped off in Ma'an to buy bread and food. Hussein and the three teams disappeared into the supermarket while the rest of us stayed by the vehicles. I climbed up on the roof rack to check the tension of the ratchet straps. Clearly this was a poor choice on my part.

The fact that only men were walking on the street hadn't rung any warning bells. Every once in a while, someone had thrown a stone at the vehicles, and they have been spat at, but frankly we can live with such expressions of disapproval. Suddenly, and without warning, an Islamic priest began to rant and appeared to be more than just upset. More and more angry men suddenly swarmed around our vehicles. Some were still talking to us, and the rather excited Arab asked what I thought about "juice". Now I am a fan of "juice" and I said so. This really got the bearded priest going and the other men seemed to have something against "juice" as well. After a few minutes it dawned on us that the Jordanians weren't talking about "juice" at all, rather they meant "Jews". It didn't help that I was still standing on the roof of the Defender while unbeknown to me on the other side of the street there was a girls' school. I was accused of having jumped on the roof in order to be able to see over the school's high wall. Unfortunately, I can't speak Arabic, so to defuse the situation down I did the most logical thing possible. I fled.

Over the radio, I told Hussein that we had to get out quickly. We jumped into the cars and left town immediately, setting the odd false trail here and there, so that no-one was able to follow us, as our next stop was camp and we didn't want to be surprised by a crowd of religious zealots. Fortunately, no one had taken up the chase.

The best way to recover from this little adventure was a trip to the ancient city of Petra. My own personal hero, Indiana Jones, had been a visitor as well. This must be a magical place. This amazing city was once the capital of the Nabataeans, and its monumental façades are carved directly out of the rock. Normally the only way to enter Petra is via the narrow Wadi Musa, and this is how we let the teams walk into the city. They didn't know that we had received permits for two vehicles to drive right into the World Heritage Site – the authorities trusted us completely, something we experienced almost everywhere in this extremely hospitable country. We found an off-road route, which the local police described as impassable – which we then proceeded to drive. After even managing to organize a genuine mounted police patrol on a camel, complete with scimitar, as a practical joke for the participants, Hans and I were beginning to think: this is how the Land Rover Discoverer Tour could work. This was pretty much how we'd always imagined it to be.

DIE RACHE
THE REVENGE

Oh Wunder: Die Teilnehmer sind etwas enttäuscht. Es ist der letzte Abend in freier Wildbahn der einwöchigen Tour und allen ist zum Feiern zumute. Zuerst wird der Biervorrat geleert, dann geht's dem Whisky an den Flaschenhals. Als die Cola alle ist, strecken einige die Spirituose mit Wasser und Brausetabletten. Das lockert die Zungen, und so erklären uns alsbald die Teams in blendender Laune, wie toll die ganze Tour doch sei – aber eben doch ein bisschen touristisch, zu wenig Abenteuer. Der Begriff der geführten Pauschalreise fällt zwar nicht, aber wir bekommen unser Fett weg, weil wir sie zum Beispiel nie allein gelassen haben.

So eine Kritik perlt an Hans und mir nicht ohne Folgen ab. Also warten wir – zugegebenermaßen nicht mehr so ganz nüchtern – in der Nacht, bis alle Teilnehmer und Journalisten schlafen, entfernen aus allen Fahrzeugen (bis auf unseres) die GPS-Instrumente und alle anderen Navigationshilfsmittel, hinterlassen in jedem Auto einen Zettel mit den aufgezeichneten Himmelsrichtungen, schnappen uns Doc Gunnar Wasmus und verlassen mit ihm und insgesamt zwei Wagen klammheimlich das Camp.

Als die sechs Teilnehmer, Hussein und das Fernsehteam dann irgendwann aufwachen, sind sie einheitlich sauer. Wir hören über Funk ihre Sprüche und amüsieren uns restalkoholisiert königlich. Die armen Kritiker müssen sich mit insgesamt neun Leuten, Kameraequipment und dem ganzen Camp-Zeug samt Müll in drei Defender quetschen und wissen nicht einmal, wohin der Rest der Reise gehen soll. Besonders das Fernsehteam kocht über: Im Auto von Hans, der sich neben mir im Sand krümmt vor Lachen, liegen die neuen Filmkassetten – sie können die ganze Aufregung nicht mal drehen. Wer uns kennt, kann sich vorstellen, wie köstlich wir unsere vorsichtige Schadenfreude genießen.

So rumpeln wir bis zur Hauptstraße, bis auch wir müde werden. Wir halten, hauen uns neben die Defender auf den Boden zum Schlafen. Nur Gunnar schafft es noch, in einem weißen Nachthemd aufs Auto zu klettern und dort zu pennen. Bis eine Polizeistreife mit angelegten Waffen kommt. Die beweisen zum Glück Humor, als Gunnar wie ein Gespenst in Weiß auf dem Auto steht und beteuert, nichts Unrechtes getan zu haben ...

Surprise, surprise. The participants were a little disappointed. The last evening in the wild on our week-long tour, and everyone was up for a party. The beer was quickly finished off before we moved on to the whisky. The cola didn't last long either, and another mixer was found using water and fizzy tablets. Suitably relaxed, the teams then proceeded to tell us how much they had enjoyed the tour – with one reservation: there had been too much tourism and too little adventure. They didn't actually use the words "package tour", but the complaint was loud and clear and meant for us, as we had never left them to their own devices.

Hans and I aren't ones to ignore criticism, and the whisky clearly played a part in our next response. We waited until the teams and journalists had all gone to sleep and then removed the GPS and any other navigational aids from every vehicle but our own, leaving a piece of paper showing the four cardinal directions. We grabbed the doctor, Gunnar Wasmus, and left camp as quietly as possible in two vehicles.

When the six participants, Hussein and the TV crew awoke, they were furious. We listened to them over the radio, and in spite of our own hangovers we enjoyed the spectacle from afar.

Our poor critics now had to organize nine people and pack the camera and all the campsite equipment, rubbish included, into the three remaining Defenders, yet without really knowing which way to go. As Hans lay in the sand next to me, his eyes filled with tears from all the laughter, the members of the TV crew were beside themselves with rage, as they couldn't film anything: the unused film cassettes were in Hans' car. Anybody who knows us also knows how much we were enjoying this.

We trundled on in the direction of the main road until exhaustion hit us, too, parked up the Defender and fell asleep underneath. Gunnar managed to climb onto the roof rack in his white nightshirt and slept on top of the car. Fortunately for us, the police unit that turned up, guns drawn, had a sense of humour when Gunnar stood up, looking for all the world like a ghost on top of the vehicle and imploring that he hadn't done anything wrong ...

ZU DEN HIGHLIGHTS GEHÖREN DIE RUINEN IN AMMAN ODER DIE FELSENSTADT PETRA IM TAL DER NABATÄER. DAS TAL IST UNVORSTELLBAR GROSS UND HAT WEITAUS MEHR ZU BIETEN ALS DIE ERINNERUNG, DASS INDIANA JONES HIER DEN HEILIGEN GRAL SUCHTE.
--
THE RUINS IN AMMAN OR THE ANCIENT CITY OF PETRA IN THE VALLEY OF THE NABATAEANS ARE AMONG THE HIGHLIGHTS. THE VALLEY IS HUGE AND HAS MORE TO OFFER THAN INDIANA JONES' SEARCH FOR THE HOLY GRAIL.

DAG ROGGE

GEBOREN AM 6.7.1962 | GELERNTER FERNMELDETECHNIKER, GESCHÄFTSFÜHRER DER LAND ROVER EXPERIENCE DEUTSCHLAND, LAND ROVER LEAD INSTRUCTOR, JÄGER, HUBSCHRAUBERPILOT, PFERDEZÜCHTER

BORN 6 JULY 1962 | TRAINED TELECOMMUNICATIONS SPECIALIST, HEAD OF LAND ROVER EXPERIENCE GERMANY, LAND ROVER LEAD INSTRUCTOR, HUNTER, HELICOPTER PILOT, HORSE BREEDER

Bei deinem Job kommt man sofort auf die Idee, du bist ein geborener Outdoorer und Offroader. Stimmt das?
Überhaupt nicht. Nach der Realschule habe ich Fernmeldetechniker gelernt, dann das Fachabitur nachgemacht, ein internes BWL-Studium absolviert und beim Fernmeldeamt 1 in Düsseldorf gearbeitet. Allerdings war mir das dann bald zu wenig.

Wovon hast du geträumt?
Zumindest von mehr, als ein Beamter zu sein. Ich eröffnete daraufhin parallel zum Postjob 1983 meine eigene Promotionsfirma. Ein Bekannter arbeitete zu der Zeit schon mit seiner Agentur für Land Rover, und er suchte manchmal jemanden zum Aushelfen. Als die Post 1988 ihr Personal verringerte und Abfindungen anbot, habe ich den sicheren Job aufgegeben und mich völlig selbstständig gemacht. 1990 konnte ich dann das Land-Rover-Geschäft übernehmen – da war mein Büro noch ein Raum im Haus meiner Eltern. 1994, mit der Einführung des Defender in Deutschland, habe ich meinen ersten Steinbruch gepachtet – heute sitzt hier die Zentrale meiner Firma APS und damit die der Land Rover Experience Germany.

Also bist du Chef über ...?
Eine der ältesten Land Rover Experience Operationen weltweit – und auch eines der größten Land Rover Experience Center von mittlerweile 37 rund um den Globus.

Welche Land Rover fährst du selber?
Viel zu selten meinen ganz frühen Land Rover Serie I aus dem Jahr 1949. Der Wagen ist voll restauriert und immer wieder bei Klassik-Rallyes zu sehen. Ein früher Serie-II-Landy ist gerade von Grund auf restauriert worden – im Look der bekannten gelben AA Road Service Fahrzeuge. Eines meiner Alltagsfahrzeuge ist ein moderner Range Rover Sport. Und dann hatte ich noch einen Defender, den ich als Winterdienstfahrzeug mit Räumschild umgebaut habe, um zu zeigen, dass es nicht immer gleich ein Unimog sein muss. Den hat allerdings ein Pflanzbetrieb gekauft – natürlich für den Winterdienst.

Wie viele Tage im Jahr bist du für die Land Rover Experience Tour unterwegs? Und wie verkraftest du den ständigen Wechsel von Zeit- und Klimazonen körperlich?
In Spitzenzeiten bis zu 200 Tage. Zeitumstellung gibt es nicht.
Es ist immer Experience-Zeit.

Hand aufs Herz: Wie kommt man zum Vornamen „Dag"?
Ganz einfach: Mein Vater verehrte Dag Hammarskjöld, den schwedischen Staatssekretär, UN-Generalsekretär und Friedensnobelpreisträger, der ein Jahr vor meiner Geburt starb.

Looking at your job, anyone would think that you were the born off-roading outdoors type. Any truth in that?
None at all. After secondary school, I was apprenticed as a telecommunications specialist, and then I went back to school to graduate, after which I completed a business studies course before starting work at the telephone exchange in Düsseldorf. Mind you, it wasn't long before I was bored.

What did you dream of doing?
I certainly wasn't dreaming of being a civil servant. I started my own event company in 1983 while I was still working for the post office. The agency of an acquaintance of mine was working for Land Rover, and every once in a while he needed assistance. In 1988, when the post office started eliminating positions they offered me voluntary redundancy so I gave up what was a secure job and went into business for myself. In 1990, I took over the Land Rover contract with my own agency – at that time I was still working from an office in my parents' house. When Defender was launched in Germany in 1994, I leased my first quarry which is where the headquarters of my firm APS and of course Land Rover Experience Germany is based.

So, you're in charge of ...?
One of the oldest Land Rover Experience programmes running – and, in addition, one of the biggest of the 37 Land Rover Experience Centres in existence.

Do you drive a Land Rover yourself?
I have a very early 1949 Series that I get to drive every once in a while. It is fully restored and often takes part in classic car rallies. I have just completed the ground-up restoration of a Series II Land Rover in the well-known yellow livery of the British Automobile Association (AA) service. One of my daily vehicles is a Range Rover Sport. I also had a Defender that I had converted into a snowplough just to show that vehicles other than Unimogs are capable of the task. It has been bought by a vegetable garden – they need it to keep the road open in winter.

How many days per year do you spend travelling on the Land Rover Experience Tour? And how do you cope with the constant changes in climate and time zones?
When it gets intense, I can be away for up to 200 days a year.
Time zones don't mean anything to me. It is always "Experience Time".

Let's be honest. Where does the name "Dag" come from?
Simple: my father worshipped Dag Hammarskjöld, the Swedish State Secretary, Secretary-General of the UN and Winner of the Nobel Prize for peace who died a year before I was born.

ISLAND
ICELAND
2001

2001
LAND: ISLAND
STRECKE: 1 400 KM
COUNTRY: ICELAND
DISTANCE: 870 MILES

6 DISCOVERY, 2 DEFENDER

DER GEDANKE
THE THOUGHT

Jordanien war ein voller Erfolg – trotz diverser Anlaufschwächen und Zeitnöte. Das erkennt auch Reinhard Künstler, der von Ford inzwischen als neuer Geschäftsführer für Land Rover eingesetzt worden ist. Da sich die Autos auch nach der Tour noch in dem Land des Nahen Ostens befinden dürfen, haben wir eine Reise für Journalisten organisiert, die ein großes mediales Feedback nach sich zog.

So ein Feuer muss man am Kochen halten. Also gibt uns Künstler den Auftrag, fürs neue Jahr eine neue Tour auszuarbeiten. Und bitte nicht mehr unter der etwas hemdsärmeligen Überschrift „Entdecker-Tour". Wir ersinnen „Experience Tour", das klingt gleich wesentlich besser.

Und wieder ist die Zeit knapp. Also suchen wir erneut ein Ziel, das uns nicht ganz unbekannt ist: Island. Mit einer Fläche von gut 100 000 Quadratkilometern wunderbar übersichtlich, als weltweit größte Vulkaninsel mit vielen tektonischen Spielarten voller Abenteuer und mit elf Prozent Gletscherfläche eine herrliche, eiskalte Glitsche. Hans hat dort bereits dreimal seinen Urlaub verlebt, auch ich war schon dort. Weitere Vorteile: ein kurzer Flug, ein sicheres Land, abenteuerliche Wetterbedingungen, beste Offroad-Möglichkeiten, sagenhafte heiße Wasserlöcher – und die Autos sind auch einfach zu importieren. Nur der Rotwein ist dort über-proportional teuer, unser Budget dagegen übersichtlich. Aber für solch schwerwiegende Fälle gibt es ja Frischwasserkanister als Transportbehältnisse.

8 000 Bewerber registrieren wir; wie auch zur ersten Tour laden wir 2 400 von ihnen in die Qualifikationscamps ein, 60 in die Endausscheidung. Und machen uns mit den sechs Besten auf, längst vergessene Wege zu finden. Aber erst kommt die Vortour.

Jordan had been a complete success despite initial planning difficulties and the short notice. Reinhard Künstler, who in the meantime had been installed by Ford as Land Rover Germany's new CEO, recognized this. As the vehicles remained in this Middle Eastern country after the tour, we immediately organized a media trip that generated a lot of press coverage.

It is important to keep the fire burning bright, so Künstler commissioned a new tour for the new year. This time, we decided to drop the rather down-to-earth "Discoverer", choosing instead to call it the "Experience Tour", which we thought was so much better.

Once again, time was short, so we started considering a new destination, albeit one which we already knew well. Iceland. With a surface area of under 40,000 square miles, Iceland was a manageable size for the tour, and as the world's largest volcanic island, it provided us with a great deal of tectonic entertainment and pure adventure. With eleven per cent of the island covered in glaciers, we had a wonderful mix of biting cold and difficult, slippery conditions. Hans had spent three holidays here, and I had also visited the island on a previous trip. Further advantages included the relatively short flight. Safety and security weren't an issue at all, the climate was challenging and thus perfect for an adventure tour, there were endless off-road opportunities and sensational hot springs, and importing our vehicles into the country would not be difficult. Unfortunately, red wine was ridiculously expensive, and our budget was modest. Fortunately, there are fresh water canisters that can be repurposed in just such eventualities.

8,000 applications flooded in, and, as with Jordan, we invited 2,400 to the selection camps and 60 to final selections. The plan was to take the six best with us to Iceland to find some long-forgotten trails. First of all, though, we had to complete the prescout recce.

DER FLUSS
THE RIVER

Mit einer erklecklichen Anzahl von Interessenten im Rücken satteln wir die Autos im Juli für die Vortour. Es gilt, abseits der Touristenwege anhand von topografischen Karten neue Herausforderungen zu finden. Und einen Einheimischen. Denn in Jordanien haben wir gelernt, wie wichtig es ist, einen Guide mitzunehmen, der sowohl die Sprache des Landes spricht als sich auch mit den Gegebenheiten und den Gewohnheiten der Einwohner, des Verkehrs und des Geländes auskennt. Wir fahren zum örtlichen BMW-Händler, der hat natürlich früher auch Land Rover vertrieben. Doch seine Vorschläge entsprechen nicht unseren Wünschen – wir wollen keine Touristenführer. Da fällt einem Verkäufer noch ein Defender-Fan ein, der von ihm einst einen 110er erworben hatte und ihn zum Bigfoot umbaute, also ihn mit riesigen Ballonreifen ausrüstete. Das war Ingo, ein Tänzer aus Reykjavík.

Mit ihm suchen wir nun zu fünft in zwei Defendern abenteuerliche Strecken – und finden sie ohne Probleme. Nur das Wetter haben wir unterschätzt: Es regnet. Ständig. Und wenn es in Island regnet, sollte man mehr als nur Gummistiefel dabeihaben.

Die erste Wasserdurchfahrt – und davon gibt es auf der Insel viele – schaffen wir noch recht problemlos: Ein paar große Steine zeigen, wo man den Fluss am besten queren kann. Bei der zweiten sind wir uns nicht sicher. Also schnappe ich mir einen Defender und probiere es ganz vorsichtig. Mit der Folge, dass der Wagen aufschwimmt und abzutreiben droht. Sofort stoppe ich den Wagen und rufe über Funk Hans um Hilfe. Er befestigt ein Sicherungsseil an seinem Auto und nach einem – mit Verlaub – schweinekalten Gang durchs knietiefe Schmelzwasser auch an meinem. So kann er mich zurückziehen. Wir beschließen, Island nicht weiter in dieser Richtung zu erkunden, sondern die 30 Kilometer zurück zur ersten Furt zu fahren und dort den Rückzug zu versuchen. Aber kaum angekommen, müssen wir erkennen: Die Steine sind nicht mehr sichtbar. Das Wasser ist auch hier rasant gestiegen.

Interest in the tour was enormous as we set about preparing the vehicles for the pre-scout in July. Using topographical maps, we needed to find challenging routes off the well-beaten tourist trails. We also needed a local. In Jordan we had learnt the importance of having someone on board who not only spoke the language but was also familiar with local traits and traditions, traffic and terrain. We drove to the local BMW dealer who had also sold Land Rovers in the past. His suggestions simply didn't match our requirements – we needed more than a tour guide. Fortunately, one of the sales staff recalled a Defender 110 customer who had converted his vehicle into a "Bigfoot" – i.e. equipped the vehicle with oversize balloon tyres. This was Ingo, a dancer from Reykjavík.

So now we were five people in two Defenders on the hunt for challenging and adventurous routes. We were more than successful. However, we underestimated the weather. It rains all the time. Wellington boots alone are not enough to defeat Icelandic rain.

Our first water crossing – and there are many on the island – succeeded without incident. A pair of large rocks indicated where the river was shallow enough to wade across. The second was a bit more difficult. I grabbed a Defender and carefully started driving across until the vehicle suddenly started floating and threatened to drift away downstream. I immediately stopped and radioed Hans for help. He attached a safety rope to his vehicle, waded through the icy cold glacial water and attached the other end to mine, thus enabling him to pull me back out of the river. Straight away, we decided to abandon this route and drove the 19 miles back to the first crossing. On arrival, at once we noticed that the rocks were no longer visible. The water level had risen dramatically.

We had no choice – we had to attempt the crossing. Hans slowly entered the river with his Defender 130, though this time his and my vehicle were joined via a snatch strap. Hans had almost made it to the other riverbank when he was forced to stop – the recovery strap was too short. I proceeded to enter the roaring torrent of water with my Defender and bogged down almost immediately.

Es nützt nichts – wir müssen es probieren. Hans rollt langsam mit seinem 130er Defender in den Fluss hinein, diesmal schon von Anfang an durch einen Berge-gurt mit meinem 110er verbunden. Hans ist fast drüben, da kann er nicht weiter, weil der Gurt zu kurz ist. Also beginne ich, meinen Defender ebenfalls in das tosende Wasser zu manövrieren. Leider fahre ich mich fest.

Jetzt wird die Situation brenzlig. Denn der Bergegurt, etwa 5 Zentimeter breit, stellt sich in der Strömung quer. Das Wasser zerrt am Gurt, an den Defendern, an unseren Nerven. Ingo, der Tänzer, muss ran. Mit Wathose (ja, so etwas hat er tatsächlich vorausschauenderweise dabei) klettert er auf den Defender von Hans und versucht, den Gurt aus dem Befestigungshaken zu ziehen. Natürlich völlig ohne Erfolg: Tonnen von Wasser drücken auf die Verbindung. Inzwischen sackt mein Auto tiefer in den Kies. Es wird Zeit für härtere Maßnahmen. Ich schnappe mir meinen Leatherman, klettere auf meine Motorhaube und schneide – die blo-ßen Hände in dem eiskalten Gletscherwasser – den Gurt durch. So kann Hans auf die andere rettende Uferseite fahren. Ich schaffe es, meinen Defender zurück ans hiesige Ufer zu dirigieren.

Hans und Ingo dort, Christian, die Journalistin Inge und ich hier – keine gute Voraussetzung für eine weitere gemeinsame Erkundung der nordischen Insel. Also was tun? „Wenn du glaubst, es geht nicht mehr, kommt von irgendwo ein Lichtlein her." In diesem Falle gleich zwei, und zwar in Form von Schein-werfern eines riesigen Traktors. Der steht inzwischen hinter mir und einem Jeep, der ebenfalls von den Wassermassen überrascht wurde und nicht weiß, wie es weitergehen soll.

Das einzige Fahrzeug, das nun noch problemlos durch den Fluss fahren kann, ist das Feldmonster. Wir bitten den Fahrer, meinen Defender an den Haken zu nehmen. Der freundliche Fahrer tut das, und drüben angekommen fragt Hans ihn, ob er auch noch unseren Discovery holt. Natürlich ersucht auch der Jeepfahrer um eine Passage. Der Traktorfahrer erweist sich als Superman: Wir seilen den Discovery an den Traktor und den Jeep an den Land Rover. So zieht uns das riesenrädrige Feldgerät durch das wilde Wasser.

Dabei entsteht ein Foto, das ich heute noch liebe: wie der Discovery den Jeep rettet. Natürlich nur rein zufällig ist der Traktor nicht auf dem Bild.

That's when things got a little hairy. The raging current had picked up the 2-inch-wide snatch strap and was slowly pulling it at right angles to the ve-hicles. The strap, the Defenders and our nerves all began to suffer from the strain. It was time for our Icelandic dancer, Ingo, to do his stuff. In his wading trousers (which he had prudently packed), he climbed on top of Hans' Defender and attempted to release the strap from the retaining hook. Naturally, the plan was doomed. The strap was weighted down by tonnes of water. Meanwhile, my vehicle was sinking deeper and deeper into the gravel. The time had come for a more radical solution. I grabbed my Leatherman, jumped on the bonnet, plunged my hands into the ice-cold water and cut the strap in two. Hans could then drive onto the opposite riverbank, and I could drive back onto the river-bank on my side of the river.

Hans and Ingo were now on one side of the river, with Christian, the journalist Inge and myself on the other. Not the best point of departure for pre-scouting this island. Yet just when it looked as though things had hit rock bottom, there was light at the end of the tunnel … or, more precisely, two headlights mounted on an enormous tractor, which was now parked behind me, and a Jeep which had also been caught unawares by the surge of water.

The only vehicle capable of crossing the river was this monstrous piece of farm machinery. We asked the driver to take the Defender in tow, which he did with-out a murmur of complaint. On the other side of the river, Hans asked him if he could bring the Discovery over as well. The Jeep driver seized his moment and asked for a tow, too. Our friendly tractor driver was obviously from the planet Krypton – the Discovery was hooked up to the tractor, and the Jeep to the Land Rover, and the huge caravan was dragged through the churning maelstrom.

We took a photo at the time, and it is still one of my all-time favourites. It shows the Discovery pulling the Jeep to safety. As chance would have it, the tractor is nowhere to be seen.

DIE TROLLE
THE TROLLS

Ich bin kein ängstlicher Mensch, sonst könnte ich solche Touren wohl weder organisieren noch durchführen oder gar leiten. Doch hier auf Island beginne ich erstmals, an mir selbst zu zweifeln.

Auch mir sind die Geschichten von Elfen und Trollen bekannt, die in großen Felsen wohnen, weswegen die Isländer ihre Straßen kurvig drumherum bauen anstatt die Felsen zu eliminieren. Ach, Humbug – oder doch nicht?

Wir sind in Islands Norden, es ist der 9. Juli, und es schneit, als wolle uns die Insel zeigen, wer der Stärkere ist (obwohl ich das nie angezweifelt habe). Wir erkunden die Gegend um Gæsavatn und suchen – wie so oft – Wege als Herausforderung. Was wir finden, ist ein Straßenschild: Askja 120 Kilometer. Prima, nur leider ist die Straße gesperrt. Aber wir wären nicht die Land Rover Experience Tour, würden wir nicht genau diese Tatsache als Einladung ansehen, es zu versuchen. Also machen wir uns auf den Weg zum Vulkan Askja.

Allerdings schneit es schnell immer stärker, die Sicht wird schlecht und schlechter, teilweise zieht Nebel auf, der über einer langsam unwirklich erscheinenden Landschaft wabert. Es wird dunkel, Schmelzwasser gluckert überall um uns herum. Und in diesem Moment denke ich: Ja, sie existieren – die Trolle, die eigentlichen Herrscher Islands, die mit uns machen können, was sie wollen. Es gibt Momente, in denen ich, der scheinbar mit allen Wassern gewaschene, weltreisende Offroad-Spezialist, nicht aussteigen will. Mir ist tatsächlich unheimlich zumute.

Was die Trolle nicht im Geringsten besänftigt. Im Gegenteil: Sie lassen mit weißen Gewändern die Straße verschwinden. Der Schnee hat sämtliche Markierungen überdeckt. Mit dem Fernglas suche ich irgendwelche Anhaltspunkte, meist vergebens. Wir bleiben andauernd in Schneefeldern stecken, müssen die Autos ausgraben, uns neu orientieren. Die Trolle haben überhaupt kein Einsehen mit den mutigen Menschen aus Deutschland und ihren englischen Autos, und die Nacht will nicht enden. Wahrscheinlich ist auch sie trollgesteuert.

Nach 13 Stunden Blindfahrt, Schneewühlen und Kampf gegen trollistische Windmühlenflügel sind wir restlos alle. In dieser Zeit haben wir gerade mal 30 Kilometer geschafft. Und dann muss der Obertroll selber müde geworden sein oder ein Einsehen mit uns gehabt haben – wir entdecken eine einsame Berghütte, die offen ist für hungrige Wanderer. Genau als solche fühlen wir uns, lassen die Autos stehen, entern die real existierende Nothütte und fallen in einen unruhigen Schlaf.

Natürlich baue ich später die Trollstrecke in die Haupttour ein. Denn das ist Experience Tour pur.

I am neither anxious nor nervous – for were that the case I wouldn't be able to organize these tours, let alone manage or lead them in the first place. However, here on Iceland and for the first time ever, I began having second thoughts about my abilities.

I had also read about the elves and trolls which lived in large rocks and which were the reason why the Icelanders built the roads around the rocks instead of simply dynamiting the stone. Just fairy tales, right?

We were on the northern half of Iceland. It was 9 July, and it was snowing as if the island were bent on demonstrating which one of us was the stronger (not that I ever had my doubts). We were exploring the region around Gæsavatn, and, as usual, looking for challenging routes. We found a road sign reading "Askja 75 miles", which was helpful – except that the road was blocked. That said, for the Land Rover Experience Tour a blocked road is just another obstacle to be overcome. So off we headed towards the Askja volcano.

Meanwhile, the snowstorm had moved up a gear, and visibility was worsening by the minute. Added to that, there was fog hanging over the ground, making the countryside look somehow unreal. It had grown very dark, and all you could hear was the gurgling of glacial water around us. At that moment I thought to myself: the real rulers of this island, the trolls, had us in their grip. I, the globetrotting off-road expert who had seen and done it all, was unwilling to get out of the vehicle. It all felt a little weird.

Not that the trolls were in any way motivated to calm down. Quite the opposite in fact. By now the road had disappeared under a white wall of snow. Whatever road signs and markings there had been were now completely covered in snow. I struggled to find any points of reference at all with the binoculars. We repeatedly bogged down in the deep snow. Again and again, we had to dig the vehicles out and figure out where we were. The trolls had no sympathy whatsoever for these courageous Germans with their English cars in this seemingly eternal night that itself seemed to be in the hands of the trolls.

After 13 hours of driving blind, shovelling snow and facing off against trolls bent on blowing us into the ground, we were absolutely exhausted. We had covered a paltry 19 miles. Either the head troll himself had had enough or had seen fit to grant us respite. Out of nowhere, we discovered a lonely mountain hut open for hungry travellers, which is of course what we were. We parked the cars and crawled into the rescue shelter, where we collapsed into a fitful sleep.

Naturally, we added the troll route to the main tour. The Experience Tour doesn't get any better than this.

DIE FARBWELTEN, DIE ISLAND BESTIMMEN, KÖNNEN FOTOS KAUM WIEDERGEBEN. PECHSCHWARZ, NEONGRÜN, SCHNEEWEISS UND AZURBLAU SIND NUR EINIGE DER FARBEN, DIE UNS BEGEGNET SIND. DIE FAHRT GEHT ÜBER RIESIGE SANDER UND ASCHEFELDER, GEFORMT DURCH VULKANE, WIND, SCHNEE UND WASSER.
--
PHOTOGRAPHY CAN'T DO JUSTICE TO THE LANDSCAPE PORTRAIT THAT IS ICELAND. INKY BLACK, NEON GREEN, SNOW WHITE AND AZURE BLUE ARE JUST A FEW OF THE COLOURS WE ENCOUNTERED. THE EXPEDITION CROSSED HUGE OUTWASH PLAINS AND ASH AND LAVA FIELDS CREATED BY VOLCANOES, WIND, SNOW AND WATER.

DIE JAGD
THE HUNT

Die Haupttour beginnt Anfang August, eigentlich die optimale Reisezeit für Island. Wir schocken die sechs Teilnehmer anfangs gleich mal mit der Straße von der viertgrößten isländischen Stadt Akureyri zum Geothermalgebiet Hveravellir, einer der anspruchsvollsten Strecken für Offroader. Kenwood als neuer Sponsor hat uns mit leistungsstarkem Funk ausgerüstet. Die Geräte besitzen zwei Kanäle, die wir als Teilnehmerkanal und als Organisationskanal einrichten. Die Teams müssen ja nicht unbedingt mithören, was Hans und ich uns während der Fahrt für sie als kleine Gemeinheiten ausdenken. Ich liebe es, mit Funk herumzuspielen. Das ist mein Steckenpferd und stammt wahrscheinlich aus meiner Zeit als Fernmeldetechniker.

Leider kennt sich auch einer der Teilnehmer bestens mit solchen Geräten aus, und es dauert nicht lange, da hat er entdeckt, dass wir uns als Organisatoren auf einem anderen Kanal über sie und ihre neuen Aufgaben unterhalten. Wir wundern uns bald, dass alle Teilnehmer alle neu gestellten Tasks so problemlos und fehlerfrei lösen – bis wir ihnen auf die Schliche kommen. Jetzt beginnt eine so unterhaltsame wie unausgesprochene Jagd nach der richtigen Frequenz. Wir wechseln unsere ständig, plappern Blödsinn über den Orga-Draht, ein bisschen Unfug über den offiziellen Kanal, um dann wieder Schwachsinn über die Orga-Frequenz zum Besten zu geben. So versuchen wir ständig, sie in die Irre zu führen. Die Teilnehmer wissen bald nicht mehr, welche Infos sie für bare Münze nehmen dürfen, und wir wissen bald nicht mehr, wie wir uns inhaltlich wichtige Dinge zurufen können, ohne dass die Teilnehmer wissen, wovon wir sprechen. Wir denken uns sogar Codewörter aus, damit wenigstens wir wissen, welche Frequenz für uns gilt.

Aber schließlich greifen wir zu klassischen Mitteln: Der persönlichen und mündlichen Absprache zwischen Hans und mir ist kein Frequenzhacker gewachsen.

The main tour began in August, which is the best time to visit Iceland. The six participants are thrust right into one of the most challenging off-road routes on the island: the road from the fourth-largest Icelandic town of Akureyri to the Hveravellir geothermal region. Our new sponsor, Kenwood, had outfitted us with powerful CB radios with two channels – one for the participants and one for the organizers. The teams didn't need to hear what we had up our sleeves for them. I love playing with radios; it has always been something of a hobby of mine – probably dating back to my work as a telecommunications specialist.

Unfortunately, one of the participants was also well versed in communications technology and in no time at all had discovered that we were using the other channel to discuss the teams and the tasks to come. We were surprised to see how well the teams solved the new tasks without a single mistake until we caught onto the scam. What ensued was an entertaining if unspoken hunt between the teams and the organization crew for the right frequency. We hopped from one frequency to the next, talked complete and utter rubbish on the organization channel, only then to talk riddles on the participants' channel before switching back to our own channel with more complete nonsense. The plan to confuse the participants worked: after a while, they no longer knew what to believe. It was a struggle communicating the organizational aspects to one another while keeping the participants in the dark. We even began using code words relating to specific frequencies for organizational matters.

Finally, we reverted back to the classic method which is impervious to radio hacking. Hans and I agreed on everything personally and exclusively by word of mouth.

INE SOLCHE FURT WIE UNTEN IST MIT VORSICHT ZU GENIESSEN.
DAS SCHNELL STRÖMENDE WASSER ZERRT AM FAHRZEUG; UNTIEFEN
UND STEINE SIND IM AUFGEWÜHLTEN FLUSS NICHT ZU SEHEN.
M HECK ERKENNT MAN DEN ALS SICHERUNG BEFESTIGTEN
ERGEGURT. TROTZDEM BEUNRUHIGT DEN FAHRER DAS REISSENDE
WASSER – EINE FLUSSQUERUNG IM GRENZBEREICH.

FORD LIKE THIS HAS TO BE APPROACHED WITH CARE. THE
AST-FLOWING WATER LITERALLY TEARS AT THE VEHICLE;
RREGULARITIES IN THE RIVERBED AND HUGE ROCKS ARE INVISIBLE
N THE FOAMING MAELSTROM. AT THE REAR OF THE VEHICLE, YOU
AN JUST MAKE OUT THE RECOVERY STRAP AS A SAFETY MEASURE.
EVERTHELESS, THE DRIVER WAS CONCERNED ABOUT THE
ORRENTIAL STREAM – THIS WAS A RIVER CROSSING ON THE LIMIT.

DER SCHLAUCH
THE HOSE

Zugegeben: Wenn wir die Teams durch deren Fehler mal auf falsche Fährten locken können, freuen wir uns wie die Kinder. Einmal lassen wir die Teilnehmer, als sie eine Abzweigung verpassen, tatsächlich durchs wilde Island irren. Als sie geknickt zurückkommen, steht das gesamte Orga-Team grinsend am Straßenrand und vollführt die La-Ola-Welle. So viel Spaß muss sein.

Just in dem Moment, als uns der letzte Discovery passiert, knallt es aus dessen Motorraum, weißer Rauch qualmt unter der Haube hervor. Ich denke nur: Motorplatzer. Sofort nehmen wir das Autoherz unter die Lupe: Öl okay, Wasser okay, Motor? Okay. Wir starten ihn, er läuft rund. Wir geben im Leerlauf Gas bis etwa 2 500 Umdrehungen – ein Knall, der Motor streikt, weißer Rauch ...

Neuerdings mit Satellitentelefon ausgestattet, rufe ich in der Zentrale in Wülfrath an, wo Harry Hemmann sitzt, der Leiter der Pressewerkstatt. Der Mann kennt einen Land Rover besser als Maurice Wilks den Grund, so ein Auto erfunden zu haben. Ferndiagnosen sind zwar immer so eine Sache, aber letztlich noch besser als in Island mit qualmendem Motor dumm herumzustehen. Harry erklärt, welche Ursachen infrage kommen können, und wir steigen tief in die Ersatzteilkisten hinab – wir haben so ziemlich alles dabei. Wir bauen, wir schrauben, wir hämmern, und das einzige Ergebnis ist, dass uns die Zeit davonläuft. Denn so frei und abenteuerlich unsere Reisen auch sind, sie unterliegen einem festen Zeitplan.

So lasse ich den großen Teil des Experience-Konvois ziehen, nur die beiden Teilnehmer, die zu dem Problemauto gehören, sowie mein Kollege Lutz Hertel, genannt „Lutz Lutz", und ich bleiben an Ort und Stelle. Es wird dunkel, Nebel zieht auf, und wir schrauben bereits geschlagene fünf Stunden an dem Havaristen. Noch einmal wagen wir einen Startversuch. Ich schaue dabei in den Motorraum, und zwar auf den Schlauch des Turboladers. Und siehe: Bei höheren Drehzahlen beginnt er, sich zusammenzuziehen, worauf weißer Rauch und das Absterben des Motors folgen. Sofort baue ich den Übeltäter aus und finde in seinem Inneren einen Produktionsfehler. Bei höherer Beanspruchung bildet sich eine Gummiblase, die den Luftdurchlass behindert. Ich schneide die Blase heraus – das Problem ist gelöst.

Nicht aber das der Müdigkeit. Im Schritttempo, bei Nebel und in tiefster Dunkelheit tasten sich Lutz Lutz und ich mit den zwei Wagen Richtung Arnarvatn. Um 3 Uhr haben die anderen die Campsite in Húsavík erreicht – wir sind morgens um 8 Uhr dort. Und ich muss gestehen: Auf dieser Fahrt glaube ich Kurven zu sehen, wo keine sind. Wir alle sind nah dran an Halluzinationen. Aber vielleicht haben sich auch nur die Trolle neue Spielchen ausgedacht.

This much I will admit: when teams make the wrong decision, it can be hilariously funny. We watched them take a wrong turn and then sat back to enjoy the spectacle that unfolded before us as they scooted here, there and everywhere through the Icelandic wilderness. When they returned looking somewhat dejected, a grinning organization team greeted them from the side of the road with a Mexican wave. At the end of the day, all one could do was laugh.

As the last Discovery drove past us, there was a bang from the engine, and white smoke started pouring out from underneath the bonnet. My first thought was: engine failure. Upon closer inspection, we established that the oil and water levels were normal. The engine appeared to be good. We started it up and it ticked over as normal. Leaving the car in neutral, we increased the throttle to about 2,500 rpm, and there it was again. A huge bang, the engine cut out and white smoke billowed out ...

We were equipped with satellite telephones on this tour, so I phoned back to the office in Wülfrath to talk to Harry Hemmann, the press fleet workshop manager. Now Harry's knowledge of Land Rovers knows no bounds – and while there are limitations to remote diagnostic analysis, even this was better than standing around looking stupidly at an engine spewing white smoke. Harry went through all the possible scenarios, and we dug deep into the spares box – we weren't short on parts. Still, the only result of our banging, hammering and extensive use of a ratchet screwdriver was that we were running out of time. For all the freedom and adventure that constitutes the spirit of the tour, the event has to run on a strict schedule.

I decided to let the majority of the convoy carry on to the next stop while the team members whose car was in trouble, my colleague Lutz Hertel – nicknamed "Lutz Lutz" – and I stayed put. It was getting dark, the fog was closing in and we had already spent five full hours working on the stranded Discovery. We tried starting it again, and I kept my eye on the engine bay, and in particular the hose leading to the turbocharger. Lo and behold, the instant the revs picked up, the hose started to contract, producing the white smoke and stalling the engine. I immediately removed the offending part and discovered a production error on the interior of the hose – under pressure, the rubber had begun to bubble, preventing the through-flow of air. Removing the bubble by literally excising it solved the problem.

It was no cure for our exhaustion, though. In the fog and in the dark, Lutz Lutz and I led our two vehicles at a walking pace towards Arnarvatn. The others had reached the campsite in Húsavík at 3 in the morning – we finally turned up at 8 am. I swear that I had seen curves in the track where there certainly weren't any. Perhaps we were just hallucinating, or perhaps it was the trolls dreaming up some other way to toy with us.

DER UNFALL
THE ACCIDENT

René Linke päppelt uns schnell wieder auf. Wir haben erstmals unseren Haus- und Hofkoch aus Wülfrath mit, der fast seine gesamte Küche dabeihat und uns mit Fleisch vom Grill, Reis und Sauce zu alter Stärke verhilft.

Nach dem Chaos mit dem Discovery läuft tatsächlich alles nach Plan. Bis zum vorletzten Tag der Tour. Wir sind auf dem Weg zurück nach Reykjavík, die Luft ist klar, der Regen macht Pause. Die Schotterpiste, deren Oberfläche konvex verläuft und die von flachen Felsen begrenzt ist, scheint gut ausgebaut. Die Teilnehmer halten sich an meine Tempovorgabe von maximal 60 km/h. Die Autos vor mir verschwinden hinter einer Kuppe, wie so oft in dieser Gegend.

Als ich den höchsten Punkt des Hügels erreiche, scheint mein Herz auszusetzen: Das Damenteam-Auto, das eben noch direkt vor mir fuhr, befindet sich nicht mehr auf der Straße. Ich registriere noch die großen Augen von Doc Gunnar, der neben mir sitzt, als ich nach rechts blicke und den Discovery durch das Seitenfenster über die Felsen wirbeln sehe. Der schwere Wagen bleibt etwa 20 Meter neben der Piste auf dem Dach zwischen großen Steinen liegen. „Es darf nie etwas passieren" ist unser Credo, und jetzt liegt ein Land Rover mit Teilnehmerinnen darin arg zertrümmert in der isländischen Wildnis.

Sofort stoppe ich den Konvoi per Funk und eile mit dem Doc zum zerstörten Auto. A-, B- und C-Säulen sind gestaucht, aber es gibt genug Überlebensraum in dem umgestürzten Offroader. Wir rufen irgendetwas in den Wagen hinein, dumme Sätze wie „Wie geht's euch?", und zum Glück erschallt sofort von innen: „Keine Sorge, alles okay." Die Damen krabbeln eigenständig aus den zerstörten Seitenfenstern heraus – Schock ja, leichte Schnittverletzungen auch, aber das ist alles. Gunnar setzt Infusionen und ist auch unersetzlich im psychischen Beistand, den er den beiden immer noch erschrockenen Fahrerinnen leistet.

Es stellt sich heraus, dass ein einfacher Fahrfehler zu der Beinahe-Katastrophe geführt hat. Die Fahrerin wollte einem großen Stein ausweichen, den sie aufgrund der Kuppe erst sehr spät am Rand gesehen hatte, verriss das Lenkrad, und wegen der konvexen Form des Untergrundes hob der schwere Wagen seitlich ab und flog in die Felsen. Am folgenden Abend feiern wir alle zusammen zwei zweite Geburtstage. Und ich schwöre, keine Tour mehr ohne Arzt zu absolvieren.

René Linke soon had us fighting fit again. We had decided to bring our Wülfrath chef – mobile kitchen and all – along with us on the tour for the first time, and his combination of barbecued meat, rice and gravy hit the right spot.

After the nightmare with the Discovery, things were actually running according to schedule. Until the penultimate day of the tour, that is. We were heading back to Reykjavík, visibility was good, and even the rain had let up. The well-constructed gravel roads have a convex surface structure and are bordered on both sides by relatively low rock faces. The participants were sticking to our set speed of maximum 40 mph. Ahead of me, the vehicles briefly disappeared from view as they drove over a slight crest.

As I reached the top of the crest, my heart sank. The ladies team car, directly in front of us just two seconds before, was now no longer on the road. I can remember seeing my co-driver Doc Gunnar's eyes widen as we both looked right, just in time to see the Discovery literally somersault over the low rock face. The heavy vehicle landed on its roof between larger rocks about 60 feet from the road. Our mantra, "Keep out of trouble," was ringing in my ears as I looked at a wrecked Land Rover with two participants on board in the middle of the Icelandic wilderness.

I immediately radioed ahead to the convoy, instructing them to stop, and the doc and I rushed over to the severely damaged vehicle. The A-, B- and C-pillars were all badly bent, but there was enough space in the upended off-roader for the team to survive. The rather stupid sounding question "How are you?" was all we managed to ask, and fortunately from the inside of the vehicle the answer was an immediate "Don't worry, we're okay." The ladies crawled out through the smashed side windows themselves, but aside from shock and minor cuts, they were okay. Gunnar put both on drips and was quick to administer psychological help as both ladies were still suffering from severe shock.

It turned out that the cause of the near catastrophe was simple driver error. The driver had turned sharply to avoid hitting a larger rock, which she only saw at the last minute as she came over the hill, and because of the convex shape of the gravel road, the heavy vehicle tilted to one side and flew into the rock face. The following night, everyone celebrated two second birthdays, and that night I swore that there would be no more tours without a doctor on board.

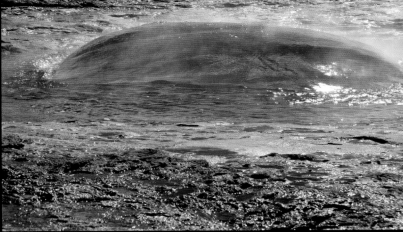

ISLAND BESITZT EINE GANZ EIGENE ENERGIE, DIE SICH DEN REISENDEN AUF ATEMBERAUBENDE WEISE MITTEILT: ÜBERALL HÖRT MAN ES IM BODEN ARBEITEN, ES RIECHT NACH SCHWEFEL, GEYSIRE STEMMEN SICH IN DEN HIMMEL. HINZU KOMMEN DIE ZAHLREICHEN WASSERFÄLLE, DIE SICH TOSEND IN DIE SCHLUCHTEN STÜRZEN.

--

ICELAND HAS ITS OWN UNIQUE AURA, ONE COMMUNICATED TO THE VISITOR IN THE MOST BREATHTAKING FASHION. THE EARTH HERE IS QUITE LITERALLY AT WORK; THE SMELL OF SULPHUR IS EVERYWHERE, AND GEYSERS LAUNCH THEMSELVES TO THE HEAVENS. ADDED TO THAT ARE NUMEROUS WATERFALLS CASCADING INTO DRAMATIC CANYONS.

HANS HERMANN RUTHE

*GEBOREN AM 6.2.1951 | GELERNTER MASCHINENBAUTECHNIKER UND WERKZEUGMACHER,
ÜBERZEUGTER WELTENBUMMLER, RECHTE (UND MANCHMAL AUCH LINKE) HAND VON DAG ROGGE*

*BORN 6 FEBRUARY 1951 | ENGINEER AND TOOLMAKER, DEDICATED GLOBETROTTER,
DAG ROGGE'S RIGHT (AND SOMETIMES LEFT) HAND*

Wie bist du zum Offroad- und Outdoor-Thema gekommen?
Ich habe mich 1990 für die Camel Trophy Sibirien beworben und auch gleich qualifiziert. Nach der Tour war ich zweitbester Teilnehmer, was das Lösen von Aufgaben anging. Von da an arbeitete ich rund zwei bis drei Monate pro Jahr für die Trophy – das Projekt Tonga/Fidschi/Samoa sehe ich heute als meinen bestbezahlten Urlaub aller Zeiten.

Und seit wann bist du mit dem Land-Rover-Virus infiziert?
Schon ein bisschen früher – und zwar seit dem Auswahlcamp für die Sibirien-Tour. Vorher fuhr ich ganz brav einen Opel Rekord Caravan, nach Sibirien aber ging es mit Defendern. Diese Autos haben mich sofort fasziniert und in ihren Bann gezogen. Da passte es, dass ich mit meiner Werkzeugfirma auch Bergsportartikel herstellte und Reinhold Messner mit meinen Produkten seine letzten Achttausender erobert hatte. Ich hatte also schon vorher eine besondere Affinität zur extremen Natur – wie Land Rover auch.

Wie hast du Dag kennengelernt?
Seine Firma bekam 1994 den Auftrag, den Defender – der ja vorher in Deutschland nicht vermarktet wurde, der stand nicht mal auf der Preisliste – für Presse und Händler einzuführen. Die damaligen Verantwortlichen bei Rover in Neuss schlugen Dag vor, doch ein paar Camel-Trophy-Trainer mit ins Boot zu nehmen. Dazu gehörte ich.

**Du bist seit Jordanien grundsätzlich bei den Planungen und soweit möglich bei den Vor- und Haupttouren der Land Rover Experience dabei.
Wie lässt sich das mit einem Job vereinbaren?**
Ich habe meine Firma im Jahre 2006 verkauft und toure seitdem etwa sechs bis sieben Monate im Jahr mit meiner Frau und meinem selbst umgebauten Defender 130 durch die Welt. Den Rest der Zeit widme ich der Experience.

Du fährst natürlich seit Langem selber Defender. Wie hast du ihn verändert, um ihn an deine Ansprüche anzupassen?
Haha, meinen gibt es so kein zweites Mal. Bei meinem jüngsten Auto habe ich nur das Chassis gekauft und alles andere selbst gebaut. Zum Beispiel wollte ich aus Sicherheitsgründen eine isolierte Glasfaserkabine, die mit dem Fahrerhaus durch eine Schiebetür verbunden ist. Das funktioniert dank eines verlängerten Führerhauses und einem Stahlhilfsrahmen, der hinten gefedert aufgebaut ist. So kann sich der Defender-Rahmen anmäßig verwinden, ohne dass es die Kabine stört. Innen gibt es Alkoven, Dusche, Toilette, 90-Liter-Kühlschrank. Alles, was schwer ist, liegt unten: Statt erstem Auspufftopf ein 120-Liter-Frischwassertank, auch der Batteriekasten und ein Abwassertank liegen unterhalb des Schwerpunktes, ebenso 45-Kilo Gas- und 120-Liter-Dieseltank. Das Ersatzrad liegt auf der Fronthaube – auch als Schutz gegen Steinschlag. Ist natürlich alles vom TÜV abgenommen.

Wo reist du am liebsten?
Zum Beispiel in Brasilien, Bolivien, Peru, Argentinien. Mit Militärkarten findet man winzige Pisten zu Geysiren in den Bergen, von denen kein Mensch etwas weiß. So etwas fordert mich heraus.

Gibt es etwas, das sich auf jeder Experience Tour wiederholt?
Vieles. Routine ist einfach wichtig, wenn es jedes Mal so viel Neues zu bewältigen gilt. Aber mir fällt natürlich sofort unser Funkruf ein, je nachdem, wer ruft: „Dag, Dag, Hans, Hans." „Hans, Hans, Dag, Dag."

How did you end up invloved in off-road and outdoors?
In 1990, I applied to go on the Camel Trophy to Siberia and qualified to go along. As far as solving special tasks was concerned, I was the second-best competitor that year. Thereafter I spent between two and three months every year working for the Trophy. I still think the Tonga/Fiji/Samoa event was the best-paid holiday I ever had.

When did the Land Rover virus infect you?
It's been a few years now – ever since selections for the Siberia Tour. Up until then, I had an Opel Rekord Caravan. After Siberia I started on Defenders. I was fascinated the moment I first encountered these vehicles, and I have been ever since. It seems appropriate that my tool company also produced the mountain-climbing equipment Reinhold Messner used on his last climbing expeditions. I've always had a thing for extremes in nature – a bit like Land Rover, I suppose.

How did you meet Dag?
His company won the contract from Land Rover to launch the Defender in Germany to both press and dealers. Up until that point, Defender hadn't been officially sold in Germany – it wasn't even on the price list. Rover management at the time in Neuss suggested he talk to a few Camel Trophy trainers. I was one of them.

Ever since Jordan, you have been involved in the planning and, whenever possible, in the pre-scout recces and main events. How do you manage to get the time off work?
I sold my company in 2006 and spend six or seven months a year with my wife touring the world in our converted Defender 130. I dedicate the rest of the time to the Experience.

You have been driving Defenders for a long time. What have you done to change your vehicle so it matches your specific requirements?
Ha-ha – my Defender is truly a one-off. For my most recent vehicle project, I literally just bought the chassis and built everything else myself. For safety I wanted an insulated fibreglass cabin that was connected to the driving compartment with a sliding door. This would only work with an extended driver's cabin and an additional steel sub-frame with its own suspension at the rear. This provides the torsional flexibility one expects from the Defender ladder frame without compromising the cabin. Inside the cabin, I have two sleeping alcoves, a shower, a toilet and a 90-litre refrigerator. Heavier items are underneath. Where normally the exhaust muffler would sit, there's a 120-litre freshwater tank. The battery rack as well as the wastewater tank are mounted below the vehicle's centre of gravity along with a 100-lbs. gas tank and a 120-litre diesel tank. The spare wheel is mounted on the bonnet – that protects against stone chips. The German Technical Inspection Agency (TÜV) has approved everything.

What are your favourite destinations?
Brazil, Bolivia, Peru and Argentina. Using old military maps, we found tiny routes to mountain geysers that nobody has ever seen. I love the challenge.

Is there some aspect of the Experience Tour that is always the same?
Lots. Routine is very important when there is always so much to discover that is new. Of course there is our classic radio call depending on who is calling who, "Dag, Dag, Hans, Hans" – "Hans, Hans, Dag, Dag".

NAMIBIA
2002

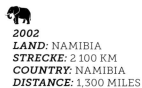

2002
LAND: NAMIBIA
STRECKE: 2 100 KM
COUNTRY: NAMIBIA
DISTANCE: 1,300 MILES

5 DISCOVERY, 2 DEFENDER,
1 RANGE ROVER

DAS KONDOM
THE CONDOM

Island ist kaum verdaut, da müssen wir schon die nächste Tour organisieren. Keine Zeit zum Verschnaufen. Aber wohin?

Nach dem abenteuerlichen, aber europäischen Island wird es Zeit, den Kontinent zu wechseln. Afrika ist traditionelles Land-Rover-Gebiet – da müssen wir jetzt unbedingt hin. Welches Land ist dort sicher? Was ist logistisch machbar? Klar: Namibia. Hans kennt das ehemalige Deutsch-Südwestafrika bereits, ich auch etwas. Es verspricht wilde Tiere, sandige Wüste, hohe Berge, unvergleichliches Licht. Kurz: Daktari-Feeling. Wer den legendären Buschdoktor nicht mehr kennt: „Daktari" (Doktor) hieß eine amerikanische Fernsehserie Ende der 6oer Jahre, die die Arbeit eines afrikanischen Tierhospitals und deren Doktoren zeigte – mitsamt der frechen Schimpansin Judy und dem schielenden Löwen Clarence. Natürlich fuhren in der Serie alle beteiligten Zweibeiner Land Rover.

10 000 Bewerber goutieren unsere Wahl. Acht Tage soll die Tour diesmal dauern, wegen des Zehn-Stunden-Fluges zum Zielort. Ich halte mich inzwischen für einen absoluten Organisationsprofi, Land Rover feiert Erfolge und verströmt Aufbruchstimmung – die Welt gehört uns.

Gernot, ein weißbärtiger Namibianer, ist schnell gefunden und als Guide vereidigt. Wie sich herausstellt, kennt er zwar jeden Vogel beim Vornamen, doch mit uns lernt er Wege kennen, an die er noch nicht mal im Traum gedacht hatte. Wir wollen die Tour mit diversen Serienfahrzeugen absolvieren: Discovery für die Teilnehmer, Defender für den Support und einen Range Rover für Begleiter wie Christian Uhrig. So touren wir durch das Land auf der Suche nach Abenteuern. Zu den größten gehört, dass uns unsere Reifen wegen der vielen spitzen Steine nur so um die Ohren fliegen. Ersatz in 19 Zoll ist kaum aufzutreiben.

Gut gerüstet durch die Erfahrungen der Vortour kommen wir zur Haupttour mit massenhaft Reifen im Gepäck in Namibia an. Und wie wir vermuten, platzt das Gummi auch diesmal ständig. Bald kennen wir jeden „Flat Tire Repair" im Umkreis von 500 Kilometern. So ein Pneu-Gemetzel habe ich nie wieder erlebt: 30 platte Reifen auf 2 000 Kilometern bei zehn Autos durch Steine und Dornen. Manchmal reparieren wir erstmal die Elektrik der Vulkanisierbetriebe am Straßenrand, weil deren Kompressoren nicht funktionieren, bevor die sich um unsere Reifen kümmern können.

Aber es kommt natürlich so, wie es kommen muss: Ein Discovery erleidet einen Reifenschaden am Brandbergmassiv, nachdem wir sämtliche Ersatzreifen bereits aufgebraucht haben. Was tun? Anhand von GPS-Informationen weiß ich, dass in etwa 30 Kilometern ein weiterer Tire Repair firmiert. Also beschließe ich, den Konvoi aufzusplitten. Drei Autos sollen beim Havaristen bleiben, der Rest muss zur Reparaturwerkstatt eilen. Da kommt unser Fotograf Thomas auf eine Idee: Man könne das Dornenloch doch durch ein Kondom flicken. Zufällig habe er gerade eines dabei. Mit einem Holzstab drücken wir das Gummi ins Loch und pumpen den Reifen vorsichtig mit dem Kompressor auf.

Aber alle, die jetzt hoffen, eine neue Ausrede für ein (an)ständiges Kondom in der Leatherman-Tasche zu haben, muss ich enttäuschen: Es funktioniert nicht. Obwohl wir extrem vorsichtig waren.

It seemed like only yesterday that we had been on Iceland, yet it was already time to plan the next tour. As the saying goes, there's no rest for the wicked. The question was: where to this time?

After an adventurous but very European-feeling Iceland, it was time to jump continents. Since Africa has always been something of a second home for Land Rover, we decided we had to head there. Where was it safe? What were the logistics like? It was obvious: Namibia. Hans was already familiar with the former colony of German South-West Africa, and I had been there, too. Wild animals, sandy deserts, mountains – it was a photographer's dream. In short: Daktari. For those not in the know, "Daktari" (meaning Doctor) was a famous 1960s American TV series about the work of an African animal hospital featuring a cheeky chimpanzee called Judy and a squinting lion called Clarence. The two-legged actors, of course, all drove Land Rovers.

10,000 applicants agreed wholeheartedly with our choice of location. A ten-hour flight meant that this time the tour would last for eight days. We were on a roll, Land Rover was striding from success to success, there was a real sense of optimism within the company, and I had become a logistics professional.

We quickly found Gernot, a white-bearded Namibian, and had him sworn in as our guide. Although he was on first-name terms with every bird in Namibia, in our company he would get to know routes that he had never dreamt even existed. We had three different Land Rover models on the tour: the participants were in Discovery, the organization team in Defenders, and we had a Range Rover for guests such as Christian Uhrig. Once again, we headed off into the bush on our hunt for adventure, and we found it immediately – in the form of numerous punctures, courtesy of the extremely sharp stones on the gravel roads. And 19-inch tyres were virtually unheard of in Namibia. After a pre-scout recce in which punctures featured far too prominently, we took plenty of spare tyres with us for the main event. As we suspected, history would repeat itself, with tyres blowing here, there and everywhere. Within a short space of time, we got to know every "flat-tyre repair" station within a 300-mile radius: 30 punctures on ten vehicles over 1,200 miles due to sharp stones and thorns remains a record in the annals of the Experience Tour. On some occasions, we first had to repair the electrical systems at the aforementioned repair shops before their compressors could be switched on to repair our tyres. Thankfully, we have not had tyre trouble like this on any tour since.

Naturally, the inevitable happened. With our supply of spares already spent, a Discovery suffered a puncture in the vicinity of Brandberg Mountain. GPS data indicated another tyre repair station about 19 miles down the trail, so I decided to split the convoy up. Three cars were to stay with the stranded vehicle, while the rest were to head on to the repair station. It was then that Thomas, our photographer, suggested using a condom to seal the hole created by the thorn, as, by chance, he happened to have one (a condom) on him ... Using a piece of wood, we forced the condom into the hole in the tyre and carefully pumped up the tyre using the compressor.

I regret to inform those in search of new and respectable reasons to carry a condom around that it didn't work – and this despite the fact that we were very careful.

Google™ earth
Map Data © 2013 AND
© 2013 Google
Image Landsat
US Dept of State Geographer

DER ELEFANT
THE ELEPHANT

Es ist phantastisch – alles das, was wir auf der zeitlich engen Vortour nicht gesehen haben, wird uns nun geboten: Natur satt, Zeit zum Genießen und vor allem wilde Tiere zum Beobachten. Das entschädigt dafür, dass die fahrerische Herausforderung in Namibia nicht so extrem ist, wie wir uns das erhofft haben. Zwar gibt es wenig asphaltierte Piste, aber die Schotterwege sind breit, und es existieren kaum Strecken, die einen Loop erlauben. Und um in eine Sackgasse zu manövrieren und den gleichen Weg wieder zurückfahren zu müssen, ist uns unsere Zeit zu schade. Deshalb sind wir für ein völlig ungeplantes Highlight ausgesprochen dankbar: eine Elefantenkuh und ihr Kalb. Die beiden stehen auf der anderen Seite eines etwa 40 Meter breiten, ausgetrockneten Flussbettes und schauen uns an.

Natürlich glotzen wir fasziniert zurück. Denn das ist so ein erhoffter Afrika-Moment für jeden Fotografen und für jedes Filmteam. Wir robben uns langsam im Flussbett vorwärts, um gute Bilder zu schießen. Da trötet jemand rechts von uns und viel zu nah: Es ist der dazugehörige Bulle. Wir haben ihn nicht bemerkt. Er stampft mit den Vorderbeinen und ist sichtlich erregt. Und er steht auf unserer Seite des Flussbetts.

Nur Fotograf Thomas und Kameramann Franky wollen nicht gleich fliehen – werden aber ziemlich schnell eines Besseren belehrt, als das tonnenschwere Tier beginnt, in ihre Richtung zu laufen. Dass unsere Knipser so schnell rennen können, habe ich ihnen vorher gar nicht zugetraut.

Wir schaffen es in die Autos, somit gelingt uns die Flucht, aber wir haben wieder etwas dazugelernt: Rechne noch mehr als bisher mit dem Unberechenbaren.

It was just amazing – everything we had missed during the tightly scheduled pre-scout recce was now laid out before us: nature as far as the eye could see, time to enjoy it and, best of all, wild animals. To some extent, this compensated for the fact that the driving wasn't quite as challenging as we had hoped. While very few roads were tarmacked, the gravel roads were wide, and there were all too few routes that allowed us to drive a loop. Because our time was too precious to drive the same route in and back out again, we were particularly fortunate that the attractions should leap before our eyepieces: an elephant and her calf. The pair stood on the opposite bank of a dry riverbed about 130 feet wide and watched us.

Obviously, we stared back – we were fascinated. It was the perfect Africa moment for every photographer and film team. We were crawling our way up the riverbed for better camera position when suddenly there was a loud trumpet to the right of and in worryingly close proximity to our position. It was none other than the third family member – the bull – and we had failed to notice him before. Stamping his front legs on the ground, he was visibly upset. To make matters worse, he was on our side of the riverbed.

Thomas the photographer and Franky the cameraman were the only ones not to get up and make a break for it. As the mighty bull began running towards them, though, they too rapidly changed their minds. I would never have imagined beforehand that our picture snappers could run so fast.

We made it to the cars and managed to escape, but we learned something that day: more than ever, expect the unexpected.

DAS AFRIKANISCHE LAND BIETET VIEL
SEHENSWERTES – ABER ETWAS GANZ
BESONDERES SIND DIE FARBENSPIELE
DER SONNE, WENN SIE AUF- ODER
UNTERGEHT.
--
THIS COUNTRY IN AFRICA HAS A GREAT
DEAL TO OFFER – OF PARTICULAR AND
SPECTACULAR NOTE IS THE EXPLOSION
OF COLOUR THAT ACCOMPANIES
SUNRISE AND SUNSET.

LIEBER ZUSAMMENBLEIBEN: DAS LAGERFEUER HÄLT AM ABEND WARM, DER MASSIVE LAND-ROVER-AUFTRITT UNLIEBSAME GÄSTE FERN. ELEFANTEN GEHÖREN ZU DEN SOGENANNTEN „BIG FIVE" UND HABEN JEDERZEIT VORFAHRT. UND DAMIT DIE LAND ROVER IMMER EINSATZ-BEREIT BLEIBEN, MÜSSEN DIE LUFTFILTER STÄNDIG VON DEM TEILWEISE SEHR FEINEN STAUB BEFREIT WERDEN.
--
BETTER TO STAY TOGETHER: THE CAMPFIRE KEEPS YOU WARM, AND THE DOMINATING PRESENCE OF THE LAND ROVER KEEPS UNWELCOME GUESTS AT A DISTANCE. ELEPHANTS RANK AMONG THE SO-CALLED "BIG FIVE" AND HAVE AUTOMATIC RIGHT OF WAY. AND TO ENSURE THAT THE LAND ROVERS ARE ALWAYS READY FOR ACTION, THE AIR FILTERS NEED TO BE CLEANED CONSTANTLY.

DER SCHADEN
THE DAMAGE

Ich sage es unseren Teams und selbst unseren Experience-Kollegen immer wieder: Fahrt im Konvoi nicht so dicht auf. Und zwar allein wegen der möglichen Steinschläge in den Scheiben der nachfolgenden Autos. Aber es ist ja so lustig, dicht hintereinander durch die Lande zu touren, und der Fotograf verlangt ja auch oft wenig Abstand, damit das Foto mit mindestens sechs staubenden, dynamisch wirkenden Wagen perfekt gelingt. Sorry, wir können viel an Ersatzteilen mitführen, aber große Frontscheiben gehören nicht dazu.

Natürlich rede auch ich manchmal gegen Windmühlen, oder aber ein besonders aufmüpfiger Stein fliegt extrem weit. Aber in Namibia unterläuft mir selber ein Kardinalfehler in Sachen Konvoifahren. Selbstverständlich haben wir auch hier Probleme mit von Reifen aufgewirbelten Steinen – das bösartigste Teil fliegt allerdings nicht in die Scheibe, sondern in den Kühler eines Discovery und zerstört ihn nachhaltig.

Neue Kühler führen wir üblicherweise nicht mit – können aber zu Hause in Schwalbach einen bestellen. Die Lodge in Palmwag besitzt einen Landeplatz, wo eine neue Gruppe begleitender Journalisten erwartet wird. Die sollen den Kühler aus Deutschland mitbringen. Nichtsdestotrotz muss der malträtierte Wagen irgendwie zur Lodge gebracht werden. Was bleibt uns übrig außer Abschleppen? So nehmen wir den Discovery ans Seil und ziehen ihn nach Hause.

Das hätten wir lieber nicht machen sollen. Denn als wir ihn endlich abnabeln, fällt mir die Kinnlade herunter: An der Front des Autos ist so gut wie nichts mehr heil. Die Scheinwerfer zerschossen, der Lack ramponiert, die Nebelleuchten zerstört. Wir sind einfach unser normales Experience-Tempo gefahren und haben ein zu kurzes Seil verwendet. Der feine Sand und die Pistensteine haben nun auch noch den Rest der Front nachhaltig zerstört. Das nächste Mal bin ich schlauer.

It is something I repeat to teams, and even our own Experience colleagues, on a regular basis. When in convoy, don't bunch up; and I say this for one very good reason – the danger of stone impact damage for the following vehicles. That said, it is more fun in close convoy, and the photographers often demand that people stick together, as the image of six vehicles in their own dust is far more dynamic. Still, while we had all manner of spares on board, our problem was that window screens weren't among them.

Sometimes I feel as though the others are to blame, and that I am talking to a brick wall. And there are times when no one is to blame and e.g. a particularly obstreperous stone flies a great distance. In Namibia, though, I was to blame: I had made a cardinal error whilst driving in convoy.

It goes without saying that we had our problems with stones being thrown up by the tyres. The most dangerous incident saw a stone flying not into the windscreen but into the radiator, where it caused significant damage.

We had no spare radiators on board but were able to order one from the Land Rover headquarters in Schwalbach, Germany. Our overnight lodge in Palmwag included a landing strip and was where we were expecting our second group of journalists to arrive, so we simply asked them to bring the replacement radiator with them. But because we had to get the Discovery back to the lodge first, we towed it home.

That was a mistake. For when we arrived at the lodge and unhooked the towline, my jaw dropped. The front end of the vehicle looked dreadful. Virtually nothing was intact. Both headlights and fog lamps had been destroyed, and the paint was scratched to hell. We had driven at normal Experience Tour speed, and the towline was far too short. Sand and gravel had finished off the front of the vehicle. It wouldn't happen again.

DAS MATTERHORN NAMIBIAS HEISST
SPITZKOPPE – EIN WUNDERSCHÖNES
LANDSCHAFTSMERKMAL IN JEDEM
LICHT. HIER GIBT ES JAHRTAUSENDEALTE
FELSMALEREIEN.
--
NAMIBIA'S OWN MATTERHORN IS THE
SPITZKOPPE. A WONDERFUL FEATURE
OF THE LANDSCAPE REGARDLESS OF
THE LIGHT. IT IS ALSO HOME TO
1,000-YEAR-OLD ROCK PAINTINGS.

DIE HIMBA LEBEN AUCH HEUTE NOCH VERGLEICHSWEISE UNBERÜHRT VON DER ZIVILISATION ALS VOLK VON VIEHZÜCHTERN, JÄGERN UND SAMMLERN, VOR ALLEM IM KAOKOLAND. EIN ZUSAMMENTREFFEN – NACH UNGLAUBLICH STAUBIGER TOUR DURCH NAMIBIAS NATUR – IST AUCH IMMER EIN KULTURELLER AUSTAUSCH UND FÜR BEIDE SEITEN GLEICH INTERESSANT UND LEHRREICH.

TO THIS DAY, THE HIMBA PEOPLE STILL LIVE RELATIVELY UNAFFECTED BY MODERN CIVILIZATION, HERDING CATTLE, HUNTING AND GATHERING FROM THE GROUND, PARTICULARLY IN KAOKOLAND. MEETING THEM IS A CULTURAL EXCHANGE, FASCINATING AND EDUCATIONAL FOR BOTH PARTIES.

DIE HILFE
THE AID

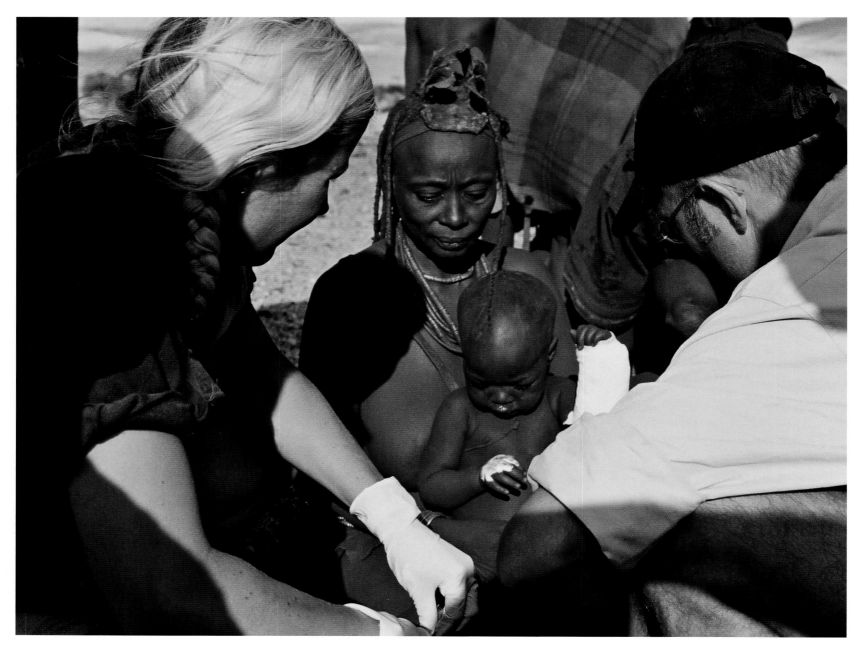

Die Land Rover Experience Tour fährt nicht nur durch die Gegend, um menschenleere Weiten kennenzulernen – im Gegenteil: Wir wollen ausdrücklich auch die Menschen und ihre Kultur besuchen, uns damit beschäftigen, ihre Botschaften weitertragen.

Das ist ein Grund, warum wir einen Kral aufsuchen, das Dorf eines traditionell lebenden Stammes. Der Dorfoberste hat eine Bitte: Der Doc möge sich um ein paar Einwohner kümmern. Einige Fälle kann Gunnar mit kleinen Pflastern und etwas Medizin heilen, aber zwei wirklich Kranke fordern sein ganzes Können. Eine Frau ist schwerkrank, sie benötigt dringend Erste Hilfe. Der zweite Fall betrifft ein Kind, das in die Feuerstelle gefallen war. Der Doc behandelt die verbrannte Haut so gut er kann. Wobei hundertprozentige Hilfe nicht an seinem Wissen scheitert, sondern an den begrenzten Hilfsmitteln, die wir mitführen.

Es ist schon immer ein Anliegen der Land Rover Experience Tour, nicht nur mit Freude am Abenteuer Teile der Welt zu erkunden, sondern auch zu helfen. Mit allem, was wir bieten können und was gebraucht wird.

The Land Rover Experience Tour is not just about discovering landscapes devoid of people – quite the opposite, in fact. We want to get to know people, the way they live their lives, and communicate their culture to others.

That is why we visited a kraal (a South African word meaning "dispersed homestead"). Before agreeing to the visit, though, the village chief had one stipulation: that our doctor attend to several of the villagers. Some of them required nothing more than a plaster and medication. Two others demanded considerably more of Doc Gunnar's medical skills. One woman was seriously ill and required immediate first aid. Another patient was a child who had fallen into the campfire. The doc treated the burns as best he could, but it wasn't possible to provide all the help needed, as we simply lacked adequate supplies of the medical equipment needed to treat an injury of that nature.

The Land Rover Experience Tour has always been about more than just the joy of adventure while exploring the world. It is also about giving something back. And that means doing whatever we can to help people.

CHRISTINE HÖFER-COLLINS

GEBOREN AM 26.3.1973 | DIPLOM-GEOLOGIN, ALS PROJEKTLEITERIN BEI LAND ROVER EXPERIENCE VON 2002 BIS 2004 ANGESTELLT, JETZT MITINHABERIN EINER AGENTUR FÜR EXTREMSPORT UND OUTDOOR-EVENTS IN SÜDAFRIKA*

BORN 26 MARCH 1973 | GEOLOGIST, PROJECT MANAGER AT LAND ROVER EXPERIENCE FROM 2002 TO 2004, CO-OWNER OF AN EXTREME SPORTS AND OUTDOOR EVENTS AGENCY IN SOUTH AFRICA

Kannst du dir ein Leben ohne extreme Outdoor-Aktivitäten vorstellen?
Nein. Ich habe dem normalen Leben immer das Abenteuer vorgezogen, und das ist auch heute noch so. Mein Geo-Studium hat mich schon früh abseits der normalen Reiseziele gebracht. Zunächst arbeitete ich in Südamerika und in den Northwest Territories, dann gehörte ich zum Support Staff der Camel Trophy, ebenso bei der G4 Challenge, und dann kam die Land Rover Experience Tour. Übrigens gehöre ich wohl weltweit zur Familie mit den meisten Camel-Trophy-Teilnehmern. Nicht nur ich, sondern auch mein Mann und sein Bruder waren dabei und ebenso die Frau meines Schwagers.

Was war deine Aufgabe bei der Experience Tour?
Ich habe das Büro München der Experience Tour betreut. In Namibia war ich bei fast allen Touren dabei, also auch bei den Kundenreisen. Darunter auch eine Tour mit National Geographic in den äußersten Nordosten des Landes. Bei der Mundo-Maya-Tour war ich als eine der Hauptverantwortlichen dabei, weil ich fließend Spanisch spreche. Und einmal Island hab ich auch mitgemacht.

Hattest du jemals Angst?
Ja, na klar. Zum Beispiel, als Hans in Belize im Dschungel verloren ging. Aber auch in Namibia. Da wurden Hans und ich einmal überfallen – dunkle Gestalten mit langen Messern nahmen uns alles ab. Es gab noch mehr Momente, aber mit solchen kompetenten und phantastischen Menschen wie Dag und Hans im Team kam oft einfach keine Angst auf. Allerdings gab es auch Zeiten, da war ich wohl etwas zu sorglos. In Namibia schlief ich etliche Nächte direkt am Lagerfeuer; am folgenden Morgen fanden wir einmal frische Löwenspuren rund ums Camp ...

Hattest du jemals das Gefühl, als Frau mit den Männern nicht mithalten zu können?
Natürlich gibt es Unterschiede in Sachen Ausdauer und vielleicht auch Leidensfähigkeit, aber ich habe immer genug Willensstärke besessen. Ich hatte übrigens auch nie das Gefühl, weniger Anerkennung als die Männer zu bekommen – im Gegenteil: Ich wurde eher hofiert und verwöhnt. Mit einer Ausnahme: Gernot, der Guide in Namibia, war ein echter Bure mit Haut wie Elefantenleder, und er hatte ziemliche Probleme mit der damals noch nicht mal 30 Jahre alten, kleinen, blonden Entscheidungsträgerin aus Deutschland.

Can you imagine your life without extreme outdoor activities?
No. I have always put adventure before everyday life, and I am no different today. My geography degree took me well off the beaten track, and initially I worked in South America and in the Northwest Territories. Then I was part of the support team on the Camel Trophy, and on the G4 Challenge before the Land Rover Experience Tour was born. By the way, I probably belong to the family with the greatest number of Camel Trophy participants. My husband and I, his brother and his wife have all taken part.

What was your job on the Experience Tour?
I ran the Experience Tour's Munich office. In Namibia, I accompanied almost all of the tours, including the customer trips and a tour we did with National Geographic in the far northeast corner of the country. On Mundo Maya I had more responsibility, because I speak fluent Spanish. I also did one tour to Iceland.

Were you ever afraid?
Oh yes, without a doubt. When Hans went missing in the Belizean jungle but also in Namibia. Hans and I were robbed. Guys with huge knives took everything. There were other moments, but working with such fantastic people as Dag and Hans in the team left no room for fear. There were other moments when I was a little reckless, such as in Namibia when I slept for a few nights right next to the campfire. Once we found lion tracks all around the campsite the following morning.

Did you ever feel that as a woman you couldn't keep up with the men?
There are obvious differences as far as stamina and one's ability to suffer are concerned but I have always been very strong-willed. I never felt that I received less recognition than the men – far from it: I was courted and spoiled, with one exception. Gernot, our guide in Namibia, was a true Boer, had skin like an elephant and problems with being told what to do by a little blonde thing from Germany who hadn't even hit 30 at the time.

MUNDO MAYA
GUATEMALA, MEXICO, BELIZE
2003

DER HINTERGRUND
THE BACKGROUND

2003
LÄNDER: GUATEMALA, MEXIKO, BELIZE
STRECKE: 1 850 KM
COUNTRIES: GUATEMALA, MEXICO, BELIZE
DISTANCE: 1,150 MILES

5 DISCOVERY, 2 DEFENDER

Jawohl, diesmal lassen wir es krachen. Drei Experience Touren sind sehr erfolgreich absolviert, und jetzt wollen wir einen drauflegen. Zum ersten Mal durch mehrere Länder, genau gesagt: drei. Eine neue Herausforderung, wieder ein anderer Kontinent – Land Rover und ich haben inzwischen gelernt, mit dem Event umzugehen. Aufkommende Routine erleichtert die Organisation. So schocken uns auch nicht die 12 000 Bewerber, die ein neues Abenteuer mit uns erleben wollen. Und natürlich die Kultur: Wir ziehen los, um auf den Spuren der Maya zu wandeln.

Naja, zunächst nur Hans, Christine Höfer-Collins, Lutz Rathmann und Claudia Lütolf. Denn meine vielen Aktivitäten fordern ihren Tribut: operative Eingriffe in die Knie. So kann ich nur von Wülfrath aus unterstützend helfen – die Vortour leitet Hans.

Yes, indeed – it's time to let loose. We have completed three very successful Experience Tours and now we want to up the ante. This time with a tour through more than one country – three to be exact. A new challenge, another continent. Both Land Rover and I have learnt how to deal with such an event. The routine makes organization simpler. We weren't even shocked by the 12,000 applicants who wanted to come with us, keen to catch the adventure buzz and to experience new cultures. We were heading off to follow in the footsteps of the Maya.

When I write "we", I mean Hans, Christine Höfer-Collins, Lutz Rathmann and Claudia Lütolf, for I had finally paid the price for being Mr 24/7: I had to have a knee operation, and that would keep me tied to my desk in Wülfrath. This time, Hans ran the pre-scout.

DER GUIDE
THE GUIDE

Auch wenn Dag am liebsten mit mir fährt und ich am liebsten mit Dag – zur Not muss es auch ohne den anderen gehen. Außerdem sind die Leute aus Dags Büro ebenfalls schwer auf Draht. Also machen wir uns zu viert und ohne den Chef auf nach Cancún, Mexiko, um einen Guide für dieses Land zu suchen. Das ist bei jeder Tour das A und O. Ohne Einheimische sind solche Reisen nicht zu machen. Aber wir treffen nicht auf die passenden Leute, also fliegen wir weiter nach Guatemala für gute Fotos, die wir für die mediale Vorbereitung zu Hause auf jeden Fall mitbringen müssen.

Doch das Schicksal meint es nicht gut mit uns: Auch in dem Zwölf-Millionen-Einwohner-Land finden wir nicht den richtigen Mann. Wir seilen uns also ab in den Kleinstaat Belize, das frühere Britisch-Honduras. Belize ist ein im Vergleich zu Guatemala völlig anderes Land, fast westlich: sauberes Englisch als Landessprache, überall Land Rover (wegen der langen britischen Herrschaft). Und obwohl es der einzige Staat Mittelamerikas mit Englisch als Amtssprache ist, werden wir auch hier nicht fündig. Wir liegen zeitlich weit hinter dem selbst gesteckten Soll zurück.

Also mit einem abenteuerlichen Flugzeug schnell zurück nach Flores, Guatemala. Wir sind ziemlich ratlos. Bis ein junger Kerl im Hotel Wind von unserer Suche bekommt und sich und seinen Vater in gutem Englisch als Guides anbietet. Der alte Herr kenne sich gut aus, und außerdem besitze man einen Land Rover, mit dem man die Gegend erkunden könne. Zudem hilft er uns, mit Kreditkarten sofort Bargeld zu besorgen. Wir haben ja gar keine Landeswährung dabei, weil wir ursprünglich nur Mexiko im Visier hatten.

Am nächsten Tag zur Mittagszeit kommt der eifrige Guatemalteke namens Juan mit einem Serie-II-Landy zurück. Der sieht gar nicht mal so schlecht aus, nur der Eimer, der unter dem Wagen hängt und offensichtlich Öl auffängt, macht uns stutzig. Außerdem ist der Wagen eindeutig zu klein. Wir zählen insgesamt sechs Leute inklusive unseres neuen Guides samt Vater und – natürlich – muss unser gesamtes Gepäck mit. Juan sieht das ein und kommt nach einer halben Stunde mit einem anderen Auto zurück: einem Toyota Hilux Pick-up. Was für ein Vehikel, um die Land Rover Experience Tour vorzubereiten.

Even if Dag preferred travelling with me, and I with him, if need be then we had to be able to go it alone. Besides, the people in his team are just as sharp as he is. So the four of us got together and headed off to Cancún, Mexico, in search of a guide. The common denominator to every successful tour is a local guide. Unable to find the right person, we headed on to Guatemala to acquire images urgently required for the pre-tour media campaign.

Clearly, luck wasn't on our side. In spite of a population just shy of 12 million, we still couldn't find a guide. We hopped over the border into Belize (formerly known as British Honduras). Compared to Guatemala, Belize was a very different cup of tea. Very Western, the official language there was British English, and Land Rovers were literally all over the place (in part due to its status as a former British colony). Despite its being the only country in Latin America where English was officially spoken, we still were unable to find our perfect guide. Up to that point, we were far behind our own targets.

Aboard an aircraft that had clearly seen better days, we returned to Flores, Guatemala, at a loss as to what to do. There, we were approached by a younger fellow who had heard we were looking for help. In good English, he offered himself and his father as guides. The older man knew a lot about the region, and they actually had a Land Rover, which we could use to explore the area. Additionally, he helped us get cash using our credit cards, as we had no money in the local currency.

At lunch time the following day, the eager Guatemalan whose name was Juan showed up with a Series II Land Rover. The vehicle looked to be in reasonable shape, apart from the bucket hanging underneath which was clearly intended to catch oil leaking from somewhere. And it was too small for six people (including the guide, his father and our luggage). Juan realized his mistake and came back half an hour later with a different vehicle: a Toyota Hilux pickup. What a car in which to prepare the Land Rover Experience Tour.

DIE LADEFLÄCHE
THE CARGO BED

In der Not frisst der Teufel bekanntlich Fliegen, also steigen wir tatsächlich in einen Toyota. Nein, nicht in, sondern auf. Vater und Sohn entern das zweisitzige Fahrerhaus, die vierköpfige Landy-Mannschaft okkupiert die Ladefläche, das Gepäck als Polster zwischen Blech- und Hosenboden. Ab in den Dschungel.

Zur Erinnerung: Eigentlich wollten wir in Mexiko einen Guide suchen, jetzt finden wir uns wieder zwischen Ameisen, Würmern, Fliegen, Moskitos und Spinnen, die auf den Toyota prasseln, während wir durch den Dschungel jagen. Denn um die Zeit zu nutzen, wollen wir jetzt neue, eventuell fahrbare Dschungelpfade kennenlernen. Mit Akribie durchpflügen unsere Fahrer mögliche und unmögliche Pisten. Die Tipps, wo es diese Pfade gibt, haben sie sich vorher bei Pflanzensammlern geholt. Das sind die einzigen Menschen, die sich noch hierher wagen.

Das bedeutet, dass die Trails mindestens zu drei Viertel zugewachsen und schon lange keine Straßen mehr sind. Das bedeutet aber auch: Äste und Blätter hängen ins Auto hinein, und beim Vorbeifahren streifen wir von Rinde und Blättern ab, was sich dort befindet und eigentlich auch dort bleiben wollte. Mit spitzen Fingern klauben wir die Fauna vom Toyota. Nie vergessen werde ich zum Beispiel die vogelspinnengroßen Achtbeiner (vielleicht waren es ja Vogelspinnen). Und während wir hinten tapfer mit fiesem Getier kämpfen, steht vorne unser junger Guide mit der Kupplung im Clinch. Besorgt lauschen wir den metallischen Geräuschen in den alten japanischen Eingeweiden. In dieser unwirtlichen Gegend hätten wir gerne ein zuverlässiges Gefährt gehabt. Egal von welchem Hersteller.

Irgendwann will der Hilux aber tatsächlich nicht mehr. Die Dichtung des Kupplungsdruckgebers ist hin. Wir schmieren das Ding voller Maschinenfett, dann geht's erst mal weiter. Tikal ist unser Ziel, und es sind noch 500 Kilometer bis dorthin. Uns tun inzwischen die Rücken weh, die Hintern, die Arme – von den ganzen Stichen der Insekten, die wir zum Glück nicht alle namentlich kennen, mal abgesehen. Noch zweimal bekommt die Toyota-Kupplung ihr Fett weg, dann sind wir endlich im Ort. Und die Kupplung ist restlos platt. Wir glauben nicht, dass hier im tiefsten und dschungeligsten Maya-Land Ersatz für das marode Toyota-Bauteil zu finden ist und gehen schon mal die gar nicht guten Möglichkeiten durch, diesen Ort im grünen Niemandsland irgendwie und irgendwann wieder verlassen zu können.

Aber Juan, unser Fahrer, ist hoffnungsfroh. Ich weiß nicht, wie er das macht, aber er findet hier in der absoluten Regenwald-Pampa tatsächlich Neuteile für den Japaner. Und während die eingebaut werden, können wir uns etwas mit Tikal beschäftigen. Erste Siedlungsspuren wurden auf das 1. Jahrtausend v. Chr. datiert, der Höhepunkt der städtischen Entwicklung wurde im 5. Jahrhundert erreicht. Etwa im 10. Jahrhundert haben die Maya die Stadt verlassen, ihre eindrucksvollen Stufentempel blieben zurück. Ganz Tikal erstreckt sich über eine Fläche von rund 65 Quadratkilometern, das Zentrum selbst umfasst etwa 16 Quadratkilometer. Der Ort ist eine der am besten erforschten Maya-Städte, obwohl viele Bauten der Stadt, in der einst wohl zwischen 50 000 und 200 000 Menschen wohnten, noch gar nicht ausgegraben sind.

So gern wir auch bleiben würden – sobald der Wagen repariert ist, müssen wir weiter. Die Zeit drängt. Es dämmert bereits, und wir haben noch viele Kilometer bis zur Grenze vor uns.

Beggars can't be choosers (or so the saying goes), so we climbed inside the Toyota. Actually, we jumped onto it – father and son climbed into the two-man cabin, while the Land Rover team occupied the cargo bed, using our luggage as cushions. Then we headed into the jungle.

Just to recap: the original plan was to find a guide in Mexico. Now we were sat between ants, worms, flies, mosquitoes and spiders racing through the jungle in the back of a Toyota pickup. To make the best of our time here, we decided to search for new jungle trails that we would drive on the tour. With meticulous dedication, our drivers ploughed through trails that ranged from driveable to impassable. The route suggestions came from plant collectors in the region, who are the only people who use them.

Three quarters of these trails are so overgrown that they can barely be described as roads at all. As we rode along them, in the back of the pickup, we involuntarily collected much of what hangs from the trees, including all manner of insects that probably would just as soon have stayed home. We carefully removed as much of the fauna from the Toyota as possible. I certainly won't forget the arachnids the size of tarantulas (which they may actually have been!) that we combated in the back of the truck while the younger guide up front had his own personal struggle with the Toyota's clutch. It was disturbing to hear the sound of metal on metal deep inside the old Japanese four-wheeler. In this particularly inhospitable region, we would have been happier with a more reliable set of wheels – irrespective of its country of origin.

Eventually, the Hilux just refused to go any further. The seal on the clutch pressure plate had gone. We packed it full of machine grease, which got it working again. We were heading for Tikal, still over 300 miles away, and besides the bites of insects – which, fortunately for our peace of mind, we were unable to identify – we had sore backs, backsides and arms. The Toyota clutch required two more helpings of grease before we finally arrived at our destination. By then, however, the clutch had finally died. The chances of finding a replacement Toyota part here in the deepest part of the Mayan jungle looked slim, and we began considering our options for leaving this green no-man's-land.

Our driver's optimism was rewarded, however, and he actually managed to source the spares for the Toyo in the middle of this rain forest.

While they repaired the clutch, we got on with the business of exploring Tikal. The first evidence of civilization there dates to 1000 B.C., and the city reached its zenith during the 5th century. The Mayans abandoned the city, with its impressive stepped temples or ziggurats, in or around the 10th century. The whole of Tikal extends over 25 square miles, with the city centre covering some 6 square miles. Tikal is one of the best-documented Mayan cities in existence, although many of the buildings in the city that was once home to between 50,000 and 200,000 inhabitants have yet to be excavated.

As much as we wanted to stay, as soon as the truck was repaired we had to make tracks. Time was tight, it was already getting dark and we still had a long drive to the border ahead of us.

DER DSCHUNGEL
THE JUNGLE

So zugewuchert wie viele der Maya-Stätten von der Flora des Dschungels sind, so muss man sich auch die Pisten vorstellen, die schon seit Langem keine Straßen mehr sind. Optimal für eine Abenteuertour mit Teilnehmern, aber suboptimal, um Kilometer zu fressen. Wir vier Deutsche hängen wieder auf der Ladefläche des Toyota, und der beste Service besteht darin, dass uns unser Fahrerduo im geschützten Führerhaus des Hilux Brote schmiert und sie aus dem Fenster auf die Ladefläche reicht. Zeit verlieren geht nicht – die Einhaltung von Zeitplänen ist eine der ganz wichtigen Grundlagen für solche Expeditionen, wie sie die Land Rover Experience ausheckt.

Trotzdem, der Weg ist zu problematisch, zu dicht bewachsen, zu unübersichtlich, um ihn im Dunkeln bewältigen zu können. Wir müssen ein Nachtcamp einrichten. Mit eindrucksvollen Macheten hacken Papa und Sohn ein Stück Dschungel an der Straße frei. Wo es geht, spannen wir Hängematten, schützen sie und damit auch uns mit Moskitonetzen. Auf dem lange nicht benutzten Weg machen wir Feuer, sehen ein paar Skorpione herumkriechen ... und tatsächlich, nach einiger Zeit schlafen wir ein. Juan und sein Vater direkt auf dem Boden. Zum Glück, wie sich herausstellt.

Denn nach viel zu wenigen Stunden Schlaf wecken sie uns aufgeregt: „Weg hier, bloß weg hier!", rufen sie. Und wenn Einheimische so zur Action auffordern, folgt man lieber, ohne überflüssige westeuropäische Fragen zu stellen. Sie werden ihre Gründe haben.

In diesem Fall ist es nur ein Grund, und der heißt „Bedford" und klingt gefährlich. Ein fetter Truck mit Pflanzensammlern auf der Ladefläche donnert über den selten befahrenen Weg und mäht alles nieder, was im Weg steht – also fast auch unser Nachtlager, den Toyota und uns selbst. Juan ist als Erster aufgewacht von den Vibrationen im Boden, die der schwere Laster vorausschickte.

Da es bereits Morgen wird und wir unsere Ruhestätte zwangsweise in aller Eile zerstören mussten, können wir auch weiterfahren. Obwohl „fahren" nicht ganz der Wahrheit entspricht. Mit Macheten und einer Motorsäge kämpfen wir uns voran. Der Truck muss irgendwo abgebogen sein, jedenfalls befuhr sicher lange niemand mehr die Strecke, die wir jetzt erforschen.

Das Vorankommen ist zeitweise extrem mühsam. Anders ausgedrückt: 200 Meter in einer Stunde. Das größte Frischegefühl genießen wir, wenn wir das getragene T-Shirt alle paar Stunden auf links drehen. Das Gepäck ist bald völlig verschlammt, der Dreck findet zusätzlich jeden Weg ins Innere. Unsere Klamotten und wir machen den Eindruck von frisch ausgegrabenen Maya.

Irgendwie schaffen wir es tatsächlich bis zum Grenzübergang Chetumal, wo wir uns wenig später dank Dusche und Hotel schon wieder fühlen wie zivilisierte Menschen. Dort findet uns Professor Ernesto Parra, ein Archäologe aus Mexiko, der sich bereit erklärt, in Mexiko unser Guide zu sein.

Just as many Mayan sites are completely covered by jungle, the same is true of the jungle tracks that have long since fallen into disuse. The tracks are perfect for an adventure tour with participants, but less than perfect when all that matters is getting from A to B. The four Germans were once again stuck in the back of the Toyota pickup, the only highlight being the sandwiches-to-go service provided by our driver team through the rear window of the cab. Once again, we had no time to lose, as keeping to a strict schedule is fundamental to the success of any expedition put together by Land Rover Experience.

Nevertheless, with the route too complicated, too overgrown and too difficult to drive at night, we made camp for the night. Using impressive-looking machetes, the father-and-son team hacked clear a section of jungle next to the track, creating an area where we could hang our hammocks between the trees, making sure to protect themselves and us with mosquito nets. On the trail, which had not seen any traffic for a very long time, we got a campfire going, watching a few scorpions go about their business. After a while, we actually fell asleep. Fortunately for us – for reasons I shall explain – Juan and his son slept on the ground, for after what seemed like minutes rather than hours, they were waking us up in a panic saying, "We have to go now." When locals demand action in this fashion, it is better to acquiesce and not ask the usual European-style superfluous questions. After all, they probably had a very good reason.

The reason was a "Bedford", and it sounded terrifying. The large truck full of plant collectors was thundering down the trail, crushing everything in its path and threatening to do the same to our campsite, the Toyota and our good selves. Juan had been woken up by the ground vibrations caused by the truck.

As it was already morning, and we had been forced to break camp in rather hurried fashion, we decided to continue driving where we had left off. Whereby "driving" was not quite accurate, as we had to chop our way through the trail with the machetes and a chain saw. The truck must have turned off the trail relatively quickly, as clearly no one had explored the section we then entered for a very, very long time.

Making progress was at times painstakingly difficult, or, to put it another way: 600 feet per hour. The most refreshing experience was turning one's T-shirt inside out every couple of hours. Our clothes were absolutely covered in mud, and the dirt clung everywhere. In our clothes, we looked like freshly unearthed Mayans.

Somehow we made it to the border crossing at Chetumal, where a hotel shower made us feel like civilized human beings again. There we met Professor Ernesto Parra, a Mexican archaeologist who offered to serve as our guide in Mexico.

DIE ANGST
THE FEAR

So eine umfangreiche Reise bedingt eine zweite Vortour – die kann ich dank heilendem Knie wieder mitfahren. Inzwischen sind auch die Autos angekommen. Eine bestimmte Stelle, die meine Vorfahrer gefunden haben, weckt mein ganz besonderes Interesse: Abseilen in unterirdisches Gewässer. Hans und sein Team haben bei der ersten Vortour eine natürliche Höhle gefunden, durch die ein Fluss rauscht. Vom etwa 120 Meter hohen Hügel über dem Fluss kann man wunderbar als Task für die Teilnehmer eine Seilaktion einbauen, zumal wir im Qualifikationscamp extra eine Aufgabe mit Seilen und Klettern geübt haben. Die Fahrrouten stehen also fest, nur die Klettertour müssen wir noch ausprobieren.

Die Idee dahinter: Die Teams bekommen Koordinaten, von dort seilen sie sich ungefähr 90 Meter auf die Wasseroberfläche ab. Danach können alle entspannt im wunderbaren Flusswasser baden – was für ein Abenteuer!

Hans, Lutz, Christine, Claudia, unser Guide Professor Ernesto, der Allrad-Journalist Bernhard Weinbacher, Land-Rover-Pressechef Paul Entwistle und ich wollen das aber vorher noch ausprobieren. Es ist 8 Uhr morgens, wir sind an der richtigen Stelle angekommen. Christine, Lutz und Ernesto schlagen sich durch den Dschungel auf dem Hügel zum Test-Klettern. Die ganze Aktion dürfte nicht länger als eine Viertelstunde dauern.

Nach einer Stunde werde ich nervös. Wir hören nichts, und erst recht seilt sich niemand ab. Ich will schon hinterher, da sagt Hans: „Lass mich mal." Ich rate ihm noch, Bernhard mitzunehmen, und weg ist er.

Ich muss gestehen, ich habe Bernhard gar nicht gefragt. Ich nehme mein Bowie-Messer und ein Funkgerät – ich weiß ja, wo es langgeht. Immerhin war ich schon zweimal oben an dem Punkt, an dem die Teilnehmer starten sollen. Ich werde unsere drei Test-Kletterer schon finden. Kann ja nicht so schwer sein.

HANS

Tatsächlich höre ich nach wenigen Fußmarsch Richtung bergauf Stimmen unserer Kollegen – die kommen aber von der falschen Seite des Berges. Ich versuche, mich durch das dichte Blattwerk zu schlagen, immer in Richtung Stimmen – aber plötzlich ist Stille. Es passiert nicht oft, aber jetzt lässt mich mein Orientierungssinn im Stich. Es ist 10 Uhr, es ist 42 Grad heiß, und es sieht überall gleich aus. Das Gezirpe von ein paar Grillen ist das einzige Geräusch, das ich wahrnehme. Kurz: Ich habe mich verlaufen und überhaupt keine Ahnung, wo ich hinmuss.

Endlich: Stimmen. Ich gestehe, ich bin die vergangenen zwei Stunden ganz schön nervös gewesen. Aber jetzt höre ich sie, die drei Vorkletterer. Sie kommen vom anderen Ende des Tunnels. Lutz erzählt, wie sehr sich der Dschungel in den vergangenen Wochen verändert hat, man fände tatsächlich keinen der einst auserkorenen Orientierungspunkte wieder. Ich renne zum Funkgerät am Auto, um Hans und Bernhard die freudige Nachricht zu überbringen und ihnen zu sagen, sie können zurückkommen – da treffe ich Bernhard. Der weiß nichts von Hans' Alleingang.

„Hans, Hans, Dag, Dag?" Ich versuche ihn über Funk zu erreichen – keine Antwort. Ich weise alle Anwesenden an, zu den Autos zu gehen und zu hupen, Lärm als Orientierungshilfe. Keine Antwort. Jetzt weiß ich: Hans hat ein Problem. Ich habe ein Problem. Wir haben ein Problem: Hans Hermann Ruthe hat sich verlaufen. Mitten in Belize, und das ist alles andere als beruhigend.

HANS

Spätestens jetzt merke ich: Ich habe ein Problem – ich habe mich verlaufen. Aber wofür gibt es Funkgeräte: „Dag, Dag, Hans, Hans! Ich glaub, ich hab mich ver... krrrrrchhhchhh." Die Funke ist tot, kein Saft. Irgendjemand hat vergessen, dieses Funkgerät aufzuladen.

„Ich hab mich ver..." krächzt es noch aus der Funke, dann ist Stille. Mit Verlaub: Scheiße. Funkloch? Akku alle? Oder ist Hans gerade Opfer einer Würgeschlange geworden? In so einem Moment gehen einem die wildesten Gedanken durch den Kopf. Als ich Hans heute das letzte Mal sah, trug er kurze Hosen – auch das noch. Hoffentlich hat er wenigstens Wasser mitgenommen.

Such a complex tour required a second pre-scout recce. Which I was able to join, now that my knee had healed. Meanwhile, our vehicles had arrived as well. One location that the team had discovered on the first pre-scout interested me in particular: abseiling into an underwater cavern. Hans and the team had found a natural cave with a river flowing through it. From the 400-feet-high mountain above the river, we could create a task for the participants that involved abseiling, as we had specifically practised rope climbing in the selection camps. The driving routes had been sorted, but we had yet to test the climbing task.

The underlying idea was that the teams would be given coordinates from which they would abseil 300 feet down to the river, where they could bathe in a beautiful stream – this was classic adventure stuff!

Hans, Lutz, Christine, Claudia, our guide Professor Ernesto, four-wheel-drive journalist Bernhard Weinbacher, Land Rover PR man Paul Entwistle and I needed to test it first. At 8 in the morning we arrived at the point where the task was due to start. Christine, Lutz and Ernesto started making their way up through the jungle to the top of the mountain to test the climbing section. We estimated this would take no longer than 15 minutes.

After an hour, I started to get nervous: We could hear no one, and nobody had abseiled down the hill. I wanted to head off up the hill, but Hans said, "I'll sort it out." I advised him to take Bernhard with him, and he disappeared.

I admit that I didn't even ask Bernhard. I took my Bowie knife and a radio; I knew where I was going, as I had already been up to the jump-off point for the special task twice. Finding our three climbing guinea pigs couldn't be that difficult.

After a few minutes' walk I could actually hear my colleagues' voices, albeit from the wrong side of the mountain. I started cutting my way through the thick undergrowth heading towards the voices – suddenly it went quiet. A rare occurrence for me, but I was completely disoriented. It was 10 am, 42 degrees Celsius (108 degrees Fahrenheit), and everything looked the same. All I heard was the chirping of a few crickets. In short, I was lost and had no idea in which direction to go.

At last: voices. Admittedly, for the last two hours I had been pretty worried. Now, though, I could hear our three test climbers coming from the other end of the tunnel. Lutz explained how the jungle had changed in the last couple of weeks, and that they hadn't been able to identify any of the reference points we had set. I ran to the radio to tell Hans and Bernhard the good news, and that they could come back, when I met Bernhard, who was completely unaware that Hans had gone off on his own.

"Hans, Hans, Dag, Dag?" I tried to reach him on the radio, but there was no answer. I told the team to go back to the vehicles to sound the horns in the hope that the noise would help him with his orientation. No answer. Now I knew that Hans had a problem. I had a problem, and that meant we all had a problem. Hans Hermann Ruthe was lost in the middle of the Belizean jungle. This was not good.

By now, I had realized I had a serious problem – I was completely lost. However, I had a radio: "Dag, Dag, Hans, Hans! I think I am lo ... Krrrrrrchhhchchch" The radio was dead. Somebody had forgotten to charge it.

"I think I'm lo ..." There was a brief crackling from the radio, and then it went dead. Poor reception? Battery dead? Or had Hans just been attacked by a snake? I make no apologies for saying this, but it was a shitty mess and no mistake. In a situation like this, all manner of potential scenarios go through your mind. The last time I'd seen him that morning, he was wearing shorts – given the terrain, not good. Hopefully, he had at least remembered to take some water with him.

I had to do something. Sitting around waiting for something to happen is just not me. At 1 pm I sent one of our vehicles to a large logging camp about 6 miles down the trail, hoping there would be someone there who knew the terrain. Of one thing I was certain. If Hans had got lost, he would do the right thing and stay put.

Ich muss etwas tun, Warten ist nun überhaupt nicht mein Ding. Um 13 Uhr schicke ich eines unserer Autos zu dem großen Holzfällercamp in 10 Kilometer Entfernung. Dort muss es doch jemanden geben, der sich hier auskennt. Denn ich bin mir sicher: Wenn Hans sich verläuft und es merkt, macht er das einzig Richtige. Er bleibt an Ort und Stelle.

Was macht man, wenn man die Orientierung verloren hat? Richtig: Man bleibt an Ort und Stelle. Ich zücke mein Messer und markiere einen Baum nach allen vier Himmelsrichtungen, die ich nach der Sonne bestimmen kann, indem ich einen Stock in den Boden ramme und mich nach dem Schatten richte. Ich weiß: Nach Westen existiert nichts anderes als 20 Kilometer dichter Dschungel bis zur Grenze nach Guatemala. Nach Osten sind es rund 15 Kilometer bis zur Hauptstraße – auch keine grandiose Aussicht. Und dann diese Hitze. Und wenn dieser Durst bloß nicht wäre.

Wir halten die Antennen hoch, rufen Hans immer wieder per Funk: nichts. In diesem Dickicht leben mindesten fünf Giftschlangenarten, ganz zu schweigen von den Skorpionen und den stechenden Insekten. Inzwischen ist ein Holzfäller vom Camp angekommen. Der zieht sich Gummistiefel an, schultert sein Gewehr und verschwindet im Dschungel. Nach einer halben Stunde kehrt er zurück mit der Nachricht, er finde Hans nicht. Wir sollten uns ans Militär wenden. Das würde die Chancen, Hans zu finden, erhöhen, weil das Gebiet Übungsgebiet der Soldaten sei. Ernesto telefoniert sofort über Satellitentelefon mit den zuständigen Soldaten, aber die winken ab: Heute nicht mehr. Erst morgen.
Es ist bereits 17 Uhr. Und es wird langsam dunkel. Ich habe Angst um Hans. Zum ersten Mal auf einer unserer Touren habe ich echte Angst.

Durst. Er kommt, und er geht nicht. Denk nach, denk an deine Camel-Trophy-Zeit. Was macht man bei Durst im Dschungel, wenn man nichts dabei hat? Man sucht eine Liane. Pro Meter Pflanze liefert sie ein halbes Glas Flüssigkeit. Ich suche und finde, sogar einige innerhalb des von mir selbst gesetzten Radius von 500 Metern um meinen Himmelsrichtungsbaum. Die Ausbeute ist nicht wirklich ergiebig, aber besser als nichts.
Wetterleuchten setzt ein, Donner grummelt in der Ferne. Unter anderen Bedingungen ein tolles Schauspiel. Ich zücke mein Messer, schnitze mir eine kleine Sitzbank, mache Feuer mit dem Feuerzeug, das ich in der Tasche habe, und warte. Inzwischen ist es 20 Uhr und stockdunkel. So etwas ist mir noch nie passiert.

Ich habe alle Journalisten und den Großteil der Experience-Mannschaft in die Lodge geschickt. Bei zwei Autos versagen inzwischen die Hupen, so sehr haben wir sie malträtiert. Ständig ist jemand am Funk, um Hans zu rufen – vielleicht kann er uns ja hören, aber nicht antworten. Dann schnappe ich mir die Landkarte: Wo ist Hans, geht es in meinem Schädel rund. Wo ist er hingegangen? Nein, er ist nicht weggegangen, er ist geblieben.
Wie sagen wir es seiner Frau?
Herrje, was war das denn eben für ein schräger Gedanke? Selbstverständlich finden wir ihn. Aber wenn nicht? Ich habe die Verantwortung, und ich habe meinen Freund „verloren". Das darf nicht passieren, das darf einfach nicht passieren. Jetzt geht noch einmal unser Guide mit dem Holzfäller los. Letzte Chance für heute.

Mein Zeitgefühl ist nicht mehr gut, meine Uhr aber immer noch genau: Es ist kurz vor halb zehn Uhr abends, da höre ich Stimmen. Ja, sie sind es, irgendwer von unserem Team, und als ich ihnen entgegenlaufen will, versagen mir die Beine. Ich bin dehydriert, habe Krämpfe, und die beiden müssen mich erst mal auf den Boden legen und meine Muskeln bearbeiten. Dann gehen wir zusammen lachend und weinend den Hügel hinunter.

Ja, auch harte Trophy- und Experience-Männer müssen, können und dürfen weinen. Hans ist zurück, und es ist wie Weihnachten im Sommer. Er war nur gut einen Kilometer von uns entfernt, aber der Dschungel schluckt alle Geräusche. Der Ärmste sieht ziemlich geschunden aus: Die Hornhaut der Augen verbrannt, voller Staub und Dreck von den Dschungelblättern, unzählige Zecken klammern sich an seinen Körper – aber er ist genauso glücklich wie wir. Trotzdem möchte ich so etwas nie wieder erleben. Und nie wieder vergisst irgendjemand der Orga, die Funkgeräte aufzuladen. Schlimmer kann es jetzt eigentlich nicht mehr kommen. Denke ich …

What is the right thing to do if you have lost your bearings? The right thing to do is to stay right where you are. I pulled out my knife and scored the four points of the compass into the bark of a tree using the sun as my point of reference, and then rammed a stick into the ground to see where the shadow was. I knew that to the west there was nothing but 12 miles of jungle to the Guatemalan border. Towards the east it was about 9 miles to the main road – not exactly motivating stuff, given the heat and the fact that I was thirsty. **HANS**

We raised the antennas and repeatedly tried reaching Hans on the radio. But it was no use. At least five different varieties of poisonous snake lived in the undergrowth, not to mention scorpions and all manner of biting insects. In the meantime, a logger from the camp had shown up. He put his rubber boots on, shouldered his rifle and set off into the jungle. After half an hour, he returned saying that he was unable to find Hans and that we should get in touch with the army. Our chances of finding Hans would be greater because the region was a military training area. On the satellite phone, Ernesto talked to the military but was told they wouldn't be able to help that day. The earliest they could send a search party would be the following day.
By now, it was 5 pm and beginning to turn dark. I was worried about Hans. For the first time on a tour, I was really afraid that something had happened.

Thirst. Once it's there, it never leaves. Think back to Camel Trophy. How do you deal with thirst in the jungle when you have no water? You look for a liana vine. A metre of vine produces approximately half a glass of fluid. Within a 1,600-foot radius of my compass tree, I found a few vines from which the yield of fluid was mediocre but better than nothing. Sheet lightning was visible in the sky, and in the distance I could hear thunder. Any other day, it would have been a marvellous spectacle. I pulled out my knife, made myself a chair, started a fire with the lighter I had in my pocket and waited. It was 8 pm and pitch black. This had never happened to me before. **HANS**

I sent all the journalists and the majority of the Experience team back to the lodge. The horns on two of the vehicles were no longer working after we had sat on them all day. One of the team stayed on the radio in the hope that Hans could hear us but wasn't able to answer. I grabbed the map. My mind raced. Where had he gone? No – I decided he hadn't gone anywhere. Hans would stay put.
What would we say to his wife?
Good God – where did that come from? Of course we would find him, but what if we didn't? I was responsible, and I'd lost my mate. This just shouldn't happen. Our guide went off one last time with the logger. This was our last chance today.

My body clock was not functioning as well as before, but my watch was fine. It was 9.30 pm, and I could hear voices. Yes, it was someone from the team, and as I attempted to run towards them, my legs collapsed beneath me. I was dehydrated and had severe cramps. The two had to lay me out on the ground to massage my leg muscles before we returned, crying and laughing, back down the hill. **HANS**

Hard-nosed Camel Trophy and Experience guys need to cry, too. Hans was back, and it felt like Christmas. He had been less than a mile away all this while, but the jungle absorbs all manner of sounds. Hans looked battered to say the least. Mildly sunblind, completely covered in dust and dirt from the jungle undergrowth, and his body a habitat for numerous ticks – but he was as happy as we were.
Nevertheless, I didn't want to experience this again. And no one in the team would forget to charge the radios in future, either.
It couldn't get any worse. Or so I thought.

DAS DRAMA
THE DRAMA

Die Vortour ist vorüber. Wir müssen nur noch die Autos zurück nach Mexiko bringen. Die Straßen, die durch den Dschungel führen, sind eng und uneben, aber teilweise schnurgerade. Ich habe endlich einen Moment Zeit zum Relaxen und dafür, die Strecke der Haupttour schon mal im Kopf abzufahren.

Plötzlich stockt der Verkehr. Vor mir steht ein Lastwagen, der die Sicht nimmt. Ich steige aus, um nachzusehen, was los ist – und mir gefrieren trotz 30 Grad die Gesichtszüge. Etwa 40 Menschen sind aus ihren Autos gestiegen und stehen tatenlos um eine gespenstische Szenerie herum. Zwei Kleinwagen sind frontal zusammengekracht. Rauch steigt unter den verknitterten Motorhauben hervor, jemand wimmert. Ich schnappe mir den Erste-Hilfe-Rucksack und renne los.

Wenn Nachdenken lähmen würde, dann jetzt: In einem kleinen Seat sitzen drei Erwachsene. Ich greife instinktiv zu ihren Handgelenken, Nacken oder was auch sonst noch nach Mensch aussieht, um den Puls zu fühlen. Aber da ist keiner, nirgendwo. Im Unfallgegner, einem nicht viel größeren Fiat, kauern auch noch zwei Menschen. Der Mann am Steuer lebt, ist sogar bei vollem Bewusstsein, die Füße sind allerdings im Fußraum eingeklemmt. Neben ihm: seine Frau, mit schwachem Puls, leise röchelnd. „Helft ihr, helft ihr!", fleht der Mann auf Spanisch. Sofort stabilisieren wir mit einem Beatmungsbalg ihre Atmung. Einen Arzt haben wir bei Vortouren bislang nicht mit.

Ihre Beine stecken im völlig zerstörten Fußraum fest. „Der Sitz muss raus!", brülle ich, und wir probieren, Schrauben zu lösen. Die rühren sich nicht. Wir versuchen, ihn mit Brechstangen auszuhebeln. Keine Chance. Wir legen das Seil der Defender-Winde über eine Umlenkrolle, um den Sitz herauszureißen. Aber wir ziehen nur den Fiat von der Unfallstelle. Wir befestigen die Winde eines zweiten Defender auf der anderen Seite. Doch so ziehen sich die schweren Wagen nur beidseitig an das Unfallauto heran. Inzwischen benötigen Lutz und der zweite Mundo-Maya-Guide Beto kurz unseren Rucksack. Sie haben

To all intents and purposes, the pre-scout recce was complete. All we had to do was get the vehicles back to Mexico. The roads that go through the jungle are narrow, uneven and at times as straight as a ruler. I finally had time to relax and to go through the route in my mind for the main event.

The traffic ahead of us suddenly slowed and then ground to a complete halt. A truck in front of us blocked our view of the road. I climbed down to see what had happened, and despite the heat my face froze at what I saw. Some 40 people had got out of their cars, staring as if paralysed at the horrible scene. Two small cars had collided head-on; smoke billowed out of the crumpled bonnet of one of the cars, and somewhere I could hear someone whimpering. I grabbed our first-aid pack and ran to the wrecked cars.

If ever there were a situation where reflection leads to a form of paralysis, then this was it. Three adults were inside a small Seat motorcar. I instinctively grabbed their wrists, necks or anything else that still looked human in hopes of finding a pulse. Nothing. In the other vehicle, a Fiat not much bigger than the first, there were two adults. The man behind the wheel was still alive; indeed, he was fully conscious, but his feet were trapped in the footwell. Next to him was his wife, groaning quietly with a very weak pulse. The man pleaded in Spanish, "Help her, help her." Christine translated for me into German. We were able to stabilize her breathing with a ventilation bag almost immediately. Thus far, we had chosen not to take a doctor with us on the pre-scout recces.

Her feet were trapped in the footwell, which had been completely destroyed by the impact. I shouted, "We have to remove the seat!", and we attempted to loosen the screws. Nothing doing. We tried to lever the seat out using crowbars. Impossible. We attached the Defender winch cable via a return pulley to the seat but only ended up dragging the Fiat further away from the accident site. We attached the winch from a second Defender to the other side, but this only

im Wald einen Mann mit gebrochenem Bein gefunden. Er ist aus dem Seat herausgeschleudert worden. Wir machen uns an die letzte Möglichkeit, die mir einfällt: Mit Leatherman, Messern und Stangen zerkleinern wir den robusten Fiat-Sitz, schneiden Teile heraus, bis wir die Frau vorsichtig aus dem Wrack herauslösen können. Endlich gibt sich ein Arzt zu erkennen und legt Infusionen. Sie ist bei vollem Bewusstsein und fragt: „Wo sind die Kinder?" Kinder? Was für Kinder? Wir haben keine gesehen. Sie sollen auf dem Rücksitz gesessen haben, erfahren wir. Gerade schreie ich – inzwischen auch an die Grenzen des Erträglichen gekommen – die Gaffenden an, sie sollen eine Kette bilden und die Unfallstelle absuchen, da erzählt ein Schaulustiger, dass direkt nach dem Unfall ein Mann beide Kinder in sein Auto verfrachtet habe, um sie ins nächste Hospital zu bringen. Ein schneller Helfer. Immerhin.

Aber jetzt bricht der Fahrer des Fiat zusammen. Nach der Bergung seiner Frau lässt seine Anspannung nach, der Kreislauf droht zu kollabieren. Wer in Mexiko so einen Unfall erleidet, hat kaum Chancen, sagen uns die Gaffer. Krankenwagen seien offene Pritschenwagen, Helfer mit Blechscheren gebe es gar nicht – der Mann habe einfach Pech gehabt. Aber das akzeptiere ich nicht. Es klingt hart, aber es ist die einzige Chance: Mit der Brechstange brechen wir dem Fahrer beide Füße. Nur so lässt er sich aus dem Auto lösen. Wir vertäuen ihn auf unsere Sandbleche und heben ihn auf den offenen Toyota Pick-up-Krankenwagen, der endlich angekommen ist und auch die Frau auflädt.

Unser Erste-Hilfe-Rucksack ist leer, unsere Köpfe sind es auch. Die nächsten drei Stunden sagt keiner von uns ein Wort. Mich holt die Geschichte erst ein, als ich mich später im Hospital nach den beiden Unfallopfern erkundige. Sie haben es geschafft, die Fußbrüche sind reparabel. Aber ihre Kinder waren tot. Hätten wir früher am Unfallort ankommen können? Haben wir etwas falsch gemacht? Hätten die Kinder überlebt, wenn wir uns um sie hätten kümmern können? Ich weiß es nicht. Aber als Vater von zwei wunderbaren Töchtern denke ich noch heute darüber nach.

winched the two heavier vehicles closer to the damaged Fiat. In the meantime Lutz and our second guide, Beto, needed the first-aid pack. They had found a man in the jungle who had been catapulted from the Seat in the crash, and his leg was broken.

Inside the Fiat, we started to hack at the solidly-built passenger seat, with Leatherman, knife and crowbars, removing it bit by bit until we could finally lift the lady carefully out of the wreckage. By now, a doctor had turned up and was able to attach her to an intravenous drip. Fully conscious, she asked, "Where are the children?"

Children? What children? We hadn't seen any children. Where was this going to end? Then we were told that they had been sitting on the back seat. By now I was at the end of my tether, with people just standing around doing nothing, and screamed at them to form a chain to search the accident site for the children. That is when one of the onlookers explained that the children had been taken to hospital by another man immediately after the accident. At least there was one person who had shown some initiative.

The Fiat driver then collapsed – he had relaxed as soon as his wife was freed from the wreckage, and it was obvious he was about to fall into a coma. Onlookers commented that anyone involved in an accident like this in Mexico normally had no chance. The ambulance was usually nothing more than an open-top truck, and cutting gear was completely unheard of. The man had just been unlucky.

I was not prepared to accept this. While it may sound brutal, we used the crowbar to break both his feet. This was our only way of getting him out of the car. We lashed him to a sand channel and lifted him along with his wife onto the open-top Toyota ambulance that had finally just arrived. It then turned round and drove off to the next town.

Our first-aid pack was empty, which was pretty much how we all felt. For the next three hours or 40 odd miles, nobody said a word.

The story really hit me when I went to the hospital to find out how the two accident victims were doing. They were fine, and the man's two broken feet would heal in time. Their children, however, hadn't survived.

Would it have made a difference if we had been able to get to the crash site sooner? Did we do something wrong? Would we have been able to save their lives if we had got to the children first? I don't know. As the father of two wonderful daughters, I still think about it to this day.

DER HURRIKAN
THE HURRICANE

Ich gestehe: Erstmals gehe ich nicht so locker auf eine Haupttour wie bislang. Sowohl die Suche nach Hans als auch der Verkehrsunfall haben mich auf brutale Art meine Verantwortung spüren lassen. Und jetzt kann Hans aus familiären Gründen nicht mit auf die Haupttour – mir fehlt mein Flügelmann an allen Ecken und Enden. Klar, die Vorbereitungen haben wir optimiert, aber trotzdem: drei Länder, zehn Autos, dazu der Dschungel, der keine Fehler verzeiht, die unberechenbare Fauna und das ebenso launische Wetter – viel Ballast für ein paar Schultern.

Aber die Tour verläuft optimal. Es gibt keine Anzeichen von Dramen jedweder Art, eher Belustigendes. Wie den Zöllner in Belize, der nur mit Schiesser-Feinripp bekleidet handschriftlich die Fahrgestellnummern der Autos in die jeweiligen Pässe schreibt. Oder die dank stundenlangem Regen wunderbar aufgeweichten Matschpisten, die das genau richtige Land-Rover-Gefühl erzeugen. Sogar das Abseilen am Hans-Schicksalshügel, das wir trotz oder vielleicht gerade wegen des unfreiwilligen Such-Abenteuers als Teamaufgabe in der Tour gelassen haben, klappt problemlos.

Nur das Wetter lässt sich nicht beeinflussen. Der Wind bläst schon ganz ordentlich, als wir unser Zeltcamp mit Genehmigung des Bürgermeisters auf dem Marktplatz von La Unión in Mexiko aufbauen. Wir sind gerade beim einfachen Essen in den Wellblechhütten, da verändert sich schlagartig die Farbe des Himmels. Der Wind wächst zum Sturm – ich habe überhaupt keine Lust zum Risiko. „Rein in die Autos!", brülle ich, und alle erkennen sofort, dass ich keinen Spaß mache. Kaum sind wir in den Landys, da wird aus dem Sturm ein Hurrikan. Er beginnt, die einfach zusammengenagelten Hütten um uns herum zu zerlegen. Fenster fliegen uns um die Windschutzscheiben, Wellbleche knallen gegen die Karosserien der Discovery und Defender.

Aber die Stürme über den Produktionshallen in Solihull in der langen Land-Rover-Historie waren manchmal existenzbedrohender als dieser mexikanische Hurrikan. Da steht ein Land Rover wie eine Eins.

Admittedly, I wasn't as keen on the main event as I otherwise would have been. The search for Hans as well as the car accident had made it brutally clear to me what responsibility really felt like. And now, for family reasons, Hans couldn't come on the tour – my wingman was missing. Our planning had improved enormously, and yet: three countries, ten vehicles, a jungle uncompromising in the extreme, the difficult vegetation and the mercurial weather – all this was a great deal for one pair of shoulders.

That said, the tour ran perfectly. There no were no real dramas – quite the opposite, there was a great deal of laughter on the tour. How could I forget the customs official in Belize who jotted down the VIN numbers of the vehicles in our passports dressed in nothing but his underwear? Or the muddy tracks through the jungle that, thanks to the incessant rain, provided the perfect Land Rover Tour feeling. Even the abseiling team exercise on Hans' fateful mountain, which stayed in the programme despite the involuntary search and rescue operation (or perhaps because of it?), was a roaring success when the time came.

The only aspect we couldn't control was the weather. The wind was already starting to pick up when we made camp in the market square of the town of La Unión in Mexico (with permission of the local mayor). We had just sat down to dinner in one of the corrugated tin huts when, without warning, the colour of the sky changed dramatically. The wind had already turned into a gale – I wasn't prepared to take any risks – when I shouted at everyone, "Into the vehicles – now!", and everybody recognized I wasn't joking. Once inside the vehicles, we watched the gale transform itself into a full-fledged hurricane as the corrugated tin huts literally disintegrated before our very eyes, with windows thrown up against our windscreens and corrugated tin flying into the bodywork of our Defenders and Discovery.

This Mexican hurricane, however, was nothing compared to the many economic storms that the Land Rover factory in Solihull had weathered over

EIN BAUM QUER ÜBER DER PISTE? MIT DEM RICHTIGEN EQUIPMENT KEIN PROBLEM.
SCHWIERIGER GESTALTET SICH DA SCHON DIE FAHRT DURCH MATSCHIGEN DSCHUNGEL
MIT TIEFEN SCHLAMMLÖCHERN UND GROSSEN PFÜTZEN. SCHILDKRÖTEN GEHÖREN
DA NOCH ZU DEN ANGENEHMEN REISEBEGLEITERN. DRECK UND STRESS FALLEN BEIM
TAUCHEN IN GLASKLAREM HÖHLENWASSER SOFORT AB.
-
A TREE STRAIGHT ACROSS THE TRACK? WITH THE RIGHT EQUIPMENT, NO PROBLEM.
THE DRIVE THROUGH THE JUNGLE, WITH ITS HUGE MUD HOLES AND ENORMOUS RUTS,
WAS A LITTLE MORE CHALLENGING. THE TORTOISE WAS ONE OF THE MORE POPULAR
COMPANIONS. A PLUNGE INTO THE CRYSTAL CLEAR WATER OF AN UNDERGROUND CAVE

LUTZ RATHMANN

GEBOREN AM 11.10.1975
DIPLOM-INGENIEUR DER ELEKTROTECHNIK, GESCHÄFTSFÜHRER DER LAND ROVER EXPERIENCE DEUTSCHLAND,
LAND ROVER LEAD INSTRUCTOR

BORN 11 OCTOBER 1975
GRADUATE ELECTRICAL ENGINEER, CEO OF LAND ROVER EXPERIENCE GERMANY,
LAND ROVER LEAD INSTRUCTOR

Du bist schon als Schüler mit dem Outdoor-Virus angesteckt worden – wie kam es dazu?

Ich kenne Hans Hermann bereits sehr lange, und habe mit ihm schon als 16-Jähriger Orientierungsläufe für die Camel Trophy organisiert. Als Hans anfing, für die Land Rover Experience zu arbeiten, ging ich mit und lernte Dag kennen. Dort gehörte es zu einer meiner ersten Tätigkeiten, die Fahrzeuge für die Jordanien-Tour in den Nahen Osten zu bringen. Kurioserweise fing diese scheinbar leichte Task schon als Offroad-Abenteuer in Europa an: Damals haben Trucker in den Niederlanden die Grenzen zugestellt, um gegen die Benzinpreis-Politik zu demonstrieren. Wir mussten aber pünktlich nach Antwerpen, um die Defender zu verschiffen – das ging zu dem Zeitpunkt halt nur über grüne Grenzen ...

Was ist jetzt deine Aufgabe?

Als CEO leite ich zusammen mit Dag die Geschäfte von Jaguar Land Rover Experience Deutschland sowie die Land Rover Experience Namibia. Seit unserem gemeinsamen Start in Jordanien ist unser Unternehmen auf 48 Festangestellte und über 250 freie Mitarbeiter herangewachsen. Damit sind wir eine der größten Experience-Operations weltweit. Wir bringen für die beiden Marken pro Jahr mehr als 40 000 Personen mit den Fahrzeugen in Berührung, etwa 4 000 davon alleine in unserem eigenen großen Offroad-Spielplatz – dem Land Rover Experience Center in Wülfrath. Auch wenn der Spaß bei Fahrertrainings, Firmen-Incentives und Spezialausbildungen nie zu knapp kommt, vermitteln wir dabei auch seriöses Wissen, von Grundlagen wie umweltgerechtem Offroadfahren bis zur knallharten Expeditionsvorbereitung. Der Renner zurzeit ist jedoch unser Fahrtraining für 11- bis 17-Jährige – früh übt sich der Profi!

Außerhalb des Geländes arbeiten wir mit einem tollen Team der deutschen Jaguar Land Rover Vertretung an Lifestyle-Programmen, Händlerunterstützung, Fahrzeugeinführungen, Messen und Presseveranstaltungen. Langweilig wird's nie.

Ist schon mal etwas Außergewöhnliches geschehen auf solchen Schulungsveranstaltungen?

Es gibt natürlich unzählige spannende und lustige Geschichten. Ein Erlebnis werde ich zum Beispiel nie vergessen. Vor einigen Jahren rief mich sonntags ein Instructor an und sagte: „Hier ist etwas passiert, aber ich kann es Dir gerade nicht erklären. Du musst kommen!" Ich wohne sehr nah am Steinbruch in Wülfrath, war also sofort vor Ort. Da sah ich einen Discovery, der mit allen vier Rädern in der Luft hing. Er lag allerdings nicht auf dem Kopf, sondern balancierte mit dem mittig verbauten Getriebe auf einem etwa 1,5 Meter hohen Stein. Der Grund: Ein Teilnehmer sollte an der Stelle einfach nur wenden, gab dabei aber zu viel Gas anstatt zu bremsen. Von anderen Steinen aufgestiegen landete der Disco mit einem Satz mittig auf dem Felsblock. Das sah aus wie eine geplante Kunstinstallation – nur die Beleuchtung fehlte. Der Wagen hatte keine Schramme. Ganz nebenbei: Die Veranstaltung war ein Incentive für Rechtsanwälte für Verkehrsrecht. Das Ereignis wurde natürlich abends noch lange am Lagerfeuer fachgerecht diskutiert.

The outdoor bug bit you while you were still a school kid – how did that happen?

I've known Hans Hermann for a very long time, so even as a 16-year-old, I was organizing orienteering exercises for Camel Trophy. When Hans started to work for Land Rover Experience, I got involved too and that's how I met Dag. One of my first tasks was to organize shipping the Jordan tour vehicles to the Middle East. However, just getting the vehicles to the Channel coast – normally a relatively straightforward task – turned into a European off-road adventure of its own. At the time, Dutch truck drivers, protesting against the fuel price, were blocking the borders, stopping us from getting our Defenders to Antwerp. We ended up having to go across country.

What do you do these days?

My job as the CEO of Jaguar Land Rover Experience Germany is to run the day-to-day business and also manage our Land Rover Experience Namibia programme.

Since our first event in Jordan, the organization now employs 48 people full-time with over 250 freelancers. Within Land Rover, we are one of the largest Experience operations in existence. In any given year over 40,000 people receive hands-on experience of vehicles from both brands with over 4,000 coming to our off-road playground at the Land Rover Experience Centre in Wülfrath. While the fun element is a significant part of driver training, corporate incentives and specialist training programmes, there is also a serious side to this and we offer courses in how to drive off-road responsibly as well as professional expedition planning. Our driver training programme for 11–17-year-olds is currently very popular – offering invaluable benefits for those who go to drive professionally in later life.

Beyond the confines of our off-road centre, we also work very closely with Jaguar Land Rover Rover's national sales company team on lifestyle events, dealer support programmes, vehicle launches, trade shows and press events. There's never a quiet day.

Has anything really unusual happened at a training event?

There are many hilarious and thrilling tales to tell. There is, however, something I will never forget. A while back, one of the instructors called me on a Sunday and said: "Something has happened, but I can't explain how or why. You need to get over here ASAP." I live pretty much next door to the quarry in Wülfrath and was there in next to no time. A Discovery was stuck with all four wheels in the air – however, it wasn't on its roof; rather, the central differential was resting on a large rock. On being told to turn the vehicle, a participant had put her foot down too hard, with the result that the Land Rover literally launched itself into the air and landed on the middle of a rock. It looked like a work of art – minus the fairy lights. The vehicle didn't have a scratch. Oh, and by the way, the event was an incentive programme for lawyers specializing in traffic law. Suffice it to say, the legal debate around the evening campfire went on for hours ...

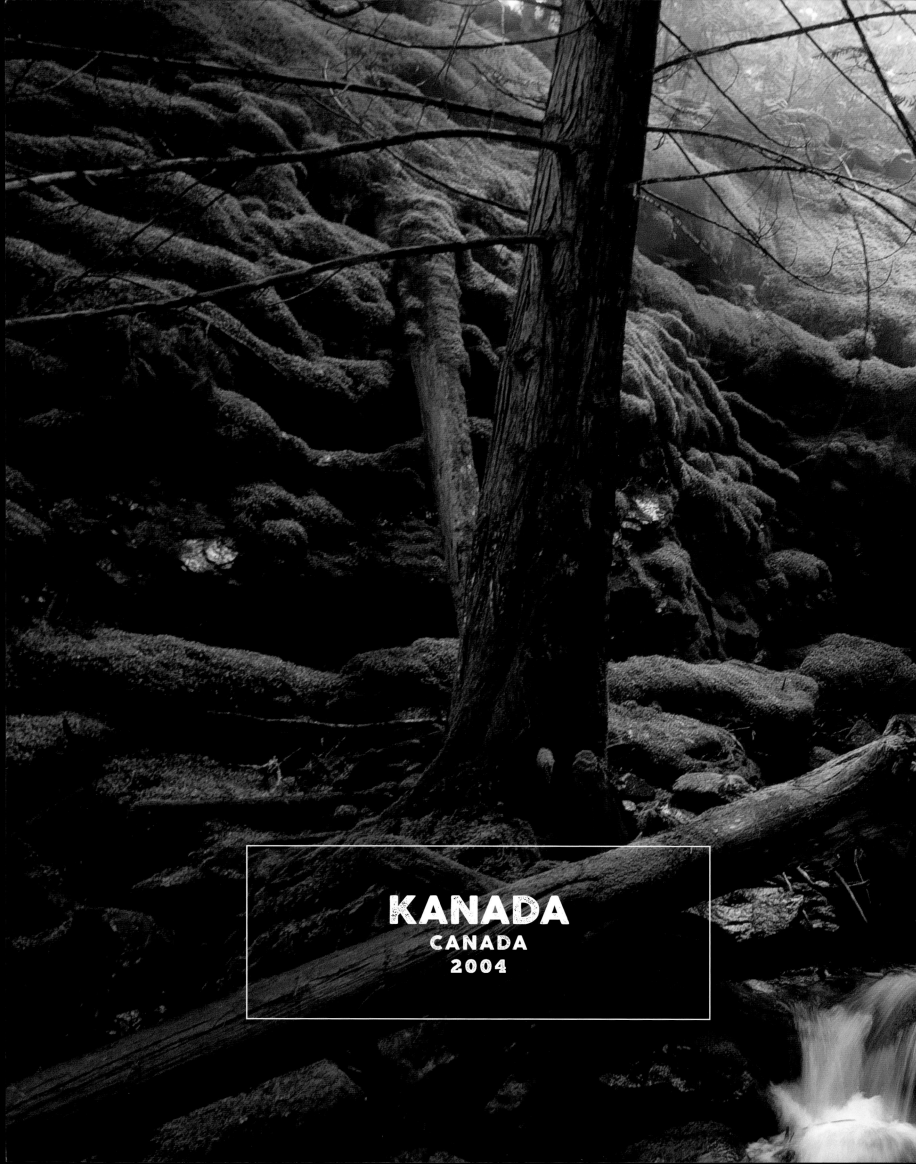

KANADA
CANADA
2004

2004
LAND: KANADA
STRECKE: 2 000 KM
COUNTRY: CANADA
DISTANCE: 1,200 MILES

4 RANGE ROVER,
3 FREELANDER, 2 DISCOVERY

DIE AUTOS
THE VEHICLES

Viel zu schnell nach der aufregenden, ereignisreichen, aber auch traurigen Dreiländertour sollen wir Land Rover wieder drei neue Ziele zur Auswahl vorlegen. Kanada ist eines davon. Aber erstmals bewerben sich weniger Menschen für die Tour als für die vorige, diesmal nur rund 8 000. Zieht Kanada nicht?

Dabei haben wir es uns wirklich nicht einfach gemacht mit der Wahl. Auf 10 Millionen Quadratkilometer Land in Kanada sollten doch wohl anspruchsvolle Offroad-Trassen abseits der rund 35 Millionen Einwohner zu finden sein? Auch Land Rover ist davon begeistert. Wir entscheiden uns für British Columbia, die Provinz am Pazifischen Ozean. Im Winter herrscht hier arktisches Klima, im Sommer wird es im Binnenland manchmal bis zu 40 Grad heiß. Wälder dominieren und damit auch Holzwirtschaft und Papierindustrie. Was aber Zivilisation bedeutet.

Trotzdem: Hoch motiviert starten wir zur Vortour. Dazu gehört, zu klären, wie wir unsere Autos ins Land schaffen können. Dass genau das zum großen Abenteuer werden soll, ist vorher nicht zu ahnen.

Defender wollen wir diesmal promoten. Was wir nicht bedenken: Der Defender besitzt in ganz Nordamerika keine Zulassung – sie ist nicht mal temporär zu bekommen. Aber auch der vorübergehende Import anderer Land Rover erweist sich als schwierig. Niemand will uns garantieren, dass wir die Autos auch wirklich aus dem Schiff ausladen dürfen, wenn wir sie in die Neue Welt schicken. Damit bricht eine unserer vier Säulen, auf die alle Touren aufbauen, weg: Hotels/Flüge, Genehmigungen, Wege und – Autos.

Was tun? Ein anderes Land aussuchen? Nein, wir laufen nicht weg vor Problemen – wir lösen sie. Idee: Wir vergessen die Defender, leasen ein paar Range Rover und ein paar Discovery beim örtlichen Land-Rover-Händler, rechnen mit 2 000 Kilometer pro Fahrzeug, zahlen dafür, und der Händler kann die Wagen hinterher als Geschäftsfahrzeuge verkaufen. Dazu hat der gute Mann aber überhaupt keine Lust. Lange verhandeln wir mit ihm und kommen nach harten Debatten zu folgendem Kompromiss: Wir kaufen die Autos komplett und er kauft sie nach der Tour zurück. Na prima.

In no time at all after the exciting, eventful but at the same time sad tour through three Central American countries we were already being tasked by Land Rover to present three new potential destinations. One of these was Canada. For the first time, the number of applications (this time around 8,000) was lower than for the previous tour. Was Canada perhaps not attractive enough?

We hadn't made things particularly easy on ourselves. About 4 million square miles should have been enough for us to find some challenging off-road routes in a country with a population of just 35 million people. Land Rover signed off on it, and we decided to focus on British Columbia, the province that borders the Pacific Ocean. It has an arctic climate in the winter, and in the summer the interior can experience temperatures of up to 40 degrees Celsius (104 degrees Fahrenheit). Dominated by forest – a fact reflected in the industries there (paper and logging) – the region's population levels were relatively high as well.

That aside, we were highly motivated as we set off on the pre-scout. First of all, we needed to find out how to ship our vehicles across the pond; little did we know that this would turn out to be a huge adventure in its own right.

This time we wanted to push Defender. We had forgotten, however, that the Defender no longer had type approval for the whole of the North American market, and that we wouldn't be able to secure temporary approval, either. There were difficulties involved in temporarily importing our other Land Rovers, too. No one could guarantee that we would be able to unload them from the ship once they had completed their journey to the "New World". Suddenly one of the four cornerstones upon which all our tours were based – hotels/flights, permits, routes and of course vehicles – was looking very shaky indeed.

Now what? Head for another country? No. We don't run away from problems. We solve them. We chose to drop the Defenders, lease some Range Rovers and a few Discovery from the local Land Rover dealer, put around 1,200 miles on them, pay the difference and let the dealer sell them on as company vehicles. Unfortunately, he simply wasn't interested. After long negotiations, we arrived at the following compromise: we would buy the vehicles outright, and he would buy them back from us after the tour. Easy.

DIE BIG BAR FERRY UND IHR LEGENDÄRER „GRUMPY OLD MAN": SO BRUMMIG IST ER GAR NICHT. ERST RECHT NICHT, WENN MAN ERZÄHLT, WIE WOHL MAN SICH FÜHLT IN DER TYPISCH KANADISCHEN TYAX-LODGE.
--
THE BIG BAR FERRY AND ITS LEGENDARY "GRUMPY OLD MAN" – WHO ACTUALLY TURNED OUT TO BE NOT SO GRUMPY AFTER ALL, ESPECIALLY AFTER WE TOLD HIM HOW GOOD IT WAS TO STAY OVER IN THE CLASSICALLY CANADIAN TYAX LODGE.

EIGENTLICH GIBT ES NUR ZWEI STRASSENTYPEN IN KANADA: HOLZFÄLLERPFADE UND ALLE ÜBRIGEN. AUF DEN LOGGING ROADS GELTEN EIGENE GESETZE – HIER HABEN DIE ÜBERLANGEN HOLZTRUCKS VORFAHRT. MAN MUSS NUR DIE FUNKFREQUENZEN KENNEN, AUF DENEN SIE SICH ANKÜNDIGEN. AUF ALLEN ANDEREN PISTEN IST „PLATZ ZUM ATMEN" – BEI BERAUSCHENDEN LANDSCHAFTEN IN UNFASSBAREN DIMENSIONEN.

--

THERE ARE ONLY TWO KINDS OF ROAD IN CANADA: LOGGING ROADS AND EVERYTHING ELSE. THE LOGGING ROADS HAVE THEIR OWN PECULIAR RULES: THE EXTRA-LONG LOGGING TRUCKS HAVE RIGHT OF WAY. ONE ONLY NEEDS TO KNOW THEIR CB RADIO FREQUENCIES WHICH THEY USE TO TELL YOU THEY'RE COMING. EVERY OTHER KIND OF ROAD ALLOWS YOU SPACE TO BREATHE AND ENJOY THE ALMOST UNBELIEVABLE DIMENSIONS OF AN INTOXICATING LANDSCAPE.

DER LOOP
THE LOOP

Doch zur Vortour reicht uns die kleine Lösung. Wir leihen uns einen Disco, einen zweiten kaufen wir. Und suchen die herausfordernden Pisten. Und finden sie nicht.

Es gibt unendlich viele Holzfällerorte, auch mit abenteuerlichen Wegen dorthin. Der Nachteil: Es handelt sich immer um Sackgassen. Mit jeder Menge Kartenmaterial setzen wir uns hin und suchen den passenden Loop – eine Schleife, die es sich zu fahren lohnt und die uns eine Woche lang in die wildesten Gebiete führt. Doch die wildesten Gebiete sind zunächst Waldbrandareale. An der Küste ist kein Durchkommen: Da hat vor Kurzem der Feuerwehrchef die Dachrinne seines Hauses repariert und dabei eine brennende Kippe auf den Rasen geschnippt. Großer Fehler.

Trotz inzwischen bester Ausrüstung – Computer, GPS-Empfänger, digitalisiertes Kartenmaterial – sind wir nicht zufrieden mit den entdeckten Pisten. Es geht eben nichts über Menschen, die eine Gegend perfekt kennen. Am Straßenrand sprechen wir einen Mann an, der neue Pflanzen in die Asche setzt. Selbstverständlich hat er eine Karte in der Tasche, handgezeichnet, mit allen geographischen Daten. Geben will er uns das wertvolle Stück nicht, das auf alten Karten vor dem Feuer basiert. Aber kurz ausleihen ist okay. So breiten wir sie auf der Motorhaube aus und fotografieren sie Stück für Stück ab. Noch vor Ort geben wir die JPEG-Daten in den Computer ein und speichern sie mit meiner Touratech-Navigations-Software maßstabsgetreu ab. So finden wir ehemalige Schotterstraßen, die jetzt bedeckt von Asche sind, und es dauert nicht lange, da haben wir den von uns so verzweifelt gesuchten Loop entdeckt. Die Teams können kommen.

For the pre-scout, we were free to proceed as originally planned. We leased one Disco and bought a second. The next step was to find our challenging routes. It sounded straightforward enough, but there was one problem: there weren't any routes to be found. There were numerous logging camps, many of them accessible only via difficult roads. The problem was that these roads were always dead ends. After purchasing every map available, we sat down and began hunting for a suitable loop that would be challenging to drive and would take us into the wilderness for a week. What wilderness there was, however, was also a high fire risk. The coast created a natural barrier. A local fire chief in the region had recently repaired the roof guttering of his house and had flicked a burning cigarette butt onto the grass. Big mistake.

While we had since upgraded our navigational equipment – route planning was now performed via computer, GPS receivers and digital maps – we were not yet happy with the routes we had found. At the end of the day, you can't beat local knowledge. At the side of the road, we got to talking with a guy planting new trees in the ash. Naturally, he had a handwritten map in his pocket, with all manner of geographical details. He wasn't prepared to give us the document, which was based on maps that pre-dated the fire, but he was prepared to lend it to us. Spreading it out on the bonnet of the vehicle, we photographed it bit by bit. Still on site, we transferred the JPEG files straight onto the computer, saving them to scale using my Touratech navigational software. Now, we were able to find the original gravel roads that had been covered in ash by the forest fire, and before long we found our way back to our loop, which we had so desperately searched for. The teams could come.

IRON CRK. RD
Freq. 153. 3

WILDERNESS
FOREST SERVICE ROAD
NOT MAINTAINED

DIE TRUCKS
THE TRUCKS

Zur Haupttour ein halbes Jahr später sieht die Geschichte schon viel entspannter aus. Die Brandschäden sind kaum mehr zu sehen und die Straßen erkennbar. Es wird eine softe Tour, die wir hier erleben (im Vergleich zu den Dschungelpisten Mexikos zum Beispiel). Wunderbare Bergpanoramen, Schneefelder, als Highlight auch mal eine weggespülte Brücke, die wir mit noch zu fällenden Bäumen ersetzen (wobei der gelernte Forstwirt Christian Uhrig einen Baum so geschickt absägt, dass er sofort in die richtige Position über den Bach kippt). Ein Blitzeinschlag in die Sandbleche neben einer Teilnehmerin, die kurz danach über Kribbeln in den Händen klagt, sorgt für Aufregung, aber nicht für Unruhe. Denn die größte Gefahr ist weder vom Wetter noch von den Wegen zu erwarten, sondern von Trucks.

Es sind riesige Holzlaster, die ständig und schnell mit Schwarz-, Weiß- und Sitkafichten, Ostamerikanischen Lärchen, Tannen und Douglasien über die Hauptstraßen donnern: den Trans-Canada Highway, Crowsnest Highway oder den Yellowhead Highway. Aber auch auf den Nebenstraßen, die alle Namen besitzen, die wir uns nicht merken können, sind sie unterwegs. Und meine Hauptaufgabe ist es, dafür zu sorgen, dass wir ihnen nicht in die Quere kommen. Denn die Trucker bremsen nicht. Es würde auch nicht viel nützen bei dem langen Bremsweg, den die tonnenschweren Lastzüge benötigen. Zum Glück sind die jeweiligen Trucker-Funkfrequenzen auf Schildern am Straßenrand zu lesen, und ich werde zum Doppelfunker. Auf der einen Frequenz spreche ich mit den Truckern und frage ihren Standort ab, auf der anderen warne ich die Teams vor den rasenden Wandschränken und hoffe, dass die Trucker mithören: „Green Creek, Kilometer 105, zehn Fahrzeuge aufwärts … "

Tatsächlich rasen die manchmal aus mehreren Anhängern bestehenden Lastzüge nur zentimeterbreit an uns vorbei – aber keiner trifft uns. Das einzige, was uns wirklich betroffen macht, ist der Land-Rover-Händler in Vancouver, als er unsere Gebrauchtwagen wieder in Empfang nimmt: Akribisch rechnet er nun jede einzelne Schramme ab. Und ein paar sind auch ohne Baumlaster-Kontakt zusammengekommen.

Six months later, the time had come for the main event, but the region looked very different. There was very little evidence of the forest fire, and the roads were visible once again. Compared to the jungle tracks of Mexico, this would be a "soft" tour. Nevertheless, we had amazing mountain vistas, snowfields and a bridge we had to replace after a flash flood. Ex-forester Christian Uhrig was a dab hand with the chain saw and could fell trees so precisely that they bridged the gap exactly. The weather provided a brief moment of excitement, too, for one participant was standing right next to a sand channel when it was struck by lightning. She complained afterwards of pins and needles in her hands but other than that there had been no cause for alarm. Yet our greatest worry remained neither the weather nor the forest tracks – we constantly had to keep our eyes peeled for the trucks.

These were the logging trucks carrying black, white and Sitka spruce trees, the eastern larch, fir and Douglas fir along the main roads: the Trans-Canada Highway, Crowsnest Highway or Yellowhead Highway. The trucks travelled numerous secondary routes as well, the names of which none of us could remember, and it was my job to make sure we avoided any head-on collisions. As a rule, trucks don't stop for anything or anyone: with articulated units weighing many tonnes, the braking distance they required made any discussion of a sudden stop relatively academic. Fortunately, the truckers' CB radio frequencies were posted on the roadside, so I was able to talk to the truckers on one frequency to confirm their locations, while on another I could warn our teams about the multi-wheel nightmares coming our way: "Green Creek Kilometre 105, ten vehicles heading north …"

At times, there was barely an inch between us and the road trains, often consisting of one artic unit with many trailers attached, that raced past us in the other direction. There was no damage, not that it made any difference to the Land Rover dealer in Vancouver, who meticulously noted every scratch when we returned the vehicles – yet not every blemish could be blamed on the trucks.

WO DER WEG VERSCHWUNDEN IST, STELLT DIE LAND ROVER EXPERIENCE IHN WIEDER HER – ZUM BEISPIEL IN FORM EINER BEHELFSBRÜCKE. EIN BISSCHEN FLORA NIMMT DER DRINGEND BENÖTIGTE UNTERFAHRSCHUTZ SCHON MAL MIT. DIE ERNTE WIRD NICHT AM ABEND ALS TEE SERVIERT, SONDERN MACHT SICH FÜR DAS LAGERFEUER ALS ZUNDER NÜTZLICH.

--

WHERE THERE WAS A WAY, LAND ROVER EXPERIENCE HAS THE WILL TO PUT IT BACK AGAIN – FOR EXAMPLE, AS A TEMPORARY BRIDGE. SOME UNDERGROWTH ALWAYS FALLS VICTIM TO THE VERY NECESSARY UNDER-BODY PROTECTION PLATES. THE HARVEST ISN'T SERVED UP AS TEA AT DINNER; RATHER IT SERVES PERFECTLY AS TINDER FOR THE CAMPFIRE.

NACH EINEM ORDENTLICHEN REGENGUSS
SIND DIE PFÜTZEN WIEDER VOLLGELAUFEN
UND SOMIT EIN LIEBLINGSMOTIV FÜR DIE
FILM- UND KAMERATEAMS. DIE MATSCHE
FLIEGT PLANMÄSSIG – PECH FÜR DIE
FOTOGRAFEN, DIE IHREN STANDORT ZU
NAH AM WASSER GEBAUT HABEN. DAS
ERGEBNIS: SENSATIONELLE AUFNAHMEN
UND EINEN TAG KAMERAS PUTZEN.
--
AFTER A SEVERE DOWNPOUR, ALL THE
RUTS ARE FULL AGAIN AND AS SUCH IN
GREAT DEMAND BY PHOTOGRAPHERS AND
FILM CREWS. AS EXPECTED, MUD FLEW IN
EVERY DIRECTION, WHICH WAS BAD LUCK
FOR PHOTOGRAPHERS WHO HAD SET UP
TOO CLOSE TO THE TRACK. THE RESULT
WAS SENSATIONAL IMAGERY AND A DAY'S
CLEANING FOR THE CAMERAS.

REINHARD KÜNSTLER

*GEBOREN AM 26.2.1949 | VON 2000 BIS 2006 DIVERSE FÜHRUNGSPOSITIONEN
BEI JAGUAR LAND ROVER, DARUNTER GESCHÄFTSFÜHRER DEUTSCHLAND VON 2000 BIS 2003*

*BORN 26 FEBRUARY 1949 | NUMEROUS MANAGEMENT POSITIONS AT JAGUAR LAND ROVER FROM 2000 TO 2006
INCLUDING MANAGING DIRECTOR OF LAND ROVER GERMANY FROM 2000 UNTIL 2003*

'n deiner Zeit als Geschäftsführer von Land Rover Deutschland fiel die Entscheidung, die LET, die Land Rover Experience Tour, aufzubauen.

Von Dr. Wolfgang Reitzle – damals Chef der Premier Automotive Group von Ford, zu der auch Land Rover ganz frisch gehörte – bekam ich im Jahr 2000 als Geschäftsführer die Aufgabe übertragen, Land Rover Deutschland zu einer funktionsfähigen, profitablen Gesellschaft aufzubauen. Stuart Daniels und ich mussten innerhalb von vier Monaten nach Auslauf der Unterstützung durch den vorherigen Eigentümer BMW eine neue Mannschaft aufstellen und Händler für zwei Drittel des Gesamtmarktvolumens finden, da die BMW-Niederassungen das Verkaufs- und Servicegeschäft in den Ballungsgebieten zum 1. Januar 2001 einstellten. In dieser Zeit lernte ich Dag kennen, der vorschlug, Experience Touren mit Teilnehmern durchzuführen, die auf Basis nationaler Ausscheidungen als Gewinner mitfahren durften.

Welche Vorteile hast du darin gesehen?

Das war eine großartige Chance, um mehrere Dinge miteinander zu verbinden. Erstens: die Markenwerte von Land Rover nachhaltig beim Handel, insbesondere bei den neuen Händlern zu etablieren. Zweitens: die PR-Arbeit regional und national zu befeuern. Drittens: die Aktivierung von Neukundenpotential durch „Probefahrten" im Rahmen der Ausscheidungen sowie die Pflege der Bestandskunden. Viertens: eine positive Einbindung und damit „Infizierung" der neuen Land-Rover-Mannschaft. Und fünftens: Dadurch, dass wir in die jeweiligen Touren-Länder von und mit Land Rover buchbare Reisen anboten, bauten wir dort eine weitere Kundenplattform auf – bei gleichzeitiger Teilabdeckung der anfallenden Kosten.

Bist du bei der Umsetzung auf Widerstände gestoßen?

Nein. Das Headoffice ließ mir am Anfang freie Hand, da niemand mit einem etwaigen Misserfolg bei der fragilen Situation von Land Rover Deutschland in Verbindung gebracht werden wollte. Erst später gab es Budgetdiskussionen, als die Gesellschaft wieder erfolgreich war.

Was macht die LET so erfolgreich?

Der Erfolg basiert zum größten Teil auf der Professionalität von Dag und seinem Team sowie ihrer ansteckenden, nicht nachlassenden Begeisterung für die Marke und die Produkte. Ebenso wichtig ist natürlich die überwiegend äußerst positive Berichterstattung durch die begleitenden Journalisten. Um es betriebswirtschaftlich auszudrücken: Ich halte die Durchführung der Land Rover Experience nach wie vor für äußerst zielführend.

During your time as Managing Director of Land Rover Germany, the decision was taken to create the Land Rover Experience Tour.

In 2000 Dr Wolfgang Reitzle, who at the time was head of Ford's Premier Automotive Group, appointed me to turn Land Rover Germany into a functioning and profitable company. Stuart Daniels and I had four months after the withdrawal of support by the previous owner BMW to put together a new team and find dealers who could supply two-thirds of the total market sales volume, as BMW franchised dealers had stopped selling and servicing Land Rovers in the major conurbations beginning 1 January 2001. It was during this time that I got to know Dag, who suggested running Experience Tours with participants who had been selected as winners on the basis of na-tional selection camps.

What opportunities did you see here?

This was a wonderful opportunity to combine a number of things. First of all, we could establish Land Rover's brand values within the dealer network (particularly the newer dealers). Secondly, it gave us an opportunity to kick-start both regional and national PR. Thirdly, the "test drives" which were part of the selection camps process were both an opportunity to generate sales as well as keep existing customers in the family. Fourthly, they were the perfect way to motivate or "infect" the Land Rover Germany team. And lastly, as we intended to offer customer holidays in the tour destinations, organized by Land Rover with Land Rovers, this was an additional sales platform with at least partial coverage of the costs.

Did you face any resistance in putting the plan into operation?

No. In the early days I was given pretty much carte blanche, as no one wanted to be associated with any failures, given the fragile situation Land Rover Germany was in. Budget discussions became more intense once the company was back on its feet.

Why is the LET so successful?

Success is in part down to the professionalism of Dag and his team as well as their infectious and constant enthusiasm for the brand and its products. Just as important is the largely positive PR effect, thanks to the accompanying journalists. To put it in a business context: I believe that the Land Rover Experience Tour makes good business sense.

SCHOTTLAND
SCOTLAND
2005

ZUGEGEBEN, WER ZUM
BALMORAL CASTLE MÖCHTE,
DEM SOMMERSITZ VON QUEEN
ELIZABETH II., MUSS DAS NICHT
OFFROAD TUN. ABER ES MACHT
MEHR SPASS – SCHLIESSLICH
WOLLEN DIE LAND ROVER AUCH
IN SCHOTTLAND BEWEISEN, WAS
SIE ALLES KÖNNEN.
--
IT IS TRUE THAT IF YOU WANT
TO VISIT QUEEN ELIZABETH II'S
SUMMER RESIDENCE, BALMORAL
CASTLE, YOU DON'T REQUIRE
FOUR-WHEEL DRIVES. HOWEVER,
IT IS MORE FUN, AS THE LAND
ROVERS WANT TO DEMONSTRATE
WHAT THEY CAN DO IN
SCOTLAND AS WELL.

🐿
2005
LAND: SCHOTTLAND
STRECKE: 1 400 KM
COUNTRY: SCOTLAND
DISTANCE: 870 MILES

8 DISCOVERY, 1 DEFENDER

DER WHISKY
THE WHISKY

Wie wir in Kanada gesehen haben: Es geht auch auf die softe Tour. Die Teams, die Journalisten, die Land-Rover-Verantwortlichen sind begeistert. Aber ist es jetzt nicht wieder Zeit für eine echte fahrerische Herausforderung? Für ein richtiges Abenteuer?

Land Rover möchte allerdings endlich mal ins Heimatland – da bietet sich in Großbritannien nur Schottland an. Knapp 80 000 Quadratkilometer groß, gut fünf Millionen Einwohner, viele Felder, grüne Wiesen, massenhaft Schafe sowie Singletrails, und Seen heißen grundsätzlich „Loch" – eigentlich gute Voraussetzungen für „Britishness on Wheels". Oder?

Ich habe da meine Bedenken. Denn nach meiner Meinung fehlt der Kick. Für mich ist es etwas wie ein Defender ohne Allradantrieb. Man ist von Deutschland aus in wenigen Stunden dort, jeder könnte auch alleine herumreisen, und wenn man sich in einem Bed & Breakfast einnistet, weiß man, dass einem nicht die Kakerlaken das Bett wegtragen werden. Wo also ist die Herausforderung? Das fragen sich wohl auch die Fans. Nur rund 4 000 Bewerber interessieren sich für die neue Tour. Für uns – Hans, Claudia, Land-Rover-Pressechef Paul Entwistle und mich – lautet die schwierigste Aufgabe auf der Vortour: Abenteuer finden.

Was wir finden, sind wunderbar asphaltierte einspurige Wege, sehr malerisch zwischen Hecken platziert, die man aber auch mit einem konventionellen Kleinwagen bezwingen kann. Klar gibt es jede Menge Grünland, aber auf Wiesen, Äckern und Blumenfeldern herumzufahren, entspricht nicht der Mentalität von Land Rover. Offroad ja, aber ohne Schäden zu hinterlassen.

Die hinterlassen wir lieber bei uns selber – und klappern zunächst leicht gefrustet, aber schon bald immer besser gelaunt, die Destillerien ab. Was bedeutet, sich mit dem wichtigsten Exportgut Schottlands zu beschäftigen. In jenem Jahr, 2005, führt dieser Teil Großbritanniens für 3,6 Milliarden Pfund hochgeistigen Whisky aus. Das Getränk belebt hier beim Highlander die Seele auf grandiose Art (nicht umsonst hieß Whisky auf Schottisch-Gälisch „uisge beatha", was „Lebenswasser" bedeutet); Aspirin übernimmt später ernährungstechnische Aufgaben.

Den Guide macht unser Presse-Paul, als „Native Speaker" können wir uns keinen besseren wünschen. Und neben dem Nationalgetränk in unendlich vielen verschiedenen Ausprägungen, Geschmacksrichtungen und Alter finden wir nebenbei auch stocknüchterne Bypass-Straßen, die meist über privates Gelände führen, und zu passender Zeit sorgen wir für alle Genehmigungen zur Durchfahrt. Geht doch. Hicks.

As we had experienced in Canada, the soft tour option worked as well. Teams, journalists and the decision-makers at Land Rover – they were all very happy. But wasn't it time for a real drivers' challenge again, time for some proper adventure?

Land Rover wanted to take the tour to the home of the brand. In Great Britain, our only option was to go to Scotland. About 30,000 square miles, with a population of five million; rich, green countryside, thousands of sheep and endless trails, and the lakes there are called "lochs". Just perfect for the brand that almost defines itself as "Britishness on wheels", isn't it?

I had my reservations. I thought that we were missing a certain buzz. It felt like a Land Rover Defender without four-wheel drive. Being but a few hours' drive from Germany, Scotland was easy for anyone to explore, and in your classic bed-and-breakfast you did not run the risk of sharing your room with an army of cockroaches. So where was the challenge? The fans asked the same question. There were barely 4,000 applicants to join us on the tour. For us – meaning Hans, Claudia, Land Rover PR man Paul Entwistle and myself – the toughest task on the pre-scout was finding any adventure at all.

We found beautifully paved, single-track roads, pretty as a picture between rows of hedges – but requiring nothing more dynamic than a two-wheel-drive runabout. We were surrounded by greenery, but driving through peoples' gardens and ploughing up their fields is not the Land Rover way. Off-road was okay, but tread lightly and don't cause any damage.

Our frustration was soon a thing of the past, thanks to the joy of visiting a number of whisky distilleries. This acquainted us with Scotland's most significant export, which in 2005 generated a handsome 3.6 billion pounds sterling in revenue. Whisky, as any Scot will tell you, is vitality for the soul. The word "whisky" comes from the Gaelic "uisge beatha", which translates approximately as "water of life". But if life is to go on normally after the imbibing is through, one is well advised to keep aspirin or something similar to hand ...

Our PR man Paul took on the role of guide – as an almost (we were, after all, in Scotland) "native speaker", the Englishman was in his element and relished the task. Thus "informed" of the endless varieties, tastes and vintages of the Scottish national beverage, we could focus on the sober business of driving shortcut routes, mostly across private estates where, equipped later with the necessary permits, we could continue the journey off-road. Though not always in a straight line.

Schottland

Isle of Man

Irish Sea

Irland

Dublin

Großbritannien

Birmingham England

-Georgs-Kanal
each

Bristolkanal

Londo

Ärmelkanal

he See

Guernsey
Jersey

GRIST

DIE MÜCKEN
THE MIDGES

Sie heißen Highland Midges, die schottischen Mücken, und sie sind bekannt dafür, dass sie in riesigen Schwärmen vorkommen und einem das Leben zur Hölle machen können. Aber uns Outdoor-Spezialisten auch?

Es ist der 6. Juli, und das weiß ich so genau, weil ich an diesem Tag Geburtstag habe. Wir haben eine Campsite am See aufgebaut – nachträglich muss ich mich fragen, ob das eine so gute Idee war. Mit Mückennetzen über den Köpfen versuchen wir zu essen, nachdem die Teams am Tage zur Abwechslung mal eine echte fahrerische Aufgabe gelöst haben: einen Pass bezwingen, dessen Weg wirklich schweres Geläuf bot. Immer wieder mussten sie Felsbrocken beiseite räumen, einige gingen zu Fuß voraus und warnten vor Löchern und spitzen Steinen. Wir sind müde, wir sind hungrig. Und wir sind voller Mücken.

Abenteuer? Ja – speisen ohne unfreiwillige Fleischbeilage. Kaum haben wir den Löffel in die Suppe getunkt, sitzen Hunderte Mücken auf dem Besteck und machen uns die Mahlzeit streitig. Wer auch nur kurz irgendwo Haut zeigt, wird sofort gestochen. Mir geht so ein Geburtstag mächtig auf den Keks, und so beschließe ich, mich mit acht Vertrauten in einen Discovery zurückzuziehen, um den zum Ehrentage geschenkten Whisky zu genießen. Myriaden uneingeladener Mücken, die den Disco belagern, werden von Insektiziden aus Sprühdosen hinweggerafft. Mit jedem Schluck Lebenswasser nimmt mein Beileid ab, bis wir nahezu gesurrfrei im Auto endlich unsere Ruhe haben. Wozu so ein Land Rover alles gut ist ...

Tatsächlich ist die Schottland-Tour letztlich fahrerisch keine große Herausforderung, trotzdem ein echter Erfolg. Erstmals berichten überwiegend Lifestyle-Magazine über die Tour – nicht zuletzt wegen der hochgeistigen Getränke. Und damit erfährt erstmals auch eine neue, nicht nur offroad-affine Klientel, wohin einen ein Land Rover bringen kann. Aufgrund des Medieninteresses soll es als nächstes für internationale Journalisten ein Winter-Event auf Island geben: es den Schreiberlingen mal so richtig zeigen, was ein Landy kann und ist.

Noch mal in klaren Worten: Island im November. Wie bekloppt muss man dafür eigentlich sein?

The mosquitoes in the Scottish highlands, commonly known as "midges", are notorious for their swarming characteristics and for generally making life hell for everyone who comes into contact with them. How would they affect the off-road specialists?

It was 6 July, and the only reason I remember the date was that it was and is my birthday. We had set up a camp at the side of a lake – in hindsight, of course, this wasn't a good idea. That day, with the teams for once having accomplished a genuine off-road challenge – a pass road that was technically very difficult to drive due to the many rocks that lay directly on the route – we were trying to dine with mosquito nets around our heads. During the drive, we had walked in front of the vehicles to check the terrain for large holes and particularly sharp stones. We were dog-tired, starving and slowly being eaten alive by the midges.

How about this for competition? – Try eating without swallowing a mouthful of insect flesh at the same time. The second I raised my spoon to my mouth, it was populated with hundreds of the little beasts, all of them keen to get my dinner before I could. Visible skin was immediately punished and punctured. This wasn't my idea of a birthday. So I retreated, joined by eight colleagues, to the safety of the nearest Discovery to enjoy my birthday present. The midges trying to crash our little party were annihilated in clouds of insect spray. Whatever sympathy I may have felt for the little creatures was rapidly vanishing with every sip of whisky, until finally the interior of the Disco was completely midge free. I'll take a Land Rover over a Scottish lakeside camp any day ...

It must be noted that, in driving terms alone, the Scotland Tour wasn't the greatest of challenges. It was a roaring success nevertheless, with lifestyle publications writing about the tour – perhaps thanks to the influence of Scotland's greatest export. A different kind of clientele, one with interests ranging beyond mudplugging, began to appreciate the breadth of the qualities that Solihull's finest had to offer. Due to so much interest from the media, the next event in the pipeline will be an international media drive to really hammer home to the scribes what a Landy was good for – in Iceland. In plain terms: Iceland in November. This was stupid. With a capital "S".

GUT DREI VIERTEL DER FLÄCHE SCHOTTLANDS WERDEN FÜR DIE
LANDWIRTSCHAFT GENUTZT – DA MUSS MAN GEEIGNETE OFFROAD-
STRECKEN SCHON SUCHEN. DIE WEGE SIND ZUDEM MEISTENS IN
PRIVATBESITZ: MEHR ALS 50 PROZENT DES GESAMTEN GRUND UND
BODENS GEHÖREN GERADE MAL 500 FAMILIEN.
--
WELL OVER THREE-QUARTERS OF SCOTLAND'S SURFACE AREA IS GIVEN
OVER TO THE AGRICULTURAL ECONOMY – SO YOU HAVE TO SEARCH
LONG AND HARD FOR GOOD OFF-ROAD ROUTES. THE MAJORITY OF
THEM ARE PRIVATELY OWNED. MORE THAN 50 PER CENT OF ALL LAND IN
SCOTLAND IS IN THE HANDS OF 500 FAMILIES.

ANDREA LEITNER-GARNELL

GEBOREN AM 21.4.1965
PRESSECHEFIN JAGUAR LAND ROVER DEUTSCHLAND SEIT 2003

BORN 21 APRIL 1965
PR MANAGER JAGUAR LAND ROVER GERMANY SINCE 2003

Was macht den Umgang mit Allradautos so besonders?
Man kann die Menschen unter ganz anderen Aspekten von Autos begeistern – eben nicht nur von Leistung und Design, sondern auch von Abenteuer und Freiheit. Ich habe 1990 bei Chrysler/Jeep angefangen und somit meine ganze berufliche Laufbahn mit den Kernmarken des 4x4-Geschäfts verbracht – und es lieben gelernt.

Immer wieder bleiben Teilnehmer von Touren und Reisen bei euch als Instruktoren. Warum?
Viele dieser Menschen wollen mit Autos arbeiten, aber nicht im Wettbewerb mit anderen Autos, wie zum Beispiel im Motorsport. Viel mehr Spaß haben sie an Autos, die in der Lage sind, Menschen zu Orten zu bringen, zu denen andere gar nicht hinfahren können. Und das gemeinsame Erlebnis, die vielen Eindrücke auf einer solchen Abenteuerreise schaffen ein unvergleichliches Gemeinschaftsgefühl, sodass sich die Teilnehmer einer Tour oder Reise auch danach immer wiedertreffen. Diese hohe Emotionalität ist auch für mich persönlich etwas, was mich an die Marke bindet.

Welche Außenwirkung haben die Experience Touren?
Für die Medienarbeit sind sie ein echtes Juwel. Denn durch die Touren zeigen wir, was die Autos können. Die Medien vermitteln das Erlebnis dieser Tour, und die Kunden können sie als Reise nachfahren. Denn einzelne Touren können auch von jedem Interessenten gebucht werden. Aber auch wenn viele Menschen im Alltag ihre Land Rover nicht an deren Grenzen bringen – die Möglichkeit, ausbrechen zu können, wird von allen geschätzt. Viele Leute kaufen ja auch eine Uhr, die 200 Meter tief wasserdicht ist, ohne dass sie jemals so tief tauchen würden. Aber sie wissen, dass ein Extremsportler damit unten war. So ist es auch mit unseren Fahrzeugen: Wir fahren in den Dschungel oder auf hohe Berge, und die Land Rover meistern jede Situation. Dieses Abenteuer holen sich die Leute nach Hause. Und wenn sie von den Touren in den Medien lesen, freuen sie sich, dass sie so ein Auto besitzen, mit denen die Experience Tour gerade wieder die schwierigsten Passagen gemeistert hat.

Aber man muss trotzdem wissen, wie man mit den Autos umgeht?
Selbstverständlich. Aber, um beim Beispiel zu bleiben: Man muss ja auch wissen, wie man taucht. Dafür gibt es unsere Land Rover Experience Trainings in Wülfrath, und bei den Reisen sind Guides dabei.

What makes four-wheel-drive vehicles so special?
Instead of appealing to the senses with performance and design, as with ordinary cars, four-wheel drives appeal to people's sense of adventure and love of freedom. I started working in PR for Chrysler/Jeep in 1990 and have spent my entire career working with the original brands in the 4x4 business, and I love it.

Tour participants seem to end up working with Land Rover as instructors on a regular basis – why is that?
Many of these individuals want to work with cars, but not in competition with other brands as one would in motor sports. They enjoy vehicles that are able to transport people to places that other vehicles can't get to. The common experience and the many impressions that an adventure trip leaves behind create an incomparable team spirit, and those who take part – whether on tour or on holiday – stay in contact with each other. This extremely emotional component is what ties me personally to the brand.

What is the impact of the Experience Tours in publicity terms?
For PR purposes, they are an absolute gift. The tours demonstrate what the vehicles are capable of. The media can communicate the experience, and customers can follow in the footsteps of the tour. Many of the tours have been marketed also as customer events. Although many Land Rover owners never take their vehicles to the limit of their abilities, it is good to know that if they wanted to, they could. There are equally people who buy a watch that is waterproof to 700 feet below the surface without ever going diving but they know that an extreme sportsman or -woman would choose that piece of equipment. The same principle applies to our vehicles. We drive in the jungle or in the mountains, and the Land Rovers take it all in stride. It is this sense of adventure that people want to take home. When they read about a tour, then they bask a little in the glory, knowing that the same vehicle that sits in their garage just made it across the most difficult terrain known to man.

Nevertheless, you still need to know how to use the technology?
Of course. But to stick with my previous analogy: you also have to know how to dive. We have Land Rover Experience training events in Wülfrath, and on the holidays there are always guides accompanying the customers.

ANNA BAUNACH

*GEBOREN AM 10.5.1984 | BACHELOR IN INTERNATIONALEM TOURISMUS,
BEI APS SEIT 2008*

*BORN 10 MAY 1984 | BACHELOR'S DEGREE IN INTERNATIONAL TOURISM,
WORKING AT APS SINCE 2008*

**Hat Dich Dein Studium Internationales Tourismus- und Event-
management auf den Job bei APS vorbereiten können? Oder hat
die Wirklichkeit der Land Rover Experience Tour damit wenig zu tun?**
Das hat es tatsächlich, allerdings nicht unbedingt inhaltlich. Die Praxis
sieht meistens ganz anders aus. Was ich aber wirklich gelernt habe, ist
perfektes Englisch sowie strukturiertes Arbeiten und mich voll und ganz
auf ein Thema zu konzentrieren. Was dann noch fehlte, habe ich von
erfahrenen Kollegen gelernt oder durch „trial and error" erfahren. Aber
auch für mich gilt: Man lernt nie aus – und ich denke, mit jeder Tour werde
ich ein kleines bisschen besser in meinem Job.

Du hast die Jubiläumsreise betreut. Wie viel Arbeit war das?
Das war logistisch die mit Abstand aufwendigste Tour, schon alleine
wegen ihrer Länge im Vergleich zu den vorherigen Events. Aber trotz Stress
und manchmal sehr langen Bürozeiten hat das richtig Spaß gemacht, weil
es eine echte Herausforderung war. Denn die größte Aufgabe ist immer,
den Überblick zu behalten.

**Hartnäckige Bewerber für die Qualifikationscamps müssen erstmal
an Dir vorbei. Gibt es viele, die sich mehrfach bewerben?**
Allerdings. Wurden die ersten Bewerber der frühen Touren noch per Telefon einzeln angerufen, geht das heute alles übers Internet. Das macht es
einfacher, Bewerber herauszufischen, die sich immer wieder bewerben.
Trotzdem rutscht auch mal einer zum zweiten Mal bis zur Endqualifikation durch. Wer allerdings einmal eine Tour mitgemacht hat, kann das
garantiert kein zweites Mal tun.

**Du kannst bei vielen Vor- oder Haupttouren nicht dabei sein,
weil das Event auch im „Back-Office" zu jeder Zeit perfekt organisiert
werden muss. Und zwar von Dir. Schlimm?**
Zugegeben: Nach einer Tour die tollen Bilder zu sehen und nicht immer vor
Ort gewesen zu sein, macht schon etwas wehmütig. Aber ich sehe ja selbst,
wie viel Arbeit während einer Tour noch anfällt, besonders wenn mehrere
Slots stattfinden und damit auch mehrere An- und Abreisen. Einer muss
die Arbeit im Hintergrund ja machen – aber auch das macht Spaß.

**Was a degree in international tourism and event management
useful for your job at APS?**
In some ways yes, though less so in terms of what actually makes up the
tours. The reality of event management is very different from the theory.
My degree taught me perfect English, how to work in a structured fashion
and how to concentrate completely on one subject at a time. I picked up
what I was lacking from experienced colleagues pretty much by trial and
error. The bottom line for me, too, is that there is no end to the learning
experience. Every tour has made me a little better at what I do.

**You oversaw the anniversary event – the Silk Road Tour. How much
work was involved?**
Logistically it was by far the most complex tour we had ever done, simply
because of its sheer length compared to previous events. However, despite
the stress and long office hours it is a lot of fun, just because it is so
challenging. The most important thing to remember is not to lose sight of
the bigger picture.

**Persistent candidates looking to make the qualification camps need to
get past you first. Do you have many repeat applications?**
Absolutely. In those early days, we had to phone each and every applicant,
nowadays, the process is run via the Internet. It's much easier to pick out
the applicants who apply again and again. Nevertheless, every once in a
while, one gets through to final selections. Anyone who has been on a tour
once certainly isn't allowed to participate again.

**You have been unable to take part in many pre-scouts and main
events because the office requires perfect back office support at all
times, which is of course your job. Is that difficult to deal with?**
I admit seeing the amazing pictures afterwards and not having been able
to be physically part of it can be frustrating. However, I know how much
work there is to be done even during the tour. This is the case when we
have more than one slot and have to make the in- and outbound travel
arrangements. Somebody has to do it, but it is a lot of fun too.

ISLAND WINTER EXPERIENCE
ICELAND WINTER EXPERIENCE
2005

DER SCHNEESTURM
THE BLIZZARD

"Above and Beyond." Ja, und weiter, und jenseits, und überhaupt – dafür steht Land Rover, und es wäre doch gelacht, wenn wir nicht ein paar Journalisten damit beeindrucken könnten, wie wir den Winter an einem der zu dieser Jahreszeit ungemütlichsten Orte der Welt mit unseren Autos besiegen. Ich weiß: Im Hinterland ist das Wetter völlig unkalkulierbar. Aber es gibt Alternativstrecken – also wage ich das Abenteuer. Denn die Experience hat schon ganz andere Probleme gelöst. Schließlich sind wir die, die Unkalkulierbares kalkulieren. Zumindest, bis wir ins Kalkül ziehen müssen, dass auch wir Heißsporne kalt erwischt werden können.

Wir, das sind erstmals die englischen und die deutschen Experience-Kollegen gemeinsam, laden 120 Journalisten ein, die sich in Zwanzigergruppen 20 Autos teilen, allesamt Discovery mit Diesel- und V8-Motoren. Jeder kann, so der Plan, drei bis vier Tage nach Herzenslust in der weißen Wildnis kurven. Start ist in Reykjavík, eine Campsite samt Hütte mit Matratzenlager für die Zartbesaiteten befindet sich in Landmannalaugar. Dort gibt es heiße Quellen, in denen man sich – so man sich denn darauf einlässt und hinabtauchen mag in die Welt der unterirdisch erzeugten Hitze – lange ausgesprochen wohlfühlen kann.

Auch ich sitze dort drinnen, wohl wissend, dass ich in drei Stunden mit meinem britischen Kollegen Dougie vor dem Konvoi starten muss, um bei einer Flussdurchfahrt schon mal das zentimeterdicke Eis zu brechen, damit die schreibende Zunft später problemlos queren kann. Aber während ich da so im heißen Wasser sinniere, merke ich, dass sich das Wetter dramatisch ändert. Vielleicht habe ich als Pilot einen siebten Sinn dafür, vielleicht achte ich als Verantwortlicher auch nur etwas mehr auf die Zeichen der Natur – ich bin

"Above and Beyond". Onward and upward, and so on and so forth. This is what Land Rover was all about. And wouldn't it be amusing to impress a few journalists by defying winter in our vehicles in one of the most inhospitable places on the planet? Winter weather in Iceland is always hard to predict, but there are several navigable routes to choose from. For this reason, I agreed to support the venture. Over the years, we had managed to solve a number of equally problematic tasks, and, after all, we had become past masters at predicting the unpredictable. That said, even hotheads like us could be caught unawares.

We – and by this I meant, for the first time, the English and the German Experience Teams – jointly invited 120 journalists in six groups of 20, split among 20 Discovery equipped with diesel and V8 petrol engines. The plan was to provide each journalist an opportunity to spend three to four days exploring the wilderness. Setting out in Reykjavík, our destination was Landmannalaugar, a campsite equipped with its own mountain hut with mattresses in a huge dormitory for the more faint-hearted. The place is legendary for its hot thermal springs, guaranteeing the perfect wellness experience for those prepared to plunge into the hot water.

Which is why I sat in just such a spring, fully aware that, three hours later, I would have to set out in front of the convoy with my British colleague Dougie to clear any water crossings of the thick sheets of ice so that the scribes could later cross without getting wet. As I sat musing in the thermal springs, I noticed that the weather had changed. Call it pilot's instinct; or perhaps I always have an eye on the weather because I am responsible for others

DER SCHNEESTURM
THE BLIZZARD

Mein siebter Sinn ist es wohl auch, der mich frühmorgens um halb vier aufwachen und nach draußen gehen lässt. Kein Zweifel: Ein Schneesturm ist aufgezogen. Es schneit bereits heftig, der Wind fegt mit Böen von etwa 100 km/h um die Hütte. Die Situation ist brenzlig, zumal einige Journalisten zeitig zurück nach Reykjavík müssen, um ihren Flieger nach Hause zu erwischen, und neu angekommene auf die Autos und ihre Tour warten. Ich wecke alle vom Orga-Team relativ emotionsfrei und gebe eindeutig zu erkennen, dass für Waschen und Frühstücken keine Zeit ist. Ich ordne unmissverständlich an, sofort die Gäste zu alarmieren und sich unverzüglich in die Autos zu werfen.

Es wird nicht so schlimm, wie ich befürchtet hatte – es wird viel schlimmer. Für die ersten 500 Meter aus dem Camp benötigen wir geschlagene zwei Stunden. Eine Straße, ein Weg oder auch nur eine Piste ist nicht mehr zu sehen. Keine Stangen, Bäume, Felsen begrenzen die Fahrbahn, es ist alles einfach nur weiß. Nicht nur am Boden, sondern auch in der Luft. Wir müssen Schneeketten montieren, und das dauert. Die Hände werden kalt, die Körper auch, wir werden immer müder, und wir sind nur 12 Kilometer von der geräumten Hauptstraße entfernt.

Die ersten Journalisten werden unruhig, besonders die, die noch in die USA zurückfliegen müssen. Andere fangen tatsächlich an, Angst um ihr Leben zu bekommen. Gerechtfertigt ist das zwar nicht, denn noch haben wir diverse Möglichkeiten – aber nicht jeder Journalist mag die volle Härte der Natur. Dennoch muss ich zugeben, auch wir als Verantwortliche waren noch nie vorher in so einer Situation. Mithilfe von GPS-Daten tasten wir uns vorwärts, aber wir kommen nicht wirklich voran. Also übergebe ich als Leader meinen Defender meinem Kopiloten, nehme eine Stange und gehe zu Fuß voraus. Mit Stochern versuche ich, den Schotteruntergrund des Weges zu erfühlen.

Das Wetter wird derweil immer schlimmer. Bei -8 Grad bleibt Schnee grundsätzlich an Scheibenwischern hängen; von den Höhenzügen mischt sich Lavaasche in den Schneesturm und peitscht schmerzhaft Körner ins Gesicht. Die Skibrille, die ich inzwischen aufgesetzt habe, bedeckt leider nicht mein ganzes Gesicht. Kurz: Es ist nicht nur ungemütlich, es ist beängstigend. Und es wird nicht besser. Als ich mich umdrehe, um nach dem mir folgenden Defender zu sehen, ist er nicht mehr da. In meinen Ohren tobt der Sturm, und tatsächlich hat mich der Fahrer verloren. Ich warte, und warte, und erst nach ein paar Minuten sehe ich seine Scheinwerfer. Damit das nicht wieder passiert, leine ich mich mit einem Abschleppseil an den mir folgenden Wagen an. Das sieht zwar bescheuert aus, ist aber sinnvoll. Und mich kann ja niemand sehen.

Die Zeit vergeht, und wir kommen nicht gut vorwärts. Hinten bleiben immer wieder Autos in Schneewehen stecken, und alle Mann müssen die Wagen ausgraben. Vier Stunden gehe ich voraus, im Schlepp den ebenso unendlich langsamen Landy. Zwischendurch telefoniere ich über Satellitentelefon ab und zu mit Keflavík und frage, ob die dortige Wetterstation vielleicht baldige Entwarnung liefern kann. Aber ich werde ein ums andere Mal enttäuscht.

Ich gebe es nicht gerne zu, aber in diesem Moment muss ich einsehen, auf Hilfe angewiesen zu sein. Unser Guide, natürlich wieder „Ingo der Tänzer", mobilisiert sofort über Telefon ein paar Freunde. Die haben an ihren Autos Ballonreifen montiert, mit denen sie oben auf dem Schnee fahren können, weil sie nicht einsinken. Inzwischen habe ich den Konvoi halbiert: Überall, wo bislang zwei Leute in den Autos sitzen, werden jetzt vier platziert. Die leeren Autos lassen wir zurück, um sie später abzuholen. Das verkürzt den Konvoi. Ein weiterer Vorteil: Die Heizungen von Dieselautos versagen völlig bei der Kälte, denn durch das langsame Herumstochern im Schnee werden die Motoren und damit die Heizungen nicht warm. Aber vier Mann im Auto schaffen eine Menge Eigenwärme!

Endlich kommen die einheimischen Bigfoots, ziehen eine Spur, helfen uns heraus – wir hätten zwar nur noch 3 Kilometer bis zur Hauptstraße benötigt, aber haben insgesamt 23 Stunden für 12 Kilometer Nebenstraße gebraucht. Kleiner Trost: Die Bigfoots basieren allesamt auf Defender-Konstruktionen.

It was probably the very same instinct that woke me up at 3.30 in the morning and saw me walk outside to take a look. There was no doubt. A weather front had closed in, and a blizzard was brewing. It had already started snowing quite heavily, and gusts of up to 60 mph were lashing the sides of the hut. The situation was critical, as some journalists needed to get back to Reykjavík to catch flights home, and new arrivals would be waiting for the vehicles to start their own tour. I woke up everyone in the organization without getting too emotional but nevertheless making the point that there was no time to wash or eat breakfast. I made it clear that we needed to inform our guests immediately and get them in the vehicles.

It wasn't as bad as I had feared – it was a lot worse. We needed over two hours just to cover the first 1,600 feet out of the campsite. Roads, tracks, even footpaths had just disappeared in the blizzard. Poles, trees, even the rock face were no longer visible in the whiteout. We had to attach snow chains, and that took time. Our hands started to get cold – our bodies, too, and we were getting tired. And all this just 7 miles from the main road, which had been cleared of snow. Some of the journalists started to grumble, particularly those with flights to the USA. Others were actually afraid that they could freeze to death. At that point in time, their fears were unjustified, as we still had a number of options; but not every journalist is capable of dealing with extreme weather. Nevertheless, the situation was a first for the organization as well. Using GPS data, we inched our way forwards but we simply weren't making enough progress. As the man in charge, I handed the wheel of my Defender to my co-driver, grabbed a crowbar, jumped out and made my way forward on foot, testing the ground as I went, in search of the gravel road beneath the snow.

The weather progressively worsened. At a temperature of -8 degrees Celsius (18 degrees Fahrenheit), the snow stuck to the wipers. The wind was also mixing up lava ash and tiny stones from the ground, and whipping this into my face. My ski goggles didn't cover my entire face. It wasn't just unpleasant – it was downright terrifying. Things weren't getting any better, either. As I turned around to check the Defender behind me, I noticed that it was no longer there. The roar of the storm was deafening in my ears, and my co-driver had actually lost me. I waited and waited, and after a few minutes I could make out his headlights. To prevent it from happening again, I attached a towrope to my belt and the other end to the Defender. It looked daft, but it made a lot of sense, for nobody could see me.

We were losing time and not making significant progress. Behind us, vehicles were stuck in snowdrifts, and everybody was helping dig them out. For four hours I was attached to the Landy, which was just as slow as I was. From time to time, I contacted Keflavík airport via satellite phone to find out whether the meteorological office had any news of a break in the weather. The news was disappointing.

I don't like having to admit this, but at that instant I realized I needed help. Our guide, naturally "dancing Ingo", organized a few of his friends on the phone. They had fitted balloon tyres to their vehicles to prevent them from sinking in the snow. By now, I had reduced the convoy by half. Vehicles that once held two people now held four. We left the empty cars behind, as we would be able to pick them up later. Another advantage was that the heaters in the diesel-engine Discovery had failed to help combat the extreme cold – the reason being that driving at barely walking pace behind a man with a crowbar meant that the engines (and thereby the heating) weren't able to reach normal operating temperatures. Putting four people into the car, however, warmed it up no end!

Finally, the local "Bigfoots" turned up, created their own track and pulled us out. The main road was just 2 miles away, but we had required 23 hours for the 7 miles of track. The only compensation, and a little one at that: the Bigfoots were all modified Defenders.

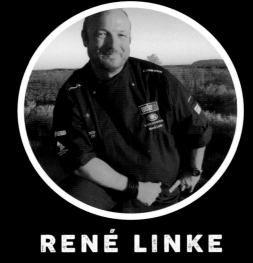

RENÉ LINKE

GEBOREN AM 31.10.1971 | KOCH UND GESCHÄFTSFÜHRER LINKE GMBH, PREMIUM CATERER

BORN 31.10.1971 | CHEF AND MANAGING DIRECTOR OF LINKE GMBH, PREMIUM CATERER

Du hast jetzt bereits sechs Land Rover Experience Touren mitgemacht. Welche hat dich am meisten beeindruckt?
Von Island, Namibia, Kanada, Schottland, Australien und Peru hat mich Island landschaftlich am meisten beeindruckt. In Namibia war es die Tierwelt, in Australien diese unglaublichen Weiten.

Wie organisierst du deine Arbeit als Koch und Caterer bei den Touren?
Anfangs wird geklärt, wo die Campsites sind, für wie viele Personen eingekauft werden muss und welche Gerichte landestypisch sind. Danach erstelle ich eine Einkaufsliste für Lebensmittel und Equipment. Letzteres wird in Deutschland eingekauft und per Übersee-Container verschickt. Die Lebensmittel besorge ich vorrangig frisch vor Ort – natürlich nationale Kost, wie in Namibia Fleisch vom Strauß, der Oryxantilope oder vom Kudu, in Australien Känguru oder Krokodil, in Peru auch mal Meerschweinchen. Die Wünsche von Vegetariern werden selbstverständlich immer berücksichtigt. Zum Einkauf bin ich schon eine Woche vor dem Start der Tour vor Ort. Hilfe bekomme ich dabei zum Beispiel von Stefan Auer, der Wahnsinnsqualitäten als Souschef besitzt. Aber auch die Teilnehmer packen mit an. In Australien habe ich mit dem Starkoch Paul Neukirch zusammengearbeitet, daraus hat sich eine echte Freundschaft entwickelt.

Stimmst du dein Essensangebot ab auf die Anstrengungen, die so eine Tour immer mit sich bringt?
Es gibt täglich eine ausgewogene Ernährung: viel Obst, frische Salate, Gemüse, Fleisch, natürlich auch viele Kohlenhydrate dank Reis, Pasta und Kartoffeln. Die Leute sind nach den zum Teil körperlich recht anstrengenden Tagen meistens extrem hungrig und verputzen fast doppelt so viel wie normalerweise.

War Australien für dich anders als die übrigen Touren? Einerseits musstest du bis zu 50 Menschen verköstigen, andererseits hattest du einen Lastwagen dabei.
Der Truck war eine neue Herausforderung. Zwei große Kühlschränke und ein geräumiger Tiefkühlschrank waren bei Temperaturen bis 46 Grad immens wichtig. Und der Arocs bietet genügend Stauraum für haltbare Vorräte. Wir sind nur jeden dritten Tag durch eine Community mit Einkaufsmöglichkeit gefahren. Und nicht immer konnten wir unseren Bedarf decken, da sonst für die Einheimischen nicht mehr genug übriggeblieben wäre. Eine Etappe war so lang, dass ich mit einem Jet nach Darwin fliegen musste, um die Vorräte wieder aufzufüllen. Ergebnis meiner Shoppingtour: eine Tonne Lebensmittel, literweise Getränke und vier Reifen. Besonderes Highlight in Australien war zudem der eingebaute Profi-Ofen im Kofferraum eines Discovery, den man auf Schienen herausziehen konnte. So viel Komfort hatte ich auf den vorherigen Touren nicht. In Namibia habe ich zum Beispiel auf einer ausgedienten Waschmaschinentrommel gegrillt.

Haben sich deine Menüpläne auch schon mal durch überraschende Umstände geändert?
Das ergibt sich ab und zu, wenn die Tagesetappen länger als geplant dauern und wir spontan und schnell etwas kochen müssen, weil alle völlig erschöpft, müde und ausgehungert sind. In Australien sollten wir in einer Community für drei Aborigines mitkochen. Es hat sich aber in Windeseile herumgesprochen, dass das Essen gut schmeckt. Und plötzlich haben wir den ganzen Stamm von fünfzig Personen verköstigt. Unvergesslich auch Island: Nach 18 Stunden Fahrt durch die Lavawüste haben wir gemeinsam unser Lager an einer heißen Quelle aufgebaut, gegrillt und sind dann in einem Thermalpool baden gegangen.

Welches der Menüs gehört zu deinen Favoriten?
Zum höchsten Outdoor-Niveau rechne ich den Riesenbarsch Barramundi mit gegrilltem grünem Spargel, frischen King Prawns, Limettenbutter und Wildreis sowie als Dessert Panna Cotta mit frischen Beeren. Danach gab es Standing Ovations – und alle leckten ihre Teller ab ...

You have taken part in six Land Rover Experience Tours. Which one impressed you the most?
Between Island, Namibia, Canada, Scotland, Australia and Peru I think it is the Icelandic terrain that really sticks in my mind. In Namibia it was the wildlife, and in Australia the huge distances.

How much planning goes into feeding the tour participants?
We need to know early on where the campsites are going to be, how many people we need to cook for and which meals will highlight local cuisine. Based on that I can put together a list of food and equipment required. The latter is sourced in Germany and then shipped overseas by container. Fresh food is sourced locally, for example, local products such as Ostrich, Oryx and Kudu in Namibia, and Kangaroo and Crocodile in Australia. In Peru, we even had guinea pigs on the menu. Of course, we also cater for vegetarians. Usually, I fly out a week before the tour starts to buy in the provisions. In my kitchen, I can also rely on the help of one of our team members, Stefan Auer, who has turned out to be an amazing Sous-Chef. More often than not, the participants like to assist too. In Australia, we were joined by star chef Paul Neukirch and that's developed into a really good friendship.

Do you plan your meals around the tasks and activities that are part and parcel of the tour?
We provide participants with a balanced daily diet: lots of fruit, fresh salad, vegetables, meat and carbohydrates with rice, pasta and potatoes. Because the tour is physically demanding, people are often very hungry and can shovel down twice as much food as they would otherwise eat.

Was Australia any different from the other tours? On the one hand, you had to feed up to 50 people. On the other, you had a truck with a kitchen on board.
The truck was a challenge in its own right. Two large fridges and an immense deep freeze were crucial with temperatures up to 46 degrees Celsius (115 degrees Fahrenheit). The Arocs also had enough room for non-perishable provisions. The opportunity to go shopping in a town only cropped up once every three days. And we weren't always able to buy what we required as that would have left the locals short of provisions. One stage was so long that I ended up having to fly to Darwin to buy a tonne of food, many gallons of water and other drinks along with four tyres. A real highlight on the Australia trip was the professional oven mounted on rails in the back of a Discovery. Such mod cons were unheard of on our previous tours – I even remember using a washing machine drum in Namibia as a barbecue grill.

Have you had to alter your menu plans because something surprising came up on the tour?
This happens every once in a while when one section of the route takes longer to complete. Then we have to be flexible and whip up something quickly as people are exhausted and starving. In Australia, we were asked to cook for three Aborigines from a local settlement. Word quickly spread that the food was tasty and suddenly the whole clan of fifty people turned up. I remember one tour to Iceland driving through an immense lava desert for 18 hours, setting up camp next to natural hot springs, getting the barbecue on and going bathing afterwards in the thermal pools.

Which is your favourite menu?
My all-time outdoor speciality must be the Barramundi giant Barra fish, with grilled green asparagus, fresh King Prawns, lime butter and wild rice followed by a panna cotta dessert with fresh berries. I remember getting standing ovations for that one and the plates were licked clean ...

ARGENTINIEN & CHILE
ARGENTINA & CHILE
2007

2007
LAND: ARGENTINIEN & CHILE
STRECKE: 1 600 KM
COUNTRY: ARGENTINA & CHILE
DISTANCE: 1,000 MILES

6 DEFENDER, 3 DISCOVERY,
1 AMBULANCE DISCOVERY

DAS INTERNET
THE INTERNET

Auch wenn uns Schottland nicht so recht an die Grenzen unserer Leistungsfähigkeit getrieben hat – jedes Jahr so eine Tour zu stemmen, ist inzwischen nicht mehr machbar. Denn es kommen immer neue Aufgaben hinzu: buchbare Experience-Reisen nach Island, Namibia und Kanada und immer mehr Arbeit in Wülfrath, wo sich der Steinbruch zum Mittelpunkt sämtlicher deutscher Land-Rover-Fahraktivitäten entwickelt. Kurz: Land Rover beschließt – mit meinem vollen Einverständnis und fast mit meiner Dankbarkeit – nur noch alle zwei Jahre zu touren. Das bedeutet ein Jahr Zeit für die Camps, bis man die sechs Teilnehmer gefunden hat, im darauffolgenden Jahr die Vor- und die Haupttour. Das hat mehrere Vorteile: mehr Zeit zum Organisieren und dadurch weniger Stress, dazu zwei Jahresbudgets für eine Tour, die dadurch wieder aufwendiger werden kann. Prompt schlagen wir Land Rover Argentinien und Chile vor. Genauso prompt bekommen wir grünes Licht dafür.

Wir fliegen zuerst in die Stadt Salta, die wir wegen ihrer für uns strategisch günstigen Lage (im Nordwesten Argentiniens am Rand der Anden in gut 1 000 Metern Höhe) als Startpunkt wählen. Salta ist eine typische Kolonialstadt. Hier beginnt auch der „Zug über den Wolken", eine der berühmtesten Eisenbahnstrecken der Welt, die über die Anden bis zum Viadukt La Polvorilla führt. Tatsächlich waren weder Hans noch ich jemals zuvor hier, aber die Recherche im Internet ist inzwischen wesentlich einfacher geworden. Und damit auch die Suche nach Wegen, Hotels und Agenturen.

Denken wir. Tatsächlich finden wir einige Firmen, die sich nach allen Regeln der Kunst anbieten, bei Reisen durch das Land behilflich zu sein. Wir besuchen sie – und erfahren einmal mehr, dass sich die Vorstellungen solcher Einrichtungen von „Reisen" und unsere von „Touren" überhaupt nicht decken. Die inländischen „Spezialisten" sind eindeutig touristisch ausgerichtet. Was wir wollen, wird als „geht nicht, zu gefährlich, kommen wir nicht hoch" eingestuft. Die Verantwortlichen haben mehr Bedenken als Ideen, mehr Sorgen als Hirn – gefrustet gehen wir erst mal Kartenmaterial kaufen und Hotels inspizieren. Ausgerechnet dabei treffen wir auf Gerry – einen so österreichischen Österreicher, wie es ihn in Österreich nicht mehr gibt. Sein Credo: „Geht nicht gibt's nicht." Er ist als Guide genau der Richtige.

Zurück in Deutschland stellen wir die Tour dank Internet und der Touratech-Software komplett fertig. Damit können Straßen und Tracks auf 100 Meter genau bestimmt werden. Google Earth beginnt zu dieser Zeit mit seinem beeindruckenden Service, und über diverse Suchfunktionen finden wir im Netz eine Geschichte von Weltenbummlern, die im Krater Galán gewesen sein wollen. Krater? So etwas ist unser Ding, da werden wir hellhörig. Von den Abenteurern wollen wir die Ein- und Ausstiegskoordinaten für den Krater erfahren – die sie uns aber nicht liefern können. Also Hochstapler? Prima! Wenn die nicht wirklich dort gewesen sind, ist es eine wunderbare Aufgabe für die Land Rover Experience Tour, ihnen zu zeigen, wo der Weg verläuft. Kurz: Wir wollen genau dort hin. Das weckt den Landy in uns ...

Even if Scotland hadn't quite tested us to the limits of our abilities, organizing and running a tour on an annual basis was no longer possible. More and more projects were landing on our desks. Customer Experience Tours to Iceland, Namibia and Canada, and more work in our Experience Centre in Wülfrath, which had increasingly become the focus of all Land Rover's driving activities. In short, Land Rover decided to run the Experience Tour now only once every two years – I could see it made sense, and to be perfectly honest I was grateful for the respite it gave us. It meant we now had a whole year to plan and run the selection camps to find our six candidates before running the pre-scout and main event the following year. We had more time to organize the event with less stress involved. We could spread one tour over two years' budgets, permitting us to do so much more per tour. Within an instant, we suggested Argentina and Chile with a programme entitled the "Road to the Clouds", and almost immediately we received the go-ahead to start planning.

First we flew to Salta, which we had already chosen as our starting point because of its ideal position in the north-west of Argentina at the edge of the Andes mountain range and its altitude of 3,700 feet above sea level. Salta, a classical colonial town, is also the starting point of one of the world's most famous railway routes, the "Train to the Clouds", which heads into the Andes by way of the La Polvorilla viaduct. Neither Hans nor I had been here before, but researching a destination online – including routes, hotels and agencies – had improved tremendously over the last couple of years.

Or so we thought. We found numerous firms claiming to be the last thing in do-it-yourself tours, only to discover, upon visiting in person, that their interpretation of "tour" was nothing like ours. Quite clearly, these national and regional "specialists" catered to the package-tour segment. Invariably, the response to our plans was something along the lines of "that won't work, that's too dangerous and that's too high." The people we spoke with spent more time expressing their reservations about what we wanted to do rather than helping us develop ideas. To combat our frustration, we went shopping for maps and explored hotels. Quite by chance, in one hotel we met an Austrian guy called Gerry – he was an original – one of a kind that has long since ceased to exist in Austria. His maxim was "nothing is impossible". He would turn out to be the perfect guide.

Once we had returned to Germany, and with the help of the Internet and our navigation software, we started to put the tour together. Roads and tracks can be identified to within just over 300 feet. Google Earth went live at around the same time, and using various search engines we discovered a story about a bunch of globetrotters who had driven in the Galán crater. Just the word "crater" got us going – this was just the kind of thing we were looking for. We contacted the adventure-seekers hoping to get the exact coordinates for entering and exiting the crater. They couldn't deliver – what kind of con trick was this? Fabulous! If that were the case, and they actually hadn't been to the crater, then it was the perfect opportunity for the Land Rover Experience Tour to show them the way. This was exactly where we wanted to go. And it woke the Land Rover in every one of us.

WAS NACH BRÄUNUNGSHILFE AUS DEN 70ERN AUSSIEHT, HAT EINEN ERNSTHAFTEN HINTERGRUND: TEEKOCHEN MIT SOLARENERGIE. REGENERATIVE ENERGIEN NUTZT MAN HIER SCHON LANGE, WEIL SO GUT WIE KEIN FEUERHOLZ EXISTIERT. DAFÜR GIBT ES UNTER DER WEISSEN SALZKRUSTE, DIE WIE EIN MEER MIT WELLEN WIRKT, BRAUNEN, ZÄHEN SCHLAMM. AUTOS AUSZUGRABEN IST IN DER HÖHENLUFT ECHTE SCHWERSTARBEIT.

IT LOOKS LIKE A SEVENTIES-STYLE TANNING STUDIO BUT HAS A MORE SERIOUS JOB: A SOLAR-POWERED TEA KETTLE. REGENERATIVE ENERGY HAS LONG FEATURED HERE, AS FIREWOOD IS VIRTUALLY UNHEARD OF. AND UNDERNEATH THE WHITE SALTY CRUST THAT HAS THE APPEARANCE OF A HUGE LAKE WITH WAVES IS TENACIOUS, BROWN MUD. DIGGING CARS OUT OF THIS STUFF AT ALTITUDE IS VERY HARD WORK.

DIE AMBULANZ
THE AMBULANCE

Unsere Recherchen bringen zunächst eine Gewissheit: Das Abenteuer wird nicht ungefährlich für die körperliche Unversehrtheit der Teilnehmer und aller anderen Mitfahrer – und das allein wegen der großen Höhen, die in den Anden bewältigt werden müssen. Bei rund 30 Menschen, die insgesamt mitfahren sollen, ist die Chance, dass einen von ihnen die unberechenbare Höhenkrankheit trifft, groß. Ich überlege lange, ob wir uns in Sachen medizinische Notfälle noch ein bisschen mehr professionalisieren sollen und entscheide mich noch vor der Haupttour für ein Ja. Das bedeutet: Aufbau eines Ambulanzwagens.

Land Rover unterstützt die Idee sofort mit einem Discovery. Ich entwerfe den Innenraum, Doc Dominik Doerr sorgt für den Feinschliff. Auf engstem Raum gibt es seitdem – natürlich auch dank vieler Sponsoren – alle notfallmedizinischen Instrumente, um über Stunden jede Intensivbehandlung durchführen zu können. Trotzdem ist innen noch genug Platz, um jemanden liegend auf einer Trage zu transportieren. „Wo andere schon aufwendig geflogen werden, werden Sie bei uns noch bequem gefahren", fällt mir schnell als Spruch zu dem rund vier Tonnen schweren Disco ein. Wert des Autos: knapp 200 000 Euro. Wir sind stolz wie Bolle auf das neue, rollende Orga-Mitglied.

Allerdings bringt uns das Gefährt zunächst ganz schön in die Bredouille, gleich zu Anfang bei der Einreise nach Argentinien. Die Zöllner haben überhaupt keine Lust, die Drogen und Betäubungsmittel, mit denen eine gut gepackte Ambulanz nun mal ausgerüstet ist, ins Land zu lassen. Sie schließen den lebensrettenden Wagen weg und üben sich in Taubheit.

Natürlich gilt es wieder, sich etwas einfallen zu lassen. Mit etwas Geduld findet Hans einen bestechlichen Zollbeamten, der uns gegen ein paar Peso zum Sperrbereich im Zoll führt, wo die Ambulanz festsitzt. Unseren bezahlten Konfidenten lassen wir seinen Kollegen erklären, dass wir dringend einen Reifen am Notarztwagen wechseln müssen.

Um unsere Aktion zu tarnen, rollen wir einen dicken Gabelstapler vor die Ambulanz. Dann schlüpfen Gerry und Hans in den Wagen und stopfen alle auf dem Index stehenden Medikamente in blaue Müllsäcke, die sie in einem mitgebrachten Defender deponieren und so verstauen, dass sie nicht auffallen. Zur Sicherheit kleben wir den großen Blaulichtkasten auf dem Dach der Ambulanz noch vollständig ab. Nur die rote Außenfarbe, die können wir nicht ändern. Das macht aber auch nichts: Trotz des auffälligen Kastens auf dem Dach und unserer grinsenden Gesichter können wir mit der Ambulanz daraufhin problemlos den Zollbereich verlassen.

Und das ist gut so, denn prompt muss eine Teilnehmerin bei der Haupttour in 4 900 Metern aufgrund von Höhenkrankheitssymptomen behandelt und unter Sauerstoffzugabe in ein niedriger gelegenes Tal gebracht werden. Sowohl unsere Findigkeit als auch die Ambulanz haben sich sofort bezahlt gemacht.

One thing was clear from our research work. Travelling at altitude in the Andes could have serious effects on the health of the participants and everyone else accompanying the tour. With approximately 30 people taking part, the chances were high that at least one of them would suffer from altitude sickness. I thought long and hard about improving our ability to respond to medical emergencies, and before the main event I decided to build an ambulance.

Support from Land Rover was immediately forthcoming, and they provided us with a Discovery. I designed the interior, and our doctor Dominik Doerr provided the final touch. For every subsequent tour, and thanks to the involvement of many sponsors, we now had a vehicle capable of dealing with all manner of medical emergencies, with a full range of intensive-care equipment on board, and which, thanks to good use of the stowage space, still had room for an injured person on a stretcher. "Costly and complicated medevac by plane, or cost-effective and comfortable by Discovery ambulance," is how we pitched the use of the four-tonne vehicle valued at around $ 232,000 (£ 178,000). We were as pleased as punch with our newest member of the organization team.

That said, our new vehicle got us into trouble the moment we arrived in Argentina. Customs had no intention whatsoever of letting the drugs and other anaesthetics with which any self-respecting ambulance is equipped into the country. The ambulance was impounded lock and key, and customs officials went deaf in both ears.

Time again to tap our creative juices. Patient as ever, Hans found a customs official not averse to a little bribery and corruption who, for a handful of pesos, was prepared to take us to the restricted area where the ambulance was parked. Our inside man told his colleagues that we urgently had to change a wheel on the vehicle.

To camouflage what we were doing, we parked a huge forklift truck in front of the ambulance. Gerry and Hans crept into the Discovery and started removing all the blacklisted substances and packing them in blue bin bags that were then hidden in the Defender we had brought in with us. As an added precaution, using masking tape we completely concealed the blue flashing-light unit. The only thing we couldn't modify was the ambulance's red paint job. Not that it mattered anyway. Despite the obvious-looking box on the roof of the Discovery and our grinning faces we were able to leave customs with the ambulance.

And it was a good job, too – in no time at all, and at an altitude of 16,000 feet above sea level, a female participant had to be treated with oxygen for altitude sickness and was transported down to a lower altitude. Our creativity with customs and the decision to build the Discovery ambulance had both paid off.

DER KLEINKRIEG
THE BORDER INCIDENT

Zunächst läuft die Haupttour lange problemlos, aber natürlich steht uns noch eine ganz spezielle, skurrile Situation bevor – so etwas können wir bei jeder Land Rover Experience Tour fast versprechen, ohne es zu planen.

Entlang der Strecke des „Zuges über den Wolken" geht es aus San Pedro de Atacama, Chile, zur Grenze nach Argentinien. Es ist stets einsam da oben, und wir bleiben selbstverständlich immer wieder in Schneefeldern stecken, aber gut gelaunt kommen wir letztlich am Socompa-Pass an. Es ist der höchste Pass für den Zug, auf immerhin 3 876 Metern Höhe, und links und rechts rosten vom Weg abgekommene Lokomotiven, Anhänger und Lastwagen in den Felsen. Hier fährt niemand außer uns freiwillig, und trotzdem halten hier je eine Handvoll Männer in zwei Zollhäuschen akribisch Wache: auf unserer Seite Chilenen, 100 Meter weiter Argentinier.

Für das Verständnis der folgenden Geschichte muss man wissen, dass sich die beiden Länder nicht gerade grün sind und strategisch auch jeden abgelegenen Posten wie diesen hier sehr ernst nehmen. Zur guten Laune der Zöllner trägt auch nicht unbedingt bei, dass eine Wachschicht hier zwei Monate dauert. Wenn sich da vier bis fünf Mann auf den Senkel gehen, und man dann auch noch böse Miene zum eigentlich friedvollen Volksfeind ein paar Meter weiter machen muss, ist klar, dass jede Abwechslung willkommen ist und ausgekostet werden will. Wir sind – eindeutig – die erste Abwechslung seit langer Zeit.

Lassen uns die Chilenen ohne jegliche Schikanen ausreisen, stellen sich die Argentinier freundlich, aber mächtig quer. Das hat einen eindeutigen Hintergrund: Uns fehlen Stempel in den Pässen für die Autos. Die Zollchefin in Salta hat uns vor ein paar Tagen die Ausreise zwar verboten, aber wir waren trotzdem gefahren. In der Hoffnung, dass Provinzgrenzer nicht so genau in die Papiere schauen. Falsch gedacht.

Na klasse. Wir sind also auf 3 876 Metern Höhe irgendwo zwischen Chile und Argentinien und kommen nicht weiter. Die Chilenen sind sehr freundlich und bieten uns Asyl an, bis alles geklärt ist – wir mögen doch bitte bei ihnen schlafen. Ein eindeutiges Angebot, um den Argentiniern da drüben eins auszuwischen.

Das wollen die Argentinier – die uns ja gerne durchgelassen hätten, aber nicht dürfen – natürlich nicht auf sich sitzen lassen. Bitte, bitte, ob wir nicht bei ihnen schlafen wollten? Schließlich seien das da drüben ja Chilenen.

Um niemanden zu verärgern, teilen wir uns jetzt schon mal auf. Die Hälfte des so genervten wie amüsierten Teutonen-Trecks schlägt ihr Nachtlager bei den Chilenen auf, die andere Hälfte bei den Argentiniern.

At first, the tour ran like clockwork. Soon enough, however, we were to be faced with another of those bizarre moments which every tour has thrown up and for which you just can't plan. Following the route of the "Train to the Clouds", we headed from San Pedro de Atacama in Chile to the Argentinian border. It is a lonely part of the world, but despite frequent intermissions where we had to dig the vehicles out of the snow we arrived in fine fettle at the Socompa Pass. At an altitude of 12,700 feet, it is the highest mountain pass that the train crosses. Rusting in the rocks below are the remains of locomotives, trailers and trucks that couldn't complete the journey in one piece. With the exception of our convoy, privateers up here were unheard of, and yet on both sides of the border, in their respective customs buildings, a handful of soldiers guarded the border meticulously: on our side the Chileans, and a hundred yards further on, the Argentinians.

To understand why the following story played out as it did, one must recall that there is little love lost between these two countries, and even border crossing points in the back of beyond such as ours are of immense strategic significance. The mood of the customs officials was also not helped by the fact that, for them, a tour of duty in this part of the world lasts two months. Four or five guys cooped up in a hut together, making evil faces at the enemy (who is actually just minding his own business) down the road, were probably looking forward with more than a bit of relish to the break from the usual monotony that our arrival at the border signified. For we were – and this was patently obvious – the only thing to have happened here for a long time.

The Chileans let us exit without any hassle. Unlike the Argentinians, who, despite putting on their broadest of smiles, were not going to be cooperative. The reason was simple. We lacked the necessary vehicle stamps in our passports. A few days prior, the head of customs in Salta had explicitly forbidden our leaving the country. We had nevertheless driven off in the hope that those working at the border wouldn't be quite as meticulous when it came to paperwork. Our mistake.

So here we were, at 12,700 feet above sea level, somewhere between Chile and Argentina, and we were stuck. The Chileans were very friendly and offered us asylum, saying we could sleep in their barracks. This was clearly an opportunity for them to poke fun at the "enemy" across the border. The Argentinians, who, as they pointed out, would have loved to let us pass but weren't allowed to, were equally unwilling to take the Chilean affront lying down and asked us whether we would like to stay on their side of the border – they wouldn't feel happy if we were forced to stay with the Chileans.

DER KLEINKRIEG
THE BORDER INCIDENT

Aber bis es ans Schlafen geht, ist der Abend noch lang. Koch Stefan spendiert deswegen Spaghetti für alle – aber wo zubereiten? Bei den Chilenen? Bei den Argentiniern? Wir wählen die Chilenen – nicht ohne die nach ihrer Meinung dubiosen Grenznachbarn auch einzuladen. Und: Es klappt! Leicht unsicher betreten die Argentinier seit weiß der Geier wie vielen Jahren (oder sogar erstmals) das chilenische Grenzerhäuschen, demontieren mit einem Rest von Pflichtbewusstsein ihre argentinischen Epauletten und sind bereit, mit Chilenen samt Deutschen zu essen. Als Nachtisch spielen wir Billard zusammen, gucken das Fußballspiel Chile gegen Kanada, und selbst die Argentinier freuen sich nach ein paar Bier mit den Chilenen, wenn deren Mannschaft ein guter Zug gelingt.

Die Zeit schreitet voran, und voller Euphorie schlachten die Chilenen morgens um 4 Uhr ein zeterndes Huftier in der irrigen Annahme, jemand hätte noch Hunger auf frische chilenische Hochlandziege. Durch diverse Touren diplomatisch geschult verspeisen wir trotz kugelrunder Bäuche noch ein paar Muskelstränge des behörnten Viehs, ehe wir uns zum viel zu kurzen Schlaf verabschieden. Nach der ungewöhnlichen Nacht lassen uns die scheinbar mit leichten Kopfschmerzen kämpfenden Argentinier auch ohne Stempel ins Land. Dass wir nach der Tour erneut und noch mehr Probleme haben werden, die Autos aus dem Land zu schaffen (wegen inzwischen diverser fehlender Stempel), ist uns in diesem Moment relativ egal.

To maintain some semblance of peace and stability and not cause an international incident, we divided the team up. Half of the crew – who by now were not sure whether to laugh or cry at the whole spectacle – put up their tents on the Chilean side, while the other half went to the Argentinians.

Bedtime was still a while away, though, so our cook Stefan set about making spaghetti for everybody – there was still the question of where to cook the noodles – at the Chilean post, or would it be better to go the Argentine ...? We chose Chile, making sure that we invited the neighbours over, too, regardless of what the Chileans thought about them. And – it worked. For the first time in who knows how many years (or perhaps at all), the Argentinians warily walked over to the Chilean border-crossing station, prudently removing their Argentinian epaulettes, to sit down for dinner with the Chileans and the Germans. For dessert we hit the pool table, watched some football as Chile was playing against Canada, and after a few beers even the Argentinians were celebrating when the Chilean national team put some moves together against the Canadians.

Time passed rapidly, and by now completely euphoric, the Chileans slaughtered one of their animals, believing in some crazy way that at four in the morning people would not be averse to grilled Chilean mountain goat. Thanks to numerous tours, and despite our full stomachs, we were diplomatically wise enough to force some of the lean meat down before hitting the sacks for a very short night's sleep. After such an unusual night, the Argentinians, clearly suffering from morning-after syndrome, let us enter their country. At that moment we didn't care a damn, but the missing stamps here and in Salta would cause us further problems later on when it came time to export the vehicles back out of the country.

MANCHMAL SIND ES DIE KLEINEN, EINFACHEN DINGE, DIE EINEM NOCH LANGE IM GEDÄCHTNIS BLEIBEN. WIE ZUM BEISPIEL DIE BEGEGNUNG MIT DEM KLEINEN MÄDCHEN, WEITAB VON JEDER ZIVILISATION. MAN TEILT SICH EINEN APFEL, ERZÄHLT, WO MAN HERKOMMT UND WAS MAN NOCH ALLES VORHAT AUF DER TOUR. „IHR SEID JA VERRÜCKT", SAGT SIE. WIR KÖNNEN NICHT VOLLER ÜBERZEUGUNG WIDERSPRECHEN.
--
SOMETIMES IT IS THE LITTLE THINGS THAT STICK IN YOUR MEMORY. MILES FROM ANYWHERE, WE MET THIS LITTLE GIRL. WE GAVE HER AN APPLE, TOLD HER WHERE WE CAME FROM AND WHAT WE PLANNED TO DO ON THE TOUR. "YOU'RE CRAZY," WAS ALL SHE SAID. WE COULDN'T DISAGREE WITH HER.

NACH DEM 4 895 METER HOHEN ABRA-EL-ACAY-PASS IN ARGENTINIEN (FESTGEHALTEN AUF DEM VERWITTER-TEN SCHILD) UND STUNDENLANGER HOCHLAND-FAHRT IST DER ÖRTLICHE SUPERMARKT EIN WEITERES ECHTES HIGHLIGHT.

--

AFTER THE 16,000-FOOT ABRA EL ACAY PASS IN ARGENTINA (WHICH CAN BE SEEN ON THE WEATHER-BEATEN SIGN) AND HOURS SPENT IN THE HIGHLANDS, THE LOCAL SUPERMARKET WAS ANOTHER HIGHLIGHT.

DER KRATER
THE CRATER

Noch in Deutschland haben wir herausgefunden, wessen Grundstück wir passieren müssen, wenn wir durch den bislang offensichtlich von noch niemandem fahrenderweise bezwungenen Krater Galán rollen wollen. Es ist ein Franzose, der in Paris lebt. Die Dienstreise nach Paris ist erfreulich kurz: Der Mann hat nichts dagegen.

Es wird Zeit, vor Ort die Tourstrecke zu testen. Die Autos für die Vortour werden nach Buenos Aires verschifft, im Konvoi fahren wir nach Salta – das sind mal eben 2 500 Kilometer. Die Tour steht bald fest: Von Salta Richtung Calama in die Atacamawüste, über San Pedro zum Socompa-Pass, von da aus zurück nach Salta. Das sind rund 1 600 Kilometer – perfekt für die neue Experience Tour. Und jetzt müssen wir nur noch den Krater einbauen.

Krater an sich sind faszinierend, dieser hier ist es auf besondere Weise. Vom Eingang bis zum Ausgang sind es etwa 30 Kilometer, wobei wir den Eingang aus dem Internet kennen, den Weg und den Ausgang allerdings nicht. Mit den Autos fahren wir über das endlos große Farmland des Franzosen, bis der Weg so eng wird, dass fast nur noch Eselskarren durchkommen. Allein die Anfahrt zum Krater dauert so lange, dass es schon Nachmittag ist, als wir den Eingang erreichen. Wir schnaufen bei der Höhe von 4 000 bis 5 000 Metern nicht schlecht, die Autos auch. Nur ganz langsam kriechen wir voran, weil wir versuchen – möglicherweise vom Höhenwahn ergriffen – die Autoelektronik zu überlisten. Die Höhensensoren in den Steuergeräten der Discovery verkleben wir mit Gießharz, sodass den Motoren vorgegaukelt wird, sie befänden sich nur auf 1 200 Metern Höhe. Das Ergebnis: Die Autos qualmen viel mehr, aber die Leistung ist trotzdem weg. Daraufhin befreien wir die Wagen wieder von dem sinnlosen Knebel.

In weiser Voraussicht habe ich erstmals bei einer Vortour einen unserer Docs mitgenommen, der auch prompt zu tun bekommt: Ein Fotograf wird höhenkrank. Gunnar muss mit ihm zurück in die argentinischen Niederungen.

Aber letztlich haben auch wir keine Chance, bei der Vortour den Krater voll zu erkunden. So verlassen wir diesen seltsamen Ort und beauftragen Gerry und seinen Schwager, die Strecke zu Fuß abzulaufen und für uns zu kartografieren, bis wir mit den Teams zur Haupttour wiederkommen.

While still in Germany, we had managed to discover whose land we would have to drive over if we wanted to explore the Galán crater – which as it turned out, had clearly not been driven by anyone thus far. The land belonged to a Frenchman living in Paris. A short flight later, we had our permit.

It was time to test the route ourselves. The pre-scout vehicles were shipped to Buenos Aires, and then we headed in convoy to Salta. A mere 1,600 miles. The tour route had finally been approved. We planned to head from Salta to Calama in the Atacama desert, via San Pedro over the Socompa Pass, and then back to Salta. A round trip of around 1,000 miles, which was perfect for the new Experience Tour. All we had to do now was to add the crater to the route.

Craters are fascinating in and of themselves – this one even more so. From entrance to exit, it was approximately 19 miles, and all we had to go on was the entrance point, which we had found online. The actual route through and the exit remained unknown quantities. We travelled across the steppe-like farmland belonging to the Frenchman until the way narrowed down to a trail barely wide enough to accommodate a donkey and cart. It was past midday before we arrived at the entrance. And at an altitude ranging between 13,000 and 16,000 feet, man and machine alike were constantly gasping for air. The only way we could make progress at all was by tricking the vehicles' electronic sensors. Perhaps we were suffering from altitude sickness ourselves; we covered the altitude sensors in the Discovery's engine management system with resin, thus creating the impression (as far as the engine was concerned) that we were at an altitude of 4,000 feet. The cars produced more smoke as a result, but with performance still down, we decided to free the engines of this unnecessary gag.

Prudently, and for the first time on a pre-scout, I had chosen to bring one of our doctors along. He was needed almost immediately. A photographer started suffering from altitude sickness, and Doc Gunnar had to accompany him back down to the Argentinian lowlands.

At the end of the day, we were also unable to completely recce the crater. As we left this unusual place I asked Gerry and his brother-in-law to complete the section on foot and map the entire stretch before we returned with the teams.

UR WER GENAU HINSIEHT, ERKENNT EIN KLEINES LAND-ROVER-LOGO
UF DEM WEGWEISER. WAREN GLEICHGESINNTE SCHON VOR UNS HIER?
DER IST ES EIN HINWEIS, DASS MAN OHNE LAND ROVER HIER NICHT
EITERKOMMT? DIE FOLGENDEN PISTEN UND OFFROAD-ABSCHNITTE
ND JEDENFALLS EINE FREUDE FÜR JEDEN ENTWICKLUNGSINGENIEUR
UF TESTFAHRT.

YOU LOOK CLOSELY, YOU CAN SEE THE TINY LAND ROVER LOGO ON
HE SIGN. WERE FRIENDS HERE BEFORE US? OR WAS IT AN INDICATION
HAT, WITHOUT LAND ROVER, THE ROAD ENDS HERE? THE FOLLOWING
RACKS AND TRAILS ARE NEVERTHELESS A JOY FOR EVERY VEHICLE-
VELOPMENT ENGINEER ON SHAKEDOWN.

DIE FINSTERNIS
THE DARKNESS

Wir sind in Südamerika zur Haupttour bereit. Gerry und sein Schwager haben ihn natürlich nicht geschafft, den mühsamen Marsch durch erkaltete Lava und brennende Sonne. Aber Hand aufs Herz: So eine 30-Kilometer-Wanderung ist selbst für einen Österreicher mit großer Klappe nicht so einfach zu erledigen. So versuchen wir erstmals seit Beginn der Land-Rover-Experience-Haupttouren, einen Weg zu finden, den wir vorher nicht bereits ausprobiert haben.

Wir wollen unbedingt durch den Krater, und die Teams wollen es auch. Obwohl wir hinter unserem Zeitplan hängen und den Krater auch umfahren könnten, wagen wir das Abenteuer. Es ist bereits 17 Uhr, als wir am Eingang ankommen. Der Plan: 30 Kilometer fahren, dann gegen Mitternacht Campsite aufbauen. Eigentlich ein wunderbares Vorhaben.

Doch gleich am Eingang zeigt uns der Boden, dass er nicht gewillt ist, sich uns anzupassen. Wir müssen uns nach ihm richten. Wir tasten uns am Rand eines Salzsees entlang – auf Google Earth war nicht zu erkennen, wie weich der Untergrund ist. Inzwischen läuft jeder Beifahrer vor dem Auto seines Piloten, um den Boden zu testen, und es wird immer dunkler. Und dunkler. Bis es stockdunkel ist. Also schwarz. Tiefschwarz.

Die erkalteten Lavamassen fressen jedes Restlicht, sodass einige Teams nun vollends die Orientierung verlieren. Und auch wir Reiseprofis müssen uns mehr auf unsere Erfahrung als auf unsere Augen verlassen. Wir erahnen Felsen und Steine am Kraterrand im fahlen Licht der Scheinwerfer mehr, als dass wir sie wirklich wahrnehmen.

Die „Fußgänger" können ihren Weg nur noch mithilfe von Stirnlampen erraten, trotzdem verlaufen sich einige. Ich muss sie zurückholen und beschließe, dass nur noch die Verantwortlichen wie Hans und ich mit unseren Autos den Weg suchen, die Teams dann nur noch vorsichtig folgen. Es ist einfach zu gefährlich für die ungeübten Teilnehmer.

Aber auch auf diese Weise kommen wir kaum voran. Immer wieder bleibt ein Auto stecken, erkennt ein Scout zu spät eine Sackgasse, muss irgendwer um einen viel zu großen Felsbrocken herumrangieren. Die Zeit vergeht, und als ich endlich eine kleine Ebene entdecke, auf die alle zehn Autos samt Zelten passen, ist es 4 Uhr morgens. Die Aufmerksamkeit ist nun völlig verbraucht, die Kraft verschwunden, die Laune durchwachsen. Ich beschließe, dass wir hierbleiben. Es ist verdammt kalt, deswegen werden die Bodenzelte extrem schnell aufgebaut. Koch Stefan kreiert ein Gebräu, das uns trotz der Strapazen glücklich macht: Kaffee mit Chilipulver.

Am nächsten Morgen um halb sieben wache ich auf und bin putzmunter, als ich nach draußen blicke. Es ist schlicht nicht ersichtlich, wie wir hierhergekommen sind. Alles, was ich rundherum sehe, ist eigentlich unfahrbar: senkrechte Wände um uns herum oder große Felsbrocken, die wir niemals hätten bewegen können. Ich weiß bis heute nicht, wie wir es in der niemals wieder so empfundenen Dunkelheit geschafft haben, das kleine Plateau zu erreichen. Aber manchmal ist das auch nicht wichtig. Wichtig ist, es überhaupt zu schaffen. Und dafür sind wir hergekommen.

Letztlich verhilft uns die Argentinien/Chile-Tour zu unserem kompletten Durchbruch in der Abenteuerbranche. Wir haben bewiesen, dass wir mit Land Rover überall hinkommen. Deswegen schaut die Company über den Tellerrand hinaus und entschließt sich, ein Presse-Event mit mehr als 120 Journalisten aus aller Welt mit den Autos hier in Südamerika zu veranstalten – das überaus erfolgreich absolviert wird.

We were ready to start the main event in South America. Naturally, Gerry and his brother-in-law hadn't managed the physically debilitating march across the solidified lava field under the burning sun. But if we're being completely honest here, the 19-mile walk was a long way, even for an Austrian with a big mouth. So for the first time ever on a Land Rover Experience Tour, we would be attempting a route that we hadn't previously tested.

For us, it was essential that we drive the crater, and the teams felt the same way. Although we were behind schedule and could have circumvented the crater altogether, we decided to take the plunge. It was already 5 in the afternoon when we arrived at the entrance. The plan was to drive the 19 or so miles and set up camp around midnight. Actually, it was a wonderful plan.

From the outset, though, the ground wasn't willing to go along with our plan, and we had to bow to its demands. We explored the edge of a salt lake – on Google Earth we hadn't been able to ascertain how soft the ground was. Meanwhile all the co-drivers had taken to walking in front of their vehicles to test the ground. It was getting darker by the minute, and very soon it was absolutely pitch black.

The solidified lava formations literally swallowed whatever light there was, and as a result, some of the teams could no longer recognize east from west or north from south. We, the travel professionals, had to rely more on our experience than on our eyes. Rock faces and stones on the edge of the crater, which can just be made out at long range using the headlights, are more figments of our imagination than real geographical features.

The "pedestrians" were now almost completely reliant on their own personal headlamps – yet some managed to lose their way. I had to go out and get them while at the same time deciding that, as Hans and I were in charge, it was our task to lead the way, leaving the teams to follow us. For the participants, who were unused to such situations, it had become simply too dangerous.

This method didn't improve our speed over the ground, however. Again and again, vehicles bogged down, and we entered one dead end after the next before recognizing our mistake and having to backtrack, or we had to manoeuvre around a large rock. Hours passed, and by the time I had discovered a flat area large enough for us to park up the vehicles and pitch our tents, it was 4 am. People's powers of concentration were gone by now, and the same could be said for their stamina – the mood was so-so at best. I decided that we would pitch camp here. It was absolutely freezing, and for that reason we put the tents up as quickly as possible. Stefan made up a drink that perked us up a bit: coffee with chilli powder.

I awoke at 6.30 that morning and was gobsmacked when I looked out of the tent. It was impossible to see how we had got here. The terrain appeared virtually impassable in every direction, as far as the eye could see. Vertical rock faces and huge boulders, which we would never have been able to move, were scattered across the landscape. To this day, I have no idea how we managed to find the plateau in the darkness. Sometimes the "how" isn't important – what is important is that you achieved it in the first place. And that was why we were here.

In the final analysis, the Argentina/Chile Tour helped to establish us as a significant player in the adventure market. We had successfully shown that we could literally go anywhere with Land Rover. Land Rover also demonstrated that it could think "out-of-the-box" and chose to run a media event for 120 international journalists with the vehicles in South America – a roaring success.

DR. DOMINIK DOERR

*GEBOREN AM 25.11.1966 | FACHARZT FÜR INNERE MEDIZIN, SPORT- UND NOTFALLMEDIZIN,
NOTARZT IN DER LUFTRETTUNG, INTERNIST, VERBANDSARZT DES BUNDESVERBANDES DEUTSCHER GEWICHTHEBER*

*BORN 25 NOVEMBER 1966 | SPECIALIST IN INTERNAL MEDICINE, SPORTS AND EMERGENCY MEDICINE,
HELICOPTER RESCUE DOCTOR AND PHYSICIAN FOR THE GERMAN WEIGHTLIFTING FEDERATION*

Du bist der zweite Doc der Land Rover Experience Tour.
Wie bist du dazu gekommen?
2006 habe ich die G4 Challenge mitgemacht, da habe ich Hans kennengelernt. Gleich darauf war ich bei den Touren 2007 in Argentinien, 2008 in Malaysia, 2011 in Bolivien und bei der Jubiläumstour auf den Spuren der Seidenstraße dabei.

Wobei wurde dein Fachwissen benötigt?
Eingreifen musste ich schon bei der G4: ein Polytrauma, ein Höhenlungenödem sowie einige leichtere Fälle von Höhenkrankheit; in Argentinien/Chile wie auch in Bolivien gab es ebenfalls leichtere Fälle von Höhenkrankheiten und Wundversorgungen, in Malaysia hauptsächlich Wundversorgungen und die Versorgung von Blutegelattacken.

Immer wieder diese Höhenkrankheit.
Ist dagegen denn gar kein Kraut gewachsen?
Nein. Grundsätzlich besteht schon ab etwa 3 000 Meter – bei manchen Menschen schon ab 2 500 Meter – ein Risiko, höhenkrank zu werden. Es gibt keine wirklich sinnvolle Vorbeugung und auch keine Faktoren, mit denen man eine Vorhersage treffen könnte, wer höhenkrank wird und wer nicht. Auch körperliche Fitness hat keinen Einfluss darauf. Allerdings kann sie dafür sorgen, dass man mit guter Konstitution in der Höhe leistungsfähiger ist.

Wie testest du auf den Touren, ob es den Mitfahrern gut geht
oder nicht?
Mit dem Pulsoximeter kann ich die Sauerstoffkonzentration im Blut abschätzen – aber nicht wirklich messen, da dies eine Genauigkeit impliziert, die unter Extrembedingungen nicht gewährleistet ist. Sie gibt aber Hinweise, ob sich eine Hypoxie, also ein Sauerstoffmangel, anbahnt oder nicht.

Welches Erlebnis ist dir besonders im Gedächtnis hängen geblieben?
Beeindruckende Momente gab es reichlich. Als ganz besonders bleibt mir unsere Übernachtung auf dem Socompa-Pass an der chilenisch-argentinischen Grenze in Erinnerung, als wir aufgrund einer sturen Zoll-Bürokratin in der Distrikthauptstadt Salta nicht gleich nach Argentinien einreisen konnten und „gezwungenermaßen" ein schönes Fest mit den Zöllnern beider (!) Seiten veranstaltet haben – und es schließlich zum Handschlag zwischen den beiden jeweiligen Kommandanten kam, was nach dem Falklandkrieg (die Chilenen haben die SAS, die Spezialeinheit der Engländer, unterstützt) auch heute noch nicht selbstverständlich ist.

You are the second doctor to take part in the Land Rover Experience
Tour. How did that come about?
In 2006, I took part in the G4 Challenge, where I met Hans. Pretty much straight after I took part in the Argentina Tour in 2007, in Malaysia in 2008, Bolivia in 2011 and the anniversary tour along the Silk Road.

On which tours were you required to go to work?
I needed to intervene on the G4 Challenge: polytrauma, a pulmonary oedema, as well as mild cases of altitude sickness; in Argentina/Chile as well as Bolivia we also had some mild altitude sickness and wounds that needed to be treated; in Malaysia it was largely wounds and treatment of leech bites.

I keep hearing altitude sickness. Is there nothing that you can do?
No. The risk of contracting altitude sickness is ever-present from about 9,800 feet upwards, for some people even from 8,000 feet. There is no really sensible prophylaxis and no factors by which one can predict who is likely to suffer and who isn't. Physical fitness has no real influence, either. Having a good constitution does mean that one is more physically able at altitude, however.

On tour, how do you test the participants' condition?
The pulse oximeter can estimate the levels of oxygen in the blood. It is not so precise as to be able to measure specific levels, as this is not possible in extreme conditions. However, it gives me an indication of whether or not there is a danger of hypoxia or oxygen depravation.

Is there any particular incident that has really stuck in your memory?
There have been many impressive moments, but one incident really stands out, and that was our enforced overnight stay on the Socompa Pass on the Argentinian-Chilean border as the result of a particularly bureaucratic civil servant in the regional capital of Salta. Given the fact that in the Falklands War the Chileans had supported the British Special Air Service against the Argentinians, the party we had with the customs officers from both (!) sides of the border, and the handshake between the two commanding officers, was something you couldn't take for granted – even in 2007, many years after the war.

MALAYSIA
2008

ERHOLUNGSREISE? NOCH GLAUBEN DIE TEILNEHMER
DER ACHTEN LAND ROVER EXPERIENCE TOUR
DARAN. SIE WERDEN IN EINEM LUXURIÖSEN HOTEL
VERWÖHNT, DÜRFEN IM WASSER PLANSCHEN UND
DIE SEELE BAUMELN LASSEN. DER BLICK IN DEN
DSCHUNGEL VERRÄT NOCH NICHT, DASS DIES EINE
DER ANSTRENGENDSTEN TOUREN WIRD – DENN DER
REGEN WIRD KOMMEN ...

THE VACATION OF A LIFETIME – OR SO PARTICIPANTS
IN THE EIGHTH LAND ROVER EXPERIENCE TOUR
THOUGHT AT FIRST. SPOILT IN A LUXURY HOTEL,
BATHING IN THE POOL, FORGETTING ABOUT YOUR
WORRIES. THE JUNGLE WOULD TURN OUT TO BE ONE
OF THE MOST STRENUOUS TOURS THUS FAR – AS RAIN
WAS ON ITS WAY ...

2008
LAND: MALAYSIA
STRECKE: 1 200 KM
COUNTRY: MALAYSIA
DISTANCE: 750 MILES

7 FREELANDER, 4 DEFENDER,
1 AMBULANCE DISCOVERY

DIE FEHLEINSCHÄTZUNG
THE MISJUDGEMENT

Australien? China? Malaysia? Wie üblich zerbrechen wir uns die Köpfe, wie wir die große vorherige Experience Tour wieder einmal toppen können. Drei Destinationen schlagen wir Land Rover vor, unser Favorit ist eindeutig Malaysia. Ziel: der Dschungel. Den kennen wir bereits aus Mittelamerika, der verspricht Abenteuer bis in jeden Bach und jede Wurzel. Wie recht wir damit behalten sollen, stellt sich allerdings erst später heraus.

Natürlich wird Malaysia gewählt. Unsere ersten Befürchtungen, organisatorische Probleme mit den Autos zu bekommen, eventuelle Sprachschwierigkeiten, asiatisches Chaos oder zu verschiedene Kulturkreise, erweisen sich als Luftblase. Die Menschen sind extrem freundlich, hilfsbereit, und die lange englische Herrschaft über das Land hilft bei der Verständigung enorm. Noch nie war es so einfach, die benötigten Autos einzuführen inklusive des voll ausgerüsteten Ambulanz-Discovery.

Unsere erste Reise nach Malaysia zur Guide-Suche endet schon bei der ersten Agentur, die wir anpeilen: Hier finden wir engagierte junge Offroad-Fans. Besonders einer sticht heraus: Shah, ein Malaie, der dort mit kurzer Hose und gelben Kniestrümpfen parat steht wie ein junger Offizier einer Fantasiearmee. Noch nie vorher konnten wir uns so schnell – und nach so herrlichem Essen, besten Hotels und perfekter Landeseinführung – wieder in Deutschland unseren Orga-Aufgaben widmen.

Die Reisestrecke ist schnell gefunden: von der Insel Langkawi vor der Nordwestküste Malaysias etwa 1 200 Kilometer durchs Land auf die andere Seite zur Ostküste ins Strandhotel. Dazwischen: Dschungel, was sonst. Und nichts anderes. Dass wir wohl auch mal den einen oder anderen umgekippten Baum zerteilen werden oder auch eine Brücke bauen müssen, ist mir so klar wie recht. Deswegen gibt es in den Qualifikationscamps bereits eine komplette Ausbildung an Stihl-Kettensägen, denn auch im Urwald kann man nicht einfach drauflos zerkleinern. Das will gelernt sein, schon alleine damit nicht irgendwem rein zufällig so ein Urwaldriese auf seinen Abenteurerkopf fällt.

Für die Qualifikationscamps melden sich nun rund 20 000 abenteuerhungrige Menschen – eine tolle Bestätigung, dass wir auf dem richtigen Weg sind. Wenn die späteren Sieger allerdings gewusst hätten, was auf sie zukommt, hätten die meisten wohl dankend abgewunken.

Where to next? Australia? China? Or Malaysia? We started scratching our heads and wondering how we could top the previous year's amazing Experience Tour. We suggested three possible destinations, our clear favourite was Malaysia. Objective: jungle. We knew the jungle from the Central American tour, where adventure could be found pouring from every stream and hiding behind every root. We would later discover just how right we had been.

Of course, it had to be Malaysia. Any initial fears – regarding vehicle shipping, possible language difficulties, Asian chaos or simply cultural diversity – turned out to be groundless. The local population was extremely helpful, and the fact that it was a former British colony helped communication enormously. Importing the vehicles, including the Discovery ambulance with all its medical supplies on board, had never been so simple.

Our first trip to Malaysia to search for a guide came up trumps with the first agency we approached. We encountered highly motivated, young off-road fans, and one in particular immediately caught our attention: Shah was a Malay wearing shorts and yellow socks, and to be honest, he looked like an extra from a Beatles movie. In next to no time, having enjoyed fantastic food, amazing hotels and a perfect introduction to the country, we were back in Germany getting on with organizing the main event.

We were able to put the route together in rapid time: starting from the island of Langkawi off the north coast of Malaysia and then heading some 750 miles across the country towards the east coast finishing in a hotel on the beach. And in-between: nothing but jungle. Removing trees that blocked our route and building the odd bridge or two were on the agenda – and ultimately what the Experience was all about. For the selection camps, we had prudently planned a complete training session on handling Stihl chainsaws, as we wouldn't be able to hack everything into matchwood in the rain forest. We needed a proper training course to ensure that the participants wouldn't start felling trees onto one another.

That we had 20,000 would-be adventurers apply for the selection camps was a fantastic confirmation that we had made the right decision. That said, if the lucky six winners had known what awaited them in the rainforest, most of them might have reconsidered coming at all.

DER BAUM
THE TREE

Wir lernen schnell. Zum Beispiel, dass eine Kettensäge, mit der man einen deutschen Durchschnittsgarten nach allen Regeln der Kunst in sämtliche Kleinteile zerlegen kann, im Dschungel nur ein stumpfer Zahnstocher ist. Natürlich treffen wir bereits auf der Vortour schnell auf einen umgekippten Baum, der den Weg – meistens alte Holzfällerpisten – komplett blockiert. Mit unserer motorisierten Kindersäge schaffen wir gerade mal einen Schnitt von 20 Zentimeter Tiefe in das Hartholz des etwa 120 Zentimeter dicken Stammes, bevor sich die Kette erstmals mit hässlichem Geräusch verabschiedet. Zunächst legen wir sie akribisch wieder in ihre Führung, aber immer öfter springt sie heraus und wird stumpf. Mit Nagelfeilen schleifen wir die Kette nach, und drei Stunden später arbeiten wir immer noch an dem hartnäckigen Stück Dschungelholz mit der Säge – und inzwischen auch mit den Winden der Autos. Für uns ist klar: Die Land Rover Experience Tour wird mit solchen Aufgaben fertig und wächst daran. Egal was kommt, wir bleiben auf dem Weg. Und lösen solche Probleme nicht so wie zum Beispiel die Rainforest Challenge: Die bricht durchs Gehölz ohne Rücksicht auf Verluste – sei es bei sich oder in der Natur. Die lassen sogar Autos im Dschungel zurück, wenn es gar nicht anders geht. So etwas kommt für uns nicht in Frage. Was mit auf die Tour kommt, nehmen wir auch wieder mit nach Hause.

Doch die Frage stellt sich auf der Vortour nicht. Ein bisschen Matsch, ein bisschen Schlamm, mal eine weggefaulte Brücke – perfekt für die Experience Tour. Dazu Kultur, zum Beispiel ein Besuch in den Cameron Highlands nahe der Hauptstadt Kuala Lumpur, wo es neben wunderbarem Tee und leckeren Erdbeeren vor allem die größte Dichte an alten Land Rover der Serien II bis III gibt. Der Grund: Viele Solihuller ließen die Briten einfach dort zurück, als Malaysia 1963 aus dem Commonwealth entlassen wurde; immer mehr kamen im Laufe der Zeit hinzu, weil sie sich als zuverlässig erwiesen. Da die nun teils schrottreifen Lastenträger hier weder Steuern bezahlen müssen noch einer technischen Überwachung unterliegen, solange sie ein großes „CH" auf den Seiten tragen und das fest definierte Gebiet der Cameron Highlands nicht verlassen, dienen die meisten von ihnen bis heute als unverzichtbare Transportmittel – wenn sie auch inzwischen mit japanischen Getrieben, koreanischen Motoren und selbstgemachten Ersatzteilen gespickt sind. Nach Schätzungen fahren hier in einem Gebiet von rund 700 Quadratkilometern etwa 7 000 Land Rover.

We learnt quickly. For example, that a chainsaw designed to chop the average German garden into bits is nothing more than a blunt toothpick in the jungle. On the pre-scout recce we encountered more than one tree blocking the logging routes. Our toy chainsaws could barely cut 8 inches into the 4-foot-wide hardwood trunk before the chain stopped with a disturbing gurgling noise. We meticulously repositioned the chain in its guide, but to no avail, as it re-peatedly jumped out of the guide before rapidly going blunt. We sharpened the chain teeth with nail files, but three hours later we were still at work on the vehicles to remove it.

For us, it was almost a matter of principle. The Land Rover Experience Tour has to deal with situations like these – they are what make the tour so special. Regardless of what is in the way, we stick to the prescribed route, in contrast to an event such as the Rainforest Challenge, which has no scruples when it comes to tearing through the undergrowth, no matter the cost to man, material or the environment. Vehicles that can't be recovered are simply left behind in the jungle. For us, this is simply out of the question. What comes on the tour goes home with the tour.

The pre-scout recce was not dogged by such issues, though. There was a bit of dirt, a bit of mud and the odd rotten bridge to repair – all of which would be perfect for the Experience Tour. On top of that, we had a true cultural highlight in the Cameron Highlands region near the capital city of Kuala Lumpur. Aside from fabulous tea blends and delicious strawberries, the region is also famous for its large population of historic Series II and III Land Rovers. When Malaysia officially left the Commonwealth in 1963, the British left many of their Land Rovers behind. Many more joined the original vehicles over the years, as they were simple to maintain. Today, the Land Rovers of the Cameron Highlands are immediately recognizable, thanks to a large "CH" painted on the side that exempts them from tax and any form of vehicle inspection but also restricts their operation to the Cameron Highlands. To all appearances now on their last legs, the workhorses are very popular and have been kept on the road with all manner of Japanese gearboxes, Korean engines and a host of other DIY parts. It is estimated that there are over 7,000 Land Rovers on the job in the 270-square-mile region.

REINE PAUSE IM KAMPF UMS
FORTKOMMEN: DIE TOUR
DURCH DEN MALAYSISCHEN
DSCHUNGEL WIRD ZUR ECHTEN
FEUERPROBE FÜR KÖRPER
UND GEIST. NOCH NIE WAR
TEAMFÄHIGKEIT SO WICHTIG
WIE HIER.
--
NO REST FOR THE WICKED KEEN
TO MAKE PROGRESS. THE TOUR
THROUGH THE MALAYSIAN
JUNGLE PROVED A TRUE
ORDEAL FOR BODY AND SPIRIT.
NEVER BEFORE HAD TEAM
SPIRIT BEEN SO IMPORTANT.

DIE SCHALTER
THE SWITCHES

Als die Haupttour startet, schauen sich die Gewinner, wie meistens bestehend aus drei Frauen und drei Männern, erst mal irritiert um. Wir bringen sie auf die Insel Langkawi, wo es keine Autos zu genießen gibt, sondern nur hellblaue Lagunen, Sonne sowie ein Top-Hotel. Und als wir schließlich mit einem Motor-segler nach einer vierstündigen Bootstour aufs Festland übersetzen, be-schweren sie sich bereits scherzhaft über diese „Urlaubsreise".

Am Festland finden sie dann ihre Freelander vor: völlig serienmäßig aus-gestattet bis auf etwas grobstolligere Reifen von der Continental-Marke Uniroyal, einen extra montierten Unterfahrschutz sowie Dachgepäckträger mit Ersatzrädern. Bereits in Jordanien hatte sich gezeigt, welchen Vorteil manch-mal kleinere und leichtere Geländewagen haben, und so bin ich guter Dinge, was die Leistungsfähigkeit der Freelander angeht. Höchstens die für schweres Gelände nicht optimale Bodenfreiheit macht mir etwas Sorgen. Aber die Vortour haben die Wagen ja auch problemlos geschafft – was soll schon werden?

Insgesamt fährt ein Dutzend Land Rover mit, die ich in drei Gruppen einteile. Die drei Gewinnerteams sollen jeweils führen, um ihrer Aufgabe – diesmal aus-schließlich Navigieren – gerecht zu werden.

Ich fahre ganz hinten in der Ambulanz nach dem letzten Dreierpack, neben mir Doc Dominik. Vor mir lenkt Journalistin Melanie den Führungs-Freelander unserer kleinen Einheit, und sie meldet sich über Funk: „Ich wollte gerade mein iPhone einstöpseln, da geht das Navi aus." Wir halten kurz an, ich fummele etwas an den Schaltern, und schon funktioniert alles wieder. Melanie ist begeistert.

Wir sind noch keine 3 Kilometer weitergefahren, da meldet sich Melanie wiederum: „Ich glaube, mein linkes Vorderlicht geht nicht." Ich gebe zu, mir ist etwas langweilig, und im tiefsten Inneren bin ich immer mal wieder ein kleiner Junge, also antworte ich: „Du hast wahrscheinlich den CO2-Schalter ange-knipst, denn die Autos sind ja Prototypen."

Stille. Eine merkwürdige Stille. Niemand nutzt den Funk. Zeit für mich, grinsend nachzusetzen: „Die Freelander haben vier CO2-Schalter. Das be-deutet, man kann die vier Lichtquellen an den Fahrzeugecken einzeln aus-schalten. Aber nie die beiden hinteren oder die beiden vorderen Leuchteinheiten gleichzeitig. Aus Sicherheitsgründen. Mit dem System wird die Generator-leistung reduziert und man senkt automatisch den CO2-Ausstoß."

Von vorn kommt nur ein trockenes „Okay" durch den Äther, und der Doc und ich haben Mühe, uns vor Lachen im Sitz zu halten. Das wird nicht besser, als nach zwei Minuten Melanies Beifahrer – logischerweise ebenfalls ein Jour-nalist – sich auf unserem Kanal meldet: „Kannst Du das bitte noch einmal wiederholen?"

Ich bin ja im Grunde ein freundlicher Mensch, deshalb erkläre ich die ganze Chose noch einmal, gespickt mit ein paar hanebüchenen technischen Raffi-nessen. Dann frage ich Melanie: „Sag mal, hast du vielleicht vor dem Start schon auf einen der CO2-Schalter gedrückt? Dann geht nämlich das Navi aus. Das ist technisch noch nicht so ausgereift." Das weckt inzwischen einen Auto-journalisten in Auto Nummer zwei unserer Dreier-Kolonne: „Echt?" Nachdem ich nicht mehr ganz so viel prusten muss, kläre ich die Geschichte auf, ehe der Redakteur die Geschichte der „neuen CO2-Schalter von Land Rover" online stellt.

As we kicked off the main event, the six winners, as always three men and three women, were initially somewhat confused. We had brought them to the fabulous island of Langkawi, where there are no cars at all, just beautiful blue lagoons. And then we put them in a luxury hotel. Finally we jumped aboard a motor yacht for a four-hour voyage to the mainland. No wonder, then, that jokes about luxury holidays started coming thick and fast.

Once on the mainland, they encountered their Freelanders. Other than specialist Continental rough-terrain, off-road tyres, additional underbody pro-tection plates as well as roof racks and spare tyres the vehicles were all standard, as they had come from the factory. We had already seen the benefits of smaller, lighter four-wheel-drive vehicles on the Jordan Tour, so I was not at all worried that the Freelanders would not be up the job. Lack of ground clearance was an issue I thought might cause us some heartache in this terrain. That said, they had mastered the pre-scout recce without a whimper.

We had twelve Land Rovers in all, which I divided into three groups. The three teams of participants were assigned the task of leading each group – and, of course, navigating their way through the jungle.

I was driving the ambulance with Dominic the doctor on board and took up my position at the end of the last team of vehicles. In front of me, the journalist Melanie, who was driving the lead Freelander in our group, radioed, "I just connected my iPhone, and the GPS screen went dead." We stopped, and I played around with the switches and got everything working again. Melanie was impressed.

2 miles down the track, Melanie was on the radio again: "I think my left front light isn't working." OK, I was bored, and deep inside I am still a little boy, so I answered, "You probably hit the CO2 switch by mistake as the cars are prototypes."

Silence. A very strange silence. Nobody was using the radio. Time for me to go one step further while grinning from ear to ear, "The Freelander is equipped with four CO2 switches you can use to switch off the lights on all four corners of the vehicle individually, but never both lights at the front or both lights at the rear simultaneously for safety reasons. The system is designed to reduce demand on the alternator, thereby reducing the vehicle's CO2 emissions."

From up ahead we heard a dry "Okay" over the airwaves, and the Doc and I struggled to prevent ourselves from breaking out in fits of giggles. After two minutes things got more complicated when Melanie's co-driver, who was also a journalist, spoke up, asking, "Can you repeat that, please?"

I am a nice guy, so I explained the whole thing once again, though this time with a topping of technical mumbo-jumbo for good measure. Then I asked Melanie, "Did you press one of the CO2 switches before we set off today? That might explain why the GPS screen went dead. The system still has a few bugs." By now, one of the car journalists in our group had woken up to the conver-sation and spoke up on the radio: "Really?" After I stopped laughing, I came clean over the tale before the journalist put the story about "Land Rover's CO2 switch" online.

Als wir als Letzter im Mini-Konvoi abends in der fast romantischen Dschungel-Campsite mit Lagerfeuer und ohne Zeitdruck ankommen, haben wir beschlossen, das Schalterspiel noch etwas fortzuführen. Als Land-Rover-Pressechef Paul auf mich zukommt, nehme ich ihn sichtlich erregt beim Kragen, schleppe ihn in eine dunkle Ecke und frage ihn, warum er mich über die CO2-Schalter nicht aufgeklärt hat. „Welche CO2-Schalter?", fragt er verdutzt zurück. „Ich dachte, man könne aus Sicherheitsgründen nur zwei Quellen auf einmal abschalten", knurre ich ihn an und kippe die Story ins Absurde, „aber es geht auch einzeln!" „Sag bloß kein Wort", antwortet Paul nach Luft schnap-pend, „das darf nicht rauskommen!" Meine Gruppe, die das Zwiegespräch planmäßig mitbekommt, macht sich vor Lachen inzwischen fast in die kurzen Hosen. Jetzt bin ich in meinem Element. Und erhöhe den Druck: „Der Auto-journalist hat das bereits mitbekommen, ich habe ihn schon telefonieren sehen." Paul ist völlig aufgelöst und informiert Christian Uhrig, unseren Marketingchef. Der antwortet: „Ich habe bereits davon gehört ..."

Bevor ich meinen Job verliere, löse ich das Rätsel dann schnell für alle auf. Ein Highlight will ich allerdings noch draufsetzen, und zwar mit einem Fernseh-interview – just for fun und für mein persönliches Video-Album. So bitte ich die mitreisenden Jungs von *Abenteuer Auto*, mit mir ein gefaktes Gespräch zu führen zu diesem Thema. So stelle ich einen Freelander vor eine Palmölfabrik, die alle 30 Sekunden eine grauenhaft schwarze Wolke aus einem Ofenrohr ausstößt, setze mich ins Auto und fabuliere über die sagenhaften CO2-Schalter, unter anderem mit einer Close-up-Aufnahme der ersten vier Radiostations-tasten. Und immer, wenn der Interviewer etwas über Zukunft und Innovation fragt, stänkert hinter dem Freelander eine schwarze Wolke hervor. Es fällt mir wirklich schwer, halbwegs ernst dabei zu bleiben.

Das Lachen gefriert mir allerdings, als ich nach der Tour erfahre, dass die Spaßvögel von *Abenteuer Auto* vergessen haben, das Pseudo-Interview heraus-zuschneiden, bevor sie das ganze Material ihrer Redaktion überließen. Ich fahre persönlich und ein bisschen zu schnell zu deren Hauptsitz nach München, um das Material noch rechtzeitig zu sichern.

That evening, as our mini-convoy rolled up in relaxed fashion in front of the almost romantic jungle campsite complete with campfire, we decided to give the switch story an extra airing. As Land Rover PR manager Paul walked over to me, I grabbed him by the arm and took him over to a corner of the campsite and asked him why he hadn't told me about the CO2 switch. "What CO2 switch?" he asked, bewildered. "I thought you could only switch two lights off simul-taneously for safety reasons," I whispered, now adding an even more absurd twist into the tale, "They can be switched off individually." Paul, who was still completely bewildered, just said, "That's enough – none of this must ever get out!" My group, which was listening to the conversation on the sly as planned, struggled to keep quiet.

Of course now I was on a high, so I turned up the pressure a little: "The jour-nalist has already found out, and I could see that he was on the phone." Paul was now more than just a little confused and informed our head of marketing, Christian Uhrig, who commented, "I've heard about this, too ..."

Before someone fired me, I once again came clean with the truth. But there was still a final chapter to the tale, one involving a TV interview – just for fun, for my own personal video album. I asked the guys from the German TV programme *Abenteuer Auto* to do a fake interview on the topic. I parked a Freelander in front of a factory producing palm oil and waxed lyrical about the amazing CO2 switches with a close-up of the four radio-station buttons. Every time the interviewer asked about the future and innovation, a cloud of black smoke billowed out behind the Freelander. It was very difficult to keep a straight face.

I soon stopped laughing, though, when I heard that the TV jokers had forgotten to remove the fake interview before handing their material over to the studio. I personally drove to their head office in Munich, and at risk of losing my driving licence, to make sure that the material wasn't broadcast.

DER SCHLAMM
THE MUD

Der Abend am Lagerfeuer wird für ein paar Tage der letzte sein, an dem wir so richtig herzhaft lachen können. Denn es fängt an zu regnen. Und wenn es im malaysischen Urwald regnet, dann bedeutet das eimerweise Wasser pro Quadratmeter Boden, was im Dschungel Schlamm bis zu den Kniekehlen und auch höher nach sich zieht.

Ich habe die Kombination von Regen und Boden tatsächlich unterschätzt. Erste Maßnahme gegen die Naturgewalten: Der Konvoi muss zusammenbleiben, damit sich die Fahrzeuge und Mannschaften gegenseitig helfen können. Daraus folgt, dass wir statt dem von uns anvisierten Schnitt von 30 Kilometern pro Stunde etwa 3 schaffen. Wieder und wieder bleiben die Freelander hängen. Aber der Ambulanz-Discovery und die Defender ebenso, der Schlamm ist verdammt tief.

Zu tief zum schnellen Vorankommen, aber nicht zu tief für die Land Rover Experience Tour. Zeitweise bauen wir Steine unter die Sandbleche, damit wir eine „Pfütze" passieren können, an anderen Stellen nutzen wir das komplette Equipment an Winden, wieder woanders müssen nicht nur die Teilnehmer und das Orga-Team in den Schlamm tauchen und schieben, sondern auch die begleitenden Journalisten. An mehreren Stellen müssen wir mit Muskel- und Motorkraft einen Freelander mit Winde durch die Schwachstelle bugsieren und ihn dann umdrehen, damit er über seine Winde samt Umlenkrollen die anderen Autos nachholen kann. Es ist knallhart, es ist teuflisch anstrengend, es ist übermäßig ermüdend, aber es funktioniert.

Der Brückenbau, der immer mal wieder notwendig wird, ist dagegen kein Problem – unsere auf der Haupttour mitgeführte Säge (diesmal im XXXL-Format) erweist sich als dschungeltauglich. Unsere Erfahrung damit ist inzwischen groß, die Arbeitsabläufe sind klar gegliedert, der Spruch der Reise lautet: „Mut zur Brücke".

Wir campen nachts direkt auf der Straße, auf dem Waldboden, in den Autos, auf den Autos, oder was sich auch immer anbietet – falls man nicht sowieso einfach am Ort der letzten Bergetätigkeit in tiefen, unruhigen Schlaf fällt. Mehr als vier bis fünf Stunden pro Nacht sind nicht drin, und bei einigen Mitfahrern schwinden Kräfte und Laune erstaunlich parallel. Alina, unsere einheimische Köchin, schafft es zwar jeden Abend, ein unendlich leckeres Mahl zu kredenzen, aber nahezu 100 Prozent Luftfeuchtigkeit, 40 Grad Hitze und immer wieder dieser Schlamm machen uns schwer zu schaffen. Nur selten gibt es Abwechslung in Form einer offiziell genehmigten Querung der einen oder

That evening around the campfire marked the last time for the next few days that people were really able to have a laugh. A day later, it started to rain. When it rains in the Malaysian jungle it comes down in buckets – meaning mud up to your knees and higher.

I underestimated the effect the rain would have on the ground. Our first countermeasure was to keep the convoy together so that everybody could help one another. As a result, rather than our average of 19 miles per hour, we managed a mere 2. The Freelanders were getting stuck on a regular basis but even the Defender and the Discovery ambulance were having problems. The mud was pretty deep.

OK – it was too deep for us travel quickly, but it wasn't too deep to stop the Land Rover Experience Tour. At times we needed to place stones underneath our sand channels in order to be able to cross the odd "puddle". There were times when the full complement of winching equipment had to be unpacked to enable if we wanted to move at all. On other occasions the whole team – meaning the participants, organizers and all the journalists – were out of the vehicles and in the mud, pushing and heaving for all their worth. At numerous locations the mix of muscle and motor was the only way to get a Freelander through a particularly difficult part, only then to turn the vehicle around to use its own winch and return pulleys to haul the following vehicles through the mire. It was really tough, physically strenuous, and just downright exhausting. But it worked.

Building bridges, however, posed no problems at all. This time we had a full-size chain saw, which was more than "jungle-approved". We had acquired a lot of experience in the team, work processes were clearly defined and the motto of the trip became "Bridge the gap with courage".

At night we slept on the track, on the forest floor, in the cars, on the cars, or wherever we could find a comfortable spot after the most recent winching session. Four or five hours of unruly, fitful sleep were the maximum. As a result, for some of the team, stamina and mood began to deteriorate almost concurrently. Our local chef, Alina, managed to work culinary miracles every night, but the 100 per cent humidity, the 40-degree-Celsius heat (104 degrees Fahrenheit) and the incessant mud started to eat away at our strength. Every once in a while, there was the welcome relief of a brief stretch of motorway between jungle sections, for which we had to first dismantle and then reassemble the Armco safety barrier …

anderen Autobahn, wofür wir die Leitplanken ab- und natürlich auch wieder anmontieren müssen.

Und dann sind da ja noch die Viecher. Nicht die großen jagen uns Angst ein, sondern die kleinen: Schlangen, Spinnen, Raupen und der ganze Mikrokosmos der fliegenden, krabbelnden, stechenden, saugenden oder einfach nervenden Insekten. Tiere, die wir in unserem Leben noch nie gesehen haben. Zum Beispiel fette Wespen, die nachts angezogen werden durch das hell erleuchtete Laptop, das als Navigationshilfe fungiert, und durch einen kleinen Spalt ins Auto geflogen kommen. Oder kleine malaysische Blutegel. Die docken gerne – aufgrund ihres körpereigenen Betäubungsmittels unfühlbar – an den menschlichen Körper an, saugen sich voller Blut und verabschieden sich selbstständig. Am Tatort hinterlassen sie ein Blutverdünnungsmittel, wodurch sofort die Blutung beim Wirt einsetzt und alle eventuellen Schadstoffe ausgewaschen werden. Und weil das so ist, sollte man sie gewähren lassen, bis sie satt sind – das ist der beste Weg, einer Infektion aus dem Wege zu gehen. Nicht schön, aber sinnvoll. Der Dschungel hat eben seine eigenen Gesetze.

Gesetze hin, Gesetze her – kurz darauf kaufe ich für ein insektenfreies Auto in einem malaysischen Tante-Emma-Laden irgendein hochgiftiges Zeug, sprühe es in mein rollendes Domizil, schließe es für eine Stunde luftdicht ab und warte. Ich muss gestehen, klammheimlich freue ich mich auf das Gemetzel im Inneren. Ob ich dabei irgendeine seltene Insektenart auslösche, ist mir letztlich nicht nachzuweisen – gesichert ist dagegen die Erkenntnis, dass später zu Hause die sonst nicht gerade zimperlichen Fahrzeugaufbereiter mit Pinzetten massenhaft fremdartige und vielbeinige Geschöpfe aus den verwegensten Ecken des Autos ziehen werden.

Richtig schlimm aber sind die Hautrötungen, einhergehend mit Juckreiz und Pusteln, die plötzlich die halbe Mannschaft befallen. Da ist selbst der Doc ratlos, denn es gibt keine Regelmäßigkeiten, aus denen sich die Ursache herauslesen lässt. Auch hier erweist sich Köchin Alina als rettender Engel: Sie tippt auf Raupen. Und sie hat recht. Viele Mitreisende sind mit Raupen in Berührung gekommen, die mit feinen, aber giftigen Härchen ausgestattet sind. Durch Kratzen verteilen die Betroffenen die tierische Essenz auf weitere Hautbereiche. Da hilft nur: Ausbaden. Was sich aber nicht überall anbietet. Ich persönlich bade grundsätzlich in keinem Bach, bei dem ich den Grund nicht sehe. Wer weiß, was da noch so alles drin ist …

Did I mention the creatures? We weren't worried about the big stuff, but the little creatures caused us sleepless nights: snakes, spiders, caterpillars and the entire community of crawling, biting, sucking or just plain nerve-wracking insects. These included things I had never seen before, such as the huge wasps that managed to fly into the car attracted by our navigation laptop's display. Or the small Malaysian leeches, which, once attached to the human body, can't be felt thanks to the anaesthetic they inject into you. They suck out as much blood as they can before going on their way, leaving a blood thinner in the bite and thus allowing whatever pollutants or other harmful substances in the body to be washed out – which is a good thing, because it is the most effective way of getting rid of infection. The jungle has its own set of rules.

Rules or not, I wanted an insect-free car and bought the bug equivalent of nerve gas at some Malaysian kiosk, sprayed the car full, closed it for an hour and waited. Of course on the quiet I was looking forward to the insect carnage to come. Whether or not I was responsible for the annihilation of a rare breed of insect is probably difficult to prove now – however, when the vehicles returned to Germany the valets took to using pincers to remove the vast range of exotic bugs and caterpillars that had died a horrible death in the inner confines of the car.

A much bigger problem were the itchy red marks and pustules that seemed to attack the team over night. Even our Doc didn't know where they came from, as there was no uniformity from which one could determine the source. Alina the cook suggested that caterpillars might be the miscreants. And she was right. Many in the team had come into contact with the caterpillars whose fine hairs were full of poisonous fluid. All the host had to do was scratch, thus spreading the fluid to other parts of the body. The only way to treat the problem was to bathe. Baths were at a premium in the jungle, and I have learned never to go bathing where I can't see the ground. You never know whom you might be sharing your bath with.

DER HANG
THE SLOPE

Mit breitem Grinsen quittieren wir das Ende der fast über-menschlichen Dschungeldurchquerung – nicht ahnend, dass Malaysia noch eine Sonderprüfung für uns bereithält. Vom Höhenzug, auf dem wir uns die Matschschlacht lieferten, führt ein schmaler Feldweg runter auf Meeresebene, wo sich unser Endpunkt befindet. Dazwischen liegt ein Gefälle von bis zu 30 Prozent. Zwischen Bäumen und Büschen schlängelt sich der Weg etwa 3 Kilometer ins Tal, mit einem Plateau zum Ausruhen in der Mitte. Schlimm ist allerdings nicht die steile Abfahrt, sondern dass der Weg ebenso nass ist wie der Dschungel vorher und damit spiegelglatt.

Hans probiert es – wie dankenswerterweise so oft – als Erster. Mit seiner Erfahrung am Steuer von Geländewagen schafft er es, seinen Defender mit teils blockierenden Rädern schadlos aufs Plateau zu setzen. Einer Teilnehmerin gelingt es auch noch, unter Einsatz ihres Lebens einen Freelander dort abzustellen, dann brechen wir die Aktion ab: zu gefährlich. Wenn ich nur an die Vier-Tonnen-Ambulanz denke ...

Aber runter müssen wir, es gibt keinen anderen Weg. Also was tun? Ich weise an, alle Kunststoffseile von den Winden zu lösen, die daran angebrachten Haken bis auf einen abzuschneiden und die Enden zusammenzuknoten. Das so entstandene lange Seil schlagen wir zweimal um einen dicken Baumstamm als Umlen-kung, haken es beim ersten Versuchsfahrzeug ein und lassen es mit Muskelkraft und im ersten Gang herunter. Es funktioniert – aber es dauert lange. Zu lange.

Da hat unser Guide Atec eine Idee. Er setzt sich in einen Freelander, fährt langsam auf die steile Stelle zu, lässt sich abkippen, knallt brutal den Rückwärtsgang rein und bremst den Wagen durch volle Pulle Gas ab, bis er ganz unten ist. Die Aktion „Rückwärts-gangbremse" ist ungewöhnlich, sinnvoll aber auch tückenreich, wir können sie also nicht den Teams überlassen. Die Instruktoren bringen auf diese Weise alle Autos ins Tal.

Wundert es jemanden, dass ich auf dieser Tour rund zehn Kilo abnehme? Und bis auf eine Garnitur als Andenken meine völlig verschlammten Klamotten noch vor Ort pulverisiere? Und wir keinen einzigen Offroad-Touristen für eine folgende Experience-Reise in dieses wunderschöne Land finden?

The first jungle crossing, which had demanded almost superhuman qualities of each and every one of us, came to an end, and, not surprisingly, we were full of beans – little did we know that Malaysia had held a little test in store for us. From the range of hills where we had fought in the mud, there was a very narrow track that took us back down to sea level and the end of the tour. With a 30-degree incline. Between trees and bushes, the 2-mile track with a plateau in the middle led all the way down into the valley. The problem, however, wasn't the incline; it was that the track was as wet as the jungle had been, and as slippery as the world-famous Cresta bob run.

Generously as ever, Hans volunteered to go first. Only thanks to his immense experience with four-wheel-drive vehicles and despite occasionally locking up all four wheels on the way, he managed to reach the plateau unscathed. One of the participants also managed to get her Freelander to the plateau, too, though she risked her life doing it. We decided enough was enough. It was simply too dangerous. The thought of taking the four-tonne ambulance down there was terrifying ...

It was the only route down, though, so we had no choice. What could we do? I advised the teams to remove the kinetic ropes from the vehicle winches, to remove all the attached hooks but one, and then to knot them all together. We belayed the rope twice around a large tree and attached the other end with the hook to the first vehicle, which went down the track in first gear, supported by our muscle on the other end of the rope. It worked, but it took too long. Atec, our guide, then had an idea. He climbed into a Freelander, drove to the top of the slope, crawled over the apex, slammed it into reverse and drove forwards down the hill in reverse using engine braking to control the vehicle until he reached the bottom. "Reverse gear braking" was unusual, made sense, but was very risky, so we decided to let the instructors bring the vehicles down the hill.

Would it surprise anybody that I lost ten kilos on this trip, and that – apart from a single shirt I kept as a souvenir – all the rest of my work clothes, which had been completely ruined by the permanent mud bath, were incinerated in Malaysia? Not one paying customer was prepared to book the Experience Tour in this beautiful country. I wonder why.

STEFAN AUER

GEBOREN AM 13.2.1966 | GELERNTER KOCH, BERUFSKRAFTFAHRER, SPRENGMEISTER, SICHERHEITSFACHKRAFT UND SEIT 2004 FLEXIBELSTES LET-TEAMMITGLIED

BORN 13 FEBRUARY 1966 | TRAINED CHEF, TRUCK DRIVER, EXPLOSIVES EXPERT, SECURITY SPECIALIST AND SINCE 2004 THE MOST VERSATILE MAN IN THE LET TEAM

Trägt man als Österreicher das Offroad-Gen von Geburt an in sich?
So ungefähr. Schon früh habe ich Spaß an Offroadern gehabt, besonders in dem damaligen Skigebiet Silvretta Nova. Da musste ich mit Allrad-Lastern hoch auf die Berge, zur Pistenrettung, zum Lawinensprengen, zum Liftbau. Irgendwann war ich dann stellvertretender Pistenchef und fuhr privat einen Puch G. 1997 hab ich an der Camel Trophy teilgenommen, es ging in die Mongolei. Prompt gewann ich mit einem Kollegen die Trophy, und von da an war ich bei den weiteren Camel-Touren als Mitverantwortlicher dabei. Dann lernte ich Dag kennen, und mittlerweile fahre ich jede Tour mit.

Als was?
Als alles. Dag kann mich für fast jede Aufgabe einsetzen. Er kann mich alleine kilometerweit vorneweg schicken, er kann mich als Lumpensammler weit hinten einsetzen, und er weiß, alles funktioniert in seinem Sinne. Zur Not schraube ich auch an den Autos herum, bis sie wieder funktionieren. Ich arbeite nebenbei als Motorradmechaniker, halte eine komplette Fahrzeugflotte in Schuss und habe meinen original Camel-Discovery von 1997 gekauft, um ihn zu restaurieren.

Gibt es etwas, was dich wirklich mal umhaut?
Nicht viel. Mein Albtraum ist eigentlich nur Schlafmangel. Wenn ich mal zwei Nächte hintereinander nur etwa zwei bis drei Stunden Schlaf bekomme, werde ich etwas grantig ...

Was hat dich auf den diversen Touren besonders beeindruckt?
Neben ein paar wirklich herausfordernden Streckenabschnitten wie der matschglatten steilen Piste in Malaysia oder der Strecke durch den Krater in Argentinien bei pechschwarzer Nacht war es ein Ausflug mit der malaysischen Köchin Alina auf einen Markt der Einheimischen in Kuala Lumpur. Als gelernter Koch war ich fasziniert von dem großen Angebot und besonders von den noch völlig unausgenommenen Tieren, die da bei 100 Prozent Luftfeuchtigkeit und 45 Grad herumlagen.

Hast du ein Rezept, in solchen Situationen auf alle Fälle gesund zu bleiben?
Klar! Am besten morgens einen Schluck selbst gebrannten Enzianschnaps. Wenn das nicht geht: Cognac oder Wodka tun's auch. Selbst abends.

Is it fair to say that Austrians are born with an off-road gene?
Pretty much. I was into off-roading from an early age, particularly in the Silvretta Nova skiing region. I had to take four-wheel-drive trucks into the mountains, as part of the mountain rescue team as well as to support avalanche blasting and ski lift construction. I became head of the ski piste team. Privately I ran a Puch G. In 1997, I took part in the Camel Trophy, which was in Mongolia that year, and won the event with a colleague. From then on I was part of the organization team for all subsequent Camel Trophy events. I got to know Dag and have accompanied every tour ever since.

Doing what?
Everything. Dag can put me on almost every task. He can send me miles up front on my own, I can play tail-end-charlie at the back, and he knows he can rely on me. If necessary, I know a thing or two about the vehicles and can get them going again. I also work as a motorcycle mechanic, keep a complete vehicle fleet on the road and bought my original Camel Trophy Discovery from 1997 with the intention of restoring it.

Is there anything that really gets you down?
Not much. My personal nightmare is lack of sleep. A couple of nights, in succession where I only get two or three hours make me a little grumpy ...

What has impressed you most on all the tours?
Alongside a couple of really challenging sections such as the slippery slope in Malaysia or the crater drive in the dead of night in Argentina, I think what impressed me most was a trip to the local food market in Kuala Lumpur with our Malaysian cook Alina. As a trained cook, I was fascinated by what was on offer, and by the uneviscerated animals which were everywhere in the 100 per cent humidity and 45-degree-Celsius heat (113 degrees Fahrenheit).

What is the secret to staying healthy in those circumstances?
Simple! Every morning I have a drink of homemade gentian schnapps. If that isn't available, then cognac or vodka works, too. Even at night.

BOLIVIEN

BOLIVIA

2011

2011
LAND: BOLIVIEN
STRECKE: 1 650 KM
COUNTRY: BOLIVIA
DISTANCE: 1,000 MILES

12 DEFENDER, 1 AMBULANCE DISCOVERY

DER DEFENDER
THE DEFENDER

War Malaysia zu hart? Zumindest sind einige der Teilnehmer an die Grenzen ihrer Kräfte gekommen. Vielleicht ist Südamerika berechenbarer? Klar, Australien ist wieder in der Lostrommel, und zur Abwechslung mal Äthiopien. Aber es wird Bolivien. Ich glaube, das Land ist etwas sanfter als Malaysia, aber mit genug Abenteuerpotenzial ausgestattet.

Sofort kommt die Frage: Ist das Land sicher genug? Südamerikanische Mafia, hohe Kriminalität und ein kaum berechenbarer Präsident – ich beschließe, Bolivien ist sicher. Und die Teamfahrzeuge sollen Defender sein, weil das Modell nun einen neuen Motor unter der Haube hat. Es wird Zeit, Land Rovers Urvieh mal wieder auf große Tour zu schicken.

Den richtigen Guide zieht Hans aus dem Ärmel: Ciro, Sohn eines bolivianischen Minenbesitzers, gebürtiger Bolivianer mit nordamerikanischem Pass. Den hat Hans im Urlaub kennengelernt. Da wir dringend einen Defender für Fotos in Bolivien brauchen, um ein bisschen für die Tour zu werben, wird Ciro als Erstes beauftragt, einen zu mieten. Wir wollen unterdessen unsere eigene Defender-Flotte aus Deutschland zum Seehafen im chilenischen Arica entsenden, um sie dann auf dem Landweg nach Bolivien temporär einzuführen – Bolivien selbst besitzt keinen Zugang zum Meer. Alles tolle Ideen. Bis auf die Tatsache, dass Ciro weder einen Wagen zum Mieten noch einen zum Leihen findet. Ich disponiere kurzfristig um: Er soll einen gebrauchten Landy kaufen.

Nach erschreckend langer Suche findet Ciro in Santa Cruz de la Sierra tatsächlich ein leidlich brauchbares Exemplar und begibt sich auf den Weg nach Cochabamba, zum Startort der neuen Tour sowie Hans' und meinem momentanen Aufenthaltsort. Doch Ciro kommt samt Auto schließlich auf einem Anhänger an. Die Karre ist schon auf diesem kurzen Weg verreckt. Freundlicher ausgedrückt: Der TDI-Motor des sehr gebrauchten Solihullers hatte bereits auf dieser Fahrt Aussetzer. Ich teste sofort den alten Wagen. Er springt an und läuft leidlich rund, aber es wird auch deutlich: Es fehlt Leistung. Keine gute Voraussetzung für Fotofahrten in der am höchsten gelegenen Großstadt der Welt, La Paz (auf 4 000 Metern). Dort denkt man ja schon, wenn man aus dem Flugzeug steigt, man hätte auf nüchternen Magen und auf ex drei große Gläser Champagner getrunken. Der magere Sauerstoff-gehalt der Luft euphorisiert einen tagsüber ein bisschen, und nachts kann man nicht schlafen.

Was Malaysia too tough? Some of the participants were well and truly at the end of their tether by the end of the tour. Perhaps the risks in South America were easier to calculate? Australia was back on the agenda, and there was even talk about going to Ethiopia. However, Bolivia got the vote. I thought the country would be easier going than Malaysia while still being able to offer enough adventure.

The first questions came soon enough: was the country sufficiently safe? South American mafia, a high crime rate and an unpredictable president – I decided Bolivia was safe. The teams would get Defenders, as it had just received a new engine. It was time to send Land Rover's original back on tour.

Once again, Hans had another ace up his sleeve – this time it was the perfect guide. Ciro was the son of a Bolivian mine owner; a native Bolivian, but with a US passport. Hans had met him on holiday. As we urgently needed a Defender for a photo shoot in Bolivia to do the usual pre-tour publicity, it was Ciro's first assignment to rent one. Meanwhile, we had also decided to ship our own Defender fleet from Germany to the deep-sea port of Arica in Chile, from whence we would import the vehicles overland into Bolivia on temporary papers, as Bolivia has no coastline. All very good ideas, except that Ciro wasn't able to rent or even borrow a Land Rover. We changed plans and told him to buy a used Defender.

After a painfully long search, Ciro found a reasonably usable vehicle in Santa Cruz de la Sierra, and immediately headed to Cochabamba, which was both where we would be starting the new tour and where Hans and I were staying. Ciro turned up, however, with the Defender on the back of a flatbed truck. The Landy had already conked out on the short trip from the capital. The truth was that the TDI engine of the rather long-in-the-tooth Solihull legend had suffered a number of misfires. I tested the vehicle immediately. It started and ran reasonably enough on tickover, but it was obvious that it was down on performance, which did not bode well for a photo shoot in the highest capital city on the planet, La Paz (13,000 feet). When you arrive in La Paz and walk off the plane, it feels as if you've just knocked back a bottle of champagne on an empty stomach. The thin oxygen produces a permanent sense of euphoria during the daytime, and at night you can't sleep.

DER DEFENER
THE DEFENDER

Aber wer kann hier in Cochabamba mal eben einen Defender-Motor reparieren? Land Rover leider nicht – ist hier nicht offiziell vertreten. Freie Autowerkstätten? Die winken ab: Japanische Massenware kriegen sie hin, aber so eine englische Wertarbeit dann doch nicht. Der VW-Händler? Zuckt freundlich mit den Achseln. Vielleicht die Lkw-Schrauber um die Ecke? Tatsächlich. Deren Antwort: „Kein Problem."

Völlig unkompliziert checken sie sofort den Kompressionsdruck, stellen fest, dass er nicht vorhanden ist, und beginnen, den Motor zu zerlegen. Über neue Kolben, Kolbenringe und so weiter sollen wir uns keine Gedanken machen, teilen sie uns mit. Ebenso seien die Kosten völlig überschaubar. Sagen sie mit dem Augenaufschlag eines anhänglichen Cockerspaniels.

Mit mulmigem Gefühl, aber in der Gewissheit, wenig Zeit, keine Wahl und den Zwang zum Vertrauen zu haben und deshalb auf die Truckerversprechen angewiesen zu sein, verziehen wir uns in ein Hotel. Um abends gegen 20 Uhr wieder in der Werkstatt aufzutauchen. Vertrauen ist gut, Kontrolle ist besser, deutsche Gründlichkeit ist am allerbesten.

Mir stockt der Atem: Der Motor liegt in gefühlten 1 000 Einzelteilen auf dem Boden – ohne dass der Block ausgebaut worden ist. Ein bolivianischer Feinmotoriker steht breitbeinig auf den Vorderkotflügeln und hont mit einer Bohrmaschine die Brennräume. Ein zweiter sinniert darüber, wo man übergroße Kolben herbekommen kann. Und ein dritter kümmert sich um die Ventile, die Ventilsitze und die Kurbelwelle – was das genau bedeutet, ist nicht so richtig ersichtlich. Mit noch gemischteren Gefühlen als zuvor verziehen wir uns für eine unruhige Nacht wieder ins Hotel.

Morgens Punkt 8 Uhr stehen wir wieder bei den Truckerschraubern auf der Matte: Der Wagen ist fertig. Der Motor läuft. Sauber und rund. Wir werden gebeten, zwei Stunden durch die Stadt zu cruisen, um den Motor einzufahren, und dann für einen Ölwechsel wiederzukommen. Der Preis für diese perfekte Arbeit: 500 Euro. Ich würde jederzeit wieder eines meiner vielen Tourenfahrzeuge bei den „Steh-Honern" in Cochabamba reparieren lassen!

We needed to find someone in Cochabamba who could repair the Defender's TDI engine. Land Rover was out of the question – there was no official dealership here. Independent workshops ran a mile. Japanese products, yes – an exotic Brit? No way. The VW dealer? He just smiled and shrugged his shoulders. What about the truck repair place round the corner? Their answer was a remarkable "No problem".

With out any ado, they checked the compression (there wasn't any) and then started to take the engine apart. We wouldn't have to worry about pistons, rings and such, and the costs wouldn't be exorbitant, either – and all this with the grateful look of a loyal cocker spaniel who has just been given a bone ...

With a sense of unease but also the realization that we had neither the time nor a choice and therefore had to trust the truck repairman, we found a hotel only to return to the workshop at 8 o'clock that night. Better safe than sorry and all that, and the meticulousness of the Germans is the best guarantee of all.

I had to fight for breath. It looked as if the motor had been reduced to a sea of 1,000 parts on the floor, not counting the block, which was still in the engine bay. A Bolivian "specialist" straddled the front wings using a drill to grind down the combustion chambers. Another technician was considering where to get hold of larger pistons, while a third was working on the valves, the valve seats and the crankshaft. What it actually all meant was not exactly clear. With more mixed feelings, we trudged back to the hotel with the prospect of an unruly night ahead of us.

The following morning at 8 o'clock on the dot we were back at the workshop. The vehicle was ready. The engine was running and sounded smooth. We were asked to spend two hours cruising around town, and then to come back to change the oil. The cost of perfection? $ 580 (£ 440).

I would repair any of my expedition vehicles at the "straddling grinders" in Cochabamba.

DAS SÜDAMERIKANISCHE LAND BIETET ALLES, WAS DAS OFFROADER-HERZ BEGEHRT: ENGE SCHOTTERPISTEN, EINSAME WEGE BIS IN DIE WOLKEN UND NATÜRLICH WASSERDURCHFAHRTEN.
--
THIS SOUTH AMERICAN COUNTRY HAS EVERYTHING AN OFF-ROADER HAS EVER DREAMED OF: NARROW GRAVEL ROADS, LONELY TRAILS INTO THE CLOUDS AND RIVER CROSSINGS.

DAS GESETZ
THE LAW

Die erste Fahrt durch Bolivien mit dem Foto-Defender überzeugt mich bereits, das richtige Land gewählt zu haben. Dennoch kommen mir die Haupt- und Nebenstraßen noch ein wenig soft vor. Doch wir werden schon die richtigen Pisten finden.

Allerdings brauchen wir dringend unsere Autos, und die stecken mal wieder fest. Und zwar in Arica. Was wir beim Verschiffen nicht bedacht haben: Es gibt ein bolivianisches Gesetz, das es nur Dieselfahrzeugen mit Motoren mit mehr als 4 Liter Hubraum erlaubt, ins Land einzureisen. Der wunderbare Defender-Motor glänzt in Deutschland aber mit einem sparsamen 2,4-Liter-Diesel, was die bolivianischen Zöllner in keinster Weise erweicht.

Hätten wir von dem uns völlig sinnlos erscheinenden Gesetz vorher erfahren, hätten wir schon bei der Verschiffung in Deutschland die Wagenpapiere (illegal, aber zeitsparend) auf 4 Liter Hubraum umgeschrieben. So ähnlich hatte es übrigens auch der Erstbesitzer des Defender gemacht, dessen Wagen wir in Bolivien gekauft haben: Die Bastelbude besitzt angeblich 4,1 Liter Hubraum. Klar, hier passt man einfach die Papiere an die Gesetze an. Die Vorschrift soll übrigens vermeiden, dass sich viele Menschen Autos mit kleinen Diesel-hubräumen kaufen – in der Hoffnung, dass sich große sowieso niemand leisten kann. So sehr ich auch dieses Gesetz drehe und wende, ich finde keine Lücke. Damit stecken nun alle Autos fest. Auch die Ambulanz, die immerhin mit 3 Litern Hubraum ausgestattet ist.

Es bleibt mir nichts anderes übrig, als mir geduldig, aber nachdrücklich den Weg zum Volkspräsidenten Evo Morales freizuquatschen. Der hat einst unser Tour-Vorhaben genehmigt und sich davor sogar für die Durchführung einer Dakar-Rallye in seinem Land starkgemacht. Ciro schafft es tatsächlich bis in die oberste Etage der Regierungsebene. Als der Präsident von unserem Debakel erfährt, erlässt er sofort eine „Lex Land Rover": „Ley 830" besagt, dass Land Rover ein Jahr lang Fahrzeuge einführen darf, die nicht an einen bestimmten Fahrer gebunden sind und die weniger als 4 Liter Hubraum aufweisen dürfen.

Our first journey with the photo-shoot Defender across Bolivia convinced me that we had made the right decision to come here. While the main and secondary roads seemed a little soft for our purposes, I was convinced we would ultimately find the right routes.

We urgently needed our own vehicles – and of course, once again, they were stuck in customs in the port of Arica. When we drew up the shipping papers, we had overlooked one important point. Under Bolivian law, only diesel-engine vehicles with a capacity of more than 4 litres may be imported into the country. The extremely efficient Defender engine performs brilliantly in Germany and elsewhere in the world with a capacity of just 2.4 litres; still, the Bolivian customs officials would not yield.

Had we known about the law beforehand (a law, by the way, that appeared to make no sense whatsoever) we could have modified the vehicle documentation accordingly, thus giving the Defenders 4-litre engines. This is illegal, but it saves time. It was also how the Defender we were already running in Bolivia had been purchased by its first owner to begin with. According to its paperwork, it had a 4.1-litre engine. In Bolivia, people adjust the paperwork to fit the law. The legislation is designed to prevent people from buying cars with small diesel engines in hopes that nobody can afford to buy larger diesel engines. The more I looked at this law, the less I saw any way of getting around it. And it meant that all our vehicles were stuck – including the ambulance, which at least had 3 litres under the bonnet.

My only chance was to remain patient and approach President Evo Morales directly. He had originally given us his approval to run the tour in Bolivia in the first place and had personally supported the Dakar rally raid in his country. Ciro managed to reach the top level of government, and when the President heard of our problem, he enacted a "Lex Land Rover" – "Ley 830" – that provided for the import of our vehicles for one year, vehicles that were not legally linked to any one specific driver and that could be under 4 litres in capacity.

DIE BLOCKADE
THE BLOCKING

Natürlich finden wir auf der Vortour die abenteuerlichsten Routen. Enttäuscht bin ich allerdings vom „Camino de la Muerte", der „Todesstraße", einst die angeblich gefährlichste Straße der Welt. Weil es inzwischen eine Umgehungsstraße gibt, sind das Gefährlichste heute Fahrradfahrer, die die Straße als sportliche Abfahrt sehen, sowie von Cocablättern vollgedröhnte Einheimische auf dem Motorrad, die weiß der Himmel wohin unterwegs sind.

Eine Herausforderung ist die Straße zumindest nicht für uns. Bis auf den Schreckmoment, als einer der oben beschriebenen Bolivianer mit seinem Zweirad hinten auf meinen Defender auffährt und ich ihn schon im unendlichen Abgrund wähne. Als ich ihn dort nicht erblicke, schaue ich hinters Auto. Da liegt er unter seinem Motorrad, grinst, platziert einen dicken Packen Cocablattmatsch zurück in die rechte Wange, faselt etwas von „Sorry, Sorry", schwingt sich wieder auf sein Gefährt und wankt weiter den Berg hinunter. Die Zeiten, in denen sich begegnende Autos so gegenseitig wie regelmäßig in den Abgrund schubsten, sind definitiv vorbei.

Aber wir finden trotz der ungenauen russischen Generalstabskarten und dank der Mithilfe grünzahniger Cocabauern, die wir über etliche Andenkilometer als Kurzzeit-Lokalguides mitnehmen, doch noch perfekte Experience-Wege – oft Minentracks. Die sind extrem schmal, bestehen aus Schotter, und die Spitzkehren sind teilweise so eng, dass wir mit den Defendern rangieren müssen. Und das ist kein Spaß. Links begrenzt eine mindestens 1 000 Meter hohe Felswand den Spielraum, rechts ein gut 1 000 Meter tiefer Abgrund. Wie gesagt: Der Camino de la Muerte ist dagegen eine Touristenattraktion für Pauschalreisende. Ich muss aber gestehen, ich baue die Straße trotzdem in die Haupttour ein. Allein schon wegen ihres Namens.

Während wir solche fahrerischen Herausforderungen selbst im Griff haben, sind wir gegen eine typisch bolivianische Protestart nahezu machtlos: Blockaden. Die hat Evo Morales erfunden, als er noch nicht Staatsoberhaupt war. Und die wenden nun unzufriedene Dorfbewohner gegen ihn selbst an. Das Prinzip ist einfach: Da es nicht so viele Straßen gibt, blockiert man bei allgemeiner politischer Unzufriedenheit die wichtigen (und manchmal auch unwichtigen) Zufahrts-, Durchfahrts-, Haupt- und Nebenstraßen durch Steine, Felsen oder Menschen. Die Folge: Eine ganze Region wird von Nachschub aller Art abgeschnitten. Zum Beispiel Kraftstoff. Oder Nahrungsmittel. Oder Unterhaltungselektronik. Völlig egal – irgendjemand wird sich schon ärgern und bei den Obersten in der Regierungshauptstadt La Paz anklopfen.

Natürlich geraten auch wir auf der Vortour in so eine Blockade. Ein ganzes Dorf ist auf den Beinen, und so ein Konvoi von vier Defendern (ohne Beulen, mit Aufschriften, gut ausgerüstet) kann keinen Einheimischen gehören. Also entweder Ausländer oder Regierungsfahrzeuge – Grund genug, sie aufzuhalten. Sofort stehen Hunderte von Menschen um uns. Guide Ciro dolmetscht das bolivianische Spanisch: mal wieder allgemeine Unzufriedenheit. Aha. Und als die Blockierer erkennen, dass wir eine Filmkamera im Gepäck haben, wünscht sich der Bürgermeister freundlich, aber nachdrücklich ein Fernsehinterview. So postieren wir die Landys als Lichtgeber um den Platz an der Hauptstraße herum, und Land-Rover-Marketingchef Christian Uhrig diskutiert eine halbe Stunde mit dem aufgeregten Dorfchef. Ciro vermittelt dabei immer diplomatisch. Mit der Zusage, das aufgenommene Gespräch bei einem deutschen Fernsehsender abzugeben, lässt uns die zwar nicht bedrohlich wirkende, aber doch deutlich in der Mehrzahl befindliche Menge ziehen.

Ich muss gestehen, wir finden nicht die Zeit, den Sender zu besuchen.

Of course, we were able to find the most challenging routes on the pre-scout recce. I personally was disappointed by the "Camino de la Muerte" or "Road of Death" that was allegedly once the most dangerous road on the planet. As it has since been bypassed, the most dangerous things left on the road are cyclists who view the route as a sporting downhill run and motorbiking locals high on coca leaves who are probably just out for the buzz.

The road is certainly no longer a challenge for us. That is, it wasn't until the moment one of the aforementioned locals rammed my Defender from behind with his motorbike. He suddenly disappeared from view, and in my mind's eye I could see him heading to a better place. I jumped out of the Defender and saw him lying on the road underneath his bike, grinning as he pushed another wad of coca leaves into his mouth. He mumbled "sorry, sorry," jumped back on his bike and headed down the mountain. One thing is certain, however: the days when one vehicle would shove another over the edge and into the abyss on a regular basis were well and truly over.

Nevertheless, despite our inaccurate Russian military maps, and thanks to the help of countless green-toothed coca farmers whom we consulted over many miles in the Andes as short-term guides, we were able to find routes (often mining roads) that suited the Experience Tour perfectly. Narrow, gravel roads with switchbacks so tight that taking a Defender through the corner nearly required a three-point turn every time. And it was no joke. To the left, a massive 3,000-foot wall of rock; to the right, a 3,000-foot drop, with nothing in-between. By comparison, the Camino de la Muerte was a walk in the park for tourists. Anyway, the famous road is part of the tour simply because of the name.

While we can control the driver-challenge aspect of the tour, we are completely helpless when faced with the common form of Bolivian protest: the roadblock – a method Evo Morales himself invented before he rose to power and that dissatisfied villagers now use against him. The idea is as simple as it is effective. Where roads are few, political dissatisfaction is expressed by blocking the major arterial (and sometimes the less important) routes, access roads and bypasses with stones, boulders and even people. As a result, a whole region can be cut off from all manner of supplies, be it fuel, food or even electronic goods. Somebody is always bothered enough to knock on the door of the head of the government in La Paz.

On the pre-scout recce, we ran into just such a protest. The whole village was on its feet, and it was obvious that our four Defenders – which lacked dents, were covered in logos and were obviously well equipped – didn't belong to locals. I.e., we were either foreigners or the government, and either way, that was reason enough to keep us there.

In an instant, we were surrounded by hundreds of people. Ciro translated from Bolivian Spanish. Once again, the issue was general dissatisfaction with the way the country was being run. And the protesters noticed that we had a camera team on board – now the mayor made it clear in friendly but firm terms that he wanted a TV interview. We positioned the Land Rovers alongside the main road, where they could provide light, and Land Rover's head of marketing Christian Uhrig debated for half an hour with the agitated mayor. Ciro played the perfect diplomatic middleman. Having agreed to pass on the material to a German TV broadcaster, the crowd, which hadn't appeared threatening but nevertheless outnumbered us considerably, allowed us to continue on our way. As it happens, we never found the time to visit a German broadcaster.

DIE TOUR LEBT NICHT NUR VON UNGLAUBLICHEN LANDSCHAFTEN, SONDERN AUCH VON BEGEGNUNGEN DER MENSCHLICHEN ART. SEIEN ES NUN ANDERE MOTORISIERTE GRUPPEN, BAUERN BEIM PFLANZEN VON COCA-STRÄUCHERN ODER EINHEIMISCHE KINDER – DIE NEUGIER, WAS DER ANDERE SO MACHT, IST STETS AUF BEIDEN SEITEN GROSS.
--
THE TOUR LIVES FROM MORE THAN JUST UNBELIEVABLE LANDSCAPES. IT THRIVES ON THE PEOPLE YOU MEET ON THE WAY, WHETHER THEY ARE OTHER GLOBETROTTERS, FARMERS PLANTING THEIR COCA CROPS OR LOCAL CHILDREN – THE DESIRE TO DISCOVER HOW THE OTHER PERSON LIVES IS OVERWHELMING FOR BOTH.

DER KRAFTSTOFF
THE FUEL

Eine Folge von solchen Blockaden ist natürlich auch Kraftstoffmangel. Für uns als Autofahrer durchaus ein Kriterium, das wir in die Planungen einbeziehen müssen. Dazu sollte man wissen: Diesel ist in Bolivien ein durchaus gängiger Kraftstoff. Aber wer den Dieselnachschub stoppt, legt Lastwagen lahm. Und alle anderen Dieselfahrzeuge auch. Es sei denn, sie sind Teil der Land Rover Experience Tour.

Aber es gehört schon ein gewisses Geschick dazu, an das bei Blockaden so kostbare Nass zu gelangen. Ciro verrät uns, dass es sich viele Bolivianer zum Volkssport gemacht haben, Kraftstoff in alten Olivenölfässern, in Essig-kanistern oder anderen Behältern zu bunkern. Wir müssen diese Menschen nur finden – und ihnen genug für ihren Schatz bieten. Dann greifen sie zu Schläuchen, schaffen durch die altbekannte Methode des Ansaugens Unter-druck, spucken den ersten Schluck aus und füllen die Tanks.

Der findige Mitarbeiter einer Baufahrzeugfirma kommt auf eine sehr lukrative Idee, uns das Selbstzündungsgebräu zu verschaffen. Er knackt den halbvollen Dieseltank des Caterpillar-Frontladers seines Chefs und füttert mit dem Stoff unsere Defender. Dafür müssen wir ihm versprechen (außer einer gewissen Summe, die sofort in bar zu entrichten ist), ihm für seinen persönlichen Defender auf der Haupttour Ersatzteile mitzubringen. Was ich natürlich auch tue. Ich bleibe nirgendwo lange, aber auch niemandem etwas schuldig.

Apropos mitbringen: Aufgrund dieser Sprit-Erfahrung der Vortour bauen wir in Deutschland auf einen neu gekauften Anhänger einen ebenso neu erwor-benen 1000-Liter-Tank mit den passenden Ventilen, um in Bolivien immer Diesel mitführen zu können. Die Einfuhr des Bausatzes ins Land ist unter anderem dank „Ley 830" nicht das Problem, aber die Straßenzustände und die Höhe umso mehr. Hänger und Zugfahrzeug kommen an ihre Grenzen, der Tank an sich aber leider auch. Denn was wir nicht bedacht haben: Bei großer Höhe dehnt sich der Kraftstoff extrem aus. Direkt vor einer Ortseinfahrt meldet sich das Überlaufventil: Diesel fließt den Plastiktank herab. Sofort lasse ich den Konvoi stoppen, in Windeseile muss jedes Fahrzeug rückwärts zum Anhänger rangieren und tanken. Tatsächlich erreicht kaum Kraftstoff den Boden.

One consequence of the roadblock tactic was the obvious shortage of fuel. It is also something we had to consider as part of the planning process. It was important to know the following: diesel is certainly a common fuel in Bolivia. But anyone in a position to interrupt the supply of diesel can prevent trucks and other diesel-powered vehicles from moving – unless, of course, those vehicles are clever enough to be part of the Land Rover Experience Tour.

Still, with roadblocks everywhere, finding juice calls for a certain skill. Ciro explained to us that it had become something of a national pastime in Bolivia, with people storing diesel in old olive oil kegs, vinegar canisters or whatever else they could get their hands on. We just needed to find these people and offer them enough cash to part with their treasure – the rest was easy: an old hose, create a vacuum by sucking up the first drops, spit it out and Bob's your uncle – fuel in the tank.

A clever employee at a construction company came up with a particularly lucrative way of providing us with diesel. He broke the lock on the tank of his boss's Caterpillar front loader, which was half full, and filled up our Defenders. The deal was (apart from an immediate cash-in-hand payment) that we bring him over some spare parts for his own Defender when we returned on the main event. Which we duly did. Wherever I go, I pay my debts as soon as I can.

Speaking of bringing things over: after the constant search for fuel on the pre-scout, once we were back in Germany we decided to build a 1,000-litre tanker trailer equipped with the right valves to enable us to carry more fuel. Thanks to our special piece of legislation, "Ley 830", importing the trailer kit into Bolivia wasn't a problem, but the condition of the roads and the altitude would give us difficulties. The trailer and the towing unit were on the limit as far as weight was concerned, and the tank had another problem, for we had forgotten the effect altitude had on diesel fuel – namely expansion. As we were about to enter a village, the overflow valve on the tank began to drip. I stopped the convoy immediately and filled up as many of the tour vehicles as quickly as we could. Fortunately, we managed to avoid spilling almost any diesel.

BUNT GEHT'S ZU IN DEN DÖRFERN UND STÄDTEN BOLIVIENS. DIE FRUCHTBAREN GEGENDEN SORGEN FÜR REICHLICH OBST UND GEMÜSE. ÜBRIGENS: DER SITZ DES HUTES NAMENS „BOMBÍN" ZEIGT AN, OB DIE DAME VERHEIRATET IST ODER NICHT – SAGT MAN IN LA PAZ. SITZT ER SCHRÄG, IST SIE NOCH ZU HABEN ...

--

LIFE IN THE VILLAGES AND TOWNS OF BOLIVIA IS A FEAST OF COLOUR. FERTILE REGIONS PROVIDE RICH HARVESTS OF FRUIT AND VEGETABLES. OH, AND BY THE WAY, IN LA PAZ ONE SAYS THE WAY A "BOMBÍN" HAT IS WORN REFLECTS WHETHER OR NOT THE LADY IS MARRIED. IF THE HAT IS

DIE SCHWESTER
THE NUN

Independencia taucht ziemlich unvermittelt in Boliviens Hochland auf, gleich hinter einer Biegung eines Reifen mordenden Schotterweges. Ich sehe Hunderte grauer Dächer plötzlich im Nirgendwo zwischen Cochabamba und La Paz. Ein Blick genügt, um zu wissen: Hier auf 17 Grad, 8 Minuten und 4 Sekunden südlicher Länge und 66 Grad, 56 Minuten und 40 Sekunden westlicher Breite gibt es keinen Reichtum.

Deswegen ist Caritas-Schwester Verena Birnbacher für die Bolivianer fast eine Heilige. Und sie ist genau so, wie man sich jemanden vorstellt, der sein Leben der Nächstenliebe verschrieben hat. Wir lernen Schwester Verena – natürlich – völlig zufällig kennen. Unser Guide Ciro hat auf der Vortour seine alte Schule San Bonifacio in Independencia besucht, die von der Bundesverdienstkreuzträgerin geleitet wird. Schwester Verena war früh aus Deutschland nach Bolivien ausgewandert und hat hier die Schule für Jungen und Mädchen gegründet. Es ist eine Art freiwilliges Internat. Die Kinder aus dem Umland müssen manchmal bis zu drei Stunden zu Fuß gehen, um ihre Schule zu erreichen. Bolivien gilt als ärmstes und exportschwächstes Land Südamerikas, zwei Drittel der Einwohner leben in Armut, 40 Prozent besitzen sogar so gut wie gar nichts. Darunter leiden besonders die Kinder – ohne Bildung haben sie keine Chance auf ein würdevolles Leben.

Mit Elan und Eigeninitiative hat Schwester Verena alles selber aufgebaut. Was stets fehlt, ist Geld. Die Schwestern, Helfer und Sozialarbeiter führen uns herum, mitten in den Unterricht im Mädcheninternat. Es war einst ein reines Jungeninternat, das 1969 fertiggestellt wurde. Zwei Jahre später eröffnete hier das Heim Papa Juan XXIII für die Aus- und Fortbildung von Katechisten. 1974 weihten die Verantwortlichen dann das Mädcheninternat Santa Elisabet ein, weil Frauenbildung noch immer ein Fremdwort in Bolivien war. Ende der 70er Jahre hat man ein Studienkreditsystem eingeführt. So wurden bis heute mehr als 300 Lehrer, Ärzte, Ingenieure, Techniker, Schneiderinnen für ihren Beruf qualifiziert, die nun durch Rückzahlungen anderen Kindern die Ausbildung ermöglichen. 2007 fasste man alle Einrichtungen als Stiftung „Fundación Centro Social San Bonifacio" zusammen, in der heute mehr als 1 200 junge Menschen lernen.

Die Schule lebt nur von Spenden der Kirche, von denen sie sogar noch einen Teil an die Kinder weitergibt und ihnen Klamotten kauft. Für mich ist es eine Selbstverständlichkeit, dass wir sie besuchen und einen Scheck dalassen. Doch Land Rover geht noch weiter und unterstützt mit fünf Euro pro Bewerber der Bolivien-Tour das bolivianische Rote Kreuz. Aber nicht nur das: In Deutschland hatte Schwester Verena eine Auszeichnung verliehen bekommen. Das Problem: Sie konnte sie nicht wirklich entgegennehmen, die Anerkennung bestand aus einer 200 Kilo schweren Gedenktafel. Und die ohne Begleitung von Deutschland nach Bolivien schicken? Sie wäre wahrscheinlich nie durch den Zoll gekommen. Natürlich haben wir das gute Stück in Deutschland gut verpackt, ins Land geschmuggelt und an Schwester Verena übergeben.

Behind a curve, while driving along the tyre-killing gravel roads in Bolivia's highlands, we stumbled across the town of Independencia. In this no-man's-land between La Paz and Cochabamba, we were suddenly confronted by a sea of grey roofs. My first thoughts were that behind the coordinates 17 degrees, 8 minutes and 4 seconds south and 66 degrees, 56 minutes and 40 seconds west was a lot of poverty.

As far as the Bolivians are concerned, Sister Verena Birnbacher, who works for the Caritas aid organization, is almost a saint. She is the living embodiment of the concept of charitable spirit. We met her purely by chance. On the pre-scout recce, our guide Ciro had visited his old school San Bonifacio in Independencia, which is run by the wearer of the Order of Merit of the Federal Republic of Germany, Sister Verena. When she was younger, she had emigrated from Germany to Bolivia, founding the school for young boys and girls. It is a form of voluntary boarding school. The children from the surrounding region have to walk for up to three hours in order to get to school. Bolivia is the poorest country in South America, with the weakest export economy. Two-thirds of the population live in poverty, 40 per cent have nothing that they can call their own. Children are the ones who suffer most in this environment, as without any education they have no chance whatsoever of improving their situation.

Sister Verena had displayed considerable elan and resourcefulness in getting the project off the ground at all – however, she needed financial support. The nuns, assistants and social workers showed us around the school while lessons were being conducted in the girls' boarding school. Built in 1969, it was initially an all-boys' boarding school. Two years later, the Pope John XXIII home for the training and further education of catechists was founded. In 1974, they opened the girls' boarding school, Santa Elisabet, at a time when education for girls and women was still unheard-of in Bolivia. By the end of the 1970s, a course credit system had been introduced. As of today, over 300 teachers, doctors, engineers and seamstresses have qualified in their respective careers and by putting money back into the school are enabling other children to benefit from an education. In 2007, the whole complex which today houses over 1,200 students, was reorganized as a charitable trust: the "Fundación Centro Social San Bonifacio".

The school lives from church donations, some of which are allocated directly to clothing for the children. It goes without saying that we wanted to pay them a visit and also make a donation. We went one step further – for every applicant on the tour, Land Rover donated five euros to the Bolivian Red Cross. There was something else, however. Sister Verena had received an award in Germany, a commemorative plaque weighing 440 lbs., but it had been impossible for her to come to Germany to take it back to Bolivia. Sending it via post to Bolivia was out of the question, as it would probably never make it through customs. We packed it well in Germany, smuggled it through ourselves and personally presented it to Sister Verena in Bolivia.

ES GIBT KEINE KURVE IM BOLIVIANISCHEN HOCHLAND, NACH DER EINEM NICHT DER ATEM STOCKT. DAS LIEGT NUR ZUM TEIL AN HÖHEN BIS ÜBER 5 000 METER; MEISTENS IST ES DER AUSBLICK, DER EINEN FESSELT. DASS DIE AUTOS WEGEN DER HÖHENLUFT AUCH LEISTUNG VERLIEREN, IST DA VÖLLIG ZWEITRANGIG – SO KANN MAN DEN WEITBLICK LÄNGER GENIESSEN.

--

ALL OF THE CURVES OR SWITCHBACKS IN THE BOLIVIAN HIGHLANDS CAN BE DESCRIBED AS BREATHTAKING. IT IS PARTLY A CONSEQUENCE OF BEING AT WELL OVER 16,000 FEET, BUT IN THE MAIN IT REFERS TO THE VIEWS, WHICH ARE SIMPLY ENTHRALLING. WHAT DOES IT MATTER THAT THE ALTITUDE AFFECTS THE VEHICLES' PERFORMANCE? YOU HAVE MORE TIME TO ENJOY THE VIEW AS A RESULT.

DER STEIN
THE STONE

Wir haben schon viele ungewöhnliche Städte gesehen, aber La Paz sticht ganz deutlich hervor. Zwei Gründe als Beispiel: Zunächst ist da die beachtliche Zahl von getrockneten Lama-Föten auf dem Hexenmarkt. Hier gibt es nicht nur Pülverchen aller Art, bei denen der aufgeklärte Europäer gar nicht wissen will, wogegen und woraus das Zeug ist, sondern auch diese staubtrockenen Tierkadaver, die einen aus hohlen Augen anblicken. Für die Bolivianer sind das Glücksbringer. Man vergräbt vor dem Hausbau in jeder Ecke des künftigen Gebäudes eines der Tiere, und alles wird gut. Beispiel zwei: Noch mehr Tiere hüpfen auf den Hauptstraßen herum. Tatsächlich, da sind Zebras. Drei, fünf, zehn. Und ein Esel dazwischen. Aber alle unterwegs auf zwei Beinen? Ja, im Regierungsauftrag. Denn der Straßenverkehr orientiert sich an der Maxime: „Erst ich, der Rest ist mir egal." Und das soll geändert werden. Also steckt Präsident Evo Morales Menschen für ein paar Peso in Zebrakostüme, und die sollen den Autofahrern beibringen, dass Fußgänger auf Zebrastreifen Vorfahrt haben, dass sie auch mal halten müssen und dass sie nicht jeden gleich umfahren dürfen, der versucht, die Straße zu überqueren. Wer es nicht kapiert, bekommt Besuch vom Esel. Und der schimpft dann kräftig.

Mit Schimpfe der harten Sorte bekommen wir es auf dem Weg nach La Paz, zum Ende der Tour, zu tun. Wir kommen gerade vom Titicacasee, diesem unglaublich blauen, riesigen Gewässer, das die bolivianische Marine (!) bewacht, und das wir auf abenteuerlichen Holzbooten mitsamt unseren Defendern gequert haben. Voller Vorfreude auf die übliche große Abschluss-party in diesem gastfreundlichen Land bekommen wir noch einmal zu spüren, was eine Blockade ist.

Wir wollen, nein, wir müssen nach La Paz, also versuchen wir, dort zu fahren, wo die Blockade noch nicht komplett steht. Das weitet sich zur Schnitzeljagd aus – Ciro und Hans huschen mit ihren Autos durch die Seitenstraßen der Vororte und melden über Funk, wo frei ist und wo nicht. 13 Wagen rasen dicht an dicht durch die kleinen Ortschaften, was den Bewohnern nicht wirklich gefällt. Einige – besonders Frauen – werfen mit kleinen Steinen, einige treffen unsere Wagen auch, sie hinterlassen aber nur kleine Lackschäden.

Aber an einer der großen Straßen ist Ende im Gelände. Steine und Menschen haben sich zu einer unüberwindbaren Barriere aufgebaut. Hans fährt vorne und entscheidet: durch geht nicht, also dran vorbei. Mit viel Speed pflügt der Konvoi über das Feld – was der anwesenden Besitzerin nun völlig missfällt. Ich fahre als Letzter und will mich gerne bei der Frau entschuldigen und ihr unser Tun erklären. Also bleibe ich neben ihr stehen und öffne das Fenster.

Keine gute Idee. Denn sie hat einen recht großen Stein in der Hand. Und droht, ihn zu werfen. Zuerst rede ich noch in Englisch, aber schnell verfalle ich etwas hektisch ins Deutsche. Denn ihre Faust mit bedrohlichem Stein und mein Kopf mit verletzlicher Hülle sind plötzlich keinen Meter voneinander entfernt. Und noch während ich rede und sie immer wieder Wurfbewegungen macht, gebe ich Vollgas.

Ich weiß nicht, ob sie den Stein letztlich geworfen hat oder nicht. Ich weiß nur, dass auch dieses Abenteuer für uns alle gut ausgegangen ist. Wie immer bei der Land Rover Experience Tour.

We have seen many unusual cities, but La Paz is certainly at the top of the list, and for two reasons. The first is the remarkable number of llama foetuses at the Witches' Market. You can buy all manner of remedies and powders made from things best left undescribed, for ailments the enlightened European wouldn't want to know about, and, of course, dried animal corpses, staring at you through their empty eye sockets. To Bolivians, they are lucky charms; if one is buried at each corner of the site of a future house, everything will be all right. The second: there was suddenly an unusual number of animals on the main roads, mainly zebras, and a mule in-between, and all of them walking on two legs, clearly on government commission. The story behind the project was to be found in the way people drive – the rule of the road being "Me first – you loser". This had to change, so President Morales put people in zebra costumes for a few pesos. The idea was to teach car drivers that people at zebra crossings have right of way, and that drivers should always endeavour to stop and not wipe out anybody trying to cross the road. Should people have problems comprehending the message, the zebras would then send the donkey to scream its lungs out at them.

We experienced another form of screaming on the way back to La Paz as the tour was winding down to a close. We had just visited the wonderful blue Titicaca Lake, interestingly guarded by the Bolivian Navy (!), which we had crossed in our Defenders aboard rustic-looking wooden boats. We were looking forward to the big party celebrating the end of the tour in this wonderfully hospitable country when we hit another roadblock.

As I said, we were headed towards La Paz and began looking for a gap in the roadblocks. This rapidly deteriorated into a sort of paper chase as Ciro and Hans darted from one side road to the next telling us over the radio which roads were open and which weren't. 13 vehicles racing through tiny villages didn't go down well with the local population; some – mainly women – threw stones at the vehicles, which caused the odd scratch or two, but fortunately nothing more serious.

Things came to a halt, though, at the end of one of the larger roads where people and stones had converged to create an impenetrable barrier. Hans drove up to the front to decide what to do. The convoy then shot at speed across the fields, which, as far as the woman who owned the land was concerned, was really the final straw. I was in the last vehicle and wanted to apologize to the lady. As I drove up to her, I wound the window down.

This wasn't a good idea, as she had a rather large rock in her hand that she seemed ready to throw. I started speaking to her in English, and then I panicked and started rabbiting at her in German as her rock and my fragile head were very near to one another. As I talked and she threatened to throw the stone at me, I put my foot down.

I don't know if she threw the stone or not. I do know that we all survived to tell the tale, which is just how it is on the Land Rover Experience Tour.

CHRISTIAN UHRIG

*GEBOREN AM 4.6.1960 | LEITER MARKETING KOMMUNIKATION BEI JAGUAR LAND ROVER DEUTSCHLAND,
EXPERIENCE-TOUR-VERANTWORTLICHER UND SPARRINGSPARTNER;
IM FRÜHEREN LEBEN U. A. MANAGEMENT SUPERVISOR BEI WERBEAGENTUREN UND STUDIUM DER FORSTWISSENSCHAFT*

*BORN 4 JUNE 1960 | HEAD OF MARKETING COMMUNICATION JAGUAR LAND ROVER GERMANY,
PROJECT MANAGER LAND ROVER EXPERIENCE TOUR AND SPARRING PARTNER;
IN ANOTHER LIFE, MANAGEMENT SUPERVISOR IN AN ADVERTISING AGENCY AND A DEGREE IN FORESTRY*

Bei welchen Touren warst du dabei?
Ich konnte bisher bei allen zwölf Tourdestinationen dabei sein. In Jordanien erst ab Start des Reiseprogramms in 2001, in jenem Jahr habe ich meinen Job bei Land Rover begonnen. Es ist wirklich unfassbar, dass wir schon zwölf so komplett unterschiedliche Abenteuer überall auf der Welt durchführen konnten.

Welche Tour hat dir am besten gefallen?
Die Frage ist sehr schwierig und eigentlich nicht zu beantworten, denn mir liegt jede Tour sehr am Herzen. Jedes Ziel hatte seinen ganz besonderen Charme und Charakter, der jeweils einmalig war. Der Dschungel in Belize, die Pampa in Argentinien, der Etosha-Nationalpark in Namibia, die Highlands in Schottland oder die Anden in Bolivien. Das nachhaltigste Erlebnis erzeugten aber ganz gewiss die Weiten des tibetischen Hochlands mit der faszinierenden Hauptstadt Lhasa auf dem „Dach der Welt" bei der Pre-Scout-Tour im Jahr 2012. Vor allem die tibetischen Mönche, mit ihrem ganz besonderen Schicksal, waren so freundlich und entspannt, als sei hier der friedlichste Platz auf der Erde.

Gibt es dazu ein Ereignis, das dir besonders in Erinnerung ist?
Ja, unsere legendäre Tour-Etappe 2008 in Malaysia. Wir waren im Dschungel unterwegs, hatten scheinbar alles unter Kontrolle und plötzlich fing es an zu regnen. Der Weg wurde schlagartig zu einer sehr rutschigen Angelegenheit. Wir hatten nur noch wenige Kilometer bis zum Ziel – nur, das war unerreichbar. Wir kamen keinen Meter mehr voran. Es ging steil bergab und die Fahrzeuge hatten keinerlei Halt. Wir versuchten es mit Palmblättern und Ästen, aber nichts hielt die Fahrzeuge. Also entschlossen wir uns, die Fahrzeuge mit aus den Seilwinden ausgebauten Aramidseilen einzeln den Berg hinunter abzuseilen. Ja, abseilen wie ein Bergsteiger. Ein paar Mal das Seil um einen Baum herum, so hangelten wir ein Fahrzeug nach dem anderen mühsam ins Tal. Das kostete Kraft und dauerte Stunden. Früh am Morgen, noch im Dunkeln, erreichten wir endlich völlig erschöpft, mit Schlamm dekoriert und gepeinigt von Blutegeln, unsere Dschungel-Lodge. Die erlösende Dusche vergesse ich nie.

Wann hattest du zum ersten Mal Kontakt mit Land Rover?
In den Jahren 1995–1998, während meiner Zeit bei Lintas, einer internationalen Werbe-agentur, war ich als Etat-Direktor für Rover verantwortlich und 1997 mit dem Freelander-Launch befasst. Wir hatten in Spanien erstmals die Gelegenheit, ins Gelände zu fahren und später auch über die Treppen an den Strand. Dabei habe ich Dag kennengelernt, der schon damals ein Offroad-Experte war.

Du bist mehr bei den Pre-Scout-Touren als bei den Haupttouren dabei – mit Absicht?
Für mich persönlich haben die Pre-Scout-Touren den größten Reiz, weil hier die Mischung aus Unerwartetem und Planungsstress, Entscheidungsfindung, Mensch und Natur so unmittelbar zusammentreffen, dass mir das, was gerade passiert, oft unwirklich vorkommt. Ich lehne beispielsweise nach gefühlten zehn Stunden Fahrt an der Motorhaube, bin im Dschungel über die Karten gebeugt, „in the middle of nowhere", und wir diskutieren über ein Thema, das banal klingt, aber essentiell sein kann. Beispiel: „Es dämmert bereits, wie weit kommen wir heute noch, bis es komplett dunkel wird und wir unser Zelt aufschlagen können?" Um dann nach Abwägung aller Pros und Cons zu entscheiden noch weitere fünf Stunden zu fahren, denn so holen wir die Zeit, die wir heute verloren haben wieder rein. Das bringt dich immer wieder an deine Grenzen und das macht den Reiz aus.

Which tours have you been able to accompany?
I have been on all twelve. I started working for Land Rover in 2001, so I was only in Jordan for the start of the customer programme. I can hardly believe that we have managed to put together twelve so completely diverse adventure trips all over the world.

Which tour was your favourite?
That's a very difficult question and almost impossible to answer, as I put my heart and soul into every tour. Each one had its own underlying charm and character, and each was unique. The jungle in Belize, the Argentinian Pampas, Etosha National Park in Namibia, the Highlands in Scotland or the Andes in Bolivia. I think the most lasting impressions were generated by the expanse of the Tibetan Highlands, with its fascinating capital Lhasa "on the roof of the world" during the pre-scout in 2012. The Tibetan monks, considering their own particular situation, were so friendly and relaxed as if they hadn't an enemy in the world.

Is there one event that really sticks in your mind?
Oh yes – one stage of the 2008 Malaysia tour event has almost legendary status. We had been making good progress along a jungle track and were on schedule when it suddenly started to rain. Within an instant, the trail transformed itself into a long, slippy, mud slide. We were only a few miles from the finish, but were literally unable to make any progress at all. The trail dropped rapidly through the jungle and it was impossible to maintain a safe, constant speed. We tried to gain some traction using branches and palm leaves but that had no effect. Finally, we decided to belay the vehicles all the way down the valley, in effect abseiling from one tree to the next as a climber would, using the winch cables. It was debilitating work and took hours. In the early hours of the morning and while it was still dark, we finally made it to our jungle lodge, physically exhausted and covered from head to toe in mud and leeches. The shower afterwards was the best I've ever had.

When did you first come into contact with Land Rover?
Between 1995 and 1998, while I was working for an international advertising agency called Lintas, I was account director for Rover and was busy with the launch of the Freelander. In Spain, we had the opportunity to drive off-road for the first time and via steps down onto the beach. This was where I met Dag, who was already an expert in all things off-road.

You spend more time on the pre-scouts than on the main event – is that intentional?
I find the pre-scout tours more interesting because their mix of unexpected events, planning stress and decision-making is often so at odds with the environment through which we are travelling. For example, I am in the middle of the jungle, in the middle of nowhere, leaning over the bonnet with maps spread everywhere, having just spent what seems like ten hours behind the wheel and we could be talking about something which sounds banal, but which is in fact crucial to the success of the tour. For example, it was already dusk, could we make camp and pitch the tents before it got dark? After considering the pros and cons we decided to drive for another five hours to make up the time we had lost. Testing your limits in this way has a real buzz to it.

ROLAND LÖWISCH

GEBOREN AM 26.9.1959
SEIT 1990 AUTOREDAKTEUR (AUTO BILD, STERN), SEIT 2006 SELBSTSTÄNDIGER JOURNALIST

BORN 26 SEPTEMBER 1959
AUTOMOTIVE JOURNALIST SINCE 1990 (AUTO BILD, STERN), FREELANCE JOURNALIST SINCE 2006

Was fasziniert dich an den Land Rover Experience Touren?
Ganz einfach: Jede Tour führt eine Gruppe von Menschen, die das alle nicht alleine erfahren würden, an Orte auf dieser Welt, die keiner von ihnen normalerweise sehen würde. Denn solche Touren sind nur möglich, weil es durch den Einsatz vieler Fahrzeuge immer einen Ausweg gibt, selbst in technisch oder geologisch höchst problematischen Fällen.

Schon selbst technische Probleme erlebt?
Kleinere gibt es immer mal, aber selbst betroffen war ich durch einen Ausfall von einigen dringend benötigten elektrischen Bordsystemen in Bolivien. Wir – meine Beifahrerin Theresa und ich – waren in meinem Lieblings-Landy, dem Defender, auf dem Weg hoch zu einem 5 145 Meter hohen Pass. Natürlich mit offenen Fenstern, weil ich auf der Fahrt immer gerne die Luft schmecken und den Wind fühlen möchte. Plötzlich merkten wir, dass nicht mehr viel von der normalerweise zuverlässigen Elektrik funktionierte. Für uns relevant: Die elektrischen Scheibenheber verweigerten die Arbeit, die Scheibenwischer samt Scheibenwaschwasserpumpe auch. Aber alle Sicherungen waren okay – der Defekt konnte also nicht mal eben beseitigt werden.

Und dann?
In großer Höhe ist es kalt, und in Trockenheit staubt es. Gegen die Kälte gab es warme Klamotten, den Staub auf der Windschutzscheibe bekämpfte Theresa mit Wasser aus Trinkflaschen – seitlich während der Fahrt aus dem Auto heraushängend. Wirklich problematisch wurde es erst, als es dunkel wurde. Denn auch die gesamte Lichtanlage hatte den Geist aufgegeben. Das einzige Licht, das funktionierte, waren die Zusatzscheinwerfer auf dem Dachgepäckträger. Allerdings auch nur durch ständiges Ziehen am Blinkerhebel, also beim Dauer-Lichthupen. Der Hebel befindet sich aber bekanntermaßen rechts, wo man auch schalten muss. Ich habe mich wohl noch nie vorher und nachher so blind, frierend, arbeitend und müde in einem Auto mehrere Stunden lang durch unbekanntes, staubiges und bergiges Terrain getastet.

Wo steckte letztlich der Fehler?
Noch in der Nacht hat die Landy-Crew den Wagen repariert. Es lag an einem Kurzschluss in der Anhängerkupplung.

What do you find fascinating about the Land Rover Experience Tours?
It's very simple. Every tour takes a group – people who would not undertake such a trip on their own – to places they would normally not get to see. The tours work because vehicles travelling in a group can always overcome technical or geological obstacles.

Have you experienced any technical problems yourself?
Little things can always go wrong, but where I was directly affected was when an electrical component failed in Bolivia. We – that is my co-driver Theresa and myself – were driving my favourite Land Rover, the Defender, up a mountain pass at an altitude of 16,900 feet. We had the windows open because I always like to taste the air and feel the wind. Suddenly, we noticed an electrical problem, which was unusual as these days the electrics are pretty reliable. The electric windows had stopped working, the windscreen wipers and the screen wash fluid pump had also ceased to function. The fuses were all okay, and it looked like this was a problem that would take a little longer to solve.

What happened?
At that altitude, it is very cold, and in dry weather you create a lot of dust. To defeat the cold you have good clothing. For the dust on the windscreen we had another solution. Theresa hung out of the passenger-door window and poured water out of her drinking bottle over the screen. By nightfall, we had a serious problem. We had lost all the lights except the additional spotlights mounted on the roof rack and they only worked by constantly pulling the indicator stalk backwards, as if one were using full beam as opposed to main beam. The switch is also on the right-hand side, near the gear stick. I have never felt so blind, cold and tired while fumbling my way forwards in a vehicle for hours over unknown, dusty and mountainous terrain.

What was the cause of the problem in the final analysis?
That same night the Land Rover guys found a short circuit in the trailer coupling.

SEIDENSTRASSE

SILK ROAD

2013

2013
LAND: DEUTSCHLAND, POLEN, UKRAINE,
RUSSLAND, KASACHSTAN, USBEKISTAN,
KIRGISISTAN, CHINA, TIBET, NEPAL, INDIEN
STRECKE: 16 000 KM
COUNTRY: GERMANY, POLAND, UKRAINE,
RUSSIA, KAZAKHSTAN, UZBEKISTAN,
KYRGYZSTAN, CHINA, TIBET, NEPAL, INDIA
DISTANCE: 10,000 MILES

7 EVOQUE, 4 DISCOVERY

DAS JUBILÄUM
THE ANNIVERSARY

Unglaublich – es ist geschafft. In 50 Tagen elf Länder durchfahren, inklusive der durchaus nicht selbstverständlichen Passagen durch China und Tibet. Alle elf Autos sind in Berlin gestartet und – fast – ohne Kratzer in Mumbai angekommen. Zwölf Teilnehmer kommen gesund zurück, rund 50 Journalisten ebenso und mein Team auch. Bis auf den Doc. Ausgerechnet er muss einen Tag früher abreisen mit Verdacht auf Denguefieber. So verpasst er mit der großen Abschlussparty den letzten Höhepunkt dieser Tour, der Königin aller Experience Touren: Es ist die längste, anstrengendste, aufwendigste, aber vielleicht auch schönste. Und vor allem: die zehnte. Die Jubiläumstour.

Die Einfahrt nach Mumbai werde ich nie vergessen. So wie man (wenn überhaupt) so eine Tour nur einmal im Leben macht und immer davon zehren kann. Ich bin noch zu aufgewühlt, um mich zu erinnern, wo genau wir langgefahren sind, zum Ziel der 16 000-Kilometer-Tour. Es war irgendwo am Strand von Mumbai, Richtung Taj Mahal Palace Hotel, das zum Tata-Konzern gehört. Ich weiß noch: Die Straße ist gesperrt, es wird getanzt, viele Leute schwenken Fahnen, eine indische Rhythmusgruppe trommelt, was das Zeug hält. Und ich höre darunter trotzdem noch mein Herz klopfen.

Und jetzt sitze ich hier alleine in meinem Zimmer, einen Gin Tonic in der Hand, und denke an alle Touren, die ich jemals geleitet habe, und an die vielen Hürden, die genommen werden mussten, bis die Jubiläumstour stand.

Die Entscheidung, wo die zehnte Tour der Land Rover Experience enden soll, ist nicht schwer zu fällen: Indien. Denn dort firmiert mit Tata die Muttergesellschaft von Jaguar Land Rover, die es möglich machte, dass es seit der Übernahme im Jahr 2008 sowohl mit Land Rover als auch mit Jaguar stetig bergauf geht. Klar, dass Mumbai – Stammsitz von Tata – das Ziel sein muss.

Aber die Tour ausschließlich in Indien zu fahren, bietet sich nicht an. Aus mehreren Gründen: Dort leben die Menschen mehr auf der Straße als in Häusern, es ist also immer und überall voll. Dazwischen stehen und laufen noch die heiligen Kühe, die man tunlichst nicht anrempeln sollte, will man heil aus der jeweiligen Ortschaft wieder herauskommen. Außerdem sind die meisten Menschen in Indien zwar überaus hilfsbereit und liebenswert, aber sie lieben auch Körperkontakt, kennen keine Scheu und kommen Mensch und Maschine oftmals so nahe, wie man das in unseren Kulturkreisen nicht kennt und schätzt. Und wer schon mal ein paar

It's unbelievable – we made it. Eleven countries in 50 days including driving through China and Tibet, which is anything but a walk in the park. All eleven vehicles started in Berlin and arrived almost without a scratch in Mumbai. Twelve participants returned to Germany as healthy as when they left, and the same went for around 50 journalists and my team. Except for the doctor, that is. How ironic that he should be the one to have to leave early with suspected dengue fever and miss the final highlight: the end-of-tour party celebrating this, the queen of all Experience Tours. It was the longest, most tiring, most complex, but perhaps the most stunning of all the tours. And it was the tenth. The Anniversary Tour.

I will never forget driving into Mumbai. A tour like this is a once-in-a-lifetime (and most don't even manage that) opportunity, and it provides a tale for a lifetime. As I write this, I am still too exhausted to remember exactly where we drove to get to our destination at the end of the 10,000 miles. It was somewhere on Mumbai's beach towards the Taj Mahal Palace Hotel, which belongs to Tata. I can remember that the road was blocked off for us, there was dancing, lots of people were waving flags, and an Indian rhythmic band were banging their drums for all they were worth – but I could still hear my own heart beating.

And now I am sitting in my room on my own, with a gin & tonic in my hand, thinking about all the tours I have led and all the obstacles that had to be overcome to make the Anniversary Tour happen.

Deciding the destination of the Land Rover Experience Anniversary Tour hadn't been difficult: India. This is the home of Jaguar Land Rover's parent company, Tata, which, after taking over the British companies in 2008, is the reason why both Land Rover and Jaguar have been able to build on their success ever since. It was patently obvious that Mumbai – where Tata is based – would have to be the culmination of the tour.

However, taking the tour to India alone was out of the question. There were numerous reasons for this: because the majority of its population spends most of their time on the streets rather than in buildings, roads everywhere are constantly teeming with people. In-between are the famous sacred cows, which are to be avoided at all costs, assuming of course you want to leave that particular town in one piece. Additionally, most people are incredibly helpful and genuine in their affection, which leads us to the next point – they are very tactile people, not at all shy, and that goes for getting very close to both man and machine, the kind of proximity rightly

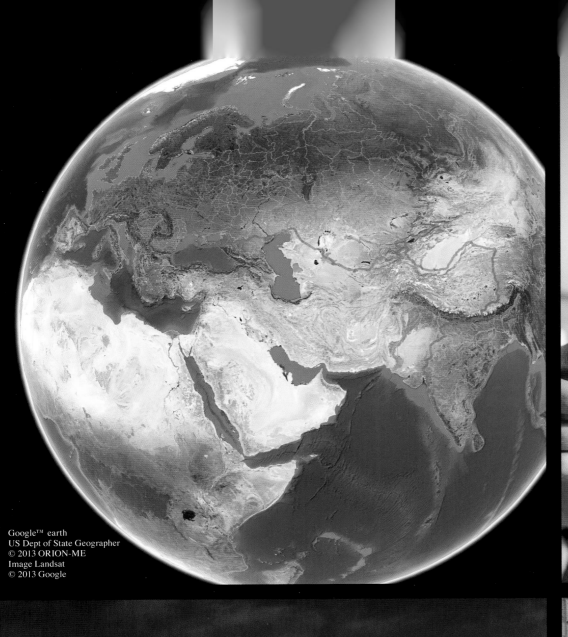

Google™ earth
US Dept of State Geographer
© 2013 ORION-ME
Image Landsat
© 2013 Google

LAND ROVER

WELCOME
SILK TRAIL 2013
MUMBAI, INDIA

DAS JUBILÄUM
THE ANNIVERSARY

so neugierige wie gut gelaunte Inder am Auto hängen hatte, weiß, dass das zwar sehr spaßig sein kann, ein Vorankommen aber doch deutlich behindert. Aus ähnlichem Grund können wir Campsites ebenfalls nicht guten Gewissens aufbauen.

Die Lösung des Problems liegt deshalb nahe, auch wenn so eine Strecke einen von uns bislang noch nicht ausprobierten und bewältigten Organisationsaufwand bedeutet. Wir fahren von Deutschland nach Indien und wandeln damit auf den Spuren der Seidenstraße. Das hat noch niemand gemacht.

Seidenstraße – schon der Name hat einen besonderen Klang. Die Seidenstraße gehört zu den ältesten Handelsrouten der Welt: ein Netz von Karawanenwegen, auf denen über Land Waren wie Gewürze, Glas, Porzellan und natürlich Seide gehandelt wurden, aber auch Religions-, Zivilisations- und Techniktransfer zwischen Morgenland und Abendland stattfand. Heute bedeutet eine Reise auf ihren Spuren vor allem massenhaft Eindrücke fremder Kulturen.

Wir wären schlechte Planer, würden wir nicht ein paar Bedenken anmelden, um sie genauso zügig wieder zu verwerfen: Sind elf Länder am Stück – Deutschland, Polen, Ukraine, Russland, Kasachstan, Usbekistan, Kirgisistan, China, Tibet, Nepal, Indien – logistisch machbar? Wird so etwas nicht zu teuer – denn höhere finanzielle Mittel als für die vergangene Tour nach Bolivien lässt das Budget nicht zu? Mal eben knappe 16 000 Kilometer in nur 50 Tagen – finden wir überhaupt jemanden, der das mitmacht?

Unsere Antworten sind ermutigend. Wir setzen nur elf statt 14 Autos ein, somit brauchen wir auch weniger Personal. Und wir machen im Gegensatz zu einigen anderen aufwendigen Touren nur eine Vortour. Da hilft es, dass wir nicht lange nach einem Guide suchen müssen: Kostja ist der richtige. Mein Freund und Kollege Hans Hermann Ruthe – wer sonst – kennt ihn bereits von einer Reise nach China, die er (selbstverständlich mit dem Auto) bereits gemacht hat. Kostja ist Spezialist und Veranstalter für Weltreisen mit Wohnmobilen. Was wollen wir mehr?

Zum Beispiel ganz offiziell am Brandenburger Tor in Berlin starten. Allerdings gibt es dafür von den Behörden vor Ort nicht die Spur einer Genehmigung. Begründung: zu großer Aufwand, Einladung für Nachahmer, Störung des Verkehrsflusses. So erteilt uns die Stadt eine klare Absage, uns dort mit Bannern, Autos und viel Tamtam zu postieren. Aber: Sich zwischen Siegessäule und Brandenburger Tor auf dem Parkstreifen zu treffen und sich von dort im Konvoi gemäß der StVO gen Polen zu bewegen, dagegen könne man überhaupt nichts einwenden. Somit ist der Startpunkt klar, ebenso das Ziel – der Rest dazwischen pures Abenteuer.

unheard of in our culture. If you have ever had a few Indians hanging onto your car, then you will probably confirm that while it was quite entertaining, it does slow you down somewhat. Similar reasons led us to conclude that building campsites would be ill-advised.

The solution to the problem was simple, even if the route required a level of planning and organization far beyond the planning required for previous tours. We were going to drive from Germany to India following the route of the original Silk Road. This hadn't been done before.

The Silk Road – even the name has a special ring to it. The Silk Road is one of the world's oldest trade routes: a network of caravan trails along which goods such as spices, glass, porcelain and of course silk were transported – but also a network in which religion, civilization and technology made the leap from Orient to Occident. To travel the Silk Road today is an opportunity to experience cultural diversity en masse.

Good planning requires considering all the possible obstacles and potential problems, even if some can be dealt with quickly. Were the eleven countries – Germany, Poland, Ukraine, Russia, Kazakhstan, Uzbekistan, Kyrgyzstan, China, Tibet, Nepal and India – logistically feasible in a single trip? Could we afford such an undertaking – we wouldn't be able to stretch our budget beyond that allocated for the Bolivia tour the previous year? We reckoned on approximately 10,000 miles in 50 days – was there anyone prepared to join us?

The answers were encouraging. Instead of 14 vehicles, we would take eleven. That would save staff. And in comparison to previous complex tours, this time only one pre-scout recce drive would be necessary. Fortunately we found a guide almost immediately. Kostja was perfect. Not surprisingly, my friend and co-worker Hans Hermann knew him from a trip he had recently undertaken to China (naturally by car). Kostja organizes global RV tours. Things were really looking up.

Except that we wanted to start from the Brandenburg Gate in Berlin, and the city authorities were not particularly interested in helping us with the necessary permits. Their argumentation: too complex, the danger of copycat events, interference with traffic flow. Our plans to put up banners, position the cars and generally give the tour a great send-off received short shrift from the town hall. However, they had nothing against our parking between the Victory Column on Strasse des 17. Juni and the Brandenburg Gate before heading for Poland in convoy while strictly observing German traffic regulations. So we knew where to start and where to finish. In-between was adventure pure and simple.

DAS BENZIN
THE PETROL

Rund 30 000 Menschen wollen uns auf dieser einmaligen Abenteuertour begleiten – wir könnten ein Auswahlcamp in der Größe von Buxtehude veranstalten. Sorry, das sind zu viele, aber eine tolle Bestätigung für unsere Auswahl der Tour und für den Hunger nach Freiheit und Abenteuer, für Reiselust und Wissensdurst. Immerhin ein Dutzend Land-Rover-Freunde haben die Chance, einen Teil der alten Handelsstraßen und die Kulturen drumherum kennenzulernen. Aber weil die Tour so lang ist und niemand 50 Tage Zeit hat, splitten wir erstmals eine Tour in drei Sektionen, wobei in jeder Sektion zwei Teams mitfahren. Die Anforderungen sind hoch: Es kommen Tagesetappen von 1 200 Kilometern vor, und wer schon mal 500 Kilometer schnurgerade Piste durch die kasachische Wüste gefahren ist, weiß, was Eintönigkeit bedeutet und wie gefährlich sie sein kann.

Aber nicht nur das legt uns die Vortour offen. Vor allem das Spritproblem holt uns ein (mal wieder, siehe Bolivien-Tour), besonders auffällig in Usbekistan und an den innerchinesischen Grenzen. Schade eigentlich, dass selbst unsere Autos noch nicht nur mit Luft und Liebe fahren.

Während Kasachstan (nach Fläche der neuntgrößte Staat der Erde) zwar extrem wenige Tankstellen besitzt, können immerhin alle, die existieren, auch Kraftstoff anbieten. Im Nachbarland Usbekistan scheint es genau umgekehrt zu sein. Das Tankstellennetz in dem Land, von dem noch gut fünf Prozent zum äußersten Osteuropa gerechnet werden, ist wohl dichter als das in der Bundesrepublik, aber die wenigsten haben tatsächlich Kraftstoff in den Tanks. Von den zehn Prozent der Tankstellen, die in der glücklichen Lage sind, überhaupt Kraftstoff anbieten zu können, haben etwa 90 Prozent nur Gas auf Lager. Der magere Rest wartet auf den nächsten Tankwagen. Der kommt eben, wenn er kommt, und das auch nicht früher, sondern meistens später. Immerhin funktioniert der usbekische Flurfunk ausgezeichnet, denn immer wieder treffen wir auf kilometerlange Schlangen von wartenden Pkw, deren Fahrer uns erzählen, gleich käme ein Lastwagen und fülle die Tanks der Tanke wieder auf. Tatsächlich sehen wir einmal, wie eine Lieferung kommt, die allerdings nicht mal für einen Bruchteil der wartenden Benzinschlucker reicht.

Womit ich unser Problem auch nur halb umrissen habe. Alle Wagen dieser Experience Tour benötigen Diesel – und das ist in Usbekistan ein noch selteneres Gut als Benzin. Selbst wenn das ölige Gemisch tatsächlich irgendwo vorhanden ist, handelt es sich meist um den sogenannten „schwarzen" Diesel – ein Treibstoffderivat aus Erdölrückständen mit einem Schuss Diesel, gedacht für die allesfressenden Kamaz-Laster, die durchs Land stänkern.

Around 30,000 people applied to join us on this once-in-a-lifetime adventure tour. We'd have to build a selection camp the size of a small airport to fit them all in. Sorry, folks, we can't take you all, even if it does confirm that the interest in the tour and the hunger people have for adventure travel and new and different cultures is still enormous. Nevertheless, a dozen Land Rover fans have the opportunity to explore the trade routes of old and experience the different cultures along the way for themselves. For the first time, though, because the tour is so long and nobody has 50 days to spare, we have split the tour into three sections with two teams driving each section. It is demanding. There are days when 750 miles have to be driven in one go, and anyone who has driven 300 miles in a straight line through the Kazakh desert knows the meaning of monotony and just how dangerous that can be.

The pre-scout also revealed that fuel would be an issue again (as we experienced on the 2011 Bolivia Tour), particularly in Uzbekistan and on the borders between provinces in China. It is a pity that our vehicles still don't run on love and air alone.

While Kazakhstan (which according to its percentage of the earth's surface is the ninth largest country on the planet) has very few fuel stations, at least all of them have fuel to sell. Across the border in Uzbekistan, the situation is exactly the opposite. The fuel-station network in a country of which five per cent is considered the easternmost periphery of Europe is, on paper, more extensive than its German counterpart – but only a very few have fuel of any kind in their tanks. Of the ten per cent with fuel available for sale, 90 per cent can offer only gas. Everybody else must wait for the fuel lorry that turns up on an "as and when" basis, with the emphasis more on "as" than on "when". Fortunately, the Uzbek "grapevine" is excellent, as we repeatedly encountered mile-long queues of cars whose drivers told us that a fuel lorry would be along shortly to replenish the fuel station. Once, we actually witnessed a delivery, but it turned out not to have been ample enough for even a fraction of the waiting gas-guzzlers.

And this brings me to the next part of the fuel problem. All our Experience Tour vehicles run on diesel, and that is even harder to find than petrol. And should you actually find something that looks like fuel oil, more often than not it is the so-called "black" diesel – a fuel derivative made from the residue of crude oil with a dash of diesel, originally manufactured for the Kamaz lorries known for their ability to run on anything and which can be found everywhere. The issue really comes to a head in the fall. Uzbekistan's complete supply of diesel is held

Im Herbst potenziert sich das Problem. Dann wird der gesamte Dieselvorrat Usbekistans an die Fahrzeuge ausgegeben, die bei der landesweiten großen Baumwollernte helfen. Wir müssen also dringend Diesel-Depots einrichten, denn wir können es uns bei der langen Haupttour nicht leisten, irgendwo lange untätig herumzustehen oder Kraftstoff zu suchen.

Was also tun eines Nachts auf der Vortour? Wir wenden uns vertrauensvoll an die so heimische wie freundliche Sprit-Mafia. Das dauert seine Zeit, aber mit den richtigen Guides, die wiederum die richtigen Fragen bei den richtigen Personen stellen, landen wir irgendwann an den richtigen Zapfsäulen. Die stehen zwar in einem stockdunklen Hinterhof, sind mit Teppichen abgedeckt und sehen aus, als sei durch ihre Schläuche seit Sowjetzeiten nichts Flüssiges mehr durchgekrochen, aber plötzlich sprudelt hier reinster Dieselsaft hervor. Der Preis ist gepfeffert, aber da Sprit das Salz in der Suppe von Automobilreisen ist, nehmen wir das hin.

Noch mehr Würze wird dem Deal verliehen (wie übrigens auch jedem anderen usbekischen Deal) durch das Begleichen der Rechnung mit der Landeswährung Sum. Der größte Schein zeigt 1 000 Sum. Das sind zum Reisezeitpunkt etwa 40 Eurocent (schwarz getauscht bei der ebenso heimischen wie freundlichen Bargeld-Mafia etwa 30 Eurocent). Die Folge: Die Usbeken laufen beim Einkaufen mit schwarzen Tüten voller Geld herum und zahlen selbst ihr Essen in den vielen Garküchen aus 100 000er-Einheiten (ein Bündel ist gleich 40 Euro), die kein Mensch nachzählt – bis auf die wenigen Touristen. Die damit aber überhaupt nicht klarkommen.

Mit Benzinproblemen ganz anderer Art werden wir an der Provinzgrenze von China zu Tibet konfrontiert. Aufgrund der langen Strecken, die wir fahren müssen, ist jedes Auto mit zwei bis drei 20-Liter-Kanistern Diesel auf dem Dach bestückt. Insgesamt führen wir auf der Vortour also etwa 200 Liter Extrasprit mit. Er ist als Notfallration gedacht, weil die Kraftstoffqualität zum Beispiel in Lhasa und Nepal nach unseren Informationen grottenschlecht ist. So haben wir zur Sicherheit auch Helikopterfilter samt Wasserabscheider und Partikelfänger im Gepäck.

Schon bei der Ankunft an der Grenze fällt uns ein riesiger Berg von Blech- und Plastikkanistern auf, die neben der Zollstation aufgetürmt sind. Ich ahne es schon: Hier will uns jemand an die Vorräte. Und tatsächlich kommen wir nicht an den Zöllnern vorbei, ohne uns der Kanister entledigt zu haben. Der Grund ist nicht Mangel an eigenem Kraftstoff oder Schikane von Weltreisenden, sondern die absolute Kraftstoffkontrolle der Chinesen in Tibet wegen der immer wieder vorkommenden Selbstverbrennungen von Mönchen.

Also keine Chance, den kostbaren Saft mitzunehmen. Allerdings möchte ich den guten Diesel nun auch nicht unbedingt den wirtschaftsboomenden Chinesen schenken. Also verteilen wir ihn an die tibetanischen Truckerfahrer, die in langer Schlange an der Grenze warteten. So happy sind die Jungs beim Warten wahrscheinlich lange nicht mehr gewesen.

over for the vehicles used to bring in the national cotton harvest. We would need to set up diesel storage depots, as we can't afford to hang around or hunt for fuel during the main event.

How does one spend an evening on the pre-scout recce? Naturally, a friendly chat with the equally friendly local fuel mafia. It takes time, but with the right guides asking the right people the right questions, we finally made it to the right fuel pumps. They were in some gloomy backyard, covered with carpets, and looked as if nothing had flowed through their hoses since the days of the Soviet Union, but all of a sudden Rudolf's finest started pouring out of the pistol. The prices are outrageous, of course, but given that a tour without diesel is like a car without wheels, we have to live with it.

The deal (like every other Uzbek deal, incidentally) gets more outrageous when paying the bill in the local Som currency. The largest-denomination banknote is for 1,000 Som. At the official exchange rate when we are travelling, this is worth 46 dollar cents or 35 pence (on the black market with the local, friendly cash mafia, around 35 dollar cents or 25 pence). The result: the Uzbeks go shopping with large black bags full of bank notes, and even lunch in one of the many hot food stalls is paid for using 1,000 Som notes bundled into a roll to make 100,000 Som (a complete roll is worth around $ 46 or £ 35). Nobody ever bothers to check, other than the small number of tourists who don't understand the system at all.

A different kind of fuel problem awaits us on the provincial border between China and Tibet. As a consequence of the distances we are travelling each vehicle has an additional two or three 20-litre jerry cans of diesel on the roof. On the pre-scout recce, that equated to a total of approximately 200 litres of extra fuel. According to our sources, the quality of the diesel in Lhasa and Nepal is so poor that we decided it was prudent to carry an emergency supply on board the vehicles. For the same reason we also had water separators, helicopter filters and dust filters on board.

On arriving at the border, we couldn't help noticing a huge mountain of steel and plastic jerry cans at the side of the customs post. It dawned on me that someone out there wanted our reserve diesel. And so it came to pass – the customs officers wouldn't let us by without relieving us of our jerry cans. The reason is not the lack of diesel or the desire to victimize the globetrotting community; no, it is simply the Chinese insistence on having their hands on every drop of fuel in Tibet because of the monks' reliance on self-immolation as a form of protest.

So taking our precious diesel with us was completely out of the question. At the same time, I was disinclined to hand it over as a gift to an economic powerhouse such as China. Instead, we shared it among the Tibetan lorry drivers waiting in the long queue at the border. Judging by the smiles on their faces, the gift was probably a rare highlight during the long wait.

DER SCHNEE
THE SNOW

Es ist April, es ist Vortour und es ist ganz und gar ungewöhnlich: In Kasachstan schneit es. Als ich aus unserem einfachen Hotel zum Parkplatz gehe, bekomme ich einen mächtigen Schreck: Wir müssen am Morgen die Autos freischaufeln, 30 Zentimeter Schnee überraschen uns total. Das bedeutet schon mal Zeitverzug, und Zeit ist das einzige, was wir nicht haben. Hinzu kommt: Weder unsere Kleidung noch die Bereifung der Wagen sind irgendwie einem Wintereinbruch angepasst. An der nächsten Tankstelle frage ich vorsichtig, ob das Wetter Richtung Süden ähnlich ist. Die ernüchternde Antwort: „Die nächsten 1 000 Kilometer bleibt es so." Dazu muss man wissen: Kasachstan ist gut 2,7 Millionen Quadratkilometer groß.

Na klasse. Uns ist erstmals auf dieser Tour nicht mehr nach Späßchen zumute. Es bleibt nichts anderes, als rein in die Autos und los. Das Schneetreiben wird dichter, die Sicht beträgt zeitweise nicht mehr als 100 Meter. Und das auf kasachischen Straßen. Kein Zuckerschlecken. Langsame, unbeleuchtete Autos und Trucks machen die Fahrt genauso gefährlich wie nicht mehr sichtbare Pistenbegrenzungen, Schlaglöcher oder plötzliche Kurven nach kilometerlanger Fahrt geradeaus. Hier muss jeder für jeden mitdenken. Der Leader im Führungsfahrzeug sagt über Funk an, wenn der Rest des Konvois überholen kann – eine Fahrhilfe, die sich unter anderem schon auf den engen Bergstraßen Boliviens bewährt hat.

Gerade noch rechtzeitig sehe ich nach langer und ereignisloser Kilometerfresserei als Fahrer des ersten Wagens, dass die Straße blockiert ist. Eine Ansammlung von Lkw behindert unsere Weiterfahrt. Und jetzt sehen wir auch das Dilemma: Der erste Kamaz hat sich eingedreht und ist mit dem Zugfahrzeug in einer Schneewehe hängen geblieben, der Hänger hat sich quer gestellt. Das Schlimmste: die Ratlosigkeit der Trucker. Es wird viel geredet und wenig getan.

Ein Großteil der russischen und kasachischen Laster ist nicht nur alt, achsenlahm und rostgeschwächt, sondern auch noch sehr schlecht mit Hilfsmitteln aller Art ausgerüstet. Aber unser Bergeequipment ist auf dem neuesten Stand. Und da wir es eilig haben, siehe oben, koordiniere ich sofort die Bergung. Oder zumindest das Vorhaben, irgendwie eine Gasse zum Passieren zu öffnen. Wir laden die Trucker ein, zu Schaufeln zu greifen, schieben selber Schnee weg und zerren dann mit Bergegurten, die an unsere Land Rover gebunden sind, an dem Lastwagen. Es braucht viele Ansätze, Versuche und noch mehr Schweiß, bis wir eine Schneise neben der Fahrbahn geschlagen haben, um passieren zu können. Das Angebot der Lastwagenfahrer, die Schneise noch zu vergrößern, damit auch sie mit ihren Uralt-Trucks vorbeikommen, müssen wir ausschlagen. Die Aktion hat bereits jetzt schon drei wertvolle Stunden gekostet. Stunden, die unsere Nachtruhe minimieren. Wie immer bei solchen Aktionen.

It's April, we're on our pre-scout recce, and how about this for bizarre: Kazakhstan was experiencing a snowstorm. As I walked from our budget hotel to the car park the following morning, I was startled and realized that we would have to dig our cars out of the snowdrift. An impressive 12 inches of snow had caught us completely unawares. This put us behind schedule – and our schedule had no time buffer built in. We lacked appropriate winter clothing, and our vehicles had no winter tyres. At the next filling station I tentatively asked whether the weather in the south was any different. The sober response: "It's like this for the next 600 miles." Just to put that in perspective, however, Kazakhstan is a good 1 million square miles in size.

Wonderful. For the first time on this trip, no one was laughing. We had no choice but to get into the cars and hit the road. The driving snow started getting thicker, reducing visibility at times to no more than 300 feet, and on Kazakh roads this was no walk in the park. Slow-moving cars and lorries without lights are a constant hazard and no less dangerous than the hard shoulder marker poles that have disappeared in the blizzard, the potholes and the sudden curves after mile-long straights. Teamwork is critical. The lead vehicle communicates to the rest of the convoy when it is safe to overtake – a method that had proved its worth on the narrow mountain passes in Bolivia.

I was in the lead car on a particularly long section that had thus far been without incident when at the last minute I noticed that the road ahead was blocked. A line of lorries prevented us from continuing on our journey. Upon closer investigation, we saw what the problem was: the first Kamaz in the convoy had lost traction in the snow, and the tractor unit was stuck in a snowdrift while the trailer had jackknifed. The worst part was that the lorry drivers hadn't a clue what to do. The standard approach to the problem appears to be to discuss at length without actually undertaking anything to solve the problem.

Most Russian and Kazakh lorries are not only old, with years of overloading and rust having taken their toll, but they also lack recovery gear (and for that matter any other kind of onboard emergency equipment.) That said, our recovery equipment was brand new and state-of-the-art. Also we had a deadline to meet (see above), so I set about coordinating the recovery – or, at the very least, freeing up a lane so that vehicles could get past. We managed to persuade the lorry drivers to grab whatever shovels they could find and started shovelling snow ourselves before attaching the recovery straps we carried on the Land Rovers to the lorry and pulling it out of the drift. A number of strategies, attempts and a great deal of sweat were required before we finally managed to clear a way next to the road enabling us to get by. We had to refuse the lorry drivers' proposal to increase the size of the passage so that they could get their oldtimers back on the road again, too. The hold-up had already cost us three valuable hours. Three hours fewer in the sack. As usual, the same old story.

DIE GRENZEN
THE BORDERS

Niemandsländer sind für mich extrem anstrengend. Das, was in Europa kaum existiert, ist zwischen den Staaten des ehemaligen Ostblocks üblich: Landstreifen von bis zu 20 Kilometern Länge, um die sich niemand kümmert, die scheinbar keinem gehören – eine Art Pufferzone zwischen Ländern, die sich nie kannten und sich deswegen auch heute noch kaum kennen. Nach Passieren einer Grenze kann man nicht zurück; auf der anderen Seite weiß man nicht, ob die Zöllner des nächsten Landes einen hineinlassen. Bei Vortouren bin ich entspannter, da habe ich Profis bei mir und wir sind nur zwei bis drei Wagen. Auf einer Haupttour wie hier auf der Seidenstraße mit elf Autos ist das etwas anderes. Erst recht, wenn etwas völlig Unerwartetes passiert. Wie auf der Fähre zwischen der Ukraine und Russland.

Will man die Grenze am Schwarzen Meer überwinden, muss man in den Zollhof der Ukraine, zeigt dort seine Fahrzeugpapiere und Pässe, fährt von dort auf eine stets volle Fähre, tuckert eine halbe Stunde übers Wasser und landet im russischen Zollhof, wo sich die Papierprozedur wiederholt. Damit wir mit allen elf Autos auf ein und dieselbe Fähre passen, habe ich ein paar Scheine lockergemacht. Der Zollbeamte dort hat mich sofort wiedererkannt, mir freundlich auf die Schulter geklopft und gut gelaunt gesagt: „Du weißt doch, wie das geht …" Erst mal auf dem Wasser, entspanne ich mich auf dem Fahrersitz meines Discovery, die Beine locker auf die geöffnete Tür gelegt. Da kommt unser Kameramann Medi angeschlendert und fragt im Vorbeigehen, wie denn die Unterlagen für die Autos eigentlich aussehen. „Wieso interessiert dich das?", frage ich misstrauisch. „Ich will nur gucken", sagt er. Das kommt mir spanisch vor und ich setze ihn auf den Topf. Was er erzählt, belustigt mich: „Da schwamm eben so eine DIN-A5-Klarsichthülle im Wasser vorbei, und ich dachte, ich hätte ein Land-Rover-Logo drauf gesehen." Ich schicke ihn weg mit den Worten, er solle sich bitte bessere Witze ausdenken.

Aber eigentlich weiß ich ja aus Erfahrung, dass es nichts gibt, was es nicht gibt, und so bitte ich dann doch kurz darauf jede Autobesatzung, mal nachzusehen, ob ihre Papiere noch vorhanden sind. Alle ziehen sie lässig aus irgend-welchen Taschen – nur Teilnehmer André klopft seine Klamotten immer hektischer ab. Und muss gestehen: Sie sind weg. Wie sich herausstellt: Während er locker an der oberen Reling stand, wollte er sie in seine Haglöfs-Weste stecken, um sie nicht im Auto zu lassen. Hat er auch gemacht – aber das Netz auf der Innenseite der Jacke dient ausschließlich dem Tragekomfort, ist also oben und unten offen und damit keine Tasche. So fanden die Dokumente den Weg ins Schwarze Meer.

Das ist nun wirklich nicht witzig: Mitten im Niemandsland plötzlich ohne Unterlagen zu stehen, zumal an einem Sonnabend, ist vielmehr prekär. In jedem Kuvert befinden sich die originalen Versicherungsunterlagen des betreffenden Autos, die originalen Fahrzeugscheine und mit der Apostille eine beglaubigte Abschrift, dass ich die Verantwortung für jedes Auto des Konvois trage. Auch die diversen Vorschläge, um sich aus dieser misslichen Lage zu befreien, halte ich eher für kontraproduktiv: „Rettungsboot zu Wasser lassen", „Käpt'n zum Umkehren und zur Suche überreden" und so weiter.

Zum Glück habe ich vor der Tour vom Büro alle Unterlagen in Farbe kopieren lassen und mitgenommen. So nutze ich also die restlichen zehn Minuten auf der Fähre, um die Kopien auf Fahrzeugpapiergröße zurechtzuschneiden und ein bisschen zu beten, die Russen mögen das nicht bemerken.

Ich gebe zu, an der russischen Grenze habe ich leicht geschwitzt und vielleicht noch etwas mehr auf die Grenzer (in diesem Fall zwei attraktive russische Grenzerinnen) eingeredet, als ich es sonst tue, um sie von den falschen Unterlagen, zu viel Medizin oder anderen nicht in jedem Land erlaubten Dingen abzulenken. Und tatsächlich: Sie bemerken den Trick nicht. Kaum in Russland

I find no-man's-land extremely tedious. Almost completely unknown in Europe, it is the norm between the states of the former Eastern Bloc. Strips of land that can extend to up to 12 miles, for which no one is responsible, apparently belonging to nobody. A buffer zone between countries that have never had relations with one another and that aren't very concerned to change the status quo today. You pass one border, meaning there is no turning back; and on the other side there is no guarantee that the customs officials will let you in at all. On a pre-scout I am more relaxed, as I am surrounded by professionals and we have two, maybe three vehicles. During a main event such as this one, we had eleven vehicles, and that is very different, especially when something unexpected happens. Such as on the ferry between the Ukraine and Russia.

If you intend to cross the border at the Black Sea then you have to enter the Ukraine customs area, show your vehicle documentation and your passport. Then you drive onto a ferry, which is always full, and steam for half an hour across the water before landing in the Russian customs area, where the whole papers thing repeats itself. Getting all eleven vehicles onto one and the same ferry had cost me. The customs official had recognized my face, patted me on the shoulder and, while smiling, said, "You know how it works …" On the water, I was relaxing for a few minutes, feet up on the open door of my Discovery, when along came our cameraman Medi and asked in an off-the-cuff kind of way what our vehicle documentation actually looked like. I was a little suspicious and asked him why he needed to know. "I just wanted to have a look," he replied. This sounded like a fairy tale to me, so I decided to grill him. What he said made me laugh. "I saw an A5 plastic folder in the water and I thought I saw a Land Rover logo on it." I packed him off, telling him to think up a better joke.

However, as I know from bitter experience, anything is possible. So I asked every team to check their papers. Cool as cucumbers, everyone pulled them out of some bag in their respective vehicle. Everyone, that is, except the participant André, who looked increasingly nervous as he checked his clothes. Then he had to admit that the papers were missing. This is how it had happened: standing up on deck, he had put the documentation in his Haglöfs vest to ensure that they wouldn't be left in the vehicle. The jacket's inside mesh, however, is a comfort feature and was open at both ends – i.e. it wasn't a pocket. This is how the documentation landed in the Black Sea.

This wasn't funny. In the middle of no-man's-land without papers, on a Saturday, is a worrying predicament for a number of reasons. Each vehicle had an envelope with the following papers: the original insurance documentation for each vehicle; the original vehicle registration document; and a certified legal copy of a document confirming that I was responsible for every vehicle in the convoy. The various methods suggested to extricate us from our plight – such as "use a rescue boat to hunt for the envelope" or "persuade the captain to turn around and look for the documents" – clearly weren't helpful.

Fortunately, I had made colour copies of all our documentation beforehand, so I used the remaining ten minutes on the ferry to cut the copies to the right size and prayed a little that the Russians wouldn't notice.

Admittedly, on the Russian border I was sweating a little and spent more time than I usually would chatting with the border guards (in this case, two attractive Russian women) to divert their attention from the falsified documents, excess medication or anything else that wasn't allowed in every country on the planet. Fortunately, it worked – they didn't notice the difference. Once in Russia proper, I contacted my office to organize new copies of all the documents, which the next group of journalists to join the tour brought with them.

eingereist, bitte ich mein Büro zuhause in Wülfrath um die Ausstellung neuer Originaldokumente, und kurz vor der Ausreise aus Russland bringen die neu angekommenen Journalisten die Papiere mit.

Permits, Urkunden, Passierscheine, Autopapiere, Pässe mit Visa – das sind neben Autos, Wasser und Brot die wohl wichtigsten Dinge auf so einer Tour. Wenn da etwas nicht stimmt, werde ich sofort nervös. Und selbst, wenn dieses Mal das Problem trickreich gelöst wurde: Das wird wohl so bleiben, solange ich die Welt erkunde.

Es war mir schon bei der Planung glasklar, dass wir mit diversen merkwürdigen Zöllnern, diversen merkwürdigen Regeln, diversen merkwürdigen Formularen und diversen merkwürdigen Landessitten an den verschiedenen Grenzen konfrontiert werden würden. Deswegen habe ich in weiser Voraussicht – erstmals auf einer Tour – ein „Bakschisch-Budget" eingerichtet. Nur, dass ich die Bestechungsgeldreserve bereits an der Grenze Polen-Ukraine anbrechen muss, damit habe ich nicht gerechnet.

Spätestens, wenn noch in Polen die Holzhütten und Panjepferde auftauchen, die Straßen fühlbar schlechter und die Rauchsäulen aus den Schornsteinen dunkler werden, landet man in einer anderen, älteren Welt. Hier lebt der graue Osten noch, der immer farbloser wird, je weiter man sich vom Westen entfernt. Wir haben keine Waren mit, die wir anmelden müssten – das sieht sogar der Zöllner an der polnisch-ukrainischen Grenze bei unserer Einreise ein. Aber leider stehen wir auf der falschen Wartespur, wie er uns zu verstehen gibt. Nun, denken wir, wechseln wir sie eben. Rein technisch kein Problem. Dagegen hat der gute Mann allerdings etwas. Mit Nachdruck untersagt er uns den nötigen Spurwechsel. Und brummt uns ein ordentliches Strafgeld auf. So macht man sich Freunde.

Die Einreise aus der Ukraine nach Russland verläuft dagegen erstaunlich entspannt. Unser Pfefferspray wird zwar konfisziert, aber wir verteilen dafür Modellautos und T-Shirts, die wir extra für diesen Zweck in beträchtlicher Anzahl eingepackt haben.

In dem Riesenreich sind es nämlich Polizisten und nicht Zöllner, die uns ans Portemonnaie wollen. Mitten in Russland wird Hans angehalten, weil er angeblich eine weiße Linie überfahren habe. Die Strafe: Konfiszierung des Passes für einen Monat, wahlweise Zahlung von 200 Dollar, dann bekäme er seinen Pass sofort wieder. 200 Dollar? Nee, das finden wir zu viel. Hans legt einen 100-Dollar-Schein in den Pass und wartet auf die Reaktion. Die kommt prompt: Weiter geht's Richtung Osten.

Die nächste Kontrolle: „Du Germansky?"

Ich nicke.

„Du Schnaps?"

Ich schüttele den Knopf. Doch das überzeugt den freundlichen Polizisten nicht.

„Du Germansky, du Schnaps!"

Und dann fordert er uns alle auf, ihm in seine Polizeistation am Straßenrand zu folgen. Dort müssen wir blasen. Das Messgerät sieht höchst modern und funktionstüchtig aus. Und es scheint die Wahrheit zu sprechen: Ich kein Schnaps, meine Kollegen kein Schnaps. Aber Hans, der als Letzter bläst, hat angeblich 0,48 Promille im Blut. Was definitiv gelogen ist.

Jetzt werden wir laut. Schiebung! Schmu! Allesamt protestieren wir mächtig. Hans besteht auf seine unnachahmliche, weltgewandte Weise auf einen Bluttest. Bluttest! Bluuuuuuutteeeeest!!! Der Lärm, den wir veranstalten, lockt nun endlich den Vorgesetzten des geldgierigen Beamten heraus. Was denn los sei? Wir beschweren uns über die Manipulation am Messgerät. Manipulation! Maaaaaanipulatiooooooooon! Und der Chef sieht ein: Hier hat er ein paar zu harte Nüsse vor sich. Und lässt uns gehen. Ich bin erleichtert, als wir Russland hinter uns lassen. Wer des Kyrillischen nicht mächtig ist, kann hier nichts lesen; wer bislang immer mal wieder auf den Rechtsstaat schimpfte, weiß plötzlich, was er an ihm hat, weil Russland damit so gar nichts gemein

Permits, certificates, passes, vehicle documentation, passports with visa – along with the cars, bread and water, these are the most important things on an expedition like this. If something is not one hundred per cent, I get nervous. Even if the problem had been solved with a bit of trickery this time, I will always be like this as long as I spent my time exploring the world.

When we started planning, we knew full well that we would have dealings with all manner of weird and wonderful customs officials with their equally weird and wonderful rules, forms and national traits on the numerous borders we had to cross. Prudently, and for the first time ever for a tour, I established a "bribes budget". That said, I hadn't anticipated breaking into this reserve quite as early as the Polish-Ukrainian border.

Wooden huts, the traditional pack horses, roads barely worthy of the name and chimneys emitting clouds of thick, sooty smoke are the clearest indication that one has landed in a very different, older world, where the colour grey grows more prominent the further east one drives.

We had no goods on board requiring declaration – this fact was registered by the customs official on the Polish-Ukrainian border. Unfortunately, we were parked in the wrong queue, as he was at pains to point out. We thought all we needed to do was change lanes, which was, technically speaking, easily accomplished. Our friendly customs official saw it differently, though, forbidding us from moving from the spot at all and immediately issuing a large fine. A lesson in how to make friends.

Entering into Russia from the Ukraine was a comparatively relaxed affair. Our pepper sprays were confiscated, but the model cars and T-shirts with which we were particularly well equipped proved to be very popular.

The thing is, in the former Soviet Union it is the police and not the customs authorities that are interested in emptying our wallets. Somewhere in the middle of Russia, Hans was pulled over for allegedly crossing a solid white line. The penalty: confiscation of his passport for a month or a no-questions-asked payment of 200 dollars and his passport would be returned immediately. 200 dollars? We thought that was over the top. Hans slipped a 100-dollar bill in his passport and waited for the reaction. It was immediate – we were free to head east.

At the next checkpoint: "You Germansky?"

I nodded.

"You schnapps?"

I shook my head. But our smiling policeman wasn't convinced.

"You Germansky. You schnapps!"

At which point we were asked to accompany him to the police station at the side of the road and subjected to a breath test. The breathalyzer looked modern enough, appeared to be in working order and seemed to be telling the truth. I, no schnapps, my colleagues also no schnapps. Hans, however, who was last up to be tested, allegedly had a blood-alcohol level of 0.48. This was clearly the stuff of fiction.

We started shouting. This is a set-up! We were being taken for a ride. We upped the tone of our protest. Hans insisted in his own inimitable and cosmopolitan way on having a blood test. By now the noise we were making had even drawn the greedy police officer's superior out of his office. We complained bitterly about the manipulation of the breathalyzer and lo and behold the boss decided to back down and let the obstreperous foreigners on their way.

I was glad to put Russia behind us. If you can't read the Cyrillic alphabet, then you are up a gum tree in Russia and no mistake. Anyone who has ever complained about the rule of law at home should take a trip there, because the rule of law in Russia is meaningless. In Russia customs and conventions fall apart more quickly than the housing. Were there any more border surprises waiting for us? Not really, just the nature of the rip-off. Such as what we experienced on the Russia-Kazakhstan border.

DIE GRENZEN
THE BORDERS

hat – hier zerfallen die Sitten genauso schnell wie die Häuser. Kann uns noch irgendeine Grenze überraschen? Nicht wirklich, nur die Art der Abzocke. Wie an der Grenze Russland-Kasachstan.

Dabei haben wir diesmal alles richtig gemacht. Korrekte Grenze, korrekte Spur, korrekte Papiere. Der Grenzbeamte will natürlich die Unterlagen sehen – ihn macht es stutzig, dass die Wagen einer Company gehören, aber Privatfahrer am Steuer sitzen. Er will die Urkunden sehen, die besagen, dass das alles seine Richtigkeit hat. Wir geben sie ihm, zunächst die deutsche Version. Er nickt, dann will er sie auf Englisch sehen. Haben wir auch dabei – seine Laune verschlechtert sich. Er nickt wiederum, dann will er sie auf Russisch sehen. Haben wir auch – wir sind wirklich bestens vorbereitet. Jetzt ist seine Laune ganz im Keller. Er gibt uns zu verstehen, dass die Papiere okay sind und wir nicht ausreisen können.

Noch schwieriger, als mit korrupten Beamten zu diskutieren, die irgendeinen Grund für die Verweigerung der Weiterfahrt vortäuschen, ist es, mit Beamten zu diskutieren, die nicht mal einen Grund vortäuschen, sondern die Weiterfahrt ohne Begründung verbieten. Ich berate mich mit Hans und dem Team und wir beschließen, als letztes Mittel die klassische Überzeugungsformel anzuwenden: ein 100-Dollar-Schein im Reisepass. Damit gehe ich zu dem Beamten zurück und bitte ihn, sich den Ausweis noch mal genau anzusehen. Vielleicht findet er ja doch noch den richtigen Stempel, das richtige Formular, den richtigen Durchfahrts-S-c-h-e-i-n. Tatsächlich wird er fündig – und lässt uns ohne weitere Fragen ausreisen.

In dieser Form ist uns das tatsächlich nur an den Grenzen der Ukraine, Russlands und Kasachstans passiert, andere Grenzen bergen andere Überraschungen. Zum Beispiel das interessante Schauspiel an einem kleinen kasachisch-usbekischen Grenzübergang, den wir auf der Vortour gewählt haben in der Annahme, hier wäre nicht so viel los. Die Straße gleicht einem monströsen, matschigen Kraterfeld. Hier stehen große Berge-Lkw, um die vielen dort havarierten Lastwagen über die Grenze zu ziehen. In den Zollhof darf aber nur eine gewisse Anzahl an Fahrzeugen, sodass davor eine riesige Schlange an Trucks auf Einlass wartet. Warum das alles Willy-Betz-Laster sind, weiß ich bis heute nicht.

Während uns die Kasachen problemlos ausreisen lassen, kommen wir in Usbekistan an einen höchst peniblen Grenzer, der seine Ausbildung anscheinend bei der Stasi genossen hat. Im Zöllnerhaus werde ich in einen neonbeleuchteten Raum geführt, den ich guten Gewissens als Verhörzimmer bezeichnen kann. Der Mann, in Zivil, will alles von mir wissen, und zwar jedes Detail der Reise. Weil so ein Vorhaben wie die Land Rover Experience Jubiläumstour durch elf Länder mit Vortour, Teilnehmern und Journalisten schwer zu vermitteln ist, behaupte ich, wir seien eine Freundesgruppe auf Sightseeing-Reise. Wir haben uns die Autos geliehen und fahren gut gelaunt

I must emphasize that this time we had done everything correctly. The right border, the right lane, the right papers. The border guard naturally wanted to see the documentation. He was suspicious that the vehicles belonged to a company, but that they were being driven by private individuals. He wanted to see the certificates confirming that everything was right and proper. We initially handed over the German documentation. He nodded and then said he wanted to see the English documentation. We handed that over, too. His mood worsened visibly. He nodded and said he wanted the documentation in Russian. No problem, he could have that, too – we had done our homework. Our border guard was furious. Yes, our papers were fine. No, we couldn't leave the country.

Dealing with a corrupt official who conjures up any old reason not to let you across their border is bad enough. But it's worse when said official doesn't even bother to say why they're not prepared to let you pass. After a quick head-to-head with Hans and the team, we decided to use the classic currency of influence: the 100-dollar-bill-in-the-passport trick. I walked back to the same official, asked him to check the passport once again in the hope that this time he might find the right stamp and the right form. As it turned out, he found what he was looking for and we were free to continue on our journey without further ado.

This particular form of harassment actually only happened on the borders of the Ukraine, Russia and Kazakhstan. Elsewhere there were different surprises lying in wait. On the pre-scout recce, for example, we were part of the following sitcom after deciding on a particular border crossing between Kazakhstan and Uzbekistan, as we thought it would be relatively quiet. The road looked like something out of a First World War battlefield – one huge, muddy crater after the next. Equally huge recovery lorries were parked and ready to pull the many broken-down lorries over the border. The number of vehicles allowed to enter the customs area, however, is limited. Hence the long queues of lorries. To this day I couldn't tell you why they were all Willy-Betz lorries (a well known German haulage company.)

While leaving Kazakhstan was trouble-free, upon entering Uzbekistan we encountered a particularly fastidious border guard who had clearly learnt his craft in the East German Secret State Police. In the customs building I was led into a neon-lit office that I can describe with some confidence as an interrogation room. The man, dressed in civilian clothing wanted to know everything about the tour. Trying to explain a project such as the Land Rover Experience Anniversary Tour, which takes in eleven countries, a pre-scout recce, participants and media is not easy, so I chose a different tack and claimed we were a group of amateur photographers on a sightseeing trip. We had hired the vehicles and were enjoying a very pleasant photo tour through these countries. We had recently undertaken a similar tour to Bolivia and put together a book full of nice holiday pics for our friends.

durch diverse Länder, um schöne Fotos zu machen – so etwas wie eine Kaffeefahrt für Laien-Knipser. So hätten wir das auch vor Kurzem in Bolivien gemacht und ein Büchlein für den Freundeskreis darüber verfasst. Mit netten Bildern vom Urlaub.

Mr. Hundertprozent will das Buch sehen. Rein zufällig habe ich natürlich eines im Auto. Ein Soldat begleitet mich nach draußen, da steht Hans. Dem teile ich in knappsten deutschen Worten und seltsam anmutenden Gesten mit, was ich dem Grenzer gerade erzählt habe, damit Hans die gleiche Geschichte erzählt, falls er auch noch verhört wird. Hans kapiert sofort – wie immer.

Der Zöllner vertieft sich in das Buch mit den fantastischen Aufnahmen von Craig Pusey, unserem Profi-Fotografen. Der Usbeke will jedes Bild erklärt haben – tatsächlich jedes einzelne. Und hat noch ein paar Zusatzfragen: Warum wir keine Mädels dabeihaben? Wann ich geboren bin? Wo Wuppertal liegt, ob eher bei Düsseldorf oder bei Köln? „Köln hat gutes Bier", sagt er plötzlich in bestem Ostdeutsch – und ich bin froh, keine dummen Sprüche während des Verhörs gemacht zu haben. Der Mann war – welch Überraschung! – einst in Ostberlin stationiert und hatte dort Deutsch gelernt. Nach vier Stunden können wir die Grenze überqueren.

Noch mehr Grenzerfahrungen? Kein Problem. Besonders die Prozeduren bei der Ein- und Ausreise nach und aus China werde ich nie vergessen. Schon während der Vortour habe ich lernen müssen, dass wir hier in einer anderen Welt sind. Bei der Haupttour verschärft sich die Situation noch. Weil in China zu Feiertagen die Grenzen geschlossen werden und wir das nicht berücksichtigt haben, streichen wir einen freien Tag in der kirgisischen Hauptstadt Bischkek und brechen vom Jurtencamp morgens um 4 Uhr auf.

Die Ausreise aus Kirgisistan mit drei Kontrollstellen klappt völlig problemlos.

Mr Perfect wanted to see the book – by chance I had a copy in the car. A soldier accompanied me to the car where Hans was standing waiting. I passed on my story to Hans in reduced form and using gestures that would have appeared rather strange to anyone observing the situation so that he would have the same story to tell the border guard in case he were asked. Hans immediately understood what I was trying to achieve – as always.

The border guard was getting more into the book with Craig Pusey's amazing photography. The Uzbek wanted to know the background behind every individual picture and had a few additional questions up his sleeve. Why are no women on the tour? When was I born? Where is Wuppertal, is it nearer to Düsseldorf or Cologne? "Cologne has good beer," he suddenly said with a very strong East German accent, and I was very happy not to have said anything stupid during the interrogation. The man had indeed been stationed in East Berlin (what a surprise!), where he had learned to speak German. Four hours later we were able to cross the border.

Any more border experiences? No problem. I will never forget the experience of entering and exiting China. On the pre-scout we had learned that we were in a different world. On the main event things got more complicated. In China, the borders are closed on public holidays. As we had forgotten to factor this in, we decided to drop our day in the Kyrgyzstani capital of Bishkek, breaking our yurt camp at 4 in the morning.

Departing Kyrgyzstan with its three checkpoints went by without incident.

DIE GRENZEN
THE BORDERS

Weitere drei erwarten uns auf chinesischer Seite bei der Einreise über den Torugart-Pass. Die erste besteht aus einem schlichten Eisentor mit müden Soldaten und wachen Schäferhunden, 10 Kilometer später müssen wir ein paar Stunden warten, um unsere Papiere checken zu lassen. Die dritte ist 70 Kilometer weiter – hier werden ausgiebig das Reisegepäck und die Autos gefilzt sowie die persönlichen Papiere ein drittes Mal gefordert. Mit der Fahrt durch eine Desinfektionsdusche betreten wir nach elfeinhalb Stunden Grenzübertritt (leicht schnappatmend, denn wir befinden uns bereits auf 3 700 Metern Höhe) endlich chinesischen Boden. In unserem Hotel in Kashgar erhalten wir dann unsere chinesischen Führerscheine, ohne die wir hier nicht fahren dürfen – später ein wunderbares Souvenir.

Die Ausreise gestaltet sich kein bisschen einfacher. Grenzübergang Zhangmu nach Kodari, Nepal: Morgens um 9 Uhr schleicht unser Konvoi durch die an einen Hang gebaute Grenzstadt, in der schon viele Lastwagen auf die Erlaubnis zur Ausreise warten. Parkende Autos blockieren den Verkehr der viel zu engen Straße, die eigentlich nur einspurig ist, aber Fahrzeuge in beide Richtungen bewältigen muss. Nach fünf Stunden Warten schauen die Offiziellen kurz auf die Fahrgestellnummern. Dann dürfen wir über eine völlig kaputte Piste zum nächsten Posten rollen, der sich unsere Pässe vornimmt. Der Fahrer muss im Auto sitzen bleiben, der Beifahrer geht zu Fuß durch ein Haus, um nach einer Serpentine wieder ins Auto zu steigen. Bei der letzten Stelle regiert nur noch das Chaos: Dicht an dicht warten Lastwagen auf die Ausreise, unser Konvoi mittendrin. Es wuselt nur so von Einwohnern dieses eigenwilligen Ortes sowie Tagelöhnerinnen, die bis zu 40 Kilo schwere Ballen mit Textilien nach Nepal tragen. Dazu noch wenig vertrauensvolle Gestalten, die immer mal wieder die eine oder andere Autotür testen – ob sie sich nicht öffnen lässt und fette Beute dahinter wartet.

Die Grenzer arbeiten erst mal nicht. Angeblich ist der Strom ausgefallen (bei der Ausreise zwei Stunden später sehen wir allerdings keinen einzigen Computer, sämtliche Arbeiten werden händisch getätigt. Das Gepäck wird übrigens akribisch nach unerwünschten Tibet-Reiseführern gecheckt). Dann geht es weiter Richtung Nepal, ab hier wirklich einspurig. Einige Autos werden durchsucht, andere nicht – ein System ist nicht erkennbar. Endlich dürfen alle – die Fahrer im Auto, die Beifahrer zu Fuß – über die „Freundschafts-brücke". Der Weg führt durch bewaffnete Soldaten sowie bereitstehende Feuerlöscher mit Niederhaltegabeln zur Bekämpfung von aufsehen-erregenden Selbstverbrennungen nach Nepal. Dort atmen wir auf. Nicht nur, weil jetzt die Hochlandetappe hinter uns liegt, sondern eher, weil wir wieder in der Freiheit sind. Zivilpolizisten legen uns zur Begrüßung einen leichten Schal um den Hals, stempeln ohne Fragen die Pässe, und schon dürfen wir in dieses bitterarme, aber wunderschöne, warmherzige und gastfreundliche Land. Für die rund 130 Kilometer von Nyalam (China) bis nach Kathmandu brauchen wir übrigens insgesamt satte 15 Stunden.

Three more were waiting for us on the Chinese side over the Torugart Pass. The checkpoint consisted of a simple iron gate guarded by tired soldiers and not-so-tired German Shepherd dogs. 6 miles further on, we had to wait for a few hours as our papers were being checked. The third checkpoint was another 40 miles down the road. This time our luggage and the vehicles were thoroughly checked, and we had to hand our passports over for a third time. Crossing into China had taken a total of 11.5 hours, and, slightly out of breath (we were after all at an altitude of 12,000 feet), we were then subjected to a disinfectant shower. In our hotel in Kashgar, we received our Chinese driving licences without which we wouldn't be able to drive here at all. Later this will be a wonderful souvenir.

Departing China was no easier. The border crossing point at Zhangmu to Kodari in Nepal. At 9 o'clock in the morning, our convoy crawled through the border town built into the side of a hill where many trucks were already waiting to depart the country. Parked cars make it even more difficult to drive along the street, which in reality is a one-track road but must service traffic in both directions. After waiting for five hours, the officials briefly checked the vehicle identification numbers. This was followed by a drive along a dreadful track to the next checkpoint, which took our passports. While the driver was expected to remain in the vehicle, the co-driver had to enter a building and, after a serpentine route, was permitted to climb back into the car. The last checkpoint was just pure chaos. Truck after truck parked up, awaiting permission to leave, and our convoy stuck right in the middle. Locals abound in this very strange place, as do day labourers carrying huge balls of textiles weighing up to 90 lbs. to Nepal. Not to mention the suspicious-looking figures who, every once in a while, test a car door in the hope that there might be something worth stealing inside.

The border guards weren't working. Apparently, there had been a power cut. (Two hours later, as we departed the country we didn't see a single computer. All the paperwork was done by hand. The luggage was meticulously checked for the highly unpopular – with the Chinese at least – guidebooks to Tibet.) After that, we were able to head in the direction of Nepal along what really is a single-track road. Some vehicles were checked, others ignored – there didn't appear to be any system to it. Finally, we were allowed to cross the "Bridge of Friendship", the drivers in the vehicles, while the co-drivers had to walk. Our route took us past armed soldiers as well as fire extinguishers and pitchforks, which were lined up just in case any one decided on self-immolation on the way to Nepal. We could breathe again. Not because the mountainous stage was now behind us, but also because we were in a free country again. Police welcomed us with light scarves around our necks, stamped our passports without asking any questions, and with that we were free to enter this dreadfully poor, but beautiful, warm-hearted and hospitable country. The 80 miles from Nyalam in China to Kathmandu had taken us a healthy 15 hours.

VON DER KIRGISISCHEN JURTE DURCHS CHINESISCHE
HOCHLAND BIS IN DIE GRÜNEN TÄLER NEPALS: WER SO LANGE
WIE WIR DURCH ASIEN FÄHRT, LERNT DIE EXOTISCHSTEN
MENSCHEN, DIE FREMDESTEN BRÄUCHE UND DIE
EINFALLSREICHSTEN TRANSPORTMÖGLICHKEITEN KENNEN.

FROM THE KYRGYZ YURT ACROSS THE CHINESE HIGHLANDS TO
THE GREEN VALLEYS OF NEPAL: ANYONE WHO SPENDS AS MUCH
TIME AS WE DO TRAVELLING THROUGH ASIA IS CONFRONTED BY
THE MOST COLOURFUL PEOPLE, THE STRANGEST CUSTOMS AND
THE MOST INVENTIVE FORMS OF TRANSPORT.

DR. BORIS KORIOTH

GEBOREN AM 10.1.1965 | LEITENDER NOTARZT

BORN 10 JANUARY 1965 | CHIEF EMERGENCY DOCTOR

DR. FRIEDRICH W. HAMMERSCHMIDT

GEBOREN AM 14.11.1980 | NOTARZT UND INSTRUCTOR

BORN 14 NOVEMBER 1980 | EMERGENCY DOCTOR AND INSTRUCTOR

Boris, haben sich Teilnehmer und Crew in Peru besonders sicher gefühlt mit dir als begleitendem Arzt?
Boris: Wahrscheinlich ist es gar nicht verkehrt, wenn man bei solchen Touren – oft weitab jeglicher Zivilisation – jemanden dabei hat, der ein bisschen breiter aufgestellt ist. Ich bin Facharzt für Innere und für Allgemeinmedizin, habe eine Hausarztpraxis in Mettmann und dort eine Gelbfieberimpfstelle. Ich habe mehr als 800 Einsätze mitgemacht und darf mich Leitender Notarzt nennen.

Welche Erwartungen hattest du an die Tour?
Boris: Natürlich habe ich gehofft, nicht eingreifen zu müssen. Meine größte Sorge war, dass sich ein schwerer Verkehrsunfall ereignet. Das ist ja nicht außergewöhnlich bei den teilweise engen Straßen am Abgrund. Eine sogenannte technische Rettung erweist sich meistens als besonders problematisch. Zum Glück ist nichts passiert.

Musstest du überhaupt eingreifen?
Boris: Klar. Mal ein Durchfall hier und ein paar Kopfschmerzen da passieren immer wieder. Eine Teilnehmerin ist auch etwas schwerer erkrankt, was mit der Höhe im Gebirge und der Serpentinenstrecke zu tun hatte – aber das hatten wir schnell im Griff.

Friedrich, du warst bei der zweiten Tourhälfte dabei. LETs führen manchmal in große Höhen, was nicht jeder gut verträgt. Welche Erfahrungen hast du damit?
Friedrich: Im Grunde jede. Denn ich bin nicht nur Notarzt, sondern auch ausgebildeter Höhenmediziner. Ich spüre die Höhe natürlich auch selbst und kann mich somit in die eventuellen Patienten hineinversetzen. So kann ich frühzeitig beratend und therapeutisch wirken. Zusätzlich nutze ich meine Erfahrung aus der Seidenstraßentour.

Und jetzt bist du zusätzlich Instructor.
Friedrich: Bei der Seidenstraße war ich noch Teilnehmer. Jetzt bin ich ein vollwertiges Teammitglied inklusive Verantwortung, auch im nichtmedizinischen Bereich. Natürlich weiß ich, dass ich noch viel lernen muss. Aber ich freue mich darauf, noch viele Abenteuer zu erleben. Die Seidenstraßentour hat mich nachhaltig verändert.

Inwiefern?
Friedrich: Ich habe zum Beispiel sehr viel über mich selbst gelernt und darüber, wie ich mich noch besser in ein Team integrieren und an meinen Aufgaben wachsen kann. Seitdem bilde ich mich auch intensiv weiter im Offroad- und Survivalbereich.

Boris, hast du dich für die Tour besonders vorbereitet?
Boris: Ich habe vor allem das notfallmedizinische Equipment zusammengestellt. Hier in Deutschland steigt man ja einfach in den Notarztwagen, da ist alles vorhanden. Aber in Peru ist das anders. Zumal der gut ausgestattete LET-eigene Arztwagen zu Hause bleiben musste, weil die Zollformalitäten zu kompliziert gewesen wären. Schließlich habe ich Kontakt zu den vorherigen Tourenärzten aufgenommen und sie nach ihren Erfahrungen gefragt.

Friedrich, war es schwer, ein Teil eines bereits gut funktionierenden Teams zu werden?
Friedrich: Gar nicht. Jeder bringt seine persönlichen und speziellen Kompetenzen auf eine Art und Weise mit ein, dass die Stärke des Teams deutlich über der des einzelnen Mitglieds liegt. Es herrscht eine hohe Akzeptanz in Sachen Fähigkeiten und Meinungen eines jeden Teammitglieds, sodass gemeinsam die beste Lösung für zukünftige Vorhaben oder akute Probleme gefunden wird. Da stimmt die Chemie ganz schnell.

Boris, did the participants and the crew feel particularly safe with you in Peru?
Boris: It's probably not such a bad idea to have someone with a broad skills base on tours like this, which are often many miles from civilization. I am a specialist in internal medicine as well as being a General Practitioner (GP) with my own family practice in Mettmann, which is also an official vaccination centre for yellow fever. I have attended over 800 emergencies as a casualty doctor and am now the Chief Emergency Doctor.

What kind of scenarios were you prepared for on the tour?
Boris: I naturally hoped that I wouldn't be needed at all. My biggest fear was that we would be involved in a serious road traffic accident, not uncommon on the narrow roads that snake along the sheer rock faces. A so-called technical emergency recovery is often very difficult in these circumstances. Fortunately, however we were spared this scenario.

Were you required at all?
Boris: Oh yes. Diarrhoea and a few severe headaches were quite common. One participant suffered a more acute form of altitude sickness – we were very high up in the mountains and the snaking roads didn't help. We were able to deal with it fairly quickly, however.

Friedrich, you were on the second half of the tour. A number of Land Rover Experience events have taken place at altitude and not every participant is able to cope with this. What kind of situations have you had to deal with personally?
Friedrich: Pretty much everything in the book. I'm not just an emergency doctor, I am also a qualified altitude sickness specialist. Because I am there with the patient at altitude, I implicitly understand what they are going through. I can advise them early on how to deal with the situation and then treat them accordingly. I can also bring the experience to bear that I gained on the Silk Road – that was my first tour.

And now you are an instructor as well!
Friedrich: I participated in the Silk Road Tour. Now I am a fully-fledged member of the team and I'm also responsible for non-medical aspects of the tour. Naturally, I am aware that I still have a great deal to learn. I can't deny, however, that I am really looking forward to many more adventures. The Silk Road Tour was a real milestone for me.

Can you elaborate how?
Friedrich: I learnt an awful lot about myself, about teamwork and how the roles I perform can help me to improve in general. I have also continued to work on my off-road driving and survival skills.

Boris – how did you prepare specifically for the tour?
Boris: I decided what emergency medical equipment was required. Back in Germany when the emergency call comes you climb into the ambulance and everything you need is on board. In Peru, it was a little different. We had to leave our own LET ambulance at home because the customs requirements were too complicated. I contacted the doctors who had accompanied previous tours to find out how they had coped.

Friedrich, was it difficult to become part of a well-integrated team?
Friedrich: Not at all. Every individual brings their own strengths and unique abilities to the table and this can only contribute to the effectiveness of the crew as a whole. As a team, we are really thankful for the wide range of skills and wealth of experience that all of us can bring to bear when we need to find a solution for potential future problems or when there is a particularly difficult issue that needs to be solved immediately. As a team, we learned how to work together pretty quickly.

HENNING LUEKE

GEBOREN AM 26.11.1986
KOMMUNIKATIONSEXPERTE UND INSTRUCTOR

BORN 26 NOVEMBER 1986
COMMUNICATIONS EXPERT AND INSTRUCTOR

Du bist seit der Seidenstraßentour ein festes Teammitglied und, wie so viele andere, ein echter Quereinsteiger. Wie kam es dazu?
Ich war bei der Hauptqualifikation für die Jubiläumstour verantwortlich für den gesamten Social-Media-Bereich. Ich habe mich intensiv mit den Teilnehmern beschäftigt und war bei allen Interviews dabei. Danach hat Dag mich gefragt, ob ich nicht Lust hätte, die gesamte Tour in diesem Bereich zu betreuen – inklusive Fotos und Videos und was sonst noch dazugehört. Da konnte ich nicht Nein sagen.

Ist es dabei geblieben?
Nein, mein Aufgabengebiet hat sich über die Australien- bis zur Peru-Tour deutlich verändert. Heute bin ich für die gesamte Kommunikation zuständig. Gleichzeitig bin ich Instructor. Genauer: Ich bin bei allen Vor- und Haupttouren dabei und Ansprechpartner für alle Themen rund um Kommunikationstechnik, vor allem im Internet. Und ich fahre das Fernsehteam von DMAX, die seit Bolivien über die Touren Reportagen drehen.

Obwohl du damit eine echte Schlüsselrolle im Team einnimmst, hat Dag etwas an dir auszusetzen. Verrätst du, was das ist?
Nun – ich vergesse gerne mal hier und da etwas. Mal lasse ich eine Kamera liegen, am nächsten Tag ist es etwas anderes. Dag hofft inständig, dass mir das zukünftig nicht mehr passiert, weil es jetzt hier im Buch steht.

Aber er hält auch große Stücke auf dich ...
Durchaus. Er behauptet immer, ich hätte das Internet erfunden. Und hat Angst, dass ich es irgendwann abschalten werde.

You've been a fully paid-up member of the team since the Silk Road Tour and like many you don't fit into the usual categories. How did you get involved with the LET?
On the anniversary event's final qualification camp, I coordinated the social media communications. I really got to know the participants and attended all the interviews. Afterwards, Dag asked me if I was interested in covering social media for the whole tour including video and stills photography and anything else that was required. Saying "yes" was the easiest decision I've ever made.

Is that still your remit?
No – my role changed considerably for the Australia tour and most recently for the Peru event. I am now responsible for all communications. At the same time, I am an instructor. More specifically, I'm involved with all pre-scouts and the main event and I'm specifically responsible for communications with particular emphasis on Internet media. I also look after the DMAX film team which has been producing the LET film documentaries ever since Bolivia.

Although yours is a key role in the organization, there is still something that bothers Dag – can you let us in on this?
Well, I can be a bit forgetful. One day it could be a camera, the next day something completely different. Dag sincerely hopes that by outing my forgetfulness in the book it will never happen again.

But he does think you have a lot of potential ...
Oh, absolutely. He tells all and sundry that I invented the Internet. And he is afraid that someday I'll switch it off.

AUSTRALIEN
AUSTRALIA
2015

DIE WAHL
THE CHOICE

2015
LAND: AUSTRALIEN
STRECKE: 3 300 KM
COUNTRY: AUSTRALIA
DISTANCE: 2,000 MILES

12 DISCOVERY SPORT 2, 7 DISCOVERY 4,
1 MERCEDES-BENZ AROCS

Australien? Niemals. Ich bin auch nur ein Mensch – vielleicht hatte ich deshalb so lange Vorbehalte gegen eine Land Rover Experience Tour auf dem kleinsten Kontinent. Gefüttert von TV-Filmen und Reportagen bestand Australien für mich bis zum Jahr 2013 ausschließlich aus ewig langen, schnurgeraden und roten Pisten, benutzt von Road Trains und Touristen. Vor meinem geistigen Auge sah ich ein paar Backpacker über den Stuart Highway irren und auf einen Jump warten – für überzeugte Offroader also wirklich keine Herausforderung.

Ich rechnete aber nicht mit der Hartnäckigkeit der australischen Tourismusbehörde. Nach dem Seidenstraßenmarathon fragt sie – mal wieder – bei uns an, ob die LET nicht doch mal in Australien Station machen könne. Nachgiebig, wie ich bin, lasse ich mich breitschlagen, mehr über das Land zu erfahren. Dafür fliege ich nach Cairns zur Tourismusmesse. Hier ist Speed Dating angesagt: Für Gespräche mit Veranstaltern erhält man je Meeting exakt 20 Minuten. Das reicht allerdings völlig. Wie ich befürchtet habe, werden uns touristische Lodges und nette Flugsafaris angeboten. Niemand versteht unser Konzept. Nur ein Vertreter des Northern Territory (NT) lässt nicht locker: Er schwärmt uns etwas von der Küste nordöstlich von Darwin vor. Und ich gebe wieder nach.

Allerdings nur in Form der Zusage, mit einer Cessna hinzufliegen und mir die Gegend anzusehen. Die kleinen viersitzigen Maschinen werden hier benutzt wie Busse – sie sind nur schneller. Filmer Henning und ich bestücken den Charterflieger außen mit GoPro-

Australia? Never. After all, I'm only human – perhaps that explains why a Land Rover Experience Tour on the world's smallest continent was off my radar for such a long time. Fed on a diet of TV movies and documentaries, up until 2013 my image of the land down under was one of dead straight earthen red tracks towards an endless horizon populated by road trains and tourists. In my mind's eye, I could picture an errant backpacker hitching a lift on the Stuart Highway – not exactly a challenge for the dedicated off-roading fraternity. However, I was surprised by the determination of the Australian Tourism board. After our marathon drive on the Silk Road they asked us – again – whether we would be interested in taking the LET to Australia. Always the accommodating softie, I was up for finding out more about the continent. This explains why I was on a plane to Cairns to visit the Travel Expo. For those not versed in tourism trade fairs, see it as an exercise in speed dating. You have twenty minutes and not a second more to talk to tourism operators. This was long enough, as we were bombarded from one stand to the next with tourism lodges and air safaris. Nobody got what the LET is about. Nobody except the rep from the Northern Territory (NT) that is. His persistence was infectious, waxing lyrical on the coast north of Darwin. I was won over.

Albeit with the proviso that they pack us in a Cessna so we could check the region out. These four-seater planes are like buses in this part of the world, except that they are much faster.

DIE WAHL
THE CHOICE

Kameras, während Anna, unsere Eventmanagerin, beim Anblick einer jungen, hübschen Pilotin ihren Berufswunsch fürs nächste Leben formuliert. Allerdings ist sie nach fünf Minuten Flug bereits dermaßen grün im Gesicht und leer im Magen, dass sie nur noch hofft, am Boden weiterhin ihren Traumjob als LET-Managerin fristen zu dürfen. Der Ausflug endet auch für mich enttäuschend: Wie befürchtet ist die Lodge ein Touristennest, die Straßen sind breit und rot, und die einzige Offroad-Piste müssten wir 30 Kilometer hin und 30 Kilometer wieder zurückfahren – nein danke. Anna möchte gern mit einer Taxe zurück nach Darwin fahren, aber als sie erfährt, dass die nächste in etwa vier Monaten vorbeikommt, zwingt sie sich wieder in den Flieger und ward bis zur Landung kaum mehr gesehen.

Also viel Aufwand für nichts? Nicht mit mir. Weil wir schon mal hier in Darwin sind, besorgen wir uns ein paar topographische Karten und schauen, ob nicht doch noch irgendwelche interessanten Pisten existieren. Der Finger rutscht über „Arnhem Land". Arnhemland? Land der Aborigines – das klingt gut. Hier auf rund 97 000 Quadratkilometern leben 64 000 Ureinwohner in rund 500 Homelands, Gemeinden im ursprünglichen Aborigines-Siedlungsgebiet. Kaum Hauptstraßen, etwas Wüste, viel Eukalyptus-Urwald. Nhulunbuy? Im nördlichsten Ort des Bundesstaates Northern Territory (NT), der 5 000 Seelen beheimatet, gibt's sogar einen Flugplatz. Mit Google Earth schauen wir uns das NT genauer an, und es fasziniert uns mehr und mehr.

Erstmalig in der Geschichte der LET nutzen wir nicht ein Auto für die erste Vortour, sondern das Flugzeug. Anna bleibt am Pool in Darwin, aber Henning und ich fliegen zunächst nach Nhulunbuy und von dort drei Stunden lang über das Arnhemland. Die Maschine ist wieder mit Kameras bestückt, die Frontscheibe mit GPS-Geräten getackert, denn eine Mindestflughöhe scheint hier nicht zu existieren. Wir finden alte Tracks, folgen ihnen, werden von Felsmassiven beeindruckt, von möglichen Wasserdurchfahrten überzeugt und von abwechslungsreicher Landschaft verwöhnt. Also doch Australien?

Na klar. Besonders, weil wir durch diesen einen Flug bereits die Hälfte der Tour – zumindest theoretisch – fertig besichtigt haben. Die Strecke Nhulunbuy bis nach Katherine steht. Als ich dann mit dem Uluru (wie der berühmte Ayers Rock bei den Aborigines heißt) das optimale Ziel der nächsten LET gefunden habe und auf dem Weg dahin einen 3 500 Quadratkilometer großen Salzsee namens Lake Mackay entdecke, steht fest: Hier müssen wir hin. Zumal wir vom Tourismusverband als lokalen Guide John Stafford bekommen – der Mann ist für den Job perfekt. Denn beruflich sucht er im Regierungsauftrag Offroad-Pisten für neue Touristenfahrten. Dank eines zusätzlichen Fünf-Stunden-Flugs von Alice Springs zum Lake Mackay und zurück kann ich die zweite Hälfte der neuen Tour fixieren. Viel schneller als gedacht ist sie fertig. Jedenfalls auf dem Papier. Australien, wir kommen!

While cameraman Henning and I covered the exterior of the charter plane with Go Pros, our event manager Anna had decided after meeting the young, attractive pilot that it was time to consider a career move. Five minutes after take-off, now somewhat greener in complexion after finding the little brown bag in the seat pocket in front of her, her focus was soon back on the dream job which she has on the ground working for the LET. The trip was a disappointment. As we suspected the lodge was full of tourists, the roads were as wide as they were red, and the one off-road track was a 30-mile round trip. Thanks, but no thanks. Anna's cunning plan to drive back to Darwin by taxi suffered a minor setback when she was told the next car was due in four months. Grimly, she climbed back into the plane and we didn't hear a wink from her until we landed.

So, was it a waste of time? Of course not. I don't waste time. As we were in Darwin we sourced some proper maps and started looking for some proper tracks. I spotted "Arnhem Land" – the land of the Aborigines. That sounded more like our cup of tea. Spread over approximately 60,000 square miles, 64,000 natives live in 500 homelands, communities in the original Aborigines settlement areas. No main roads, some desert, a lot of indigenous eucalyptus forest. Nhulunbuy? In the northernmost town of the Northern Territory, home to a population of 5,000, there was even an airstrip.

We checked out NT on Google Earth and were hooked.

This was an LET first. Instead of pre-scouting in vehicles, we used an aeroplane. Anna stayed poolside in Darwin while Henning and I flew to Nhulunbuy and then for three hours over the Arnhem Land. Once again, we plastered the aircraft full of cameras and attached our GPS to the front windscreen – which out here made complete sense – for even if there was a minimum flight altitude, we didn't stick to it. We flew along ancient trails, were surprised by massive rock formations that came out of nowhere, river crossings that would be the business for the tour, and were taken aback by a landscape that changed constantly. Could we really take the LET to Australia?

And how we could. This one flight had enabled us to pre-scout half of the tour. The route from Nhulunbuy to Katherine was a done deal. Once I had established that the destination would be Uluru (the name the Aborigines give to the world-famous Ayers Rock) and discovered that the 2,200 miles Lake Mackay was on the way, it was clear to me that we had to do this. The icing on the cake was the guide we were provided with by the local tourism board. John Stafford was perfect. Working for the government, it was his job to source new off-road routes for tourists. A quick five-hour plane trip from Alice Springs to Lake Mackay and back and we had the second half of the tour in the bag. On paper at least, the LET was looking good. Australia here we come.

AUSTRALIEN PUR: DER KONTINENT IST NICHT SO, WIE MAN SICH ERZÄHLT? OH DOCH, ER IST GENAU SO – EINSAM, KARG, FASZINIEREND.

--

AUSTRALIA ON THE ROCKS: WHAT YOU'VE HEARD ABOUT THIS CONTINENT IS ABSOLUTELY WHAT YOU GET – A BARREN, LONELY BUT FASCINATING PLACE.

DER LASTWAGEN
THE TRUCK

Mir ist sehr schnell klar: Australien wird nicht nur fahrerisch eine Herausforderung, sondern auch logistisch. Viele Autos und viele Menschen (wir planen mit 50 Reisenden und etwa 20 Autos) benötigen viel Treibstoff, Proviant und Sitzgelegenheiten. Und problematisch kann werden, dass so selten Tankstellen und Supermärkte unseren Weg kreuzen. Also müssen wir Diesel, Essen, Getränke sowie Tische und Bänke transportieren. Die Discovery Sport sind aber voll mit Zelten, Ersatzrädern, Reisetaschen und mehr. Und wohin mit zusätzlichem Werkzeug und der Notarztstation, die wir sicherheitshalber bei solchen Mammuttouren mitführen?

Ganz einfach: Tankstelle mitnehmen, Restaurant mitnehmen, Mini-OP mitnehmen. Und zwar alles in einem. Land Rover stellt keine Lastwagen her, also muss es die Basis eines anderen Herstellers sein. Und zwar von einem, für den es weltweit problemlos Ersatzteile gibt: Mercedes.

Meine Wahl fällt auf einen Arocs 3345 AK 6x6. Anders ausgedrückt: 13 Liter Hubraum, 450 Diesel-PS, Zwölfganggetriebe mit Untersetzung, drei angetriebene Achsen. Während Mercedes das Chassis fertigt, lasse ich einen Kofferaufbau maßschneidern. Damit er schwingen kann, sitzt er auf einem dreipunktgelagerten Hilfsrahmen. Innen lasse ich ein Regalsystem auf Rollen erfinden, Tiefkühltruhen einrichten, eine unabhängige Computeranlage sowie die Notarztzelle installieren. Aufs Dach kommt die aufwendige Klima- und eine Satellitenanlage. Unter dem Koffer wird ein vom Lkw-System unabhängiger 450-Liter-Dieseltank installiert, ebenso ein 350-Liter-Wassertank und eine Luftdruckregelanlage, mit der man nicht nur die Lkw-Reifen befüllen oder entleeren kann, sondern auch die der „kleinen" Autos. Vorne wartet die schwerste Elektro-Superwinch, die zu haben ist, auf Arbeit, hinten hängen zwei Ersatzräder, die durch einen elektrischen Galgen bedient werden können. Zusätzlich wird eine Beleuchtungsanlage angeschraubt und, und, und. In Rekordzeit ist der Lkw perfekt. Naja, fast jedenfalls: Mit 22 Tonnen Gewicht (beladen) und einer Höhe von 4 Metern ist das Auto ganz schön groß und schwer geraten.

Was soll ich sagen: Den Lastwagen zu bauen und mitzunehmen erweist sich als goldrichtig. Unsere Köche René und Paul zaubern Schmackhaftes auch im letzten Winkel des Outbacks, wir benötigen tatsächlich sämtliche Anlagen (bis auf die Rettungswagenfähigkeiten). Allerdings ist der Truck meistens langsamer unterwegs als der Konvoi – manchmal steht das LET-Team auf dem Dach des Koffers und fräst mit Kettensägen oben Platz, damit der Laster passieren kann.

Trotzdem: Auf der Tour ereilen die Trucker keine besonderen Vorkommnisse. Bis Fahrer Christian etwa 50 Kilometer vor dem Ziel Ayers Rock über Funk meldet, dass das Luftbefüllungssystem spinnt. Er steigt aus, schaut nach und staunt nicht schlecht: Die gesamte (zur Böschungswinkelvergrößerung klappbare) Hecktraverse hat sich verabschiedet. Das bedeutet: Luftbefüllungssystem kaputt, keine Heckleuchten mehr, keine Blinker. Und der Truck muss noch zurück nach Darwin fahren zur Verschiffung. So fragen wir in Alice Springs bei einem Mercedes-Händler nach Ersatzteilen. Der hat zwar noch nie einen Arocs gesehen, aber schafft es, am nächsten Tag sämtliche Teile vor Ort einzubauen. Inklusive LED-Rückleuchten. Chapeau. Übrigens: Mercedes übernimmt die Kosten. Das Abvibrieren gilt als Garantiefall.

One thing was immediately apparent. Australia wasn't just going to be a challenge to drive. The logistics would be enormous. Lots of vehicles and people (we were planning on taking 50 people in 20 Land Rovers) require a lot of diesel, food and chairs. Another problem was the lack of fuel stations and supermarkets on the route. We would have to take diesel, food, drinks and furniture – our Discovery Sport were full to the brim with tents, spare wheels, travel bags and a whole bunch of other items. Where would we store our additional tools and the emergency first-aid station that we always take on this these mammoth-scale expeditions?

The solution was simple. Take the fuel station, restaurant and first-aid centre with us in one vehicle. Land Rover doesn't build a truck so we needed to look elsewhere. And it had to be a manufacturer where getting spares wouldn't be a problem anywhere. The answer was Mercedes.

I chose an Arocs 3345 AK 6x6. A 13-litre capacity 450 hp diesel, 12-speed transmission with reduction gearbox and three driven axles. While Mercedes manufactured the chassis, I commissioned a coach-built box body. For it to be able to oscillate independently of the chassis, it sits via three mountings on its own sub-frame. I came up with a shelf system on rollers for the interior, plus it is equipped with deep freezers, its own computer system and emergency first-aid station. Air-conditioning and a satellite communications system were mounted on the roof. Directly below the coach-built body we fitted a separate 450-litre diesel fuel tank, a 350-litre fresh water tank and a compressor capable both of adjusting the truck's own tyre pressures and those of the Land Rovers. Up front, we installed the largest electrical winch on the market, while two spare wheels were mounted on electrically operated gallows at the rear. Did I mention the floodlights? I could go on ... In no time at all the truck was ready to roll. Well almost. With a fully laden weight of 22 tonnes and a height of 13 feet this was no lightweight.

Nevertheless, the decision to build and take the truck with us was the right one. Our cooks René and Paul could whip up the most delightful meal in the farthest corner of the outback and everything bar the first-aid station came into its own on the tour. But, the six-wheeler was slower than the rest of the convoy. Every once in a while, the LET team had to jump on to the roof to clear a passage with chainsaws so that the truck could continue on its way.

That said the tour was largely incident free for the truck team. 31 miles from the final destination Ayers Rock, Christian (the driver) radioed in saying that the compressor was doing strange things. A quick inspection revealed a much greater problem. The rear cross-member (which could be folded up to increase the vehicle's angle of departure) was completely missing. The result: a broken compressor and no rear lights or indicators. And we still had to get the truck to Darwin to be shipped back to Europe. After contacting a Mercedes dealer in Alice Springs and despite never having seen the vehicle before, he sourced the missing parts including the LED rear lights and the repair work was completed the following day. Respect. And another thing – Mercedes footed the bill. The vibration that caused the problem was covered by the warranty.

DAS UNWETTER
THE STORM

Wie immer bleibt nach der theoretischen Routenfestlegung die Frage: Können wir das auch praktisch fahren? Am Boden sieht es immer anders aus als von oben. Und werden wir die entdeckten Pisten nach der Regenzeit noch so vorfinden wie aus dem Flieger begutachtet? Es wird Zeit, die Tour mit Autos abzufahren. Wir leihen uns vom lokalen Importeur drei Discovery aus, bestücken zwei mit Dachzelten, stopfen zusätzlich Einmann-Armeezelte (Swags) hinein plus Treibstoffvorräte. Jedes Auto erhält zwei Ersatzräder und was man sonst noch alles gebrauchen kann.

Das Northern Territory zeigt sich erstaunlicherweise von seiner sanften Seite. Es regnet nicht, die Sonne scheint, und nachts leuchten oben Tausende Sterne und unten Tausende von Spinnenaugen, die das Licht aus unseren Kopflampen reflektieren. In einer der seltenen bewölkten und deshalb stockschwarzen Nächte, nach einer anstrengenden Fahrt, campieren wir an der ersten Stelle, die uns flach und geeignet erscheint. Am nächsten Morgen machen wir trotz viel zu früher Weckzeit große Augen: Wir haben unsere Zelte direkt am Ufer des Mackay-Salzsees aufgeschlagen. Land-Rover-Pressemann Mayk hat sogar direkt auf dem See genächtigt. Traumhaft …

Die Vortour ist fast beendet, und die letzte Nacht vor dem Ziel Ayers Rock wollen wir ein bisschen zelebrieren. So suchen wir eine besonders schöne Stelle und finden sie nach einem Abzweig auf dem höchsten Hügel der Sir-Frederick-Kette, der steinig ist und fast keinen Bewuchs hat. Wir sammeln Brennholz – Stefan und Marvin holen aus dem Tal fette Äste – und transportieren es auf dem Dach zum Hügel. Am Lagerfeuer verarbeiten wir das Erlebte, wir gönnen uns ein, zwei oder drei Bier und beobachten den Buschbrand auf der einen Seite und die geballten dunklen Wolken auf der anderen – alles weit weg, etwa jeweils 200 Kilometer entfernt. Dann fallen wir schnell in tiefen Schlaf; unser Schreiber Roland und ich je in einem der Dachzelte, die anderen in ihren Swags auf dem Boden. Und plötzlich bricht die Hölle los.

Ich weiß nicht mehr, ob es ein Donnerschlag ist, prasselndes Wasser in Form von dicken Regentropfen auf dem Zeltdach oder der starke Wind, der am mobilen Haus zerrt, was mich und alle anderen weckt. Die Zeit zwischen Blitz und Donner ist erschreckend kurz, das Zentrum des Unwetters liegt keine 2 Kilometer entfernt. Aber noch schlimmer sind die Windböen: Sie fegen von unten gegen die Böden der zweiteiligen Dachzelte (nur das Kopfteil ist am Dachgepäckträger fest verankert) und klappen sie zusammen.

Roland, der im zweiten Dachzelt gegen die Urgewalten kämpft, kann sich gerade noch rechtzeitig auf den nach oben klappenden hinteren Teil des Zeltbodens werfen, um ihn auf den Dachgepäckträger zu drücken. Ich dagegen liege so, dass ich nicht genug Druck auf das Fußteil ausüben kann. Der Wind klappt das Zelt gnadenlos zusammen, und so werde ich zum Fleischklops im Zelt-Burger. Meine Rufe verhallen ungehört im tosenden australischen Monstergewitter. Nur ab und zu höre ich draußen jemanden kurz fluchen, weil er bei der Flucht aus dem Swag zum Auto restlos durchnässt wird.

Mir kommt der unangenehme Gedanke, dass ich die absolute Spitze auf der höchsten Erhebung der Gegend darstelle – sollte man so etwas bei Gewitter nicht unbedingt vermeiden? Wir haben vor dem Schlafengehen in weiser Voraussicht zwar die Aluleitern der ARB-Touring-Zelte auf die Gummimatten der Autos gestellt, aber die sind inzwischen auch weggeflogen. Was wir gar nicht gebrauchen können, ist ein Blitzeinschlag ins Metall.

Wir haben Glück. Kein Blitzschlag, der Wind flaut ab. Erst jetzt kann ich mich befreien. Die Anspannung lässt nach, und dem Schrecken folgt Erleichterung, weil niemandem etwas passiert ist. Es ist 4.30 Uhr, und die Nacht nach dem Schrecken vorbei. Die abziehenden Wolken lassen den Blick auf einen wunderschönen Sonnenaufgang zu. Wir brechen auf. So kurz diese Nacht auch war – wir werden sie nie vergessen.

It's always the same. You have the route down on paper but you ask yourself: can we actually drive the trail? On the ground things can be very different. This was the case concerning specific routes, which we had mapped out from the air, yet potentially they could no longer exist after the rainy season. It was time to test the route with the vehicles. A local dealer lent us three Discovery, two of which were fitted out with roof-tents. In addition, we loaded up each vehicle with one-man tents (Swags), stores and two spare wheels for the tour.

The Northern Territory was surprisingly on its best behaviour. Sun from dawn till dusk and not a drop of rain. A panoply of a thousand stars in the night sky above us, and a thousand spiders' eyes below, was reflected in the light of our head-torches. On one of the few cloudy days when the nights are inky black, a particularly strenuous drive ended with us setting up camp at the first flat spot we could find. The following morning after waking up far too early we saw to our surprise that our camp was on the shore of Lake Mackay. Our press manager Mayk had even pitched his tent directly on the salt flats. It was stunning.

The pre-scout was all but over. Wanting to celebrate our final night at Ayers Rock we pitched camp on the highest spot that can be reached after following a branch of the Sir Frederic Chain route up the rock. It was steep and had no vegetation. With their usual foresight, Stefan and Marvin had collected firewood in the valley stowing it on the roof of their vehicle. Around the campfire we went over the trip again in detail enjoying a few well-earned beers while watching the bush fire on one side of the rock and the ominous dark clouds on the other – both panoramas a good 120 miles in the distance. It didn't take long to fall into a deep sleep, our writer Roland and I were in the two roof tents, the others were in their swags on the ground. It was then that all hell broke loose.

Looking back, I don't know what it was that woke us all up, a crack of thunder, the patter of heavy drops of rain on the tent roof, or the forceful wind. The time between each flash of lightning and the accompanying roar of the thunder was terrifyingly short – the centre of the storm was about a mile away. The gusts of wind were the most frightening aspect of all. The storm lashed at the base of the roof tent, which is a two-piece construction (only one end of the tent is firmly secured to the roof rack), with the result that the other half was forced up, crashing down on itself.

Roland was just able to flatten himself on the flapping lower end of the tent pressing it down onto the roof rack. I was unable to do the same with my own tent, as I couldn't get my weight onto the tent floor such was the force of the wind. Like a Venus flytrap, the tent halves crashed together and I was the fly. In the midst of the rising crescendo of an Australian bush storm I could hear curses as someone made a run from their swag to a vehicle getting completely drenched in the process, but nobody could hear me bellowing for help.

It occurred to me that sat in my roof tent sandwich, I was in the most exposed spot – not a pleasant thought in the middle of a thunderstorm. With some foresight, before we went to sleep, we had placed the aluminium frame rods of our tents on the vehicles' rubber mats but the storm had literally thrown them to the four winds. The last thing we needed was a lightning strike hitting the poles. However, luck was on our side. We were spared the lightning and the wind died down. I was finally able to get out of the tent. After the shock of this experience we were just relieved that no one had been hurt. It was 4.30 am, and as the clouds dissipated we were treated to an amazing sunrise. It was time to break camp. As short as the night had been, it was one that we wouldn't forget in a hurry.

DIE QUARANTÄNE
THE QUARANTINE

Es ist schon seit Längerem Usus, eine Land Rover Experience Tour hauptsächlich mit einem gerade neu eingeführten Land-Rover-Modell zu bestreiten – etwas Werbung muss sein. Für Australien bietet sich der neue Discovery Sport an. Das Auto ist so neu, dass wir zwölf Stück – vorrangig als Transportautos für die Teilnehmer und Journalisten – aus England kommen lassen müssen. Sie stammen direkt vom Band. Hinzu gesellen sich sieben Discovery der vierten Generation und der Küchen- und Notfall-Arocs. Allesamt werden per Schiff nach Australien gesendet. Sie kommen problemlos in Darwin beim Zoll an. Allerdings erst eine Woche vor dem geplanten Start der Australien-Tour.

Wir haben erwartet, dass der Lkw die meisten Probleme bei der Einreise bereiten wird, weil er unter anderem mit Blaulicht ausgestattet ist, aber der Riese wird als Erster freigegeben. Es folgen die (gebrauchten) Discovery als Support-Autos. Und dann kommt … eine sehr resolute Zollinspektorin. Die setzt mal eben die Discovery 4 fest.

Der Grund: Dreck. Die Australier passen höllisch auf, dass keine Krankheiten ins Land geschleppt werden. Und mit „höllisch" meine ich „höllisch". Die Australier haben jedes Recht dazu, Seuchen auszuschließen, aber diese Beamtin scheint die Sache persönlich zu nehmen. Sie fordert penible Sauberkeit. Mit ein bisschen Wischen ist es nicht getan. Mit jedem Lappen in unseren Händen verdunkelt sich ihr sowieso nicht gerade freundlich gesonnenes Antlitz mehr und mehr.

Wir hätten zwar auch anderes zu tun, aber nun muss ich mein gesamtes Team – immerhin fünf Mann – zum Autoschrubben abstellen. Neudeutsch heißt das kärchern: Mit fetten Dampfstrahlern bewaffnet kriechen die Jungs um die Autos herum. Sie nehmen jede Ecke und jede Kante ins Visier und kennen bald jede Profilrille der Reifen mit Namen.

Miss Zoll allerdings reicht das ewig lange Desinfizieren nicht. Kurz vor Ablauf der Woche schaut sie unter die – geklebten – Teppiche im Innenraum. Und was sie sieht, gefällt weder ihr noch uns. Denn unter den Fußbelägen hat sich Schlamm eingenistet. Anscheinend wurden die Discos in englischem Wetter nahe Eastnor Castle mit den typischen Offroad-Zutaten konfrontiert: Wasser und Erde. Schlamm. Also müssen wir alle Teppiche rausreißen und erneut mit passenden Wasserwerfern anrücken. Die Zeit wird verdammt knapp. Denn das Team ist noch in der Nacht vor der geplanten Abfahrt dabei, die zwölf Autos durchzuspülen. Für uns gerade noch rechtzeitig erhält die Gnadenlose dann aber doch den Befehl von oben: Lass sie fahren!

Tatsächlich kann die Tour pünktlich starten, weil meine Männer die gesamte Nacht hindurch die kurz zuvor freigelassenen Autos packen, bestücken, vorbereiten. Dass sie allerdings auch noch die ersten Tage während der Tour mit bestimmten Arbeiten an den Wagen die verlorene Zeit wieder aufholen, merken nur die ganz Aufmerksamen.

For many years now we have built the Land Rover Experience Tour around the introduction of a new Land Rover model – after all, a little bit of marketing is not a bad thing. For Australia it was the turn of the new Discovery Sport. The vehicle was so new that the twelve cars for the event had to come directly from Great Britain. They were fresh from the factory. In addition, we had seven Discovery 4 and the mobile kitchen/emergency response truck. They were all shipped off to Australia arriving in Darwin where they had to go through customs exactly one week before the tour was due to start.

We had anticipated that the truck would cause us most problems on entry, however the truck was the first to make it through customs. Next on the list were the seven Discovery 4. It was then we met a very resolute customs officer who was determined not to release the Discovery 4.

The reason was simple: dirt. The Australians are extremely pedantic about preventing disease from entering the country, and when we say pedantic, we mean obsessive. While their regulations are clearly justified, it seemed to us that this customs officer was taking it personally. Fastidious cleanliness was the order of the day. A wipe down wasn't going to work – just the mere sight of cloths in our hand resulted in the stern face of authority getting darker with every minute that passed.

Time was short, but we were now forced to put the team (five guys) on to scrubbing the cars clean. Equipped with industrial pressure washers, the boys set about the vehicles giving them an intimate makeover.

Our customs officer was not impressed by our efforts to disinfect the vehicles. The week was almost up and she decided to inspect the surfaces underneath the carpeted interior. Neither she nor we were happy with what she found. Mud had collected under the floor carpet. Clearly the Discos had experienced everything that British weather and an off-road tour at Eastnor Castle could throw at them: water + earth = mud. We were forced to remove all the carpets and hose the interiors down again. Time was short. Really short. The night before our departure we were still busy washing inside the vehicles! In the nick of time, the one who must be obeyed received her own orders from above: let them go!

The only reason for our punctual start the following day was that as each car was hosed out again, my lads immediately packed the kit, fitted the extras and generally got the vehicle roadworthy for the tour. Only the most eagle-eyed participant noticed that early on during the actual tour we were still busy fitting kit because of the time we had lost disinfecting the vehicles.

SCHEU UND NEUGIERIG ZUGLEICH: BEGEGNUNGEN MIT ABORIGINES BLEIBEN
UNVERGESSEN. BEI GEGENSEITIGEM VERTRAUEN BEKOMMT MAN EINEN
EINBLICK IN IHRE UNVERGLEICHLICHE KULTUR UND LEBENSWEISE.
--
SHY AND CURIOUS IN EQUAL MEASURE: ENCOUNTERING THE ABORIGINES
WAS AN UNFORGETTABLE EXPERIENCE. A MUTUAL SENSE OF TRUST GAVE US
AN INSIGHT INTO THEIR INCOMPARABLE CULTURE AND WAY OF LIFE.

DAS RITUAL
THE RITUAL

Arnhemland wird seit etwa 60 000 Jahren vom Aborigines-Stamm der Yolngu besiedelt, allerdings können sie erst seit Kurzem dort auch wieder selbstverwaltet leben. Die Ureinwohner haben es sich in diesem von Wüste, Eukalyptus-bäumen und Termitenhügeln geprägten Landstrich so wohnlich wie möglich gemacht, auch wenn unter anderem der Alkohol der Weißen ihnen teilweise ihre Kultur geraubt hat. Die Supermärkte im Arnhemland sind wie Gefängnisse vergittert, die lokalen Polizeidienststellen logieren in direkter Nachbarschaft. Kein Wunder, dass manche Communitys keine Weißen dulden, ihnen die Durchfahrt verweigern oder das Fotografieren verbieten. Unser Guide John Stafford hat in mühsamer Arbeit alle nötigen Durchfahrtsscheine besorgt, mit Landlords geredet, Tankstellen ausfindig gemacht.

Unsere Tour beinhaltet auch die Fahrt durch den faszinieren-den Gregory-Nationalpark. Der gehört ebenfalls den Aborigines. Es sind spezielle Erlaubnisschreiben nötig, um bestimmte Teile davon durchqueren zu dürfen. Wer ohne erwischt wird, muss bis zu 20 000 australische Dollar Strafe zahlen (rund 13 000 Euro). Das liegt auch daran, dass ein bestimmter Abschnitt der Strecke über heiligen Boden führt. Und den dürfen wir nur in Begleitung von Larry passieren.

Larry Johns ist zwar nur Halb-Aborigine, aber trotzdem ein „Traditional Owner", wie die Aborigines-Landlords auch genannt werden. Was er sagt, ist Gesetz. Und das Gesetz steht auch auf Schildern: Heiliges Land darf nicht betreten werden. Das ist wörtlich gemeint. Wer hier seinen Fuß auf das Land setzt, wird sterben. Wer einen Zweig abbricht, wird sterben. Wer Blumen pflückt, wird sterben. Damit die Götter trotzdem auf uns aufpassen, führt uns Larry zu einem heiligen Tümpel, einem sogenannten Billabong, der heiliges Wasser führt. Er und seine Begleiter tauchen Emaillebecher hinein und bestreichen unsere rechten Arme mit dem trüben Nass. Danach werden die Haare beträufelt. Das Ritual soll uns schützen – wir aufgeklärten Europäer machen den Hokus-pokus mit. So fasziniert wie zweifelnd.

Und dann geht es los. Nur die Reifen dürfen den Boden be-rühren. Die Landschaft ist rau: Mal nehmen uns große Bäume die Sicht, mal hat Feuer über weite Flächen das Unterholz geschwärzt. Stolze, riesige Esel streunen durchs Gelände, Kamele rennen erschreckt weg – und plötzlich entdecken wir zwei fette Bullen. Ein weißer und ein schwarzer, sie kämpfen heftig. Das muss natürlich aufgenommen werden mit Fotoapparat und TV-Kamera. Aber wie?

Tatsächlich klettern wir aufgeklärten Europäer alle aus den Autos – durch die Fenster, in Verrenkungen um die Türen herum, aufs Dach, auf die Trittbretter. Bloß nicht den Boden berühren, man weiß ja nie so genau. Larry bleibt cool im Auto sitzen. Und lächelt: Der schwarze Bulle gewinnt.

Arnhem Land has been inhabited by the Yolngu aboriginal clan for over 60,000 years but they have only recently been able to administer the territory themselves. The Aborigines have made this harsh region with its characteristic desert, eucalyptus trees and termite hills habitable despite the destructive effects of the white man's alcohol on aboriginal culture. Supermarkets in Arnhem Land look more like prisons than shops and the local police are usually housed next door. Not surprisingly, communities are often no-go areas for whites, some even going so far as to prevent whites from passing through or taking photographs. Our guide John Stafford went the extra mile to get the necessary permits, talk to the landlords and identify where the fuel stations were. Part of the tour took us through the amazing Gregory National Park which also belongs to the Aborigines. Special permits are required to drive certain parts of the park, otherwise there can be a fine of up to Australian $ 20,000 (US $ 15,300 / £ 11,700). The reason being that part of the route goes over sacred ground and for this we needed to be accompanied by a man called Larry.

While only half-aboriginal, Larry Johns is still a "traditional owner", the term used to describe Aborigine landlords. What he says is law in these parts. And the signs at the side of the road confirm this: you are not allowed to enter this area, as it is sacred ground. The warning is to be taken at face value. You put one foot on the ground, you die. To guarantee us the protection of the Gods, Larry took us to a pool, a so-called billabong, which is a source of holy water. Larry and his mates dipped enamel cups into the pool and coated our right arms with the murky water. And then he sprinkled it over our hair – the ritual was supposed to protect us. We, the enlightened Europeans, let the hocus-pocus literally wash over us with an equal measure of fascination and scepticism.

And with that we were off. Our tyres were the only things allowed to touch the ground. This is a raw and unforgiving place. In an instant we were enveloped by immense trees reducing visibility to zero, followed by huge tracts of land bearing the blackened scars of bushfires. Large and rather self-confident donkeys wandered across the countryside and camels shocked by our sudden appearance, ran off in fear. We discovered two bulls locked in combat, one black, and the other white – of course we had to capture this on film, but how? The enlightened Europeans exited the vehicles any way they could without touching the ground including going through the windows, hanging on doors, climbing on to the roof and the running bars. Only Larry stayed inside with a smile on his face. The black bull won.

SIR-FREDERICK-KETTE, GANZ OBEN: SELBST IN
AUSTRALIEN WÜTEN UNWETTER – UND WEHE,
MAN IST DANN AM FALSCHEN ORT ...

– –

AT THE TOP OF THE SIR FREDERICK CHAIN: EVEN
AUSTRALIA CAN BE HIT BY STORMS AND HEAVEN
HELP YOU IF YOU'RE IN THE WRONG PLACE ...

WER SUCHT, DER FINDET NICHT IMMER: DIE PISTENSUCHE QUERFELDEIN IST EIN SPEZIELLES ABENTEUER. MANCHMAL MÜSSEN WIR RÜCKWÄRTS ZURÜCK.
--
THE JOB OF A NAVIGATOR HAS ITS UPS AND DOWNS. TRAILBLAZING ACROSS COUNTRY IS A PARTICULAR KIND OF ADVENTURE. SOMETIMES REVERSE GEAR IS THE ONLY OPTION.

DIE PISTEN
THE TRACKS

Ich habe bei meinen vielen Touren und Vortouren ja schon eine Menge Pisten erlebt: matschig, steinig, weich, hart, staubig, gefroren, eng, breit. Aber die in Australien sind besonders extrem. Und extrem unterschiedlich.

Da sind zum Beispiel die geraden, roten Pisten, die so typisch für Australien sind. Für kurze Verbindungsetappen müssen wir sie benutzen, und die rund 15 Meter breiten Schotterpisten sind tatsächlich so langweilig, wie ich schon immer befürchtet habe. Bis ein Road Train kommt. Das ist ein Lastwagenzug von bis zu 55 Metern Länge und mit 700 PS, der bei 100 km/h die Luft genauso zerteilt wie alles andere in seinem Weg. So ein Truck fährt grundsätzlich mittig, weil die Straßen konvex gebaut sind, damit Regenwasser ablaufen kann. Und ein Trucker denkt nicht dran, bei Bedarf auszuweichen. Kann er auch gar nicht. Die Bullenfänger der Road Trains sind dicker als die Schranken vor dem Bundeskanzleramt und könnten wilde Storys erzählen.

Dann sind da – zumindest auf der Vortour – Pisten, die aussehen, als wären sie welche, aber eigentlich sind es keine. Wir probieren einige davon aus, weil noch leichte Autospuren zu entdecken sind. Auf der schlimmsten befindet sich links und rechts trockenes, dorniges Gestrüpp. Bald greifen die harten Äste abgebrannter Büsche nach dem Neulack der Landys, selbst das Einklappen der Außenspiegel nützt nichts. Als würden Fingernägel über eine Schiefertafel ziehen, jammern malträtiertes Scheibenglas und Blech ihr Lied von der Pein. Und ich verziehe das Gesicht, als fräße sich die borstige Flora direkt in meine Haut. Schließlich breche ich ab, es bleibt nur der Rückweg. Mangels Platz zum Wenden müssen wir rückwärtsfahren. Kilometerlang ...

Dann sind da Sanddünen. Für die Range Rover Sport auf der Vortour stellen sie kein Problem dar, für die kleineren und voll beladenen Discovery Sport mit ihrer geringeren Bodenfreiheit allerdings schon. So bleiben einige stecken, und ihre Ausgrabung kostet Schweiß und Zeit.

On numerous tours and pre-scouts, I have experienced every possible kind of trail: muddy, stony, soft, hard, dusty, frozen, narrow and wide. The Australian variant can be summed up in two words: extreme and diverse.

Take the archetypal Australian red dirt outback roads. We used them to link up various parts of the tour. The 50-foot wide gravel roads were just as dull. I always feared they would be – that is until a road train turned up. These articulated trucks up to 180 feet long put out over 700 hp and at a steady speed of 60 mph blaze their own trail on the highway. They dominate the middle of the road, and for good reason. The roads are convex so that rainwater drains off them. Evasive manoeuvring is not in your average trucker's vocabulary. Why would it be? The kangaroo bars fitted to road trains are thicker than the security barriers in front of Parliament.

Then there are the lookalike trails – on the pre-scout tour, for example – that in reality are nothing of the kind. We tested a few where the faint remains of vehicle tracks were still visible. The worst were often hedged in on both sides by thick, thorny bush land. The burnt hardwood branches soon leave their unique fingerprint all over the shiny new Land Rover paintwork. Even retracting the outside mirrors doesn't help. Imagine the sound of a hardened fingernail scratching across slate, amplified tenfold, and you can begin to sense how the glass and bodywork of our vehicles was made to suffer. After a while, we had to go back. Because we couldn't turn around we had to drive all the way back down the trail in reverse ...

Next on the agenda – the sand dunes. On the pre-scout they hadn't been a problem for the Range Rover Sport. For the smaller, fully loaded Discovery Sport with less ground clearance it was a different matter. A few of them got stuck and digging them out cost us time and no little effort.

DIE PISTEN
THE TRACKS

Und dann sind da die „normalen" Pisten: hart, bestückt mit Steinen oder abgebrochenen Ästen und Zweigen. Zum Beispiel durch die Strauchwüste. Eine Piste führt in die Community Yagga Yagga. Das Dorf wurde von der Regierung für die Aborigines gebaut, aber die scheinen sich hier nicht wohlgefühlt zu haben. Die Häuser stehen leer, die Kinderschaukel schwingt im Wind, als sei der Nachwuchs eben erst abgesprungen. Ein paar Regale im Supermarkt sind noch mit Konserven bestückt, die Pumpe am Brunnen funktioniert einwandfrei. Orte wie dieser wirken gespenstisch – aber unser größtes Problem hat keinen überirdischen Ursprung.

Es besteht aus Gummi: die Reifen. Auf der Vortour nutzen wir handelsübliche Offroad-Reifen (je Auto zwei Ersatzräder auf dem Dach) und wir bereuen es bitterlich. Denn jedes Auto muss mit fünf (!) Plattfüßen kämpfen. Im Schnitt zwei Reifen pro Wagen werden irreparabel aufgeschlitzt, der Rest ist zum Glück mit Bordmitteln zu reparieren. Damit uns nicht die Reifen ausgehen, suchen wir in jeder Ortschaft einen Reifendienst, der noch professioneller reparieren kann. Der Grund für die vielen Schäden: die Hitze. Herrschen in den Reifen normalerweise Temperaturen von 50 bis 60 Grad, sind es in Australien bis zu 90 Grad. Der Gummi wird weich, und alles, was spitzer ist als ein Tennisball, bohrt sich in die Pneus, wenn man nicht aufpasst. Zur Sicherheit nehmen wir auf die Haupttour drei Ersatzräder pro Pkw mit, die mit den festesten Reifen bestückt sind, die wir finden konnten: dicke Wände, große Stollen. Bei der Haupttour kosten die Pisten durchschnittlich immerhin nur zwei Platten pro Pkw, was immer noch 38 beschädigte Reifen insgesamt bedeutet. Unser Truck leidet übrigens außergewöhnlich: Wegen seines Gewichts von 22 Tonnen machen seine Pneus besonders schnell schlapp. Acht Platten müssen repariert werden. Zwei der riesigen Schlappen sind rettungslos hinüber.

Nicht zu unterschätzen als Reifenkiller sind übrigens auch die Bauten der heimlichen Herrscher des Northern Territory, die sich neben und auch auf den Pisten türmen: die Behausungen der Termiten. Die ameisenartigen Insekten bauen mit den knallharten, bis zu 3 Meter hohen Sandhügeln perfekte Klima-anlagen für ihre unzähligen unterirdischen Gänge und Kammern. Sie schaffen damit aber auch Barrieren, und wer sich nicht den Unterboden aufreißen will, umfährt die Kunstwerke lieber. Was nicht jeder begreift: Ein begleitender Journalist ist zu schnell unterwegs und übersieht so eine Naturkathedrale mit der Folge, dass die gesamte Vorderachse des Discovery Sport ausreißt. Die drei zum Glück unverletzten Insassen werden ebenso wie alles Transportable aus dem Wagen auf andere Autos verteilt. Es bleibt nichts anderes übrig, als den jungen Gebrauchtwagen mitten im Nirgendwo stehen zu lassen, nicht weniger als 1 500 Kilometer von einerseits Katherine und andererseits Alice Springs entfernt.

Der Abschleppwagen, ein 4x4-Laster, braucht eineinhalb Tage, um das Auto zu erreichen und ebenso lange, um mit dem Havaristen zurückzukehren. Der Land Rover ist in der Zwischenzeit nicht angefasst worden. Kein Wunder: Die Bevölkerungsdichte beträgt hier 0,18 Menschen pro Quadratkilometer. Wahrscheinlich haben sich nur ein paar Dingos, Dromedare, Vögel und Eidechsen über das Designerstück in der Wildnis gewundert. Was beweist: Wir suchen wirklich nur die besten Abenteuerpisten.

There was nothing "normal" about the "normal" trails which were hard-bedded and often filled with stones or splintered branches. Take the route through the bush desert. One trail led straight to the Yagga Yagga Community. The village was originally built for the Aborigines by the government but it would appear that they weren't that fond of the place. It had the atmosphere of a ghost town and a playground swing rocked to and fro in the wind, as if some errant child had just jumped off it. In the supermarket a couple of tins were still on the shelves and the pump in the water well was in full working order. It felt like the spirits had taken over here, but our biggest problem was far more down to earth.

More specifically our tyres were the problem. We had used the standard off-road rubber you can buy over the counter for the pre-scout tour (two each per car, stowed on the roof). And we regretted the decision almost immediately. Each vehicle suffered at least five (!) punctures. On average, two tyres per vehicle were damaged beyond repair, while we managed to patch the others together with our onboard tool kits. The first task in every settlement we drove through was to find a professional tyre repair service. One of the reasons for the many punctures was the heat. Normally, tyre temperatures between 50 and 60 degrees Celsius (120 and 140 degrees Fahrenheit) are to be expected. In Australia, this shot up to 90 degrees Celsius (190 degrees Fahrenheit). The rubber softens up and anything that is sharper than one of your granny's teeth can go through it like a knife. Just to be on the safe side on the main event we took three tyres per vehicle with us – tyres with much thicker walls and studs. We still went through two tyres per vehicle on the main drive, which added up to 38 tyres in total. Our truck was particularly badly affected. 22 tonnes put enormous pressure on the tyres leading to 8 punctures. For two of the tyres, it was a one-way trip.

A tyre killer we hadn't reckoned with were those constructions belonging to the real bosses of the Northern Territory – the termites. Their hills can be found on and at the side of every trail. These solidly built ant mountains can reach a height of 10 feet and contain a myriad of underground tunnels and chambers for their occupants. If you don't want to lose your underbody protection plates then it is better to treat these cathedral-like works of art as a roundabout rather than plough through them. Not every journalist on the tour took this advice seriously. For one who had a little too much speed on the clock there was no time to manoeuvre and it was good-bye Discovery Sport front axle. Fortunately, nobody was injured and both occupants and kit could be divided among the other vehicles. For the unfortunate Discovery Sport, however, the tour was over and we had to leave it in no-man's-land 930 miles from Katherine in one direction and Alice Springs in the other.

The recovery vehicle – a 4x4 truck – took a day and a half to reach it and the same to drive back. In the outback, the vehicle hadn't been touched the whole time it was parked up. Not surprising, given the population density of 0.5 people per square mile. The only witnesses to its lonely vigil were probably a few Dingos, dromedaries, birds and lizards. Proof positive that we only look for the best adventure trails we can find.

MARVIN VERHEYDEN

GEBOREN AM 8.3.1984 | GELERNTER TIERARZTHELFER, LET LEAD INSTRUCTOR UND SENIOR PROJECT MANAGER

BORN 8.3.1984 | TRAINED VETERINARY ASSISTANT, LET LEAD INSTRUCTOR AND SENIOR PROJECT MANAGER

Wie und wann bist du zur Land Rover Experience Tour gestoßen und was ist deine Hauptaufgabe?

2008 habe ich bei den Qualifikationscamps zur Malaysia-Tour als Freelancer die GPS-Station betreut. Danach war ich bei jeder Vor- und Endqualifikation dabei, ab der LET Seidenstraße als verantwortlicher Organisationsleiter. Meine erste Haupttour habe ich 2013 begleitet, da war ich bereits fest bei Dags Agentur APS angestellt. Meine Aufgabe: dem Chef den Rücken freihalten. Während so einer komplexen Tour stehen ·täglich Hunderte von Entscheidungen an und es gilt, ebenso viele Details zu kennen, um einen sicheren und reibungslosen Ablauf zu gewährleisten. Da braucht man ein gut funktionierendes und verlässliches Team an seiner Seite.

Ich bin derjenige, der als Erster ins Zielland fliegt und es als Letzter verlässt. Wenn Dag noch nicht vor Ort ist, übernehme ich seine Position, leite das Team und treffe alle Entscheidungen. Meine Vorbereitung auf die nächste LET beginnt an dem Tag, an dem ich von der aktuellen LET zurückkehre. Denn jedes Ziel erfordert unterschiedliches Equipment aufgrund unterschiedlicher Schwierigkeiten und Aufgaben.

Du warst bislang bei drei Haupt- und fünf Vortouren dabei. Was hat dich unterwegs besonders nachhaltig beeindruckt?

Es ist sehr schwer, die Touren zu vergleichen. Aber für mich war es ein ganz besonderer Moment, als ich mich bei der Seidenstraßentour in Nepal mitten auf die Straße gesetzt habe und minutenlang den freien Blick auf den Mount Everest genoss. Der Gedanke, dass man von seiner eigenen Haustür auf 5 000 Höhenmeter gefahren ist und nun das „Dach der Welt" sehen darf, geht unter die Haut. Ein weiterer unbeschreiblicher Moment ist es, wenn ich nach zwei Jahren Vorbereitung, sehr viel Schweiß, Arbeit und Zeit die letzten Meter einer LET fahre und mir klar wird, dass die Tour erfolgreich und sicher endet.

Egal, welche Probleme, Action oder Aufgaben anstehen – du behältst unterwegs stets die Nerven und vor allem die Ruhe. Hast du ein Rezept dafür?

Ich habe gelernt, dass auftretende Schwierigkeiten und Komplikationen am besten nach und nach analysiert und abgearbeitet werden sollten. Manchmal muss ich als Feuerwehrmann mehrere Brände löschen und gleichzeitig den Teilnehmern, Journalisten, aber auch·dem Team gegenüber Ruhe und Professionalität ausstrahlen. Wenn ich ruhig und konzentriert agiere, überträgt sich das auf alle – das Problem lässt sich so viel schneller und besser lösen. Ich glaube, ich brauche Stress, um gut zu arbeiten. Aber nach den oft extrem anstrengenden Zeiten drehe ich in der Regel eine Runde durch den Duisburger Zoo. Dort habe ich fast 20 Jahre lang gearbeitet. Und deshalb kenne ich dort alle Winkel, wo ich mich entspannen kann.

Gab es mal eine Situation, in der selbst du nicht mehr weiterwusstest oder am liebsten aufgegeben hättest?

Aufgeben war noch nie eine Option. Mit dem Wissen, dass ein tolles Team hinter mir steht, ist jede extreme Situation zu meistern. Und davon gibt es viele. Zum Beispiel in Australien, als Stefan Auer und ich in einem Discovery zweieinhalb Tage quer durch die Wüste am Lake Mackay gefahren sind, um eine Strecke für den Support-Truck zu erkunden. Neben einem heftigen Unwetter waren dort die Distanz, die Zeit, die Müdigkeit und die Einsamkeit extreme Gegner. Oder die eine Nacht in den Anden Perus, in der wir während der ersten Vortour -13 Grad im Zelt aushalten mussten. Überhaupt Peru: Zwischen Satipo und unserem Camp am Río Ene erlebten wir die Schlammschlacht unseres Lebens.

An welchen Ort der Welt würdest du gerne noch einmal – oder überhaupt – reisen?

Wenn es ginge: an jeden. Reisen wird immer ein Thema in meinem Leben sein. Egal ob mit Boot, Kanu, zu Fuß oder in meinem Land Rover 110er Defender – die Welt hat noch so viel zu bieten. Und das will ich alles sehen.

How and when did you hear about the Land Rover Experience Tour and what is your role?

I was lucky to be taken on as a freelancer to monitor the GPS exercise for the Malaysi Tour Qualification Camps in 2008. From then on I was involved with every pre- an final qualification camp before becoming an organizational manager at the start of th Silk Road LET. I joined Dag Rogge's agency APS full time in 2013 and took part in m first experience tour that same year. My job is largely supporting Dag in the day-to-da organization. During a tour, hundreds of issues need attending to daily to guarante people's safety. It helps to have a reliable team in the background that knows exactl what must be done.

I am the first to check out the destination and the last to leave when the tour is ove When Dag isn't there, I'm his deputy; I run the team and make all the decisions on hi behalf. I start work on the next LET the day I return from the current event as ever destination presents us with unique difficulties for which we need to be prepared.

You have attended three main tours and five pre-scouts thus far. Is there anything that you have experienced that has really stuck with you?

It is always difficult to compare the tours. One moment that truly stands out was durin the Silk Road tour in Nepal. I recall just sitting down on some track with a completel uninterrupted view of Mount Everest and staring at it gobsmacked for what seemed lik an eternity. The idea that I could walk out of my door, drive to an altitude of 16,000 fee and take in this view of the "roof of the world" just blows my mind. Another momen which is difficult to quantify in words, is that sense of satisfaction when after two year of hard work, you are driving the final yards of a tour and you know that it has been success and everyone is safe.

Regardless of the problems, activities, or tasks that need to be dealt with, you have a reputation for remaining cool, calm and collected. How do you do it?

Having attended numerous LETs and helped to organize international events for ou Land Rover colleagues in England, I have learned to be structured in the way I respon to problems, dealing with each issue as it happens. At times, you need to fight multipl fires while presenting a professional face to the media, participants and of course th team. If I stay calm, then the team remains calm so enabling us to find a quicker an better solution to the problem. I thrive on stress – and I'm a better team player for i When I have had a particularly taxing day I often go for an hour's walk in Duisburg zoo where I worked for 20 years. I know a few places that bring me back down to earth.

Have you ever experienced that feeling of not knowing how to carry on or of wanting to give up?

Giving up has never been an option for me. Of course, there are days that are determine by Murphy's Law. However, knowing that there is an excellent team behind me give me the confidence to deal with every extreme situation. And there are many of those I recall when I shared a Discovery in Australia with Stefan Auer for two-and-a-hal days in the desert near Lake Mackay looking for a route for our support truck. A violen storm, the unfathomable distances, exhaustion and a sense of extreme isolation al combined to test us to the limit. Equally unforgettable was a night spent in the Peruvia Andes during the first pre-scout when the temperature dropped to -13 degrees Celsiu (9 degrees Fahrenheit) – inside the tent. While I think about it, Peru and the rout between Satipo and our camp on the Río Ene was the mother of all mud baths.

Is there one place on the planet that you would like to visit or return to?

There is no one place. Travel will always feature large in my life. Whether in a boat, canoe, on foot, or in my Defender 110 there is still so much to see. And I want to see it al

CRAIG PUSEY

GEBOREN AM 16.8.1966 | GEBORENES MULTITALENT,
FOTOGRAF SEIT 2003

BORN 16.8.1966 | BORN MULTI-TASKER,
BECAME A PROFESSIONAL PHOTOGRAPHER IN 2003

Wie gestaltete sich dein erster Kontakt mit Land Rover?
Land Rover habe ich bei der Armee kennengelernt – auf dem Rücksitz in zu vielen Stunden auf schlechten Straßen. Dank meines Bruders habe ich dann aber Offroadfahren genießen gelernt: Er kaufte sich einen neuen Range Rover und begann, für Land Rover zu schreiben. Ich fing trotz meines Jobs als IT-Manager bei einem großen Konzern an, für den bekannten englischen Autofotografen Nick Dimbleby zu fahren. Wir haben einige Storys zusammen gemacht. Das Fotografieren habe ich mir autodidaktisch beigebracht: Irgendwann reichte es mir nicht mehr, Autos für Fotografen zu bewegen – ich wollte selber knipsen. Bald darauf kaufte ich eine gebrauchte Kamera ...

Wie bist du zur LET gekommen?
Für die LET wurde ich 2005 erstmals gebucht, als der bisherige Fotograf keine Zeit für die Schottland-Tour hatte. Seitdem bin ich dabei. Allerdings hatte ich von der Reise etwas ganz anderes erwartet: Ich hatte für ein paar Hotelnächte gepackt und nicht fürs Camping. Aber es war großartig. Da habe ich erst gemerkt, wie mir vorher bei der Büroarbeit das Abenteuer gefehlt hat.

Hat sich die Art deines Fotografierens im Laufe der Zeit verändert?
Mein Fotostil hat sich dramatisch weiterentwickelt und ich gehe davon aus, dass das auch so bleibt. Jeder Profi, der glaubt, seine Bilder könnten nicht besser werden, lügt sich in die Tasche.

Was ist das Schwierigste bei deiner Arbeit auf einer Tour?
Es ist nicht – wie man denken könnte – Autos „dynamisch" abzulichten, also in einer Art und Weise, dass man auch auf einem Foto sehen kann, dass sie fahren. Darin habe ich viel Übung durch meine Arbeit im Motorsport oder bei Trackdays. Eine der großen Herausforderungen ist es immer wieder, Menschen zu fotografieren. Man muss erst mal ihr Vertrauen gewinnen – und ebenso Vertrauen zu ihnen haben. Und dann ist Respekt das beste Werkzeug; wir wollen ja auch nicht völlig unvermutet irgendwo eine Kamera vors Gesicht gehalten bekommen. Aber wirklich schwierig ist manchmal, unter Zeitdruck die gewünschten Resultate liefern zu können, auch wenn der perfekte Schuss nicht machbar ist. Hinzu kommt zeitweise noch große Müdigkeit. Das perfekte Nachtbild zu machen nach gerade mal drei Stunden Schlaf ist schon etwas Besonderes.

Welche LET hat bei dir die nachhaltigsten Spuren hinterlassen?
Schwer zu sagen. Argentinien war besonders hart und faszinierend, das Team passte perfekt zusammen. Die Seidenstraßentour war aus Sicht eines Fotografen extrem: so viele Motive und nie genug Zeit, sie alle festzuhalten. Egal wo ich hinsah, gab es etwas, was sich zu fotografieren lohnte. Zur spannendsten Tour gehört wohl Bolivien – da wurden wir ein paarmal mit Steinen beworfen und einmal fast gekidnappt. Das war wirklich aufregend.

How did you first come into contact with Land Rover?
I knew Land Rover from my time in the British Army – usually too many hours sat the back on dreadful roads. Through my brother, I got involved with off-roadin He bought a new Range Rover and started writing about Land Rovers for magazine I was working as an IT Manager and began driving for the well-known Briti photographer Nick Dimbleby. We worked on a few stories together. Basically, I taug myself photography: it got to the point where it wasn't enough for me just to be the g driving the car in the shot. I wanted to be taking the picture myself. I bought myself m first used camera soon after that.

How did you hear about the LET?
I was booked to go on the 2005 Scotland tour after the previous photographer ha confirmed that he was unable to go. I have been involved ever since. For that first tri I thought I would just be staying in a hotel for a couple of nights and packed accord ingly – I didn't think I'd be in a tent. That said – I loved every minute of the tour. It was a eye-opener for me living that life of adventure that I had been missing working in an office.

Has your photography changed over the years?
My style of photography has moved on quite dramatically since I started and I thin it will continue to do so. A professional photographer who claims that their picture could not be any better is lying through their back teeth.

What is the most difficult aspect of photography on the tour?
It isn't what you would think – namely, capturing the vehicles dynamically so that yo get the impression of movement. Many hours spent in motorsport and at track day taught me how to do that. One of the greatest challenges on every tour is photographin people. You need to win their trust as well as trusting your own instincts that they ar right for the photograph. The best tool you have is respect; none of us wants to have camera shoved in their face out of nowhere. Sometimes it is hard to deliver the image that are required when time is short and you know that the prize-winning shot isn going to happen. Exhaustion is also a factor at times. Getting that perfect night shot afte only three hours' sleep is a bit special.

Which LET made the greatest impression on you?
Difficult to say. Argentina was hard work and at the same time immensely fascinating and the team bonded well. From a snapper's perspective, the Silk Road Tour wa extremely difficult with far too many amazing shots and too little time to capture them Regardless of which direction you pointed the camera, there was always somethin begging to be photographed. Bolivia probably had the greatest thrill factor. We had t put up with people throwing stones at us and were almost kidnapped. That helps yo to stay alert.

PERU

2017

RESPEKT IST ALLES: RESPEKT VOR DEN MENSCHEN, VOR DER KULTUR, VOR DER NAHRUNG, VOR DER NATUR – SO LERNT MAN LAND UND LEUTE AM BESTEN KENNEN. DAS GILT GANZ BESONDERS FÜR DAS UNFASSBARE PERU.
--
IT'S ALL A QUESTION OF RESPECT. RESPECT OF PEOPLE, CULTURE, FOOD AND NATURE – THIS IS THE BEST WAY OF GETTING TO KNOW A COUNTRY AND ITS INHABITANTS.

2017
LAND: PERU
STRECKE: 1 800 KM
COUNTRY: PERU
DISTANCE: 1,100 MILES

15 DISCOVERY 5, 3 RANGE ROVER SPORT

DER ZOLL
CUSTOMS

Südamerika war bis jetzt bei jeder Land Rover Experience Tour ein Knaller. Da ist es kein Wunder, dass es uns wieder dorthin zieht. Und wenn man die bisherigen Touren toppen will, bietet sich eigentlich nur ein Land an: Peru. Der Andenstaat beherbergt drei Klimazonen innerhalb der Landesgrenzen. Wir haben Strand und Wüste, Hochland sowie Dschungel, und die unvergleichliche Inkakultur fasziniert jeden, der gerne reist und an Zivilisationshistorie interessiert ist. Man kann einfach nichts falsch machen.

Startpunkt der Vortour ist der örtliche Land-Rover- und Jaguar-Händler in Perus Hauptstadt Lima. Wir wuseln uns vom Flughafen per Taxi durch die Zehn-Millionen-Metropole und werden herzlich empfangen. Der Betrieb ist groß, und es stehen drei Range Rover Sport aus Brasilien für die Suche nach geeigneten Pisten bereit. Zwar haben die Wagen kein Untersetzungsgetriebe und für die wegen der großen Bremsanlagen sehr breiten Felgen gibt es in Peru keine passenden Offroad-Reifen, aber wir haben zumindest in Sachen Pneus vorgesorgt: Aus den USA wurden bereits 24 grobstollige „General-Grabber-AT"-Reifen eingeschifft. Also alles kein Problem.

Denkste. Während wir die Range Rover Sport einrichten, mit Funk versehen, beladen, mit Ersatzkanistern bestücken, kümmert sich der Händler vor Ort um die Zollformalitäten, damit wir die Reifen abholen können. Doch das ist kompliziert. Die Papiere sind nicht fertig. Und werden es auch nicht. Eigentlich sind wir abfahrtbereit, die Räder könnten jeden Moment freigegeben werden. Deshalb richten wir uns beim Händler häuslich ein. Hier und da eine Besprechung, Essen gehen in der Nachbarschaft, lesen, Essen gehen, besprechen. Der Tag verstreicht, ohne dass etwas passiert. Uns rennt die Zeit weg, aber es hilft nichts: Wir müssen noch eine zusätzliche Nacht im benachbarten Hotel verbringen.

Der nächste Tag ergibt zunächst nichts Neues. Außer dass ich auf die geniale Idee komme, eine Kameradrohne zu kaufen. Eine Einfuhr wäre problematisch gewesen, deshalb entscheide ich, bei einem lokalen Fachhändler eine Phantom 4 zu erwerben. Da sich beim Zoll nach wie vor nichts tut, probiere ich sie aus. Aus Langeweile ausführlich. Was ich hätte lassen sollen …

Zunächst geht alles klar. Das gute Stück fliegt unter meiner Regie wunderbar und ruhig durch die Werkhallen des Landy-Händlers. Aber Lima von oben zu sehen, wäre auch mal schön. So lenke ich das technische Wunderwerk durch die große Einfahrtshalle nach draußen, wo die Thermik den weißen Quadrokopter erfasst und schnell in die Höhe treibt. Über das angeschlossene Smartphone bewundern wir die Umgebung von oben. Und dann mache ich – erfahrener Hubschrauberpilot, der ich bin – einen echten Anfängerfehler: Ich will die Drohne durch den Halleneingang wieder nach innen fliegen. Die Drohne reagiert natürlich viel zu sensibel und ist viel zu filigran, um dem Kamineffekt irgendetwas entgegensetzen zu können. Kaum im Gebäude, fängt sie an zu trudeln, und ich kann sie nicht mehr lenken. Sie berührt leicht den Boden und macht sich dann unkontrolliert auf den Weg, einen nagelneuen und auslieferungsbereiten Jaguar XJ zu zerkratzen. Das will ich nicht zulassen und begehe meinen zweiten Anfängerfehler: Ich greife in die Drohne, deren Propeller noch voll rotieren.

Every Land Rover Experience Tour we have run in South America has been an unmitigated success. Not surprisingly, we found ourselves drawn to the region again. Peru was capable of topping every tour thus far. While everyone has heard of the Andes, Peru is also home to three different climate zones. Beach, desert, highlands and jungle are in abundance here, not forgetting the unique cultural heritage of the Incas, which is a magnet for any ancient civilization buff. This was a veritable no-brainer.

We kicked off the pre-scout tour at the local Jaguar Land Rover dealer in the Peruvian capital Lima. After snaking our way from the airport through this mega city by taxi, we received a warm welcome from the local team. Being a large dealer with good contacts, they had managed to source us three Range Rover Sport from Brazil to help us work out the route. However, the vehicles lacked low range and we were unable to find any suitable off-road tyres to match the large road-biased wheels and brakes fitted. Fortunately, we had already organized the import of 24 sets of off-road "General Grabber AT" tyres from the United States. So it looked like we were ready to roll.

My optimism was a little premature. While we sorted out the Range Rovers, fitting radios, loading up and packing the spare jerry cans, the dealer took care of the customs formalities so that we could pick up the tyres. Things got complicated. The documents we required weren't ready. The process had ground to a halt. We were itching to get on the trail and as the tyres could turn up at any moment we chilled as best we could, held the odd meeting, went for a bite to eat in the neighbourhood, caught up on some reading, ate some more. The hours passed without anything actually happening. We were stuck facing another night in the hotel next door.

The following day was no different. I had the bright idea of buying a camera drone. Importing one would have been complicated, so I chose to buy a Phantom 4 from a local dealer. As the customs people still hadn't got in touch, I tried it out. And I thought why not make the test a thorough one. With hindsight, a stupid idea …

At first, inside the dealer workshop it seemed quite easy to fly, however, I wanted to see Lima from on high. I flew this piece of technical wizardry right through the entrance hall and outside where the quadrocopter was immediately carried upwards by the thermals at a rapid rate of knots. Via my phone screen I was able to take in the view from above. What happened next was a typical rookie's mistake (and that despite me possessing a helicopter pilot's licence!) I wanted to fly the drone back into the workshop. The drone is far too sensitive and delicate to counteract the chimney effect and started spinning inside the building as I realized it wasn't responding to my inputs. As it gently scraped the floor, it began to make its way towards a brand-new Jaguar XJ saloon about to be delivered to a customer. This could not happen and the rookie made his second mistake. I grabbed hold of the drone although the propellers were still rotating.

DER ZOLL
CUSTOMS

Was soll ich sagen: Die Schnitte in meinem Unterarm werden in der benachbarten Klinik mit 18 Stichen genäht. Die Drohne ist wieder einsatzbereit, nachdem wir einen beschädigten Propeller ausgetauscht haben. Und die Reifen sind noch immer nicht da. Erstmals seit Bestehen brennt es im Zoll. Alle Mitarbeiter werden evakuiert. Es ist wirklich verhext. Dann, nach 46 Stunden Warten, gibt der Zoll gelbes Licht. Okay, das ist zwar nur die Vorstufe zum nötigen grünen Licht, aber immerhin. Nach weiteren zwei Stunden können wir die Räder endlich abholen.

Prima – es ist Sonntagabend, und der Händler hat zwar eine Maschine zum Wechseln, aber niemanden, der sie bedienen kann. Was tun? 500 Meter weiter ist eine Tankstelle, und dort betreiben zwei Peruaner einen Reifendienst. Die bekommen jetzt den Auftrag ihres Lebens: 24 Reifen in Rekordzeit von einer Felge auf die andere ziehen. Mein Team rollt die Räder teilweise per Hand den holperigen Bürgersteig zur Tankstelle und zurück, einige werden auch per Taxi transportiert. Dann werden sie montiert, die Ersatzräder auf den Dächern verzurrt. Nach genau 50 Stunden Wartezeit sind wir endlich bereit.

Es ist Abend, 22 Uhr. Wir können los. Wir fahren noch vier Stunden bis nach Chincha, quartieren uns für drei Stunden in einem Hotel ein und starten morgens bei Sonnenaufgang. Darauf folgen 22 Stunden Fahrt – irgendwie müssen wir die verlorene Zeit ja wieder aufholen. Das Team macht das wie immer hochprofessionell mit, natürlich ohne zu murren. So mag ich das. Nur mein Arm schmerzt.

The rest is inevitable. In the clinic next door, I had to have eighteen stitches in my lower arm. The drone was ready to fly once we had repaired the damaged propeller. The tyres, however, still hadn't turned up. We heard that for the first time ever there had been a fire in the customs building and all the staff had been evacuated. It was beginning to feel like a conspiracy. After 46 hours of twiddling our thumbs, customs came up trumps with our wheels. Two hours later they were on their way.

Good news, right? It was Sunday evening and although the dealer had a tyre stripper on the premises there was no one around who knew how to operate it. Time to put on our thinking caps again. A third of a mile down the road at the fuel station two Peruvians ran their own tyre service. They got the contract of a lifetime to swap the tyres on 24 wheels. My guys literally rolled some of the wheels by hand along the pavement while the rest were taken by taxi. The new wheels were fitted on to the axles, the spares strapped on to the vehicle roof racks and after 50 hours we were finally ready.

It was 10 o'clock at night. We drove out of the dealership heading for Chincha four hours distant. After three hours in a hotel, we were up at the crack of dawn and on our way again. We had a 22-hour drive in front of us – we needed to make up for lost time. Professional as ever, there wasn't a sound of dissent within the ranks. That's how it should be. But my arm was painful.

DIE WÜSTE
THE DESERT

Ich habe schon eine Menge Wüsten gesehen, zum Beispiel in Jordanien, Namibia und China. Aber auf das, was Peru bietet, bin ich nicht vorbereitet. Wenn mir von offizieller Stelle geraten wird, bestimmte Gebiete nur mit speziellen Guides zu durchqueren, richte ich mich grundsätzlich danach. So auch hier: Wir würden keine Chance haben in dieser Wüste am Rande des Südpazifiks ohne einen Spezialisten, wird mir eindringlich eingebläut. Und der könne nur Maiki Nieto heißen, genannt „Desert Fox", Wüstenfuchs. Maiki fährt lokale Rallyes wie die Baja Inka mit seinem allradgetriebenen Dodge Ram 2500 Heavy Duty samt 7,2-Liter-Lkw-Motor und kann „lesen", wie man dieses Sandmeer relativ gefahrlos durchquert, ohne ständig stecken zu bleiben. Maiki ist nicht besonders gesprächig, aber seine Führung ist Gold wert. Schon der Beginn der Wüste fasziniert mich: Wir sind südlich von Ica, die Felder sind grün, die Granatapfelplantagen hängen voller Früchte. Dann: Sand. Massenhaft Sand. Wüste, von jetzt auf gleich. Sozusagen ohne Übergang. Wir senken den Luftdruck in den Reifen und folgen dem Desert Fox.

Wie er sich orientiert, ist nicht zu erkennen. Er folgt keinem Track, weil es keinen gibt. Die Oberfläche der Silikatmassen sieht absolut jungfräulich aus. Aus Hügeln werden Dünen, aus Dünen werden verdammt große Dünen. Das Fahrgefühl ist wie im Tiefschnee, weich und absolute Konzentration erfordernd. Trotzdem können wir nicht verhindern, dass das eine oder andere Auto sich festfährt. Wir müssen schaufeln und benötigen die Sandbretter, aber wir bekommen jedes Auto wieder flott – natürlich.

Irgendwann wird der Boden fester, wir scheinen auf Kalk zu fahren. Jedenfalls sehen die Wagen von hinten aus, als würden sie brennen, so sehr werfen die Reifen Staub auf. Und dann hält der Wüstenfuchs an, und wir müssen ein-, zwei- oder dreimal hinschauen, bevor wir begreifen, welche Art Steinhügel da vor uns liegt: ein versteinerter Blauwal. Freigelegt, aber der Erosion schutzlos ausgeliefert. Es ist nicht schwer, noch den Kopf zu erkennen, sogar die einzelnen Barten am Maul sind perfekt erhalten. Um uns herum befinden sich noch mehr Hügel. Darunter sollen sich weitere Balaenoptera Musculus befinden, sie sind nur nicht ausgepackt. Die Geschichte dazu: Einst hätten Ur-Haie eine Herde Wale in flaches Wasser gejagt, letztlich seien dort alle nicht mehr herausgekommen. Mit etwas Geduld lassen sich auch noch Haizähne im Sand finden, so groß wie eine Handfläche. Heute liegt dieser Ort 40 Kilometer von der Küste entfernt – nur ein Schild lässt erkennen, dass die Regierung schon weiß, welchen Schatz sie hier hat: Im Namen des Kulturministeriums ist das Fossilienareal zur Schutzzone erklärt. Um keine Plünderer anzulocken, taucht es auch in keinem Reiseführer auf. Ich bin völlig geflasht.

Weiter geht's. Maiki zeigt uns Reste von markierten Inka-Pfaden, der Sand wird wieder tief, die Dünen höher. Und dann: einer der schönsten Ausblicke, die ich je genießen durfte – rundherum nichts als Sand und in kilometerweiter Entfernung das Meer. Dort wollen wir hin. Hier, nah am Meer, sind die Dünen am höchsten, und Maiki weiß, wie man wieder runterkommt: rollen lassen. Einige seiner Routen führen fast senkrecht 100 Meter hohe Dünen hinunter. Wenn man das Auto lässt und nicht in irgendeiner Art und Weise zwingt, rollt es problemlos bergab. Man muss nur unten früh genug Gas geben, um den nächsten Berg wieder ein Stück hinaufklettern zu können, was wiederum die nächste Abfahrt vereinfacht. Das funktioniert natürlich nicht immer, aber das Ausgraben haben wir ja schon vorher geübt.

Endlich: Eine letzte Abfahrt, wir erreichen das Meer. Fette Möwen empfangen uns. Kein Wunder, ganz in der Nähe bei Santo Domingo befindet sich das Nationalreservat Paracas, ein 335 000 Hektar großes Vogelnaturschutzgebiet. Maiki führt uns zu einer Höhle, die perfekte Campsite. Wie gesagt: Es ist die schönste Wüste, die ich je erleben durfte.

I have done a lot of desert in my time including Jordan, Namibia, Chile and China but even I wasn't prepared for what we faced in Peru. When the authorities advise taking a guide, this is advice I usually stick to. This was the case in Peru. Slowly but surely, it dawned on me that in this desert on the edge of the Southern Pacific Ocean, it would be irresponsible to travel without a guide. The best one around was a certain Maiki Nieto. Appropriately nicknamed the "Desert Fox", Maiki has made a name for himself driving local rallies such as the Baja Inka with his 7.2-litre 4WD Dodge Ram 2500 Heavy Duty truck. The man has an uncanny ability to "read" the terrain ahead and cross deserts without constantly getting stuck. Maiki wasn't exactly talkative, but his navigational abilities were spot on. South of Ica, lush, green fields of pomegranate plantations ripe with fruit suddenly vanished. We were in the middle of a desert. We dropped the air pressure in the tyres accordingly and followed the Desert Fox.

Just exactly what our guide used for orientation was beyond me. He didn't stick to tracks because there weren't any. The smallest hills metamorphosed into dunes. Driving across them was akin to powder skiing, soft and undulating, while at the same time demanding every ounce of concentration. Inevitably one or other of the vehicles got stuck. To get them going again we needed the sand channels and started digging.

At some point the ground firmed up – it felt like driving on chalk. From behind, our vehicles were throwing up so much dust they looked like they were on fire. The Desert Fox stopped his vehicle and it took us a while to understand what the stony outcrop in front of us had once been. We were looking at the fossilized remains of a blue whale – in one sense free, but completely exposed to the effects of erosion. One could still recognize the head even down to the individual hairs around its mouth. We were surrounded by many similar hillocks, each of which had its own Balaenoptera musculus waiting to be unpacked. There was a reason why they were here. Many thousands of years ago prehistoric sharks had forced a herd of whales into shallow water from which they had been unable to escape. With a little patience one could even find sharks' teeth in the sand. Today the site is over 25 miles from the coast. A Ministry of Culture sign informs tourist visitors that this display of fossils is a specially protected scientific site. To ward off plundering there is no mention of the place in any guidebook either. I was speechless.

Time to move on. Maiki showed us what was left of ancient marked Inca trails, the sand got softer, the dunes higher. Then we were served up with one of the most amazing vistas I have had the privilege to enjoy – a 360-degree panorama of sand and in the distance you could just see the sea. This was where we were headed. The majority of the time we had spent climbing, so at some stage we would have to start descending. The dunes are at their highest in the vicinity of the coast. Maiki showed us the best way to get back down – just let it roll. Some of his routes involved driving down an almost 330-foot vertical drop. If you let the vehicle go on its own and refrained from trying to force the process, it worked. You just had to remember to stroke the accelerator early enough in the dip to get over the next crest and repeat the process. It didn't work every time, but we at least knew how to dig ourselves out.

Finale. One last drop and we had finally reached the ocean. Huge seagulls were waiting to greet us – hardly surprising given that just outside Santo Domingo is the Paracas National Reserve, an 828,000-acre bird sanctuary. Maiki led us to a cave where we set up camp. It doesn't get better than this – undoubtedly the most beautiful desert I have ever seen.

UND DANN IST PLÖTZLICH DAS MEER
DA: WIE GUT, DASS EINEM AUTO BEI
SO EINEM ANBLICK NICHT DER ATEM
STOCKEN KANN.
–
ALL OF A SUDDEN WE WERE FACING
THE SEA. FORTUNATELY OUR
VEHICLES ARE LESS PRONE TO
BREATHLESSNESS AT THE SIGHT OF
SOMETHING SO BEAUTIFUL.

MACHU PICCHU: DIE INKA-RUINEN SIND JEDE ANREISE WERT. ERST RECHT MIT DEM LAND ROVER – AUCH WENN DAS EXEMPLAR OBEN NUR EIN MODELLAUTO IST.

--

MACHU PICCHU: THE INCA RUINS ARE ALWAYS WORTH A VISIT. PARTICULARLY WITH A LAND ROVER – EVEN IF THE EXAMPLE SHOWN HERE IS ONLY A TOY.

Ich versuche grundsätzlich, eine Land Rover Experience Tour so auszurichten und durchzuführen, dass alle Teilnehmer, alle Journalisten und selbstverständlich auch Land Rover als Veranstalter zufrieden sind. Das ist meinem Team und mir bislang auch immer gelungen. Aber eine Aufgabe in Peru bringt uns an unsere Grenzen: Wir sollen ein Foto mitbringen, das mindestens eines unserer Expeditionsautos gemeinsam mit den berühmten Ruinen von Machu Picchu zeigt. Die Idee ist durchaus nachvollziehbar – die Kultmarke am Kultort. Allerdings gilt es davor, ein paar Schwierigkeiten aus dem Weg zu räumen.

Erstes Problem: Es gibt keinen Weg für Autos nach Machu Picchu, egal wo man starten möchte. Man kommt um die Bahnfahrt nicht herum: Von Santa Teresa dauert das Gerumpel eine halbe Stunde, die meisten Touristen übernachten aber in der ehemaligen Inka-Hauptstadt Cusco, und von dort fährt die Bahn mit Glasdach durch sehenswerte und wilde Bergregionen mehr als drei Stunden.

Zweites Problem: Am Bahnhof von Machu Picchu gibt es tatsächlich ein paar Straßen. Aber nur für hier auf ewig gestrandete Busse. Die schleppen die Touristenströme in Serpentinen auf den Ruinenberg und bringen sie auch wieder runter. Es gibt tatsächlich auch einen Fußweg auf Naturstufen – wir haben ihn aber nur bergab benutzt, und schon das war abenteuerlich ...

Drittes Problem: Perus Regierung hat schon seit Langem herausgefunden, dass man mit deftigen Eintrittsgeldern die Staatskasse aufmöbeln kann. Also gibt es unterhalb der Ruinen ein Gebäude mit Kasse, Drehkreuzen und Restaurant. Von dort sieht man nicht mal ein paar müde Mauerreste, man kann erst recht nicht motorisiert dorthin gelangen.

Natürlich haben wir das alles schon früh in Erfahrung gebracht. Also was tun? Wir besorgen uns bereits bei unserem Händler in Lima ein 1:32-Modell des neuen Discovery, und unser Henning – dank seiner Film- und Fotoaufnahmen verfügt er über eine ruhige Hand – bemalt den weißen Wagen mittels Filzstiften mit den Logos unserer Sponsoren und mit den Motiven unserer eigenen Aufkleber. Unser Fotograf Craig braucht nicht lange, um das so täuschend echt aussehende Mini-Auto auf einem Stück Rasen etwas abseits und oberhalb der Ruinen so zu drapieren, dass es wie echt aussieht. Dazu noch ein gutes Auge und das richtige Objektiv – und knips: Steht der Discovery vor den Ruinen von Machu Picchu.

Bei der Präsentation der Ergebnisse von der Vortour in England fragt doch tatsächlich einer der Anwesenden, wie wir es geschafft haben, ein Auto auf einer der Terrassen über den Ruinen zu platzieren. Aufgabe erfüllt. Irgendwie jedenfalls.

My priority in setting up and running the Land Rover Experience Tour is to make it work for the participants, the media and ultimately for Land Rover as the event organizer. Thus far, the team and I have always been able to achieve this balance. One request for the Peru tour really got our creative juices flowing. Our paymasters required a photograph of one of our expedition vehicles in front of the ruined city of Machu Picchu. I could see the attraction of having a cult brand in front of a cult location. There were, however, a few hurdles to clear first.

Problem No. 1: Regardless of how you look at it, there is no way of approaching Machu Picchu by car. The only way up is by train. Departing from Santa Teresa, the journey is only half an hour, but most tourists stay in the ancient Inca capital of Cusco before taking a three-hour train trip through vibrant and stunning mountain scenery.

Problem No. 2: Machu Picchu's railway station does have a few roads, but they are exclusively for buses to transport tourists up the serpentine track and bring them back down again. There is also a stone path, which we used on our way back down, and that was hair-raising enough.

Problem No. 3: Peru's government realized a long time ago that substantial admission ticket prices go a long way to help fill the state's coffers, explaining why there was a building below the ruins with ticket counters, turnstiles and a restaurant. But don't expect to see the ruins from there and certainly not with your own vehicle.

Of course, we had checked this out beforehand. We needed to find a "work around". Via the dealer in Lima we managed to get hold of a 1:32 scale model of the new Discovery and Henning our cameraman painted our sponsor logos and copies of the vehicle decals on the white toy. Craig the photographer didn't need long to position the realistic looking miniature Discovery on an area of grass just above the ruins so that it looked like the real thing. With the right lens, a photographer's eye and there we had our publicity shot in front of the ruins of Machu Picchu.

Back in England when we presented the results of the pre-scout we were actually asked how we managed to park a vehicle on one of the terraces above the ruins. Job done. Sort of.

DER MATSCH
THE MUD

Es gibt Dinge, die ich nicht zweimal erleben möchte. Dazu gehören zum Beispiel Unfälle, Ausfälle und Regenfälle. Besonders nicht im Dschungel. Nach den Schlammerfahrungen in Malaysia wollte ich eigentlich nie wieder durch irgendeinen restlos nassen Regenwald. Matsch raubt Zeit, ist anstrengend, macht alles dreckig und ist verdammt ungemütlich. Was soll ich lange reden – wer sich in den Dschungel begibt, kommt um Schlamm eben doch nicht herum. Bereits auf der ersten kompletten Vortour bekommen wir einen Eindruck, was Nässe mit peruanischen Pisten macht: Sie verwandelt sie in Rutschbahnen. Wir haben in einem kleinen Ort vor dem Rio Ene übernachtet, mit den Zelten unter einem Dach für den lokalen Wochenmarkt, und das war gut so, denn in der Nacht hat es zwei Stunden lang heftig geregnet. Haben wir uns am Vortag noch über die wilde Staubentwicklung beim Fahren beschwert, steht uns nun eine ganz andere Aufgabe bevor.

Die Oberfläche der Naturpiste nach Satipo hat sich aufgelöst. Der rote Lehm setzt sich sofort in die Profile der Grabber-Reifen. So wird unsere Berg- und Tal-Tour, die bei normalen Bedingungen für Land-Rover-Geländewagen eine Lachnummer zwischen grünen Riesen wäre, zur schweißtreibenden Dauerschleicherei. In jeder abfallenden Links- oder Rechtskurve wäre Schrittgeschwindigkeit blechgefährlich, weil die Landys bei nur einem km/h zu schnell in die von den Bewohnern der Gegend angelegten Wassergräben rutschen würden. Ein Schnitt von 10 km/h lässt uns vermuten, dass der Tag verdammt lang werden wird. Den Eindruck verstärken Baumstammbrücken und Wasserfurten. Erstere sind nicht nur wegen des nassen Holzes glatt, sondern auch voller Matsch, was ein Abrutschen möglich werden lässt. Letztere sind wegen des Regens teilweise recht tief. Aber natürlich schaffen wir es. Was mich glauben lässt, dass es noch schlimmer nicht kommen kann.

Tut es aber, und zwar bei der finalen Vortour. Gleicher Regen – nur viel länger. Gleiche Piste – nur noch viel aufgeweichter, sodass man von Piste schon nicht mehr sprechen kann. Diesmal bezweifle sogar ich, dass wir ankommen. Der Matsch ist stellenweise knietief. Er setzt sich nicht nur ins Reifenprofil, sondern gleich auf die kompletten Räder. Die Gefahr des Wegrutschens ist diesmal nicht so hoch, weil der ganze Unterboden der Range Rover auf der roten, nassen Erde aufliegt. Hier ist das volle fahrerische Können gefragt.

Wir robben uns förmlich Meter für Meter voran. Traktion können wir nur erreichen, indem wir viel mit der Lenkung arbeiten und uns Matschkanten suchen, an denen sich die Reifen irgendwie orientieren können. Irgendjemand muss ständig aussteigen: erstens, um die Autos zu erleichtern, zweitens, um vorauszugehen und die Bodenkonsistenz unter dem Schlamm zu erkunden. Und drittens, um zu schieben. Es dauert nicht lange, da sehen wir aus wie Gollum nach der Reise durch Moria, und wir haben viel Mühe, die nur geliehenen Autos nicht völlig einzusauen.

Ein Übergang über einen Wassergraben bereitet uns richtig großes Kopfzerbrechen. Quer zur Fahrtrichtung liegen zwei fette, aber absolut glitschige Baumstämme darüber. So schaffen das selbst die hochbeinigen Range Rover nicht. Also müssen dünnere Stämme und dicke Äste gefunden werden, um die Zwischenräume zu füllen, damit die Wagen nicht aufsetzen. Und dazu müssen wir – natürlich – so richtig durch den Matsch. Wir haben es letztlich wieder geschafft. Nach 32 Stunden für 8 Kilometer. Ich möchte solche Eskapaden jetzt aber wirklich nicht noch einmal erleben.

You know that rule of thumb "once bitten, twice shy". I apply that to things like crashes, breakdowns and rainfall. It is worse still when all three happen in the jungle. After getting very muddy in Malaysia, I vowed never again to tackle a rainforest, particularly in the rain. Mud is bad for your schedule, and it's exhausting, it leaves your kit filthy and is generally thoroughly unpleasant. However, if you want jungle, you get the mud for free. Our first complete pre-scout was a lesson in how rain can transform a Peruvian dirt track into a toboggan run. Stopping in a small village near the Rio Ene, we prudently set the tents up on a covered market place. A wise move as during the night it rained solidly for two hours. After moaning the day before about the crazy clouds of dust we were kicking up on the trail, now we had a very different problem to deal with.

The surface of the track to Satipo had simply disappeared. Our Grabber tyres were caked solid with red clay. On any other occasion, the mix of mountainous and valley driving would have been no test at all for the Land Rovers – today our progress ground to an exhausting crawl. Even at walking pace, one mile an hour too fast going through the corners could result in the vehicles sliding uncontrollably into the ditches at the side of the track. We were managing an average speed of 6 mph, which confirmed my fears that it was going to be a long day. This assessment was further underlined by the state of the log bridges and the water crossings on the route. The former were slippery like ice rinks and covered in mud, making them treacherous to drive over and the latter were now very deep thanks to the incessant rainfall. We made it through this time and I remember thinking that it couldn't get more difficult than this.

It did, however. On the final pre-scout we had the same rain. This time it didn't stop. Same track, though it had now softened up so much that "track" was something of a misnomer. Normally, I'm more optimistic and yet even I thought we wouldn't make it. We were up to our knees in mud. The goo actually covered not only the tread pattern on our tyres, but the whole wheel. Sliding off the track was no longer an issue as the Range Rover underbodies sat firm on the red muddy morass of earth. We required every ounce of driving ability to get out of this.

We crept forward. Our only hope of traction was by plying the steering wheel back and forth to cut an edge in the walls of mud where the tyres could bite. Every once in a while somebody had to get out of the vehicle, to reduce the weight, check whether the ground below the mud was actually firm enough to gain traction and to push. It wasn't long before we looked like Gollum from Tolkien's *Lord of the Rings* after his travel through Moria and it became a real problem keeping the interiors of our hired Range Rovers clean.

One river crossing presented us with a real headache. Two huge, slippery tree trunks lay at 90 degrees to the trail – they were too big to climb over with the Range Rovers without grounding out. The solution was to find enough smaller logs and branches to fill the gaps to give us a clear chance of driving over them. It meant jumping into the brown stuff – again. 32 hours to drive 5 miles. I have had my fill of mud for a lifetime.

DIE PLANUNGSUNSICHERHEIT
PLANNING AHEAD

Planung ist nötig, gut und – mit Verlaub – manchmal „fürn Arsch". Beispiel gefällig? Perus Hochland, 60 Kilometer vor unserem Ziel, ein kleines Dorf auf dem Weg nach Huancayo namens Tana, wo wir Tische und Bänke für eine Schule gespendet haben. Wir wollen an diesem liebenswerten und ruhigen Fleckchen Erde auf 2 200 Metern Höhe übernachten. Es liegt auf einem Short Cut zur Hauptstraße – die absolut atemberaubende Strecke durch Felsschluchten und über uralte Holzbrücken erlaubt es, dass wir uns nicht einen halben Tag lang auf einer Ebene in rund 5 300 Metern Höhe herumquälen müssen.

Da meldet sich mein Freund und Koch Réne per Funk. Er ist schon vorgefahren, weil er einen Journalisten im Auto ins Tal bringt, dem die bisherige Höhe nicht gut bekommen ist. Seine Info: 6 Kilometer vor dem Ziel liegen Felsbrocken auf der Straße. Keine Weiterfahrt möglich – er alleine kann die fetten Steine nicht bewegen. Mit drei Kollegen düse ich nach vorne, und zu fünft rollen wir die Folgen eines Erdrutsches beiseite. Währenddessen fragt uns ein entgegenkommender Zweiradfahrer, warum wir uns diese Mühe machen – in 3 Kilometer Entfernung würden Bauarbeiten die Passage sowieso blockieren.

So war das nun nicht geplant. Ich fahre vor, um mich schlau zu machen: Nach 3 Kilometern ist die Straße tatsächlich gesperrt. Bauarbeiter reparieren einen Wasserabfluss, auf einer Länge von etwa 10 Metern ist die Schotterpiste schlicht weg. Die Männer sind dabei, das fehlende Stück einzuschalen und alles mit Beton auszugießen. Das bedeutet für uns: 57 Kilometer zurück und bergauf fahren, um dann die Hochebene zu durchleiden. Nein danke.

Wir reden kurz mit den Bauarbeitern, und sie sind mit meiner Idee einverstanden: Wir sammeln Steine und befestigen damit unsere eigenen Fahrspuren inklusive spezieller Ausfahrt. Tatsächlich rollen alle 19 Autos unseres Konvois langsam, aber problemlos über das Stück Straße, das eigentlich unpassierbar sein soll. Noch im Hellen und zeitig genug, um ohne Stress unser Camp aufzubauen, erreichen wir das Ziel. So mag ich das.

Am nächsten Tag geht's weiter nach Huancayo. Die bislang gute Straße führt wieder bis auf 4 600 Meter Höhe und wird immer schmaler, immer kurviger. Damit sich die Fahrzeuge unseres Konvois nicht ständig auf den Stoßstangen hocken, habe ich ihn in vier Gruppen geteilt. Ich bin relativ weit vorne, als es wieder heißt: kein Fortkommen möglich. Diesmal ist ein Lkw Schuld. Ein Sattelzug mit Dreiachsauflieger hat sich verkeilt. Der Container des Brummis hängt trotz weitem Ausholen des Fahrers in einer Rechtskurve an einem Felsvorsprung über der Straße fest. Der Fahrer versucht, rückwärts aus der Klemme zu kommen, aber die Räder drehen durch. Gewonnener Platz zum Rangieren: etwa 20 Zentimeter. Die verzweifelten Einheimischen wissen nicht weiter.

Aber wir. Dabei hilft uns unsere Ausrüstung. Es gilt, den Hänger mit dem Container so weit zu kippen, dass er um den Felsen herum geführt werden kann. Wir laden die Maxtrax ab, das sind variable Sandbleche aus dickem Plastik. Vor die drei kurveninneren Aufliegerräder schichten wir Steine, darüber die Maxtrax. Das kippt die Ladung um rund 10 Grad, und der Laster kann die Engstelle passieren. Gut übrigens, dass mir meine Jungs erst hinterher zeigen, was vorne am Laster prangt: Gefahrgutzeichen in allen Formen und Farben bis hin zum Totenkopf. Aber ich will es ja nicht anders. Denn normal wäre langweilig. Bei aller Planung …

Planning is important and sometimes – with respect – a complete and utter waste of time. How about this for an example? We were on our way to Huancayo, travelling across the Peruvian plateau, 40 miles out from our overnight camp in the adorable peaceful village of Tana at an altitude of 7,200 feet above sea level. We had donated a set of chairs and tables for the local school, hence the shortcut to the main road – an absolutely breathtaking trail along gorges and ancient wooden bridges, which saved us spending an extra half day gasping for air at 17,400 feet.

My mate and our chef René called up on the radio. He had driven on ahead to transport a journalist back down the valley who was suffering from altitude sickness and had some disturbing news. 4 miles out from the next town there had been a landslide and the trail was impassable – René couldn't move the rubble on his own. I took three colleagues and set off ahead of the convoy. Between the five of us we started to clear the fallen rocks. While we were at it, a cyclist appeared from the other direction asking why we were bothering to clear the track at all – 2 miles further on roadworks blocked the trail completely.

We hadn't planned for this. I drove on to check the situation for myself. The road was well and truly blocked. Road gangs were busy repairing a water channel, which had required removing about 30 feet of the gravel track completely. The men were building the moulds to take the concrete for the final section. We would have to turn round and drive 35 miles before climbing and driving back along the plateau. No thanks. We talked to the road crew and they agreed to my plan. We collected enough rocks to bridge the gap for our vehicles with a special exit route out of the ditch. All 19 vehicles slowly drove over the "impassable" obstacle coming through with no problems. We reached our destination in daylight and with enough time to set up camp without having to rush things. Just the way I like it.

The following day we headed onto Huancayo. Once again, the road had taken us to an altitude of 15,000 feet and while it was in good condition, it had started to get narrower with more and more switchbacks. To prevent the convoy from literally sitting on each other's bumpers, I divided the vehicles up into four groups. I was quite a way forward when I received the message that there was something holding us up again. This time a truck was to blame. An articulated lorry with a triple-axle trailer had jack-knifed. Despite the driver having taken a wide angle to get round the corner, the container was jammed under an overhanging part of the cliff on the right hand side of the road. His efforts to reverse and free up the trailer hadn't worked and his wheels were spinning uselessly with a gain of a paltry 8 inches for manoeuvre. The locals were pretty desperate.

We came up with a plan. It helped that we had some useful equipment on board. The idea was to tip the trailer enough to allow it to be pulled around the corner. We unloaded our Maxtrax sand channels made from extremely durable, robust plastic. To get the trailer plus container to lean the required ten degrees we piled up stones in front of the trailer's inside wheels and placed the sand channels on top thus enabling the truck to manoeuvre around the corner. As it turned out, it was a good job that my lads waited until after we were finished before showing me the hazardous cargo warning sign including the all too obvious skull and crossbones symbol on the front of the truck. But hey, this is what I live for. Normal is for other people. You can't plan for everything.

DAS PECH
BAD LUCK

Wenn Sie, liebe im Geiste Mitreisende, nach der Lektüre der vielen abenteuerlichen Kapitel den Eindruck haben, dass die diversen Land-Rover-Modelle sowie mein Team und ich von der Land Rover Experience Tour eigentlich überall hin und durch können, wo wir es wollen, haben Sie grundsätzlich erst mal recht. Und Sie haben inzwischen bestimmt auch mitbekommen, dass ich mir eher die Nacht um die Ohren schlage, um eine praktikable Lösung für ein Problem zu ersinnen, als mit den Achseln zucke, das Problem delegiere oder aufgebe. Die gefundenen Alternativen sind niemals Hexenwerk, sondern das Ergebnis von meist logischem Denken.

Das ist der Natur allerdings völlig wurst. Ich will zwar nicht behaupten, dass sie bei allen unseren Touren gnädig war, aber sie hat uns nie einen so großen Streich gespielt, dass wir umkehren mussten. Sie ahnen, was kommt?

Peru, mittendrin, Haupttour, zweite Etappe. Wir nehmen die rund 190 Kilometer lange Straße von Huancayo in den Dschungel nach Satipo in Angriff. Normalerweise braucht man dazu etwa sieben Stunden. Wir sind pünktlich und im Zeitplan – der einzige Überpünktliche ist El Niño. Es regnet aus Eimern, in wenigen Stunden etwa 30 Zentimeter Wasser. Unsere Piste besteht teils aus Schotter, teils aus Asphalt – es gibt Schlimmeres. Zunächst geht auch alles gut, selbst wenn das Fahren bei Sturzfluten nicht gerade ein Genuss ist. Und dann passiert das, was ich eigentlich bei jeder Tour irgendwann befürchte, was aber noch nie eingetreten ist: Ein Erdrutsch mit Steinen und Geröllmassen hat die Fahrbahn unter sich begraben, etwa eine Fahrstunde vor unserem Ziel. Und es ist diesmal leider nicht ein Erdrutschchen, sondern ein ausgewachsener halber Berg, der uns an der Weiterfahrt hindert.

Und nicht nur uns: Ein Linienbus voller Menschen wartet schon seit geraumer Zeit. Auf was? Sie haben einen Bagger angefordert, erzählen sie uns, und sie würden es begrüßen, wenn wir uns an den Kosten beteiligen, um weiterfahren zu können. Neugierig wie ich bin, frage ich, wann der Bagger denn eintreffen soll: „In einer Stunde." Allerdings bin ich oft genug in Südamerika unterwegs gewesen, um zu wissen, was hier „eine Stunde" bedeutet: halber Tag. Oder ein ganzer. Oder noch länger.

Ich sage es ganz offen: Ich hasse es, wenn ich klein beigeben muss. Aber selbst ein Land Rover Discovery kann zwar Berge bezwingen, aber sie nicht versetzen. Und ich auch nicht. Bleibt nur: umkehren – die gesamte Strecke zurück nach Huancayo fahren. Dort übernachten wir. Eine andere Strecke nach Satipo am nächsten Tag ist ebenfalls unmöglich. Wir müssten durch einen normalerweise harmlosen Fluss – der ist aber zum reißenden Gewässer mutiert. Also fahren wir neun Stunden lang nach Pisco und bieten den Teilnehmern als Ersatz für den Dschungel eine Extratour durch die Wüste.

Und wenn man schon mal so richtig Pech hat, ist Murphy's Law nicht weit: Ein Charterflieger sollte uns von Pisco nach Cusco bringen, damit wir von dort aus die berühmte Ruinenstadt Machu Picchu besuchen können. Was passiert? Zuerst ein Gewitter in Cusco. Und zwar so, dass der Flieger am Boden bleiben muss. Und dann lässt die Crew über Nacht das Licht an, so dass er am nächsten Morgen keinen Strom zum Starten hat. Bei allen Hürden: Wir haben Machu Picchu trotzdem noch erreicht.

So eine Land Rover Experience Tour ist und bleibt – trotz aller akribischer Vorbereitungen – ein pures Abenteuer. Auch in Zukunft.

You, the reader, accompanying us in spirit on our many adventures, may think that the Land Rover Experience team and their vehicles can go anywhere they want and in one sense you'd be right. By now, you will have realized that I am more likely to stay up all night to solve a problem before shrugging my shoulders, delegating the task to someone else or simply giving up. Working our way around a problem is not the stuff of magicians – more the result of approaching the issue in a logical way.

Not that Mother Nature really cares much for logic. There have been moments on our tours when she has made life difficult for us, but we have never been forced to turn around. Until now, that is.

We were in Peru, right in the middle of the second stage on the main tour making our way along the 190-kilometre route from Huancayo in the jungle to Satipo. Normally, this would take around seven hours. We were on schedule and making good progress. El Niño soon changed that. It was raining cats and dogs – in less than a couple of hours we had already seen almost 12 inches of rain. The road itself was a mix of gravel track and tarmac – we had seen much worse and although it was hard work, things initially looked OK. The thing I fear most on any tour is a landslide. It had, however, never happened. Until today. An hour out from our destination, the road ahead had just disappeared under a mass of rocks and debris. And this wasn't just any old landslide: in front of our windscreens, a significant portion of the mountain prevented us from continuing on our way.

And we weren't alone. A coach full of tourists had obviously been there for some time, waiting, it transpired, for an excavator to come and clear the road. What is more, they would be grateful if we could contribute towards the cost of clearing the road. Curious, I asked when they expected the digger to turn up. We were told an hour. I have spent a lot of time in South America and it was immediately clear that this meant at least half a day, more likely a full day or even longer.

I'll be honest. I HATE giving up. The Land Rover Discovery is great at climbing mountains, not so good at clearing them out of the way. Our only choice was to turn around, drive all the way back to Huancayo and overnight there. Another route to Satipo the following day was equally off the cards. We would have to cross a river, normally no problem whatsoever, but the weather had transformed it into a raging torrent. We headed for Pisco – a full nine hours' drive – it meant that we would have to do without the jungle – instead, the participants faced another drive through the desert.

A small portion of bad luck is often followed by a dollop of Murphy's Law for good measure. Our charter aircraft was due to take us from Pisco to Cusco; and from here, we were going to visit the ruined city of Machu Picchu. The thunderstorm in Cusco prevented the aircraft from taking off. The crew cleverly left the lights on overnight with the result that the following morning the aircraft's battery was dead. By some miracle we nevertheless we made it to Machu Picchu.

Despite the best planning in the world, even the Land Rover Experience Tour sometimes needs a bit of luck.

In Peru waren Sie zum ersten Mal bei einer
Land Rover Experience Tour dabei.
Mit welchen Erwartungen sind sie nach Südamerika gereist?
Über die Chance, mit der Land Rover Experience Tour durch Peru zu reisen, haben meine Frau und ich uns sehr gefreut. Wir hatten diese Reise als Urlaub gebucht, wohlwissend, dass es keine Erholungsreise werden würde. Wir waren gespannt auf die Fülle der Abenteuer und die faszinierenden Erlebnisse, die mir immer wieder von der Land Rover Experience Tour berichtet wurden. Diese Erwartungen sind in der Realität nicht nur erfüllt, sondern sogar weit übertroffen worden. Peru präsentierte uns eine unglaubliche Vielfalt an Abenteuern und Begegnungen, an Kultur und Natur, sowie an Traditionen und Entdeckungen. Wir danken Dag Rogge und seinem Team, dass wir diese Tour erleben konnten.

Gab es besonders beeindruckende Erlebnisse?
Davon gab es eine ganze Menge – und ich bin froh, dass es dieses Buch gibt. Denn hier finden sich zahlreiche dieser außergewöhnlichen Momente dokumentiert. Man benötigt eine gewisse Zeit, um die vielen überwältigenden Eindrücke zu verarbeiten. Unvergesslich bleibt sicherlich die Campsite am Pazifik unter einem klaren Sternenhimmel und begleitet von einem fantastischen Essen mit einem guten Schluck peruanischen Rotwein. Oder der Erdrutsch bei der Fahrt in den Regenwald – und wie gelassen die Peruaner mit solchen Naturereignissen umgehen. Oder die Fahrt mit dem gläsernen Zug aus dem historischen und sehr bunten Cusco zu unserem finalen Traumziel Machu Picchu. Darüber hinaus gibt es Dutzende kleine und große Momente, die die Faszination Land Rover Experience Tour ausmachen.

Welche Bedeutung besitzt die Land Rover Experience Tour
für die Marke Land Rover? Immerhin handelt es sich hier
um ein besonders aufwendiges Event.
Das stimmt ganz sicher – die Land Rover Experience Tour ist aufwendig. Sie fordert den Organisatoren und uns als Unternehmen einiges ab. Aber die Tour ist auch einmalig und einzigartig – und damit ist sie typisch für Land Rover. Denn nur unsere Marke besitzt die Authentizität und diese lange Tradition, wenn es um Expeditionen und Abenteuer geht. Unsere Modelle verfügen seit 1948 über eine Bandbreite an Fähigkeiten, die sie fast überall hinführen. Nicht umsonst wurden sie z. B. als UN-Fahrzeuge eingesetzt und werden vom Roten Kreuz in vielen unwegsamen Gebieten genutzt. In Peru haben wir diese Fähigkeiten immer wieder erlebt: Der Land Rover Discovery und Range Rover Sport müssen vor keiner Aufgabe zurückschrecken, sie kommen mit jedem Untergrund und jeder Herausforderung zurecht; ob Wüstensand oder fast 5 000 Meter Höhe. Insofern ist jede Land Rover Experience Tour für die Teilnehmer eine Probefahrt unter extremen Bedingungen, und sie liefert Bilder und Erlebnisse, wie sie eben nur von Land Rover kommen können. Auch bereitet sie den Weg für die Land Rover Experience Reisen, die Kunden und Interessenten ebenfalls buchen können.

Blicken wir in die Zukunft: Welche weiteren Ziele können Sie sich
für die Land Rover Experience Tour vorstellen?
Grundsätzlich kann ich mir für Land Rover alles vorstellen, schließlich sind wir in über 150 Ländern weltweit vertreten. Insofern dürfte es nur wenige Winkel der Erde geben, in denen noch kein Land Rover gewesen ist. Wenn man nun auf dem Globus nach Zielen für die Land Rover Experience Tour Ausschau hält, gibt es unter den Erdteilen nicht mehr viele weiße Flecken. Europa hat die Tour ebenso bereist wie Nord-, Mittel- und Südamerika. Auch Asien war bei den zwölf Auflagen unter den Tour-Zielen, ebenso wie Australien vor zwei Jahren. Eine der ersten Land Rover Experience Touren führte nach Afrika – damals war es noch eher eine interne Veranstaltung. Deshalb könnte ich mir vorstellen dorthin zurückzukehren. Seit Jahren bieten wir bereits sehr erfolgreich Land Rover Experience Reisen durch Namibia oder Botswana an. Aber Afrika bietet noch viel mehr. Ich bin fest davon überzeugt, dass das Land Rover Team ein spannendes Ziel finden wird. Aber man kann auch Land Rover Abenteuer „zu Hause" erleben. In unserem Land Rover Experience Center bieten wir allen Interessenten und Kunden die Möglichkeit, unsere Fahrzeuge abseits des Alltags und abseits asphaltierter Wege zu testen und zu erleben. Ich freue mich darauf, Sie dort oder auch auf einer unserer Land Rover Experience Reisen begrüßen zu können.

Peru was the first time you took part in a Land Rover Experience Tour.
What did you expect?
My wife and I were overjoyed at the opportunity to take part in the Land Rover Experience Tour to Peru. Although we booked the tour as a holiday, we were both aware that this wasn't going to be a vacation in the traditional sense. We were keen to experience for ourselves the adventures and the fascinating tales that I have heard time and again from previous Experience tours. Our expectations weren't only met – they were surpassed many times over. We met some amazing people, experienced culture and landscapes very different from our own and were thrown into the odd adventure or two. We can only express our gratitude to Dag Rogge and his team for making it all possible.

Was there anything that sticks particularly in your mind?
Many things – which is why I am so pleased about the book. Countless unforgettable moments on the tour are documented within these pages. One needs some time to process many of these remarkable experiences. Our campsite on the Pacific under a starlit sky, accompanied by a fantastic dinner and a glass of Peruvian red wine for example. Or the landslide we experienced in the rainforest and how relaxed the Peruvians are when faced with natural disasters. Or the journey in the vista dome train from the historical and colourful town of Cusco to the destination of our dreams Machu Picchu. There are literally dozens of moments, some more significant than others, that make a Land Rover Experience Tour so special.

How important is the Experience Tour for the Land Rover brand? After
all, it requires a considerable amount of effort to make it happen.
Absolutely. The Land Rover Experience Tour requires a huge amount of effort – both from the organizers and from the company. However, the tour is one of a kind – it's both unique to and characteristic of Land Rover. We are the only brand to possess this kind of authenticity and tradition with regard to expeditions and adventure per se. Ever since 1948, our vehicles have been characterized by their broad range of abilities enabling them to drive pretty much anywhere. This explains why they have been the vehicle of choice for organizations like the UN and the Red Cross operating in inaccessible regions everywhere. We have had to call on these abilities time and again in Peru. Neither our Land Rover Discovery nor the Range Rover Sport let us down once regardless of the terrain or the task at hand, whether in the desert or at an altitude of 16,000 feet. As such, every Land Rover Experience Tour can be seen as a test drive in extreme conditions, delivering pictures and experiences as only Land Rover can. The Tour also prepares the way for the Land Rover Experience safaris which can be booked by paying customers.

Let's take a look at what the future holds: Are there any particular
destinations, which you believe would be a good fit for
the Land Rover Experience Tour?
In principle, nothing is impossible as Land Rover is currently present in over 150 countries worldwide. That implies there are only a few far-flung corners of the earth, which have not yet seen a Land Rover. Searching the globe for possible future destinations for a Land Rover Experience Tour also reveals that there are few regions left on the map still to be explored. Europe, North, Central and South America have all featured in the Experience programme. The twelve tours thus far also include Asia and Australia, which was visited two years ago. One of the first tours went to Africa – but it was more of an internal event. For that reason alone, I could imagine returning to this great continent. For many years the Land Rover Experience Tour programme has included Namibia and Botswana – but there is so much more to Africa. I am convinced that the Land Rover team can come up with an exciting destination. Fortunately, there is a way to experience adventure with your Land Rover "at home". Our Experience Centres offer prospective customers and those who have already been bitten by the Land Rover bug the opportunity to test our vehicles off the beaten track and away from the daily grind. I look forward to welcoming you at one of our centres or perhaps on one of the next Land Rover Experience Tours.

EPILOG
EPILOGUE

Wenn ich behaupten würde, zwölf Land Rover Experience Touren hätten mich um 20 Jahre altern lassen, wäre das gelogen. Aber ebenso flunkern würde ich, wenn ich konstatierte, ich wäre dadurch jünger geworden.

Würde jemand dagegen sagen, die Zeit hätte mich um 20 Jahre weiser werden lassen – nun ja, ich würde mich zumindest nicht nachhaltig dagegen sträuben.

Richtig ist wahrscheinlich: Ich habe unglaublich viel dazugelernt. Ich habe so wahnsinnig viele tolle Menschen kennen und schätzen gelernt, denen ich sonst wahrscheinlich nie begegnet wäre.

Ich kann Gefahren besser einschätzen als vorher, ich kann ihnen eher ausweichen, und ich weiß genau, auf wen ich mich hundertprozentig verlassen kann.

Na, wenn das nicht die perfekte Grundlage für weitere Touren ist. Ich bin noch lange nicht satt.

If I were to say that twelve Land Rover Experience Tours had put 20 years on me, I'd be lying. It would be equally untrue to claim the opposite and say that they had made me feel younger.

However, if someone were to point out that I had gained 20 years' worth of experience in the same time frame, I wouldn't argue with that.

Truth be told, I have benefitted enormously from the experience. I have met and learned to respect a group of wonderful people whom under normal circumstances I would never have had the pleasure of meeting at all.

My sixth sense for danger has improved dramatically; I am quicker to avoid trouble today than I was as a younger man, and I know on whom I can rely one hundred per cent.

Now if that isn't the best reason for planning more Experience Tours, I don't know what is. I, for one, am still hungry.

100 EXTREME
DIE INTENSIVSTEN MOMENTE AUS ZWÖLF LAND ROVER TOUREN

- **die gefährlichste Straße:** ein extrem schmaler Minenweg (Bolivien)
- **der gefährlichste Moment:** ein überlaufender Tankanhänger (Bolivien)
- **der schönste Sonnenaufgang:** in der Wüste (Namibia)
- **der schönste Sonnenuntergang:** in den Bergen (Kirgisistan)
- **der offenste Guide:** Tenzin (China)
- **die schwierigste Passage:** ein Flussbett (Argentinien)
- **der problematischste Einkauf:** auf dem Frischmarkt (Malaysia)
- **das furchtbarste Hotel:** lieber keine Beschreibung (Bolivien)
- **das beste Hotel:** ein Haus in Colomé (Argentinien)
- **das seltenste Tier:** ein wilder Puma (Kanada)
- **die tiefste Wasserdurchfahrt:** fast bis zur Mitte Seitenscheibe (Island)
- **die höchste Bergstraße:** Gyatso La mit 5 228 Metern (Tibet)
- **das schlimmste Essen:** Gammelfleisch zum Selberkochen (Bolivien)
- **das leckerste Essen:** diverse Restaurants (China)
- **der größte medizinische Eingriff:** ein schlimmer Verkehrsunfall (Mexiko)
- **die komischste Situation:** eine erfundene Technikgeschichte (Malaysia)
- **die längste Tagesetappe nach Zeit:** 19 Stunden (Island)
- **die längste Tagesetappe nach Kilometern:** 1 161 Kilometer (China)
- **der untalentierteste Fahrer:** ein deutscher Journalist (Guatemala)
- **die problematischste Benzinsuche:** täglich (Bolivien)
- **das größte Geldbündel:** Barzahlung beim Tanken (Usbekistan)
- **die höchste Bestechungssumme:** 2 000 … (aber wo war das noch?)
- **der längste Grenzaufenthalt:** 13 Stunden (Usbekistan)
- **die schwierigsten Visumanträge:** bitte nicht daran erinnern (China)
- **das teuerste Telefonat:** eine Satellitenverbindung wegen Luftschlauchproblem (Island)
- **die schwierigste Teilnehmeraufgabe:** eine Abseilaktion (Guatemala)
- **die teuerste Fahrzeugpanne:** das eigene Auto abschleppen (Namibia)
- **das größte Missverständnis:** zum Glück noch nicht passiert
- **der längste Umweg:** 500 Kilometer wegen einer Blockade (Bolivien)
- **die kürzeste Nacht:** zwei Stunden (Island)
- **die meisten Insekten:** mindestens Abermillionen (Schottland)
- **der fieseste Stich:** ein Blutegelangriff (Malaysia)
- **der ungewöhnlichste technische Defekt:** ein Kabelbaumfehler im Defender (Bolivien)
- **das höchste Bier:** auf 5 124 Metern (Bolivien)
- **die größten Grenzschikanen:** diverse (Ukraine, Usbekistan, China)
- **der dichteste Dschungel:** verschiedene (Malaysia, Guatemala)
- **die scheuesten Kinder:** bei der Dorfbevölkerung (Argentinien)
- **der albernste Unfall:** ein leichter Auffahrunfall Land Rover/Land Rover (Malaysia)
- **die steilste Straße:** der Kraterweg (Argentinien)
- **die engste Straße:** eine Bergtrasse (Bolivien)
- **das wildeste Überholmanöver:** an einer Grenz-Baustelle vorbei (Usbekistan)
- **die niedrigste Temperatur:** -23 Grad (Argentinien)
- **die längste verschneite Straße:** rund 1 000 Kilometer (Kasachstan)
- **die größte geleistete Hilfe:** an Schwester Verena (Bolivien)
- **das schlimmste Getränk:** Rotwein, der ein schlechter Rosé war (China)
- **der abartigste Brauch:** Trockenfisch essen (Island)
- **der naheste Moment des Verzweifelns:** schwimmende Autopapiere (Niemandsland Ukraine/Russland)
- **die fieseste Fingerfalle:** Kachelrand im Bad (Tibet)
- **die dreckigsten Klamotten:** völlig verschlammte Garnitur (Malaysia)
- **die treuesten Land-Rover-Fans:** die LET-Gemeinde (weltweit)
- **die beste Idee:** feuriges Spritfilteraufheizen unterm Defender (Chile)
- **die dümmste Idee:** Benzinabzapfen aus dem Spritfilter zum Grillen (Bolivien)
- **die aufwendigste Reparatur:** Motorüberholung beim Defender (Bolivien)
- **der schrägste Bewerber:** ein ungeeigneter Deutschrusse (Deutschland)

- **der/die älteste Teilnehmer/in:** eine 64-jährige Tierärztin (Deutschland)
- **die größte Fehleinschätzung:** eine vermeintlich tolle Abkürzung wählen (China)
- **der sympathischste mitreisende Promi:** Jessica Schwarz (Argentinien, Seidenstraße)
- **die merkwürdigste Anfrage an den Doc:** Arztgeheimnis (irgendwo)
- **das schwerste Auto:** die rund vier Tonnen wiegende Ambulanz (diverse Länder)
- **das leichteste Auto:** Land Rover Freelander (Malaysia, Jordanien)
- **der treueste Sponsor:** Continental und Haglöfs (Deutschland)
- **die größte Bewerberanzahl:** 30 000 für die Seidenstraße (Deutschland)
- **die schwierigste Bewerbercamp-Aufgabe:** nachts vergrabene Räder suchen (Deutschland)
- **die krasseste Bewerberlüge:** „Ich bin kein Eventhopper." (Seidenstraße)
- **die heißeste Temperatur unterwegs:** 43 Grad (Usbekistan)
- **die tougheste Teilnehmerfrau:** ein Journalist (!) aus München (Deutschland)
- **der härteste Teilnehmer:** ein LR-Fan aus Krefeld (Deutschland)
- **die längste Ansprache:** bleibt ein Geheimnis (geheim)
- **der langsamste Abschnitt:** 2 km/h im Durchschnitt (Guatemala)
- **der schnellste Abschnitt:** Autobahn Berlin-Polen ohne Tempobegrenzung (Deutschland)
- **der schlechteste Treibstoff:** Kamaz-Diesel-Fusel (Usbekistan)
- **der hilfreichste Tipp von außen:** bergab fahren im Rückwärtsgang (Malaysia)
- **der schrägste Mitfahrer:** ein Cocablätter kauender Bergbauer (Bolivien)
- **die gefährlichste Kurve:** Spitzkehre einer Minenstraße (Bolivien)
- **die längste Kolonne:** 18 Autos (Indien)
- **die längste Tour:** 16 000 Kilometer (Seidenstraße)
- **die wenigsten Tageskilometer:** 2 Kilometer (Guatemala)
- **die größte Hürde:** der Zoll (Jordanien)
- **der wichtigste telefonierte Satz:** „Wir haben's geschafft!" (Indien)
- **die größte Hilfeleistung:** Erste Hilfe bei einem schweren Verkehrsunfall (Tibet)
- **die längste Suche:** der verschwundene Hans (Guatemala)
- **der anstrengendste Meter:** letzter Schritt zum Pinkeln auf 5 200 Höhenmetern (China)
- **der beste Spruch:** „Sneidn wer rauuuus" (China)
- **der dümmste Spruch:** Teilnehmerin: „Wo sind meine Hupen?" (Nepal)
- **die größte Zeitverschiebung:** acht Stunden (Kanada)
- **der längste Tag:** Sonnenaufgang bis Sonnenaufgang (Island)
- **die geringste Autokraft:** 30 PS im Defender (Defender)
- **die größte Fehlkalkulation:** ein Touristenfallen-Abendessen (Russland)
- **die größte Fehlinvestition:** zu viele Ersatzreifen mitnehmen (Seidenstraße)
- **das bestangelegte Geld:** das Dankeschön an Zöllner (nahezu weltweit)
- **der überraschendste Laden:** eine Autowerkstatt (Bolivien)
- **der meistkonsumierte Drink abends:** Bier (weltweit)
- **der coolste Moment:** Eine Neun-Mann-Geburtstagsfeier im Discovery (Schottland)
- **das schärfste Essen:** in einem Restaurant in Golmud (China)
- **der verrückteste Guide:** Adil aus Kashgar (China)
- **die skrupelloseste Tat:** ein heftiges Insektengemetzel (Malaysia)
- **das sicherste Gefühl:** erzeugt von offiziellen Inoffiziellen in Toyota Land Cruisern (China)
- **die heftigste Kommandoübernahme:** eine Flugzeugkanzel-Okkupation (Argentinien)
- **die ungewöhnlichsten Tankwarte:** auffällig unauffällig verkleidete Zivilpolizisten (China)
- **der größte Erfolg:** die Seidenstraßentour (Deutschland, Polen, Ukraine, Russland, Kasachstan, Usbekistan, Kirgisistan, China, Tibet, Nepal, Indien)

100 EXTREMES
THE MOST INTENSE MOMENTS IN TWELVE LAND ROVER TOURS

- **the most dangerous road:** an extremely narrow mining road (Bolivia)
- **the most dangerous moment:** a leaking tanker trailer (Bolivia)
- **the most beautiful sunrise:** in the desert (Namibia)
- **the most beautiful sunset:** in the mountains (Kyrgyzstan)
- **the most candid guide:** Tenzin (China)
- **the most difficult route:** a dry riverbed (Argentina)
- **the most difficult shopping trip:** a fresh produce market (Malaysia)
- **the worst hotel:** better left unsaid (Bolivia)
- **the best hotel:** a house in Colomé (Argentina)
- **the rarest animal:** a wild puma (Canada)
- **the deepest river crossing:** water almost halfway up the side windows (Iceland)
- **the highest mountain road:** Gyatso La 17,152 feet (Tibet)
- **the worst food:** rotten meat that we had to cook ourselves (Bolivia)
- **the best food:** numerous restaurants (China)
- **the most serious medical task:** a serious road traffic accident (Mexico)
- **the funniest situation:** a phoney technology story (Malaysia)
- **the longest driving stage (in hours):** 19 hours (Iceland)
- **the longest driving stage in miles:** 721 miles (China)
- **the least talented driver:** a German journalist (Guatemala)
- **the most difficult search for fuel:** every day (Bolivia)
- **the largest wad of cash:** paying for fuel (Uzbekistan)
- **the largest bribe:** 2,000 ... (but which country was that again?)
- **the longest wait at a border:** 13 hours (Uzbekistan)
- **the most difficult visa application process:** don't remind me (China)
- **the most expensive telephone call:** a satellite link to discuss a problem with an air hose (Iceland)
- **the most difficult participants' special task:** abseiling (Guatemala)
- **the most expensive breakdown:** towing our own vehicle (Namibia)
- **the biggest misunderstanding:** it hasn't happened yet (fortunately)
- **the longest detour:** 310 miles because of a blocked road (Bolivia)
- **the shortest night:** two hours (Iceland)
- **the most insects:** millions (Scotland)
- **the most painful bite:** leeches (Malaysia)
- **the most unusual breakdown:** a short circuit in the wiring loom of a Defender (Bolivia)
- **the highest beer:** 16,811 feet (Bolivia)
- **the worst border shenanigans:** numerous (Ukraine, Uzbekistan, China)
- **the thickest jungle:** various (Malaysia, Guatemala)
- **the most shy children:** villagers (Argentina)
- **the most ridiculous accident:** a rear-ender involving two Land Rovers (Malaysia)
- **the steepest road:** the crater route (Argentina)
- **the narrowest road:** a mountain road (Bolivia)
- **the craziest overtaking manoeuvre:** past a building site at the border (Uzbekistan)
- **the lowest temperature:** -23 degrees Celsius (-9 degrees Fahrenheit) (Argentina)
- **the longest road covered in snow:** 621 miles (Kazakhstan)
- **the greatest delivery service:** Sister Verena (Bolivia)
- **the worst drink:** a red wine that was a very poor rosé (China)
- **the most disgusting tradition:** eating dried fish (Iceland)
- **the moment of greatest despair:** watching our vehicle documentation float in the water (no-man's-land between Ukraine and Russia)
- **the worst finger trap:** the bath rim (Tibet)
- **the dirtiest clothes:** tour kit completely covered in mud (Malaysia)
- **the most loyal Land Rover fans:** the global LET community
- **the best idea:** "flame grilling" the fuel filter underneath the Defender (Chile)
- **the worst idea:** drawing off diesel from the fuel filter to get the barbecue going (Bolivia)

- **the most complex repair job:** engine overhaul on Defender (Bolivia)
- **the most off-the-wall candidate:** a particularly unsuitable German of Russian descent (Germany)
- **the oldest participant:** a 64-year-old vet (Germany)
- **the greatest miscalculation:** a "fantastic" shortcut (China)
- **the nicest VIP we ever took with us:** actress Jessica Schwarz (Argentina, Silk Road)
- **the strangest request made of the doctor:** medical secret (that goes for the country, too)
- **the heaviest vehicle on the tour:** the ambulance, weighing around four tonnes (numerous countries)
- **the lightest vehicle:** Land Rover Freelander (Malaysia, Jordan)
- **the most loyal sponsors:** Continental and Haglöfs (Germany)
- **the largest number of applications:** 30,000 for the Silk Road (Germany)
- **the most difficult selection camp task:** hunting buried wheels at night (Germany)
- **the most blatant applicant lie:** "I am not an event hopper" (Silk Road)
- **the hottest temperatures on tour:** 43 degrees Celsius (109 degrees Fahrenheit) (Uzbekistan)
- **the toughest female participant:** a male (!) journalist from Munich (Germany)
- **the toughest male participant:** a Land Rover fan from Krefeld (Germany)
- **the longest speech:** remains a secret (classified)
- **the slowest section:** 1.2 mph (average) (Guatemala)
- **the quickest section:** the motorway between Berlin and the Polish border (no speed limits) (Germany)
- **the worst fuel:** Kamaz-diesel (Uzbekistan)
- **the best driving tip ever:** driving downhill in reverse gear (Malaysia)
- **the most bizarre passenger:** a coca-leaf-chewing miner (Bolivia)
- **the most dangerous corner:** a switchback on a mining road (Bolivia)
- **the longest convoy:** 18 vehicles (India)
- **the longest tour:** 10,000 miles (Silk Road)
- **the shortest distance travelled in one day:** 1.2 miles (Guatemala)
- **the biggest obstacle:** customs (Jordan)
- **the most important sentence on the phone:** "We made it" (India)
- **the most significant rescue operation:** first aid at a serious road traffic accident (Tibet)
- **the longest search:** Hans after he went AWOL (Guatemala)
- **the most exhausting walk:** taking a leak at 17,000 feet above sea level (China)
- **the best adage ever:** "Cut it out" (China)
- **the daftest quote:** participant "Where's my horn?" (Nepal)
- **the greatest time difference:** eight hours (Canada)
- **the longest day:** sunrise to sunrise (Iceland)
- **the least horsepower:** 30 hp in the Defender (Argentina)
- **the greatest miscalculation:** dinner in a tourist trap (Russia)
- **the biggest investment error:** too many spare tyres (Silk Road)
- **the best investment:** thank-you money to customs officials (everywhere)
- **the most surprising shop:** a vehicle workshop (Bolivia)
- **the evening drink consumed most:** beer (everywhere)
- **the coolest moment:** a nine-person birthday party in one Discovery (Scotland)
- **the spiciest food:** a restaurant in Golmud (China)
- **the craziest guide:** Adil from Kashgar (China)
- **the most ruthless thing we ever did:** massacring insects (Malaysia)
- **the greatest feeling of security:** the unofficial officials accompanying us in their Toyota Land Cruisers (China)
- **the most dramatic takeover:** the cockpit of a light aeroplane (Argentina)
- **the most unusual filling-station attendant:** the oh-so-obvious undercover policeman (China)
- **the greatest success:** the Silk Road Tour (Germany, Poland, Ukraine, Russia, Kazakhstan, Uzbekistan, Kyrgyzstan, China, Tibet, Nepal, India)

IMPRESSUM | IMPRINT

© 2018 Jaguar Land Rover Deutschland GmbH
© 2018 teNeues Media GmbH & Co. KG, Kempen
Alle Rechte vorbehalten

Herausgeber | Editor: Land Rover Deutschland
Vorwort | Foreword: Prof. Dr. Ralf Speth, CEO Jaguar Land Rover &
Christian Uhrig, Head of Marketing Communication Jaguar Land Rover Germany &
Dag Rogge, Head of Land Rover Experience Germany
Text: Roland Löwisch & Dag Rogge
Übersetzung | Translation: Graham Paul Entwistle
Lektorat | Copy editing: Dr. Simone Bischoff (Deutsch),
Schmellenkamp Communications & Dr. Suzanne Kirkbright (English)
Redaktion | Editorial coordination: Nadine Weinhold
Design & Layout: Christin Steirat
Design Assistance: Iris van Kempen, Therese Giemza
Bildbearbeitung & Proofs | Photo Editing & Color separation: Jens Grundei
Herstellung | Production: Alwine Krebber

ISBN 978-3-96171-084-3
Library of Congress Control Number: 2017958249

Printed in the Czech Republic

Bibliografische Information der Deutschen Nationalbibliothek
Die Deutsche Nationalbibliothek verzeichnet diese Publikation in
der Deutschen Nationalbibliografie; detaillierte bibliografische Daten
sind im Internet über http://dnb.dnb.de abrufbar.

Bibliographic information published by the Deutsche Nationalbibliothek
The Deutsche Nationalbibliothek lists this publication in the
Deutsche Nationalbibliografie; detailed bibliographic data are available
on the Internet at http://dnb.dnb.de.

**Wir danken allen, die dazu beigetragen haben, dass zwölf Land Rover Experience Touren
so sicher und erfolgreich stattfinden konnten.
Special thanks to all those who made the twelve Land Rover Experience Tours possible.**

Jaguar Land Rover Deutschland GmbH
Campus Kronberg 7
61476 Kronberg im Taunus
Germany
Phone: +49 (0)2131 15 12 370
lrhilfe@jaguarlandrover.com

Published by teNeues Publishing Group

teNeues Media GmbH & Co. KG
Am Selder 37, 47906 Kempen, Germany
Phone: +49-(0)2152-916-0
Fax: +49-(0)2152-916-111
e-mail: books@teneues.com

Press department: Andrea Rehn
Phone: +49-(0)2152-916-202
e-mail: arehn@teneues.com

teNeues Media GmbH & Co. KG
Munich Office
Pilotystraße 4, 80538 Munich, Germany
Phone: +49-(0)89-443-8889-62
e-mail: bkellner@teneues.com

teNeues Media GmbH & Co. KG
Berlin Office
Kohlfurter Straße 41–43, 10999 Berlin, Germany
Phone: +49-(0)30-4195-3526-23
e-mail: ajasper@teneues.com

teNeues Publishing Company
350 7th Avenue, Suite 301, New York, NY 10001, USA
Phone: +1-212-627-9090
Fax: +1-212-627-9511

teNeues Publishing UK Ltd.
12 Ferndene Road, London SE24 0AQ, UK
Phone: +44-(0)20-3542-8997

teNeues France S.A.R.L.
39, rue des Billets, 18250 Henrichemont, France
Phone: +33-(0)2-4826-9348
Fax: +33-(0)1-7072-3482

www.teneues.com

Bildnachweise | Photo Credits

Front cover photo by Craig Pusey
Jordanien/Jordan: Dag Rogge, Hans Hermann Ruthe, pp. 12/13 © Shutterstock, Inc./
nicolpetr, p. 17 © iStockphoto LP./stevenallan,
p. 18 © Shutterstock, Inc./Max Topchii, p. 19 © Shutterstock, Inc./Marco Tomasini,
p. 21 © Shutterstock, Inc./Rossillicon Photos,
p. 22 © Shutterstock, Inc./sbarabu, pp. 26/27 © Shutterstock, Inc./Waj
Island/Iceland: Nick Dimbleby, Dag Rogge, Hans Hermann Ruthe,
pp. 32/33 © Natalie Tepper/ArcaidImages/GettyImages
Winter Experience: Nick Dimbleby
Namibia: Thomas Grimm, Dag Rogge, Hans Hermann Ruthe
Mundo Maya: Thomas Grimm, Dag Rogge, Hans Hermann Ruthe,
pp. 74/75 © Shutterstock, Inc./Zai Aragon
Kanada/Canada: Thomas Grimm, Dag Rogge, Hans Hermann Ruthe
Schottland/Scotland: Craig Pusey, Dag Rogge, Hans Hermann Ruthe
Argentinien/Argentina: Craig Pusey, Hans Hermann Ruthe
Malaysia: Craig Pusey, Hans Hermann Ruthe
Bolivien/Bolivia: Roland Löwisch, Craig Pusey, Hans Hermann Ruthe
Seidenstraße/Silk Road: Pierre Johne, Craig Pusey, Hans Hermann Ruthe

Australien/Australia: Craig Pusey, Henning Lueke, Alexander Seger, Timo Peters
Peru: Craig Pusey, Henning Lueke, Alexander Seger, Jonas Egert

Satellitenkarten/Satellite maps: Google™ earth

Icons
Camel icon (Jordan) Created by Edward Boatman from the Noun Project
Puffin icon (Iceland) Created by parkjisun from the Noun Project
Elephant icon (Namibia) Created by parkjisun from the Noun Project
Panther icon (Mundo Maya) Created by M. Turan Ercan from the Noun Project
Reindeer icon (Canada) Created by VectorBakery from the Noun Project
Squirrel icon (Scotland) Created by Tracy Hudak from the Noun Project
Armadillo icon (Argentina & Chile) Created by Amanda Sebastiani from the Noun Project
Cobra icon (Malaysia) Created by parkjisun from the Noun Project
Flamingo icon (Bolivia) Created by Brand Mania from the Noun Project
Eagle icon (Silk Road) Created by M. Turan Ercan from the Noun Project
Jackal icon (Australia) Created by M. Turan Ercan from the Noun Project
Llama icon (Peru) Created by M. Turan Ercan from the Noun Project